THE RADICAL AMERICAN JUDAISM OF MORDECAI M. KAPLAN

THE MODERN JEWISH EXPERIENCE
Deborah Dash Moore and Marsha L. Rosenblit, editors
Paula Hyman, founding coeditor

Mordecai M. Kaplan in his office at the seminary.
Courtesy of the Library of the Jewish Theological Seminary

THE RADICAL AMERICAN JUDAISM OF MORDECAI M. KAPLAN

MEL SCULT

INDIANA UNIVERSITY PRESS

Bloomington & Indianapolis

This book is a publication of

INDIANA UNIVERSITY PRESS
Office of Scholarly Publishing
Herman B Wells Library 350
1320 East 10th Street
Bloomington, Indiana 47405 USA

iupress.indiana.edu

Telephone orders   800-842-6796
Fax orders   812-855-7931

Manufactured in the United States of
America

Library of Congress
Cataloging-in-Publication Data

Scult, Mel.
  The radical American Judaism of
Mordecai M. Kaplan / Mel Scult.
    pages cm. — (The modern Jewish
experience)
  Includes bibliographical references and
index.
  ISBN 978-0-253-01075-9 (cloth : alk. paper)
  — ISBN 978-0-253-01088-9 (e-book)
1. Kaplan, Mordecai Menahem, 1881–1983.
2. Reconstructionist Judaism. I. Title.
BM755.K289S395 2014
296.8'344—dc23

2013019522

1 2 3 4 5   19 18 17 16 15 14

As for me, I shall behold thy face in righteousness.
Psalms 17:15 *

ואני בצדק אחזה פניך

In gratitude to Rabbi Neil Gillman, for his generous appreciation,
and to my brother,
Allen Scult, my most significant intellectual Other

---

*Biblical verse on a stained-glass window at the Society for the
Advancement of Judaism, Kaplan's Congregation.

CONTENTS

ACKNOWLEDGMENTS

There are always many people to thank when one writes a book, and this book is no exception. I am grateful to Professor David Kraemer, librarian at the Jewish Theological Seminary, for permission to quote from the diaries of Mordecai Kaplan, the originals of which are at the Seminary. I also want to express my thanks to Rabbi Deborah Waxman, director of the Eisenstein Archives at the Reconstructionist Rabbinical College, for permission to quote from the Kaplan papers.

I want first to thank people who have edited my work. At the top of the list stands my wife Barbara, whose sense of style and perfection are evident throughout this book. She is a hard critic, but the end product more than justifies the difficulties in getting there. David Lobenstine was enormously devoted in editing this work, and for that I cannot thank him enough. He is the most careful reader that I have ever dealt with, and I am grateful for his skill and effort. Next is Rabbi Richard Hirsh, director of the Reconstructionist Rabbinical Association. Richard is a good friend and colleague with whom I have spent countless hours on the phone discussing Mordecai Kaplan and the many issues raised by this work. In addition, he has also edited a significant number of chapters in this book. I told Richard rather early on that, in the event of my death or incapacity, I wanted him to finish the book. I have great faith in him, in his writing ability, in his intelligence, and in his knowledge of Kaplan and Reconstructionism. Amy Gottlieb has also edited a number of chapters with great skill and thoroughness. Others who have edited various parts of this work include Robert Seltzer, Barbara Heyman, Marilyn Silverstein, and Baila Shargel. My thanks also go to

Professor Lenny Levin for his help in connection with transliterations. Any inaccuracies are my own.

Among my academic colleagues, there are many with whom I have shared my thoughts on Kaplan. Foremost is Neil Gillman. With his help I was able to teach a course at the Jewish Theological Seminary on the philosophy of Mordecai Kaplan. This course mobilized my efforts and motivated me to organize my Kaplan material. The organization for that course is the organization for this book. Arnie Eisen, now chancellor at the Jewish Theological Seminary, has been a friend for a long time. Not only has he been encouraging and supportive, but the conference that he organized at Stanford University in 2004 was a landmark in my career. The conference was devoted exclusively to Kaplan, and the proceedings were eventually published. Professor Robert Seltzer, colleague and long-time friend, has read parts of this manuscript and is always encouraging. I have also shared parts of this book with Professor Shaul Magid of Indiana University, Nancy Fuchs-Kreimer of the Reconstructionist Rabbinical College, Yossi Turner of Schechter Institute in Jerusalem, and Rabbi Jack Cohen of Jerusalem, z"l. Professor Yehoyada Amir of Hebrew Union College, Jerusalem, has also been consistently encouraging in all my work on Kaplan.

Others who have read selected chapters include Rabbi Shel Schiffman, Jane Susswein, Anne Eisenstein, and Miriam Eisenstein. Both Miriam and Anne have been very generous with their help, and their close-up insights have been invaluable. Paula Eisenstein Baker, a fellow scholar, has also been helpful through the years. I am indebted to the extended family of Mordecai Kaplan, especially Hadassah Musher and her son Daniel, for their support.

In addition to the people named above, I am much in debt to certain individuals who have supported me from the beginning. At the top of this list are Jack and Kaye Wolofsky of Montreal, loyal disciples of Mordecai Kaplan and continually helpful in my work. The members of my congregation, West End Synagogue—A Reconstructionist Congregation, have been unfailingly encouraging over the years. They have afforded me a continuous opportunity to share and refine my ideas. Their positive response is dear to me. I want to single out my WES friends Joe Gurvets and Jerry Posman.

I am profoundly grateful to my fellow board members at the Kaplan Center for Jewish Peoplehood. The efforts and ongoing concern of Dan Cedarbaum, Eric Caplan, and Jack Wolofsky are of fundamental importance in helping people understand the message and relevance of Mordecai M. Kaplan. I want to thank Ellen Kastel, former archivist at the Jewish Theological Seminary, whose help and encouragement I value very much. In addition, I am grateful to the members of my book club with whom I have shared my concerns during the past fifteen years. My Florida friends, Bill, Molly, Henry, Jim, Sherry, and Linda, have been with me over the long haul and their companionship has been extremely valuable.

Last but certainly not least is my brother, Allen Scult, Professor Emeritus of philosophy at Drake University. Allen is my constant conversational other about Kaplan and many other intellectual matters. His suggestions always lift my work to a higher level.

PREFACE

I have been studying Mordecai Kaplan, his life and his thought, continually since 1972. One might reasonably ask, as my wife often has, how someone could remain with one subject for so long. Part of the answer lies in the wealth of material Kaplan left behind. In addition to the books and articles that appeared during his lifetime, there is a mass of unpublished material. The Reconstructionist Rabbinical College in Philadelphia, which I have been affiliated with, houses a very large Kaplan archive, containing box after box of everything from sermon notes to lecture notes, personal letters to comments on the Torah, and much else in between.[1]

But beyond the almost infinite paper trail, other, more potent reasons draw me to Kaplan. I have for much of the past six decades struggled to define the exact meaning of my Jewishness. Midway through this journey, Kaplan came along. He told me, both in person and through his books and articles, that being a Jew was not primarily about accepting a particular belief system. Rather, being a Jew was a matter of biography and community. "Belonging is more important than believing," as Reconstructionists like to say.[2] His perspective has been revelatory and liberating. If my relationship to the Jewish people is a matter of biography—if my Jewishness, in other words, is a question of my life story and the life story of the Jewish people—then I am free to evaluate any and all traditional beliefs and reject what makes no sense to me. There is no way in which my being a Jew could be undermined.

Within the liberation that Kaplan has fostered, there are other intellectual and philosophical issues that attract me to him. For many years

I have been interested in the thought of Friedrich Nietzsche; his ideas about "overcoming," or personal transcendence in particular, have been enormously inspiring for me. After studying Kaplan for some time, it dawned on me that his notions of salvation and personal fulfillment were strikingly similar to Nietzsche's.

Some years later, I also discovered a connection between Kaplan and Ralph Waldo Emerson, which paralleled my interest in Nietzsche. Despite their major differences, Nietzsche and Emerson share some important convictions, particularly the notions of fulfillment and self-transcendence.[3] Kaplan and Emerson and their ideas of self-fulfillment all fit beautifully together as a way to live a Jewish life. Kaplan actually crafted a prayer based on an essay by Emerson,[4] and as we shall see, he intended to insert this Emerson prayer into the Sabbath morning services. Thus, as a Kaplanian, I could pray from Emerson.

Kaplan additionally attracted me because of his help in resolving certain theological problems, which went back to my study with Abraham Joshua Heschel (1907–72).[5] In my youth, I studied at the Jewish Theological Seminary; Heschel was my professor in Jewish philosophy for three consecutive years. Although the curriculum called for us to study medieval Jewish philosophy, we only studied Heschel. *Man Is Not Alone,* Heschel's first theological work, had just appeared. I remember quite distinctly our discussions about the matter of wonder, radical amazement, and the mystery of the human condition and of the universe altogether. I was enthralled. After the mystery, in Heschel's words, came what he called "the meaning beyond the mystery." But, enthralled though I was, the meaning beyond the mystery eluded me. I could never understand what Heschel meant. Many years later, Kaplan's naturalistic theology came to my rescue, resolving much of my confusion on this and other religious problems.[6]

As Kaplan helped me decode ideas that had stumped me for so long, I felt an urgent need to understand the way in which Kaplan related to Heschel. To my amazement, I found that Kaplan was instrumental in bringing Heschel to the Jewish Theological Seminary. I also discovered a prayer that Kaplan had crafted based on a Heschel essay. Kaplan, it seemed, was exhorting me to pray from Heschel, just as he had urged me to pray from Emerson. Sometime afterward, as if some power were guiding me, while researching the papers of Rabbi Ira Eisenstein, Kaplan's primary disciple and his son-in-law, I discovered an early loose-leaf prayer book of the Society for the Advancement for Judaism, Kaplan's original congregation.[7] To my astonishment, I found that the Emerson prayer and the Heschel prayer were on facing pages. Heschel and Emerson, united by Kaplan in his Sabbath prayer book—I was moved to tears.[8]

As I explain my interest in Kaplan, the above list of reasons feels only partial. If nothing else, Kaplan is multidimensional. He thought broadly; he was unafraid to express his thoughts. And he had thoughts, it seems, about pretty much everything. The result is that he is both maddening and mesmerizing. Quite the opposite of a traditional philosopher, who aims for consistency, who attempts to resolve all uncertainties, he seemed to revel in life's ambiguities. Such multiplicity, as we shall see, plagued him for much of his life and is a large part of his legacy today. Kaplan is easily misunderstood because often he will stand on both sides of an issue; it is always a challenge to try to clarify his ambivalence. As we approach and try to analyze Kaplan's thinking, we should keep in mind Walt Whitman's famous assertion in *Song of Myself:* "I contradict myself, I am large, I contain multitudes." Though such complexity has damaged his stature within Judaism, Kaplan's "multitudes" and contradictions have provided me with a seemingly boundless framework for self- and community exploration.

* * *

There are no limits, it seems, to the ways in which Kaplan has been misunderstood. Here let one example suffice—a recent celebration at the Park Avenue Synagogue, the home for many years of Rabbi Milton Steinberg [1903–50]. The purpose of the gathering was to mark the publication of Steinberg's posthumous novel *The Prophet's Wife.*[9] Steinberg, a preeminent conservative rabbi in his time, was decisively influenced by Kaplan, his teacher and hero. Practically every speaker at the event mentioned Kaplan in one connection or another. Steinberg, who had also written *As a Driven Leaf,* the novel about the heretical ancient rabbi Elisha ben Avuya, was Kaplan's most outstanding student at the Jewish Theological Seminary. While it was not surprising that all the speakers

mentioned Kaplan, what was startling was the sheer volume and depth
of misunderstanding and misinformation about Kaplan and his beliefs.

One of the key speakers quoted Steinberg's attack on Kaplan in 1949,
where he stated that Kaplan had no theology but only discussed what
it meant to have a theology. Harold Kushner, the well-known author
of *When Bad Things Happen to Good People,* told the five hundred or
so people gathered at Steinberg's Park Avenue Synagogue that Steinberg wrote the now-famous *As a Driven Leaf* to remedy the fact that
his teacher, Mordecai Kaplan, had no theory of evil. Another speaker
described Kaplan as a rational, unemotional person who had no sense
of the metaphorical.

I was confounded by the lack of real understanding of Kaplan and
the vehemence of these attacks. This work is an attempt to correct distor-
tions like these, which are pervasive and which extend far beyond that
event. One of the best-known Kaplan scholars recently said to me that
he did not understand why Kaplan needed a theology in the first place
when his whole system centered on the notion of peoplehood rather than
godhood. I have found that today Kaplan is identified with his famous
concept of "Judaism as a civilization" and with the notion of "living in
two civilizations" and a few other ideas that have been reduced to little
more than slogans or sound bites. Most people, including many of his
devoted followers, seem to think there is little of real value in Kaplan's
thinking beyond these primary concepts.

Within the scholarly community, there is a corresponding lack of
knowledge about Kaplan and his philosophy of Jewish life. Whenever
modern Jewish thinkers are analyzed, academics place Hermann Cohen
or J. B. Soloveitchik or Franz Rosenzweig or Abraham Joshua Heschel
at the center of attention. If Kaplan is mentioned, it is only a nod. This
situation is changing, but the change has been long overdue and is still
slow in coming.

Though frustrating, the lack of attention to Kaplan is understandable
both on a popular and scholarly level. His best-known work, *Judaism as
a Civilization,* stands at five hundred pages and is written in a wooden
prose all but unreadable. It is also difficult to take Kaplan seriously as a
religious philosopher when he is so often ambivalent about the key issues. At the same time, his preoccupation with the sociological and the

pragmatic seems to place him in a bygone era, behind the more spiritual concerns of our own day. It is my fervent belief, however, that, if we determine to immerse ourselves in the unforgiving prose and if we allow ourselves to embrace the ambiguities, we shall discover that Kaplan can play a very significant role in the intellectual and spiritual controversies both of the past and of the present.

* * *

Bringing Mordecai Kaplan back to life, and to relevance, will have much to do with an unappreciated but vital document: his diary. This amazing work, only recently made available to the public, is extraordinarily long—twenty-seven volumes, each volume containing 350 to 400 handwritten pages. His is the largest diary ever written by a Jewish person and may be one of the most extensive on record in human history. Starting in 1913, when he was thirty-two, Kaplan wrote almost weekly until 1978, when he was ninety-seven. These pages offer provocative insights into Kaplan's constant struggle in formulating his ideas and his frustration in implementing them. He withholds nothing. Here are revealed his religious complexity and the paradoxes of his inner life, in abundance and with startling intimacy. I have been reading his private thoughts for more than half of my own life, and I am as fascinated now as I was almost four decades ago.[10]

Although Kaplan published a great deal during his lifetime, in his own opinion—and mine—the journal is his most significant work. Emerson, a compulsive diarist himself, realized the value of the private diary: "Only what is private, & yours, & essential, should ever be printed or spoken. I will buy the suppressed part of the author's mind; you are welcome to all he published."[11]

I became aware of the diary during my first meetings with Kaplan. I met him for the first time in 1972, when I interviewed him at Camp Cejwin in Port Jervis, New York where he often spent the summer.[12] We talked for three days; rather, I should say, he talked, and I listened. We talked morning and afternoon. He wanted to continue in the evening, but I was exhausted and could not go on. He was ninety-one years old.

When Rabbi Kaplan returned to Manhattan, I continued to visit him at his apartment. My first time there he took me into his study.

Opening a closet and pointing to its contents, he exclaimed with pride, "You see—that is my diary!" The closet was filled from floor to ceiling with large accountant-type volumes. In the subsequent months, he permitted me to make a copy for myself.[13] The family and those close to Kaplan undoubtedly wondered, "Who is this young man with the *chutzpah* [nerve] to expect a personal copy of the diary?" Fortunately, in the course of time, their opinion changed.

For my part, I was so overwhelmed with the embarrassment of riches that I did not quite know what to do. I soon realized that the diary would alter the course of my professional and personal and spiritual life. Without a personal copy of the journal, my work on Kaplan—a biography, published in 1993; a series of excerpts from the journal, published in 2001; numerous essays; and this intellectual history—would never have come to fruition. Despite Kaplan's many publications, I am of the firm belief that the journal is primary in understanding his thinking and, without it, any investigation of his philosophy remains incomplete and superficial. Any serious student of Kaplan's life and work must have a thorough knowledge of the diary.

The best way to think about Kaplan's diary is as he thought of it—a tangible proof that he lived, that he thought, and that he had something worthwhile to bequeath to the world. In his irritation with finding a way to communicate his deepest personal thoughts, he often turned to the diary: "In my frustration, I turn to writing in this journal as the only means left me to externalize and render transferable that aspect of my being I experience as my soul, self or reason."[14] The journal, thus, becomes the repository of his self, his very soul.

The diary helps us understand that, despite his public involvements, Kaplan was very much a private person. It is a great irony that this man who emphasized the importance of community was so isolated. It may be that his emphasis on community was an expression of his own psychological need for some kind of social bonding. The diary, one might say, became his "universe" and, in a way, substitutes for the realities of community for which he longed but never found.

The journal is a revelation of Kaplan's inner life and of the complexity of his thought and of his own sense of incompleteness. It is also a record of his persistence in bringing his message to the Jewish people.

In talking to a reporter, Kaplan once stated that all religious innovation should be measured by the standard of "spiritualized intelligence."[15] Indeed, "the quest for spiritualized intelligence" might be fitting as a description of the diary and as the epitaph for the life and mind of Mordecai Kaplan.

Over the last nearly forty years, Kaplan's diary has taught me a great deal about myself and has given me insights into how I might see and live in our world. It has also inspired the bulk of my life's work. It is a great sadness to me that Mordecai Kaplan is not appreciated as I believe he should be. My hope is that, by plumbing Kaplan's diary, along with his published works, we will gain new insight into the thinking of one of our era's most important Jewish thinkers and, in the process, gain new insight into the world we might create.

THE RADICAL AMERICAN
JUDAISM OF
MORDECAI M. KAPLAN

INTRODUCTION

Mordecai M. Kaplan was one of the most radical Jewish thinkers of the twentieth century. When it came to expressing his opinions, Kaplan had much courage and never hesitated to speak his mind. He vehemently rejected the belief in the Jews as the chosen people of God. The center of his radicalism focuses on his theology and his concept of God. Kaplan rejected the belief in a supernatural being and did not envision God as a super self. God, Kaplan firmly believed, does not issue commandments or speak to anyone or direct history. In his commitment to a religion of naturalism, Kaplan denied the reality of the traditional biblical miracles—from the parting of the Red Sea to the extraordinary powers granted to the lost Ark. Though the Torah is central to the religious life, he felt it was the creation of the Jewish people and not from the "mouth of God."

Kaplan was an ardent disciple of Baruch Spinoza, the seventeenth-century Dutch philosopher ("Too bad we only had one Spinoza," he once wrote). If he had his druthers, he would have employed Spinoza in saving the Jewish people. Kaplan was a process thinker and, like another of his intellectual mentors, Ralph Waldo Emerson, believed that we are dominated by the tyranny of nouns. To free us from this tyranny, he advocated that we think with verbs, that is, in terms of process and action.

Kaplan lived the Emersonian ideal of self-reliance. Though he does not often mention Emerson's name, he was clearly influenced by the great Sage of Concord. *Self-reliance,* for our purposes, is the ability to stand back from one's culture, so that intelligence and rationality triumph over conformity and tradition. It is about having the courage of one's convictions, regardless of the consequences.

There are some who have branded Kaplan an atheist because of his rejection of the supernatural. Nothing could be further from the truth, and our impulse to see him as an atheist reveals the depth of our misunderstandings. Kaplan, like his forefather Spinoza, was God-obsessed. He contemplated the divine all the time.

The fact that Kaplan was excommunicated in 1945 because of his "heretical" prayer book reveals the extent of the anger that he generated among traditional Jews, even among his "friends" and colleagues at the Jewish Theological Seminary. The story is told that, in the 1950s, when Chaim Herzog, the chief rabbi of Israel, came to New York, he would not even step inside the seminary building because Kaplan was on the faculty.

* * *

The origin of Kaplan's revolutionary ideology is associated with his teachers, Emile Durkheim and John Dewey, and with the sociological view of religion as embodying the collective consciousness of the group. It would, however, be a distortion to think of Kaplan's ideology solely in societal and naturalist terms. Kaplan was indeed a naturalist and a sociological thinker, but he went beyond naturalism and consistently attempted to articulate a vision of the intertwining of the spiritual and natural worlds, a vision he termed *transnaturalism*. As we shall see, we can think of this mode of experiencing as a realm between naturalism and supernaturalism, a realm that has much in common with contemporary spiritual concerns. It transcended the natural realm yet was not supernaturalist; in other words, it did not involve miracles or any phenomena beyond the natural. We can call it *supranaturalism,* or a naturalism pushed to the limit. Despite Kaplan's naturalist, antitraditionalist tendencies, he must, I believe, be described as a pious man. Although he and Abraham Joshua Heschel became rivals, it should not surprise us that Kaplan deeply appreciated Heschel and was instrumental in bringing him to the Jewish Theological Seminary.

The best way to approach Kaplan is to keep in mind that he was a rabbi obsessed with the survival of the Jewish people. He was not a philosopher; if we look to him for a consistent and rigorous philosophy, we will be confused and disappointed. Inevitably, he stands on both sides of a question; we might describe his approach as a philosophy of mood. He is the dedicated Zionist who edits a book of prayers for American holidays; he is the religious naturalist par excellence yet has no problem in resorting to traditional God-language when he needs to; he is the committed pragmatist who, in general outline, accepts the views of Hermann Cohen, the famous neo-Kantian. This notion of a philosophy of mood will play a major role in our analysis of Kaplan.

For the most part, Kaplan may be described as a pragmatic believer. His first question in understanding a ritual or any kind of historical phenomenon was to ask how it had traditionally functioned. Did it continue to function as it had in the past? If it did not, how could its function be restored? If it could not be "reconstructed," he concluded, that element of Judaism should be discarded, no matter how painful. In his decades-long quest for religious renewal, the liturgy became a primary area of innovation. He was quite radical in his attempt at Reconstruction but always preferred the use of traditional modes and formulas when a particular custom or prayer was at issue. The concept of obligation, even though in a radically altered form, was also significant in Kaplan's approach to ritual. He was firmly committed to a minimum core of observance, though he also believed strongly in the individual's right to choose and mold the nature of his or her religious life.

Mordecai Kaplan's approach to Judaism and his theology must be understood as one manifestation of the Americanization of the Jewish experience. His philosophy was an attempt to introduce a way of thinking that would appeal to the children of immigrants who were born in this country, were Americanized, and were attending institutions of higher learning in large numbers. He is a product of the Progressive Era, the bourgeoning social sciences and the pragmatic school of American philosophy. He was more influenced by John Dewey, the pragmatist, than he was by the explorations of William James; when he was young, Kaplan found it difficult to relate to James's concern for the individual that forms the backbone of *The Varieties of Religious Experience*. Kaplan, like Dewey, emphasized intelligence over tradition as a major tool in the religious and moral quest.

Nonetheless, Kaplan gradually grew into a deep appreciation for the individual in religious life and eventually even sought to appropriate democratic individualism as a major component of Jewish civilization. In his radicalism, he would have us pray on the Sabbath from the works of Emerson and Dewey. "Davening from Dewey" was a regular practice of his own spiritual life. Kaplan, as we shall see, is the ultimate pluralist.

Yet if we only see Kaplan in terms of James, Dewey, and the sociologists, such a portrait would be a gross distortion of who he was and what he stood for. For him, the pragmatic always needed to be considered in the service of the religious. One scholar has called his approach "religious pragmatism," an expression that perfectly describes his multiple goals. For Kaplan, the sociological understanding of Emile Durkheim and the numinous of Rudolf Otto were not exclusive but complementary. Both Otto and Durkheim were central to Kaplan's naturalistic piety. Would it stretch the issue too far to call him "Kaplan the Pious"? I think not.

We must also keep in mind that Kaplan came from a traditional background and was thoroughly conversant with the traditional rabbinic corpus. Indeed, in the first thirty-five years of his tenure at the Jewish Theological Seminary, his efforts were principally devoted to the teaching of *midrash,* not to modern philosophy. Only in the mid-1940s did he begin teaching a course titled "Philosophies of Judaism." His students, including Louis Finkelstein and Robert Gordis, saw him as a master of *midrash.* Kaplan was a congregational rabbi throughout his life and was occupied in a major way with preaching Torah to his congregation.

He is certainly the most important American disciple of the cultural Zionist Ahad Ha-Am. He was critical of his teacher, however, and advocated what has been called a "transnational Zionism," which sees the center of Jewish life in a rebuilt Israel but also accepts the need for a permanent and robust diaspora.

Kaplan is the apostle of the group and the community, but his thinking contains an important emphasis on democracy and on the individual. He firmly believed that, though religion functions only within the group context, it is the individual and his or her development—or perfection—that constitute the sole aim of religion. Indeed, he stands with Emerson as seeing that the path to the divine begins with the individual and the search within.

Especially in his later life, Kaplan's concern with self-fulfillment (what he called salvation) and moral perfection never left him. These ideas are central both to Emerson and to *Mussar,* the Jewish ethical tradition. Emerson's ideal of moral perfectionism was of major significance in molding Kaplan's thought and fit perfectly with the *Mussar* tradition he inherited from his father.

Though Kaplan did not advocate a new denomination in his major works, it was clearly something he considered. A denomination may be defined as a movement that has a distinct ideology and a separate set of institutions. Kaplan had a distinct ideology, but a new seminary was something that was out of the question. His profound attachment to the Jewish Theological Seminary meant that he would not leave to start a new rabbinical school; as a result, Reconstructionism was established as a denomination only after he left the seminary. Out of necessity, he spoke of Reconstructionism as a school of thought. Following his retirement, however, the Reconstructionist Rabbinical College was established, and no one was happier than Mordecai Kaplan. Though the Reconstructionist movement is part of Kaplan's legacy, his ideology is larger than the denomination.

* * *

We are today in the middle of a fundamental struggle between the religiously devout and the scientifically skeptical. A spate of volumes has appeared recently attacking religion and pointing to its destructive influence on history. This debate has been going on for a long time but has recently heated up. Few dedicated religious thinkers stand in the middle—accepting modernity and democratic individualism and at the same time embracing a religious naturalism compatible with a contemporary understanding of the world. Mordecai Kaplan is a prime example of this most unusual combination. This volume attempts to present the many-sided ideology of Kaplan in ways relevant to current religious debates and, in the process, to reveal the abiding importance of his thinking.

Kaplan's relevance for our day is clear. For those who have moved past the fundamentalism of neotraditionalism, for those who cannot accept the esoteric categories of neo-Kabbalism, for those who will not be bound by the strictures of the traditional Jewish law, Mordecai Kaplan is a compelling alternative. Liberal Jews still wrestle with the nature and essence of our Judaism (whether God-given or man-made), with the status of the *halakhah* (whether cultural custom or divine law), with the proper relationship between the sciences, democracy, and religion. Kaplan confronted all these issues in an honest and provocative way; our own lives and the health of our communities will be the richer for engaging with the bounty of his brain. Those concerned with the survival of the Jewish people and of Jewish civilization would do well seriously to consider Mordecai Kaplan and his philosophy of Jewish life.

ONE

EXCOMMUNICATIONS: KAPLAN AND SPINOZA

Too bad we had only one Spinoza.

—*Mordecai M. Kaplan, 1939*

Most of us think of Mordecai Kaplan as the founding father of the Reconstructionist movement. Indeed he was, but his life was marked equally by another, quite different, biographical event: he was the first rabbi in the United States to be excommunicated by the ultra-Orthodox. Excommunication is usually associated with the Catholic Church and not with the Jews, but, alas, this painful act has been part of Jewish life for centuries. Indeed, the enemies of Maimonides—Jews, of course—burned his books after he died in 1204 and excommunicated anyone who read them. The most famous excommunication in Jewish history took place in Amsterdam in 1656. Its recipient was Baruch Spinoza, one of Kaplan's intellectual inspirations.

The excommunication of Mordecai Kaplan, which occurred as a result of a prayer book he published in 1945, is a good place to begin a study of Kaplan's thought. Thinking of Kaplan in connection with Spinoza will also raise some fundamental and perhaps disturbing questions about Kaplan. Did Kaplan fully embrace Spinoza's philosophy, or were there issues on which the two differed? And how do these paired excommunications, nearly three hundred years apart, enable us to understand twentieth-century Jewish thinking?

Spinoza, the best-known Jewish heretic, was born in Amsterdam in 1632. Rather a precocious young man, he began to think independently about religious matters at an early point and did not hesitate to speak with other members of the Jewish community about his beliefs. A *herem* (literally, ban) or excommunication was pronounced against him in 1656 by the leaders of the Amsterdam Jewish community. Although the *herem* does not specify the particular beliefs that were at issue, the community leaders certainly had in mind the following: he rejected the immortality of the soul, as well as the providential personal God—the God of Abraham, Isaac, and Jacob—and claimed that the Hebrew scriptures and Jewish law were neither literally given by God nor binding on the Jewish people. Excommunication meant that the person involved was to be cut off completely from the Jewish community. Jews were to have no contact with him whatsoever.

In the last century, a number of prominent Jews have wanted to reinstate Spinoza as a member of the Jewish people. Among them are Joseph Klausner, the noted Jewish scholar, and David Ben-Gurion. Klausner, who came to the Hebrew University in the late 1920s, advocated bringing back Spinoza in his inaugural lecture at the university. It is perhaps also noteworthy that a course in Spinoza's thought was taught in 2006 at the Rabbinical School of the Jewish Theological Seminary. Until recently, it was nearly unimaginable that future Conservative rabbis would be studying Spinoza! In addition, Steven Nadler, a well-known Spinoza scholar, asserts in his recent book *Spinoza's Heresy* that the whole matter of Spinoza's status must be reconsidered since the reasons for the excommunication are still unclear.[1] Although Spinoza is still considered a heretic by some, he nonetheless occupies an honored place in Jewish history (at least for most non-Orthodox Jews, and even some Orthodox ones).[2]

Kaplan's place in Jewish history is much clearer than Spinoza's, though Kaplan's transgressions are no less profound. The actual excommunication of Rabbi Mordecai Menachem Kaplan took place in New York City at the McAlpin Hotel on June 15, 1945. His "crimes" were multiple, as we shall see. In addition to attracting the ire of Orthodox Jews for several decades, two of Kaplan's actions were particularly objectionable and became the occasion of the ban: the publication of a new prayer book in May 1945, with multiple deletions and additions, and the lesser appreciated but as important act of publishing a new Passover *haggadah* four years earlier, which also differed significantly from the traditional text.

The Torah portion for the week of Kaplan's excommunication was *Korah*, which contains the narrative of the quintessential biblical dissenter who challenged the authority and wisdom of Moses. The rabbis' rush to judgment (the *herem* was issued only a month after Kaplan's prayer book appeared) was certainly influenced by their desire to classify Kaplan with Korah, that most "despicable" of biblical rebels, but was also a result of the concentration camp revelations from Europe then appearing.[3] The ultra-Orthodox organization of rabbis, calling itself the "*Agudat Harabbanim* [Society of Rabbis] of the United States and Canada," came together a month after V-E day to issue a formal ban against Kaplan. Kaplan, thus, occupies a singular place in American Jewish history, for no other figure has been condemned so fiercely, much less made the object of a ban.

How could it happen that a well-known and generally respected rabbi in the American Jewish community was excommunicated? How could it happen in the mid-twentieth century that a group of respected rabbis would decide not just to criticize one of its brethren but to burn his offending book? The incident makes little sense to us today but reveals something crucial about the power of Kaplan's thinking and the dilemmas of mid-century American Jewry. The explanation for this bizarre set of circumstances lies not only in the early years of Kaplan's life but also in the evolution of his intellectual and religious development. It would also help if we understand the fears and concerns of the Orthodox community during this period.

Kaplan was born not far from Vilna, the Lithuanian center of Ashkenazic Jewry, in June of 1881. He claims that he was so firmly located in the traditional Jewish world that he did not know the English date for his birth until he came to America and decided one day to look it up in the Jewish collection of the New York Public Library.[4]

Rabbi Israel Kaplan, Mordecai's father, was a well-educated, traditional Ashkenazi Jew. In 1888, he was invited by Jacob Joseph, the newly appointed chief rabbi of New York City, to become a member of the chief rabbi's entourage. The creation of the office of chief rabbi reflected the deep concern of a group of New York Jews to bring some order into traditional Judaism in the city. The massive immigrations of the late nineteenth century exposed rifts and conflicts within the Orthodox population. Some of the new immigrants were much more observant of Jewish law than others. The function of the chief rabbi was to help preserve Orthodox life, to unify the various Orthodox communities, and to increase their self-respect.[5]

Kaplan senior enrolled his son in a local yeshiva on the Lower East Side soon after arriving in New York City. Rabbi Israel Kaplan, however, remained his son's most important teacher until Mordecai was well into his twenties.[6] Though he lived within the Orthodox tradition, not known for its receptiveness to outsiders, Israel Kaplan was an unusually tolerant person. Arnold Ehrlich (1848–1919), a biblical critic who was shunned by much of New York Jewry, was a regular visitor to the Kaplan household. Ehrlich had converted to Christianity in Europe and aided Christian missionaries in their Hebrew translation of the New Testament. Though he eventually returned to the Jewish fold, it was difficult for him to integrate into the Jewish community. Ehrlich accepted the canons of biblical criticism—which in the late nineteenth century meant post-Mosaic authorship of the five books of Moses and the existence of multiple biblical documents that were forged by an editor into the final Pentateuchal text. There is no doubt that Ehrlich had a significant "heretical" influence on the teenage Kaplan.[7]

Another very significant influence during Kaplan's teenage years was the famous cultural Zionist Ahad Ha-Am. Though Ahad Ha-Am (Asher Hirsch Ginsberg, 1856–1927), was a deeply dedicated Jew from a traditional background, he had no place in his Zionist ideology for God or the synagogue. He was accurately referred to as the "secular rabbi," and the young Kaplan was strongly attracted to his philosophy.[8]

Kaplan's conflicts with the ultra-Orthodox began when he applied for his first rabbinical position in 1903. It was just about this time that the Union of Orthodox Rabbis of the United States and Canada, which would excommunicate him in 1945, had come into being. The ultra-Orthodox were deeply troubled by the many immigrants who were calling themselves rabbis but who lacked credentials and appropriate knowledge.

The Jewish Theological Seminary, founded in 1886, was reorganized under Solomon Schechter in 1902 with the goal of helping to Americanize these immigrants.[9] The ultra-Orthodox were highly critical of the Seminary and its nontraditional curriculum. These Orthodox rabbis attempted to prevent congregations from hiring Seminary graduates. When they learned that Kehilath Jeshurun, an established Orthodox congregation on the Upper East Side, was going to hire a graduate of the Seminary as its rabbi, they strongly condemned this action. The Seminary graduate involved was Mordecai Kaplan.[10]

Kaplan had received his B.A. from City College in 1900 and was ordained at the Jewish Theological Seminary in 1902. He was hired at Kehilath Jeshurun in 1903 and officiated there from 1903 until 1909. During this period, he also studied for his Master's at Columbia University, majoring in philosophy and sociology. It is clear from his writings of this period that he had profound conflicts about his religious faith. Though he strictly adhered to the daily round of prayers and rituals, he felt cast adrift from his moorings as a traditional Jew and grew impatient with the traditional prayer texts. In an early diary entry from May 1905, we find the following: "[A]re not these [entries in the journal] more truly prayer and confession than the infinite repetition of the daily prayers in our ritual, from which I find it necessary to desist occasionally in order to be able to recite it all without getting nausea." His religious conflicts would give him no respite. "Oh God what anguish of soul! How doubt tortures me," he wrote in his journal in 1905.[11] Or again: "I little thought that at this time of my life, I would find myself so aimless. . . . I find a perfect 'photograph' of my mental life in the book of *Koheleth* [Ecclesiastes], in its skepticism, in its fear of God, in its worldliness and in its threadbare spirituality."[12]

Kaplan was rescued from this intolerable existential situation by Solomon Schechter, who in 1909 hired him to direct the Teachers Institute at the Seminary. For the next decade, Kaplan devoted himself to his duties at the seminary and, toward the end of that decade, also helped organize the Jewish Center. The Jewish Center, founded in 1918 in a magnificent building still standing on West 86th Street in Manhattan, was a combination of an orthodox synagogue and a Young Men's Hebrew Association (YMHA). The "*shul* with a pool and a school," as the Jewish Center was called, was the perfect embodiment of Kaplan's concept of Judaism as a civilization.[13] The Center, however, was an Orthodox institution, and we should not be surprised that, as time went on, Kaplan developed significant disagreements with the its leadership.

A major incendiary event was an article Kaplan published in 1920 in which he expressed his belief that Orthodoxy had no future in America.[14] The article appeared in the *Menorah Journal,* a leading liberal monthly of the time and became a cause celebre in the Orthodox community. How he expected to continue as rabbi of an Orthodox institution after he published this article I still do not understand. In the article, Kaplan states his conviction that, if Orthodox Judaism was to survive, it had to adjust to democratic culture in America. One might say that, with this article and Kaplan's exodus from the Jewish Center, he ceased to be an Orthodox rabbi.[15] In the winter of 1922, Kaplan moved one block down the street from the Center and organized the Society for the Advancement of Judaism.

Kaplan's crowning achievement during this period was his magnum opus, *Judaism as a Civilization,* published in 1934. This foundational work is crucial in understanding his alienation from the Orthodox. Though few Orthodox rabbis were likely to read it, Kaplan's hard-hitting theological naturalism and his dismissal of the concept that Jews are a "chosen people" received much publicity.[16]

One of Kaplan's most radical proposals in *Judaism as a Civilization* is that rituals be considered as customs or folkways, instead of laws. In explaining the way that the concept of custom might be applied to *kashrut* (dietary laws), Kaplan states the following:

> Once these practices lose their character as laws and become folkways, Jews will be able to exercise better judgment as to the manner of their observance. There need not be the feeling of sin in the case of the occasional remissness nor the self-complacency which results from scrupulous observance.... from the standpoint observed here it would not be amiss for a Jew to eat freely in the house of a Gentile, and to refrain from eating *trefe* [non-Kosher food] in the house of a fellow Jew.[17]

As a consequence of such "heresy"—that is, considering *mitzvot* as custom and not law—Kaplan was strongly criticized by prominent Orthodox leaders, including Rabbi Leo Jung (who succeeded him at the Jewish Center) and Rabbi Joseph Lookstein (who succeeded him at Kehilath Jeshurun). Kaplan did not think this proposal regarding *kashrut* particularly extreme, since he did not "give outright license to violate *kashrut*," but only wanted to illustrate what it meant to treat rituals as folkways instead of as legal certainties.[18] Rabbi Jung believed that Kaplanism reduced the Jews to the level of "Eskimos, Poles and Magyars." He maintained that nationalism plus reform was the essence of Kaplanism and a most dangerous threat to Orthodoxy. He did not deny that Orthodoxy was in trouble and indeed felt that the Orthodox were indebted to Kaplan, who by his threat helped to whip the remnant of Israel back into shape.[19]

With respect to *kashrut* and his own religious regimen, Kaplan for the most part continued traditional observances. To be accurate, however, we should say that the matter of Kaplan's personal religious life was complex and not strictly Orthodox. As important as the minutiae of *kashrut* were, it is also evident that his radical ideology seemed to grow more and more threatening by the year. During the 1930s, Kaplan proceeded to spell out the implications of his naturalist theology. He moved from the metaphysical to the practical in detailing the way that the *mitzvah* system could be explained and justified not as the will of God but as an embodiment of the ideal of self-fulfillment.

This brings us to what, unbeknownst to Kaplan, was the first major precipice of his life: the creation of a new *haggadah* text. Today, there is a plethora of new *haggadot*, liturgies for the Passover service, each of which introduces new material, new political concerns, new interpretations of the biblical story of the Exodus. But in the late 1930s, there was only the traditional text, created two millennia ago. Like all elements of the Jewish diaspora, it had been translated into numerous languages and took on new resonances as the centuries wore on, but the Hebrew text itself was essentially unchanged.

Kaplan's *New Haggadah*, which he published in 1941, was a shock. To begin, Kaplan eliminated from the Passover story the ten plagues that befell Egypt and dropped most of the references to the rabbinic interpretations of the Exodus. Instead of the traditional emphasis on the saving power of God, in Kaplan's *haggadah*, Moses is the focus, and Passover is the holiday of freedom, rather than divine deliverance. The distinction is subtle but fundamental. Most importantly, Kaplan's *haggadah* dropped the call for divine vengeance against the nations, embodied in the *Sh'fokh hamat-kha* prayer ("Pour out thy wrath upon the nations, oh Lord." Psalms 79:6). This prayer is said after the Passover meal, when the door is opened for Elijah, the prophet who traditionally is supposed to usher in the last days. Part of that scenario is, of course, the punishment of all the enemies of Israel.[20]

This "hatred" formula is especially important in understanding the *herem* that brought down upon Kaplan four years later. Although scholars have always naturally assumed that the occasion for the excommunication was Kaplan's 1945 prayer book, it is obvious that *The New Haggadah* was as important if not more important than the prayer book. The evidence here is quite simple. Rabbi Israel HaLevi Rosenberg (1915–55),[21] a member of the executive committee of the *Agudat Rabbanim*, stated in his opening remarks to the official declaration of Kaplan's excommunication, "We are gathered here today to vehemently protest against one of the [Conservative Rabbis] who has issued a new *siddur* [prayer book] in Israel. These Conservatives are worse than the Reform (Jews). Every traditional Jew knows the Reform but the Conservative Jews dress themselves in [the garb of] a new Judaism, a modern Judaism which traditional Jews follow thinking it is our own."[22]

Rosenberg then went on to decry the Kaplan *haggadah,* calling attention especially to the elimination of the hate formula. This rabbi accused Kaplan of taking out these words "in order to curry favor among the non-Jews." These same nations, Rosenberg pointed out, stood by while the "cursed killers [Nazis] eliminated whole Jewish communities. It was these same nations who stood by and did nothing while more than five million Jews were slaughtered. . . . if these words, 'pour out thy wrath' had not been in the *haggadah* it would have been our obligation at this time to add them."

Although the decree of excommunication does not mention the *haggadah,* its timing speaks volumes. The Kaplan *haggadah* came out in 1941, as Nazi Germany was bludgeoning its way through Europe. Over the next several years, awareness of the slaughter of Europe's Jews slowly grew among American Jewry; at the same time, the radical message of Kaplan's *haggadah* made it infamous among the leaders of the ultra-Orthodox community.[23] We should point out that, though Kaplan eliminated the "hate prayer," *The New Haggadah* contains numerous original readings in which the tyranny of the ancient pharaoh is brought into contemporary focus by means of comparison with fascist dictatorships.

Nonetheless, the ultra-Orthodox could not forget or forgive the elimination of the hate prayer. They had four years to consider what to do about *The New Haggadah*. When the Kaplan *siddur* came out in May of 1945, they jumped at the chance to issue the decree of excommunication. The horrors then being revealed about the concentration camps help us understand the mood and the swift reaction of the Orthodox community. The speeches offered to justify Kaplan's excommunication referred explicitly to the camps. The anger of the rabbis, though terribly misdirected, is understandable considering the still-looming threat of Nazism and the catastrophic assault on the heart of Judaism.

After a number of other speeches given by members of the executive committee, the decree of excommunication was read by Rabbi Rosenberg to the assembled audience. The decree reads, in part:

TEXT OF THE DECREE OF EXCOMMUNICATION

My help comes from the Lord, the maker of heaven and earth

—(Psalm 12 1:2)

> The leaders of the people, rabbis of Greater New York and surroundings, heads of yeshivos, hasidic leaders, and scholars from the great yeshivos of this community, gathering together on the third day of the week of the *parashah* of *Korah* [Numbers 16:21], the second day of Rosh Hodesh Tammuz, 5705—at the calling of the executive body of the Union of Orthodox Rabbis of the U.S. and Canada [*Agudas HaRabonim*] and of the Rabbinic Committee [*Va-ad HaRabonim*] of Greater New York, because of the terrible scandal done in a high-handed and openly insolent manner by a certain person called Dr. Mordecai Kaplan, in publishing a new monstrosity by the name of *Siddur Tefihlos* in which he demonstrated total heresy and a complete disbelief in the God of Israel and in the principles of the law of the Torah of Israel—and the future of a heresy that continues like this who can contemplate?—therefore, it has been decided unanimously and in one congregation to banish him and to excommunicate him and to separate him from the community of Israel until he fully repents in accordance with law and custom.

> We hereby publish and declare, by the authority of the King of the Universe and by the power of our holy Torah, with complete fortitude and strength and with the full weight of the law, **A Total Prohibition and Total Ban on This Siddur,** which must be neither seen nor found throughout all the territory of Israel, and by the bite of the snake [of excommunication], the curse of the rabbis that has no remedy is upon anyone who holds this *siddur* in his hand or who looks at it, whether in private or in public. Anyone who obeys all of the above will be doubly blessed.

After the meeting, Kaplan's *siddur* was burned,[24] as the *halakhah* demands of a *Sefer Torah* (Pentateuchal scroll) written by a *min* (heretic). The whole event was painfully symbolic of all-too-recent events. The group of rabbis burned Kaplan's *siddur* just five weeks after Germany surrendered to the Allied forces and the war officially came to an end (V-E Day, May 8, 1945). In the weeks after, Allied soldiers began the horrific discovery of countless charred bodies in the concentration camps across Germany and Poland. As reports of these horrors crossed the Atlantic and entered into the American consciousness, it is inconceivable that Jewish leaders would burn a document created by a fellow Jew. The procedure in 1945 seems especially bizarre and offensive. The rabbis, however, could not suppress their anger against Kaplan for eliminating the call for hatred from the *haggadah*. If there was a time for hatred, after all, the shocking events between 1941 and 1945 was certainly that time. In 1941, the horrors of the Holocaust were not fully known, but it was clear that the Jewish people were threatened. Nevertheless, Kaplan was adamant that hatred was not central to the religious consciousness and equally adamant that such hatred would never lead to peace and security.

The issue of hate, as we all know, is still very much alive today within the fundamentalist ideologies of each of the Abrahamic religions, Jewish, Christian, and Muslim alike. The destruction such emotion has caused is incalculable. Particularly as we contemplate a shadowy world of terrorist attacks and near-constant chaos in the Middle East, the simple acceptance of Kaplan's *haggadah* seems like a beautiful possibility. Yet we can almost understand the reactions of the Orthodox rabbis in 1945. The Jewish people were threatened with extinction at the hands of a well-armed and ideologically driven nation; what other weapons did Jews have but to call down the wrath of God upon their enemies? It seemed a deeply emotional affront to eliminate the hate formula. Many of the Orthodox thought Kaplan was undermining Judaism as a whole. The ultra-Orthodox were threatened twice it would seem—not only by the Holocaust but by modernity as a whole, which seemed ever more at odds with their values. Many of those who were murdered in Europe were religious Jews, and many of those in the Union of Orthodox Rabbis came to America before the war, and many others had relatives in Europe who had not been so fortunate. In the face of such threats, hatred seemed an essential weapon in the Jewish arsenal. Their anger against Kaplan, though obviously misplaced, is understandable.

According to Jewish law, a person under the ban is excluded from the community more than cursed to eternal damnation. Jews are not allowed to talk to, do business with, or relate to the excommunicated person. Kaplan, nonetheless, received hundreds of supportive letters during the months after the excommunication, including one from Albert Einstein. Obviously, there were few ultra-Orthodox Jews in Kaplan's life; thus, the effect of the ban was largely symbolic. Kaplan related that some years later when the chief rabbi of Israel was in New York and invited to the Seminary, he refused to enter the building because Mordecai Kaplan was a member of the faculty.[25]

There was, however, at least one recorded incident where Kaplan was actually shunned by a fellow Jew because of the ban. It occurred at the Jewish Theological Seminary and involved another member of the seminary faculty, Professor Saul Lieberman, a great Talmud scholar and a relative of the Hazon Ish (Avraham Y. Karelitz, 1878–1953), who was at the time the leader of *haredi* [ultra-Orthodox] Jewry in Palestine.[26] The incident, which later became quite famous, is recorded in Kaplan's diary:

> Last Saturday morning, after the services, Rabbi Joel Geffen called my attention to the fact that an advertisement had appeared in *Morning Journal* of Friday, June 8, announcing a special conference of rabbis for the purpose of denouncing a so-called prayer book issued by atheists and common heretics who call themselves rabbis. This convention was called by the Union of Orthodox Rabbis. That advertisement appeared again in the last Monday's and Tuesday's "Morning Journal." The third ad was more strident than the preceding.
>
> Last Wednesday "The Jewish Morning Journal" and "The Jewish Day" carried reports of the conference. According to these reports the rabbis present not only carried through the formal ceremony of *herem* against me, which was concluded with the reading of the first Psalm, but also had a copy of the prayer book burned on top of the table at which the presiding officers sat. The one who applied the match was a certain Rabbi Ralberg.
>
> On Wednesday morning at 10:30 I presided at a meeting of the special committee of the Rabbinical Assembly to deal with the problem of enlisting young people for Jewish professional leadership and service. At 1:00 PM I went to Prof. Marx's room in the fourth floor to attend the special luncheon in honor of Finkelstein whose fiftieth birthday anniversary had come round. As I entered the room I noticed that Prof. Lieberman did not give the slightest sign of recognizing my presence. I was a bit flustered for a moment, but soon adjusted myself

to the situation, because I had always known him to be violently antagonistic to me and my works. At the table later, I noticed that he sat at the very end together with Moshe Davis, instead of at a place near the head of the table, according to his status on the Faculty. When the luncheon was over and I was waiting for the elevator to take me downstairs, Lieberman was coming in my direction. As soon as he noticed me, he lowered his eyes and hastened his steps. "Why are you angry with me," I said in all innocence. "I am not angry," he replied and ran on. Later it occurred to me that possibly, he regarded it his duty to obey the *herem* of the rabbis. Sure enough, when I was at the Seminary on Friday, I learned that that was actually the case!

Though the consequences for Kaplan and his status within the community were negligible, the *herem* definitely affected him. Just as the rabbis saw the excommunication within the context of Holocaust and the ongoing revelations of its horrors, so did Kaplan. He was disgusted and depressed by the situation. The day after the *herem* was published in the paper, he confided to his diary:

I had always had nothing but profound contempt for the rabbis associated with the "Union &c." I had had enough of a close-up view of them to know their immoral dealings. I could not help seeing in them the unfailing demonstration of the low moral level of at least 50% of the *Tannaim* and *Amoraim* [early rabbinic leaders] as reflected in the Talmud. This dastardly action of theirs at the present time when even the greatest reactionaries are still lying low and dare not violate publicly the four freedoms for which the war against Germany was supposed to have been fought and won is liable to render us Jews odious even to the more liberal elements of the general community. What a shattering effect this exhibition of moral degeneracy on the part of men who call themselves rabbis has upon me I can hardly express. All my efforts depend upon faith in the Jewish people. With so much corruption wherever I turn, I find it exceedingly hard to carry on the struggle for Jewish survival. Truth to tell, I experience neither the sufferings nor the consolations of a martyr.[27]

Though the excommunication did not cut Kaplan off from the Jewish community in any significant sense, it did highlight and deepen his radicalism. For the Orthodox, this event would forever brand him as a heretic.

The act of excommunication seems quite out of place in the twentieth century, especially at a hotel conference room in mid-town Manhattan. This act—medieval both in its historical origins and its aggressiveness—seems more appropriate to the era of the *auto da fé* and the various inquisitions that named heretics between the twelfth and seventeenth centuries. Kaplan's bizarre fate cannot but help us think back to the most famous excommunication of all—Baruch Spinoza. Considering Spinoza will afford us an opportunity to evaluate Kaplan's naturalistic tendencies and his affinity to "the great heretic."

Born in 1632, Spinoza lived in Holland where the Jews had only recently come in large numbers, fleeing the horrors of the Inquisition both in Spain and then in Portugal. Spinoza had a traditional education, which, in Holland at that time, meant primarily Torah study and Hebrew grammar. (It is interesting to note that late in his life he authored a Hebrew grammar.) Although there is some dispute among scholars, it is probable that Spinoza was not well acquainted with either the Talmud or the classics of rabbinic Judaism.

As a child, Spinoza was quite precocious. Rather early on, he became involved in the pursuit of secular learning, but his extrareligious inclinations are not likely to have been the cause of his conflicts with the Jewish community. In his early twenties, Spinoza studied with a certain Franciscus Van den Enden from whom he learned the classics in Greek and Latin and also fell in love with his teacher's daughter, who is rumored to have been thirteen years old at the time.[28] His studies were productive, but the romance did not bear fruit. Van den Enden had many radical political ideas and believed strongly in democracy. He also believed that religious leaders should have no part in a democratic state. Van den Enden "insisted on strict, political, equality between all members of the state, absolute freedom of speech, religion and opinion; and freedom of 'philosophizing.'"[29] For the two years before his excommunication, Spinoza fell under the spell of Van den Enden.

The ideas of Spinoza's Latin teacher about freedom were far from the political realities of the day. The Jews, recent immigrants to Amsterdam, were deeply apprehensive about the safety and the stability of their community. Their grandparents had been exiled from Spain and more recently from Portugal, so the dangers were certainly real. Amsterdam's Jewish leaders believed that their survival in Holland depended on avoiding scandal; anything that sounded heretical was an immediate threat. The *herem*, or excommunication, was the primary mechanism they had for disciplining and controlling the members of their community.

Excommunications were not infrequent. Sometimes they were for such transgressions as "banal" as adultery, but more often they concerned matters of religious belief. The most famous excommunication before Spinoza concerned one Uriel Da Costa (1585[?]–1640). In his writings and conversations, Da Costa raised doubts about the immortality of the soul and questioned the Mosaic authorship of the Bible. Amsterdam's leaders found this intolerable. At one point, he recanted his beliefs but then later relapsed into heretical arguments. In 1633, he was flogged in his synagogue; afterward, the synagogue leaders laid him in the doorway, and all those attending walked over him as they left, in his words, "stepping with one foot over the lower parts of my body."[30] A short time later, he killed himself.

Spinoza's treatment was much less harsh, although the mere exclusion from the community was very serious. He had published nothing that could be deemed heretical and was a loyal member of the congregation, having the previous year finished saying Kaddish for his father. He attended synagogue more or less regularly in the year before the *herem*. The members of the *ma'amad*, the synagogue's central committee, even went so far as to offer him a type of bribe. They were more concerned with appearance than substance and asked Spinoza to attend services more frequently. His response, in the phrasing of one scholar, was that "even if they offered him ten thousand guilders 'he would not accept such hypocrisy,' for he sought only truth and not appearance."[31]

And so, on July 27, 1656, three days before the ninth of Av—which commemorates the destruction of the First and Second Temples in ancient times—a decree of excommunication was read in the synagogue against Spinoza. Not surprisingly, his reaction as recorded by one of his biographers seems aloof and detached, even arrogant: "All the better, they do not force me to do anything that I would not have done of my own accord if I did not dread scandal. But, since they want it that way, I enter gladly on the path that is opened to me, with the consolation that my departure will be more innocent than was the exodus of the early Hebrews from Egypt."[32] Such sentiments clearly indicate how alienated Spinoza was.

Although Kaplan identified with the great philosopher and embraced much of his philosophy, at the same time he was critical and believed that Spinoza felt only scorn for the Jewish people. In 1944, Kaplan vented his anger against those who seemed to be enemies of the Jews: "Marx and

Spinoza hated the Jewish people," he asserted in his journal in November of that year, "and [they] looked forward to its demise." At the same time, Kaplan like so many others considered Spinoza to be among the most important of modern thinkers: "Spinoza's importance consists in his crystallizing the spirit of modernism. . . . He altered radically the [traditional] universe of thought and has virtually established the contemporary universe."[33]

If Kaplan was a heretic, and many have felt that he was, it must be clearly understood that his heresy was in the service of saving the Jewish people.[34] Spinoza's transgression, by contrast, was in the service of reason. He was interested in saving humanity, but not the Jewish people in particular. Nevertheless, Kaplan did not hesitate to include "the great heretic" in his course for rabbinical students on the philosophies of Judaism at the Jewish Theological Seminary. In the early 1940s, this was certainly a brave move. Emerson's statement about the burdens of heroism is pertinent: "Popularity is for dolls; a hero cannot be popular."[35]

Though Kaplan despised Spinoza because of his disdain for the Jewish people, he nonetheless believed that Spinoza "achieved the highest conception of God,"[36] a concept that centered on the naturalistic rather than on the supernatural super "self" of traditional religion. It was because Spinoza's theology emphasized "reason as the true law of our being" that his concept of God appealed so deeply to Kaplan.[37] Ever the rationalist, Kaplan had deep respect for Spinoza's methods and for his emphasis on "blessedness," which he considered equivalent to salvation (a central concept, as we shall see, in Kaplan's philosophy).[38] Kaplan comments on Spinoza and salvation in the following terms: "He [Spinoza] identified salvation with the fulfillment of that which constituted human nature, which for him consisted in a life of the body and of the emotions in the service and under the control of reason."[39]

Of course, Jewish philosophy has always had a strong rationalist strain. The contemporary French Jewish philosopher Emmanuel Levinas (1906–95) similarly praised Spinoza for this trait. In a very moving passage on the great philosopher, Levinas writes,

> Freedom of spirit, in a very precise manner, announces the wish to maintain an inner link with the truth: to be self-effacing before the truth, but to feel the master in this effacement, like the mathematician who bows before the evidence,

conscious of a supreme freedom. This marvelous coincidence of obedience and commandment, subjection and sovereignty, bears a well-worn but handsome name: reason. It is to reason that Spinoza's work offers supreme and certainly approving homage.[40]

It is not at all surprising that Kaplan resents the fact that Spinoza was put "outside the tribe," particularly in the fight for reason and for "spiritual independence" that Kaplan so deeply identified with. The following passage sums up Kaplan's thought on this complex issue:

> We rightly blame the "Goyim" [non-Jews] for isolating us and for the resulting degeneration. But if our culture were intrinsically worth anything, it ought to have been able to ward off that degeneration. I can't forgive our Jewish great men—Maimonides, the Gaon of Wilna, the Besht and others of like repute—for having contributed nothing to make us culturally and spiritually self-sufficient, for having left us on the contrary, bound hand and foot by tradition, so that we have become helpless cripples. Too bad, we had only one Spinoza and that he too preferred [sic] to fight from without instead of from within.[41]

Indeed, Kaplan explicitly challenges the Jewish people to carry on the work of Spinoza in bringing about the third revolution in religious thought. Kaplan emphasized that the first revolution was brought about by Moses who changed thinking about God as many to thinking about God as one. The second revolution was brought about by medieval Muslim philosophers who, under the influence of the Greeks, moved thinking from considering God as corporeal to God as incorporeal.[42] The third revolution, initiated by Spinoza, shifted thinking from the God of miracles to the God of nature. In a very instructive passage, Kaplan then calls upon the Jews to storm the barricades of ignorance and continue Spinoza's work: "Is it too fantastic," he asks," to suggest that it devolves upon us Jews to take a leading part in the third revolution as we did in the first?"[43] Kaplan would thus heartily agree with current scholars who seek to bring Spinoza back into the fold,[44] but his thinking goes even further and advocates a kind of Jewish Spinozism. Indeed, we can sum up much of Kaplan's philosophy by calling it a Spinozist approach to God and religion in the service of saving the Jewish people.

From the time of Philo of Alexandria, philosophers have believed that faith and reason lead to the same conclusions, even when such similarity was not obvious. Spinoza struggled to free reason from the dominance of religious authority. This required him to attack the primary source of ecclesiastical dominance—the Bible. Spinoza became, unwittingly, the father of biblical criticism. He believed that the books of the Torah were written over many generations by different people and that they did not directly reflect the voice of God. Spinoza insisted that the miracles of the Bible were all imaginary, and the prophets were not literally the messengers of God but rather talented men who eloquently elaborated fundamental moral insights. The truths of the Bible are not literally true but rather morally true. Such truths are rather the products of their specific time, unlike the truths of reason, which are eternal.

Spinoza believed that the only way to examine scripture was outside the burdens of religious tradition. In his words, "I resolved in all seriousness to make a fresh examination of Scripture with a free and unprejudiced mind, and to assert nothing about it, and to accept nothing as its teaching, which I did not quite clearly derive from it."[45] Spinoza believed that, in this way, he could understand the Bible in terms of its original historical context and thus extricate it from the interpretations of tradition that grew more cumbersome across the ensuing centuries.

Spinoza's target was religious authority, both Jewish and Christian. He railed against religious authorities of all types who "denounce those who deny miracles . . . because the dispelling of ignorance would entail the disappearance of that astonishment which is the one and only support . . . for safeguarding their authority."[46] Spinoza condemned religious leaders for promoting a literal understanding of the Bible in order to keep people ignorant. He believed that the purpose of the state was to serve its citizens but said that religious authorities believed the purpose of the state was to serve God and perpetuate their authority.

Kaplan certainly agreed with Spinoza on the problems of religious authority. He believed that traditional faith entailed a great deal of ignorance. He did not consider the Torah to be the literal word of God. The Torah revealed the Jewish people, rather than the other way around. Kaplan urged his fellow Jews to give up their belief in miracles and in the literal truths of the Torah and to substitute a more rational, rather than mythological, view of Jewish tradition.

The heart of the Kaplan-Spinoza attack on religious authority and on biblical interpretation was based on the long-standing tendency of interpreters to read their particular perspective back into a text without acknowledging it. This time-honored tradition of homiletical interpretation, both men argued, was fundamentally dishonest. Spinoza put it this way: "We see most people endeavoring to hawk their own commentaries as the word of God, and giving their best efforts, under the guise of religion, to compelling others to think as they do."[47] Kaplan terms this notion *transvaluation,* a process that "consists in ascribing meanings to the traditional content of a religion or social heritage, which could neither have been contemplated nor implied by the authors of that content."[48]

Spinoza believed that people must be liberated from the authority of the Bible and its interpreters so that they might pursue the truth through a life of reason. Kaplan, in a parallel move, sought to free the Jewish people from the authority of tradition to rescue their holy text from irrelevance and impotence. For these thinkers, the use of reason must begin with the understanding that the words people speak, including the holy words of scripture, are most often a product of the context in which they live and the culture they inhabit. The Bible is time-bound, as all human documents are, and in many instances is a very primitive document.[49]

For Spinoza, after we are freed from ecclesiastical authority, we can use our own reason to find truth and blessedness. For Kaplan, after we honestly state what is in the Torah, without any admixture of our own opinion, we are then free to update this vital document so that it remains relevant to our lives and our own views of the world. This last step Kaplan called *revaluation.* He insisted that there is always a core of eternal truth that lies behind the mythology and the contextual totality of the Jewish tradition.[50] But for this eternal truth to remain meaningful and not rigid, this core must be understood in contemporary terms. If it is, then the Bible can be become a fresh and compelling document once again. The new is always compelling and echoes Martin Buber's conviction that "all religions are true at the beginning."

Kaplan thus advocated that first we must see the Bible for what it is—a very human document, a product of its time that reflects the struggles of a very special people to find meaning and truth. Kaplan understood that Jews in every generation recreate the tradition to meet their needs and thereby keep it alive. He insisted that the Jewish people must continue the work of the past by doing the same thing—which is to say, by reconstructing it.

The ultimate religious question about Spinoza and Kaplan concerns their belief in God. Spinoza was considered an atheist even during his lifetime. In that era, it was believed that an atheist would lack all morality and discipline. Nothing could be more mistaken especially when it came to Spinoza. Nonetheless, it is true that both Kaplan and Spinoza rejected the personal God of traditional religion. According to both, God neither feels nor has a will nor speaks to anyone. God does not intervene in history or formulate laws. God does not reward or punish.

Kaplan's detractors often dismiss him as an atheist because they maintain that only a supernatural, personal God can be considered divine. Neither Kaplan nor Spinoza were atheists, and both of them thought about God continually and spent much of their lives trying to articulate the meaning of divinity in terms of human experience. One of the many reasons that these two men are so important is that the complexity of their thinking challenges us to expand our normal definitions. So let us put aside the reductive notion of "atheism," with its negative connotations. Instead, let us consider two extremes of the divine: transcendence, which describes a God who is above the world, and immanence, which describes a God who is in the world. If we understand that both Spinoza and Kaplan were primarily immanentists, then we can no longer dismiss them as atheists.

At a rather early point in the 1920s, Kaplan put the matter this way:

> while I believed in God as a transcendent Being I could not conceive of that Being having any meaning for us except through and in terms of human experience. The more real and immediate such experience is of the realities of life the more can we appreciate the spiritual values that signify God. The experience of reality is, in my opinion, as essential to experiencing God as the harp is for the production of music. The music is not evolved out of the harp but is conditioned by it. So our appreciation of the reality of God is not evolved out of our every day experience but conditioned by it.[51]

Spinoza believed that God was totally immanent or, to put it in more conventional terms, that God was totally identified with nature or all that is. He rejected all supernatural explanations. With Kaplan, the picture is more complicated. Kaplan, the genius of immanence, was never entirely satisfied with a God who was totally identified with the world and with nature. Yet, ultimately, I believe that Kaplan's heart and mind were on the side of immanence. In one striking statement explaining Spinoza, he asserted, "perhaps . . . what Spinoza understood by the statement 'God is' is . . . namely that the process of being as such is synonymous with God."[52]

Additionally, Kaplan points out a very curious fact mentioned by the Hasidic leader Shneur Zalman of Liadi (1745–1812) that, in "gematria," or Hebrew numerology, the word for God (*elohim*) and the word for nature (*hatevah*) both equal the number eighty-six.[53] According to traditional thinking, a numerical equivalence denotes a connection of meaning. Whether we believe in this traditional mode of logic or not, we should note that the mere fact of this equivalence fascinated Kaplan.

A number of times in his early career,[54] Kaplan stated his support for the views of the sociologist Emile Durkheim (1858–1917).[55] According to Durkheim, God was primarily identified with the highest ideals of any society.[56] But such conviction was never entire, and Kaplan also rejected the view that God was totally immanent or solely identified with social ideals.

It is clear that Kaplan at times expresses his belief in a transcendent God. As he put the matter in another early diary entry, "The moment God is merely identified with the world and conceived as being immanent but not transcendent, His divinity is denied and He is dissolved into the world. This is the atheism and pantheism which religion so vigorously contends against."[57] Nevertheless, Kaplan maintained that it is only in terms of immanence that God is meaningful in our lives.

Though Kaplan and Spinoza shared a common rational orientation, they differed in their goals. Kaplan was obsessed with rescuing the Jewish people; Spinoza believed that only reason—and not religion or cultural affiliation—can save us and was the apostle of the secular. Kaplan, drawing on Spinoza's achievements, desired to Judaize the secular (although many accuse him of the opposite, of secularizing Judaism). Although the forces of secularism were extremely powerful, Kaplan believed they could still be harnessed in the service of religious renewal.

Clearly, Kaplan's views on God, like so much of his thinking, are complex and multilayered. Across the eight-decade arc of his intellectual development, Kaplan says things that seem at opposite ends of the philosophical spectrum. Such seeming contradictions have led many to dismiss Kaplan as a philosopher and to criticize him for what seems to be a lack of intellectual rigor. But as we challenge ourselves to expand our definitions, we will find that these inconsistencies are crucial reflections of different moods. We should not simply dismiss his contradictions as inconsistent thinking. Kaplan is, rather, exploring alternative theological possibilities. Within this alternate world—a world that requires flexible definitions but also offers revelatory answers—we shall be able to expand our own sense of the theologically possible. Just as Kaplan continued to consider life's most important questions throughout his own life, resisting a fixed answer in favor of a more satisfying multiplicity of answers, so too shall we return again and again to the many different threads of his thinking.

We are left, then, with two men separated by several centuries yet united by a common "punishment." Their "crime?" To think wildly, to speculate rashly, to dream with great abandon about the things they cared for most.

TWO

SELF-RELIANCE:
KAPLAN AND EMERSON

Know your soul and you will come to know your creator.

—*Joseph Albo, as quoted by Mordecai Kaplan, 1954*

For the modern Jew, the needs of the autonomous self threaten the coherence of the Jewish community. Individualism is the greatest problem facing the Jewish people. For Mordecai Kaplan, as for so many other twentieth-century Jewish leaders, the primary problem was how to deal with the new sense of self that is at the root of both American culture and modernity. We cannot flee from it. It is precious and yet problematical. We cannot simply dismiss it. If we are to rise above its lowest expression—as narcissism and self-absorption—we must understand it.[1]

Kaplan's theology is complex, but I believe that the place of the individual holds the key to understanding his system. As we know, he was a fierce, lifelong advocate of the notion of Judaism as a civilization; he championed the concept of community and of the collective consciousness of the Jewish people. He devoted almost a decade of his life to organizing and running the Jewish Center, and he was a follower of that great cultural Zionist Ahad Ha-Am. While all these are significant, his views on individualism and individual fulfillment are the linchpins that hold the elaborate structure of his thought together.

Kaplan, of course, is not alone. When we speak historically of the individual in American religious life, we naturally think of Ralph Waldo Emerson; we shall see that Emerson plays a major part in molding Kaplan's religious views. Let me put it another way. There are several voices in Kaplan's head, voices that are quite disparate. We have called this a philosophy of mood. There is Henri Bergson and John Dewey and Baruch Spinoza. There is Emile Durkheim and Rudolf Otto. There is Ahad Ha-Am and Ralph Waldo Emerson. These advocates of the collective and the individual, of the mystical and the rational, are all held in a creative tension by Kaplan throughout his life. Kaplan moves back and forth. He rarely resides in one mood for very long, and his moves from one to the other are always provocative.

Understanding Kaplan's theology and his reinterpretation of salvation means to see him within his American context, within the broad outlines of religion in America. Salvation is a very old concept that refers to the goal and purpose of religion and is usually associated with Christianity. Throughout the Middle Ages, the term was taken to mean life everlasting in the next world. Kaplan was comfortable with the concept and reinterpreted it in a very American way, to refer to self-fulfillment in this world. This reconstructed notion of salvation is one of the foundational concepts of Kaplan's system.

Religion in America means Emerson. As Sidney Ahlstrom, the great scholar of American religion, puts it, "Emerson is in fact the theologian of something we may almost term 'the American Religion.'"[2]

At first glance, Kaplan and Emerson seem an unlikely pair, a very odd couple: Jew and Christian, rationalist and near mystic, one devoted to peoplehood, the other elevating the individual to divine status. They seem divergent in the extreme. Yet Kaplan not only appreciated Emerson but used him freely.

I first happened on the vast and poignant connection between Kaplan and Emerson purely by accident, while studying Kaplan's diary. In the summer of 1942, Kaplan was eagerly logging his thoughts about the prayer book that would come out in 1945 and would lead to his excommunication.[3] Kaplan finally decided to take seriously a piece of advice he had given many years before to one of his students, Louis Finkelstein. To create liturgy, he told Finkelstein in the early 1920s, you must take a theological essay and turn it into a prayer. Throughout the summer of 1942, Kaplan did just that, pondering essays by Leo Baeck, Abraham Joshua Heschel, and Ralph Waldo Emerson.[4] His entries on the first two writers made immediate sense to me, as Kaplan shares his Jewish commitment and liberal theology with both Baeck and Heschel. But when I came across his first references to Emerson, I was confounded. Kaplan a transcendentalist—how was this possible?

Yet Emerson's presence is undeniable, both in Kaplan's journal and in numerous published writings. I can think of no better example of the pluralistic nature of Kaplan's mind. Heschel and Baeck made it into the final edition of 1945 prayer book. Emerson did not. It should be noted, however, that, at the Society for the Advancement of Judaism before the 1945 prayer book appeared, Kaplan had instituted a loose-leaf prayer book, perhaps the perfect metaphor for his attitude toward the liturgy— a core of prayers to which the congregation could easily add or subtract. In the loose-leaf prayer book, Emerson and Heschel exist side by side.[5]

Abraham Joshua Heschel (1907–72) is perhaps the most important spiritual presence in the American Jewish community today. Coming from a traditional home, his religious ideology bound him to his Hasidic and mystical forebears. Born in Poland and descended from a distinguished line of Hasidic rabbis, Heschel fled the persecutions of Hitler's Germany and was brought to the United States by Reform leader Julian Morgenstern, who was intent on rescuing religious leaders of all stripes from the Nazi onslaught.[6]

Heschel, a master stylist in Hebrew, Yiddish, and English, eventually became a faculty member at the Jewish Theological Seminary where he spent many years teaching Jewish philosophy and mysticism. His philosophy seems, on the surface, completely antithetical to Kaplan's pragmatic naturalism, yet Kaplan, a pluralist to the core, was able to embrace Heschel as he had Emerson.

The Emerson essay Kaplan used for constructing the prayer we are considering was written in the late 1830s, when Emerson was at the height of his creative powers. Born in 1803 and educated at Harvard, he had been appointed minister of the Second Church of Boston in 1829, which he left three years later because of his conviction that he could no longer administer communion. Leaving the post of minister was but one manifestation of Emerson's growing rebellion against organized religion. Perhaps it was this rebellion that attracted Kaplan.

A prolific diarist and essayist, Emerson wrote and thought and preached his philosophy of individualism, which he called "self-reliance." His approach to religion was revolutionary, advocating that divinity was to be found within the moral conscience of each person. This particular brand of individualism has been called "moral perfectionism."[7] People had only to listen to their higher selves and were not doomed to an eternal struggle with their essential sinfulness as traditional Protestant thinkers, particularly John Calvin, had taught.

Emerson's theology was naturalistic, as Alfred Kazin, the well-known literary critic and Emerson apostle, has emphasized:

> Emerson's God did not make this world or provide salvation in the next. He did not lay down commandments, reward the righteous, or condemn sinners. He was another side of oneself, the ideal, the ultimate—to be reached in the perfection of one's consciousness.[8]

Emerson always emphasized that religion is an experience that must exist in the present, rather than as a past tradition, and he was drawn away from any supernatural understanding of Christianity. The prayer that Kaplan composed reflects the individualism at the center of Emerson's philosophy, as well as a bias against tradition and establishment.

Kaplan composed the prayer from key sentences that he took from Emerson's 1839 address to the Harvard Divinity School.[9] Most of the language here is Emerson's but the prayer is Kaplan's.

Needed Prophets for Our Day[10]
by
Rabbi Mordecai M. Kaplan
in the name of
Ralph Waldo Emerson

He who makes me aware that I am an infinite soul heartens me.
He who gives me to myself lifts me.
He who shows God in me fortifies me.
He who hides God from me destroys the reason for my being.
The divine prophets, bards and lawgivers are friends of my virtue, of my intellect, of my strength.
Noble provocations go out from them, inviting me to resist evil.
But let us not speak of revelations as something long ago given and done.
Only by coming to the God in ourselves can we grow forevermore.
Let us not say that the age of inspiration is past, that the Bible is closed.
Let us learn to believe in the soul of man, and not merely in men departed.
The need was never greater of new revelations than now.
The faith of man has suffered universal decay.
The heart moans, because it is bereaved of consolation and hope and grandeur.
We feel defrauded and disconsolate.

Our religion has become spectral.
It has lost its grasp on the affection of the good and on the fear of the bad.
What greater calamity can befall a nation than the loss of worship?
Then all things go to decay.
Genius leaves the Temple.
Literature becomes frivolous.
Science is cold.
The eye of youth is not lighted by hope of a better world.
Society lives for trifles
In the soul let redemption be sought.
Let the keepers of religion show us that God is, not was.
That He speaketh, not spoke.
And thus cheer our fainting hearts with new hope and new revelation.

Kaplan tells us in that journal entry that we ought to pray from Emer-son regularly in the Sabbath *Musaf* service, the additional prayer for the Sabbath.[11] Such an assertion constitutes a very significant theological statement, challenging our understanding of Kaplan and his theology. He is saying here that the divine is within, that the divine is revealed to us continually through moral reflection and that inspiration is to be found not only in the scriptures but in ourselves and our contemplation of the larger universe. While we may think of Kaplan primarily as a sociologist, his insistence on the Emersonian ideal of individualism reveals that he is one with the naturalist religious tradition we associate with the Roman-tic poets and the deists of the eighteenth century.

Emerson is, thus, a major part of Kaplan's lifelong project: his recon-struction of American Judaism. One might say that, in a sense, Emerson functioned as a part of Kaplan's subconscious. In the choices of what we read and in the texts we return to, we often discover lost parts of our-selves. Kaplan's Emerson offers just such a retrieval—of a part of Kaplan that has been lost (or misunderstood) today, and also of a part of him that he himself grew unaware of over time but is retrieved for him and for us through the Kaplan-Emerson prayer.

There are hints of Emerson in Kaplan's writing from the beginning. Let us look at the very first paragraph of Kaplan's journal. The year was 1913; Kaplan was thirty-two. He was preparing a series of talks to dif-ferent Menorah Societies around the country. The Menorah Societies consisted of groups of university students organized to further the study of Jewish culture. Kaplan's first stop was Harvard. In the journal, as he

would do for the next six decades, he began to work through the ideas
for his talk.

> Religion is primarily a social phenomenon. To grasp its reality, to observe its
> workings and to further its growth we must study its functioning in some social
> group. The individual and his development or perfection may constitute the sole
> aim of religion, but the fact and substance of religion cannot exist completely
> and exhaustively in an individual.[12]

This passage shows Kaplan at his best and is extraordinarily instructive.[13]
If we read these words, and Kaplan's writing in general, while keeping
in mind Ahad Ha-Am and Durkheim, we will emerge with one image:
Kaplan the sociologist. If we keep Emerson in mind, we fashion quite
another. One might say that, in a sense, Kaplan is often "speaking" Emerson but is barely aware of it. He states in the above passage an idea that
Emerson calls "self-culture."[14] The individual and his perfection, Kaplan
believes, is the goal of group life and the "aim" of religion. This thought
is perfectly Emersonian. We might call this individualism *bildung* [Ger-
man word for self-culture], since, for Emerson, this truth is inherited
from his teacher Johann Wolfgang von Goethe and Matthew Arnold,
as we shall see below.[15] Kaplan, in turn, eventually calls it "salvation."

It is well to remember that to talk about a religion of the individual
does not mean to advocate self-indulgence or narcissism. On the con-
trary, as we shall see, it means to rise above these, to find the divine
within each of us.

In this same journal entry, Kaplan states that the group is never the
end of our struggle; it is only the means to survival. But if we dare to
look beyond mere survival, we must ask, "survival for what?" Any such
question of larger purpose will naturally bring us back to the self and to
the religion of the individual.

There are times when the connections between Kaplan and Emerson are explicit and overwhelming. In a fascinating diary passage written
during World War II, Kaplan considers the evils of fascism and the way
that individuals are drawn by societal pressures toward evils they are
not always fully aware of. Only an inner freedom, he writes, can save
the individual when the multitude is bent on mischief. Kaplan's mind
jumps to Exodus 23:2, "Thou shalt not follow a multitude to do evil." But
in interpreting the verse, he thinks immediately of Emerson and quotes

one of the many famous lines from "Self-Reliance": "Society everywhere is in conspiracy against the manhood of its members." "Inner freedom," Kaplan continues, "is only the nay of which the yea spells truth, justice and peace. In saying nay to brute force in all its manifestations man qualifies himself for partnership with God to build the city of God."[16] Thus, the divine lies in the individual's courage to transcend his fears and to stand against the pressures of his society—in short, to stand for the transcendent.

For Kaplan, Emerson sometimes served as a "holy" text that precisely expressed what he was thinking; or, to put it another way, in his journal, Kaplan would be working through a situation or an idea, and a statement from Emerson would pop into his mind. In 1943, for example, Kaplan was reading about the Battle of France a few years before and was deeply impressed by the bravery of the French. The vital spirit expressed in the heroism of the French reminded him of a passage from Emerson about the individual, which he then inserted into his journal. The passage Kaplan quotes at this point is actually unrelated to heroism but links to vitality—a central notion in Kaplan's system:

> Consider that the perpetual admonition of Nature to us is, the world is new, untried. Do not believe the past. I give you the universe new and unhandselled every hour. . . . In your sane hour you shall see that not a line has yet been written. . . . It remains for you; so does all thought, all object, all life remain unwritten still.[17]

Emerson's call to renewal illustrated for Kaplan the ever-present potential to remake ourselves. That potential is the core idea in Kaplan's notion of salvation. As we shall see, Kaplan has always been much more interested in salvation than in God—a point that has caused great anger in his critics and, just as important, great misunderstanding among his disciples. My hope is that, if we come to this foundational aspect of Kaplan's thinking through the seemingly roundabout notion of the self-reliant individual, we will be better able to appreciate both of these concepts.

Kaplan is continually searching for a proper formulation for this hybrid, and profoundly nontraditional, version of salvation. At one point in the journal, as if to quote John Dewey, he says that salvation means growth. Additionally, we must remember that growth for Kaplan takes

place only within the group. Though Kaplan's theology bears a striking resemblance to Emersonian transcendentalism, his ideology is only
completed through his appropriation of Dewey.[18] Emerson never emphasizes the group as much as his disciples do. To complete the circle,
we must remember that, for Dewey, the group exists for the benefit of
each individual in it.

Kaplan's most frequent formulation is that salvation means to become fully human. The more pragmatic articulation of this idea is that
salvation enables us to become fully effective. Again and again, Kaplan asserts the ideal of individual perfection and embraces democracy
as Emerson and Dewey understood it. (We should mention here that
Dewey serves as Kaplan's other *"rebbe,"* and Dewey's progressive pragmatic philosophy provides a corrective to Emerson's unabashed search
for the divine.) Stephen Rockefeller, one of Dewey's most articulate contemporary disciples, says that Dewey's "concept of growth is one of the
big unifying ideas in his evolutionary philosophy of human nature and
society. It ties his theory of the moral life together with his psychology,
theory of education, and social thought."[19] Kaplan summed up his own
ideology in a similar vein:

> Salvation is redemption from those evils within and outside man which hinder
> man from becoming fully human, or which obstruct his urge to self metamor-
> phosis [i.e., self-fulfillment]. Salvation is unhampered freedom in living and
> helping others to live a courageous, intelligent, righteous and purposeful life.[20]

Throughout the 1940s, Kaplan wrote much about creating a scientific
schema of religion that he called "soterics"—from the Greek word *soter,*
to save. His hope was to create a scientific theory of salvation, a "pragmatic metaphysics," if you will. Over the years, I have found fragments
in English from Kaplan's work on soterics, including the quotation at
the beginning of this chapter. This work was apparently translated into
Hebrew in the 1955 and appears under the title *Ha-emunah ve-hamusar*
(Belief and Ethics). On the first page of *Ha-emunah ve-hamusar,* we find
the striking quotation that began this chapter, which I believe illustrates
the thrust of Kaplan's whole theology. The quotation is from Albo, the
fifteenth-century Jewish philosopher, who himself was quoting Al Gazzali, the eleventh-century Muslim philosopher whose thought, of course,

goes back to Aristotle and Plato. The statement Kaplan quotes is *"Dah et naphshekhah ve-tedah et borekha"*—which translates as "know your soul and you will come to know your creator." The direction here is clear: it is from, and through, the individual that we get to the divine. In Kaplan's thinking, the term *soul* is always equivalent to the self, or the individual. The self, in other words, is the key to the divine. We cannot get more Emersonian than this.[21]

Kaplan's connection of the self and the divine finds a provocative echo in Emerson's own diary, as he explores the hoped-for unity of the self. The unity of the self is another way of articulating the goal of self-fulfillment or self-reliance, to use Emerson's phrase. In the quotation below, we feel Emerson's sense of frustration as he struggles to achieve the unity that is his goal and that is a manifestation of the divine within.

> I am not united, I am not friendly to myself, I bite and tear myself. I am ashamed of myself. When will the day dawn of peace and reconcilement when self united and friendly I shall display one heart and energy to the world?[22]

* * *

The "Divinity School Address," on which the above Kaplan prayer is based most completely, sums up Emerson's attitude toward established religion. It stirred great controversy. One eyewitness comments on the lecture: "The discourse was full of divine life,—and was a true word from a true soul. . . . [Nonetheless, it] gave dire offence to the rulers at Cambridge. . . . The harshest words are not spared, and 'infidel' & 'atheist' are the best terms poor E. gets." This friend and supporter summed up what many others felt about Emerson: "He is a seer, who looks into the infinite, & reports what he sees."[23] The greatest "crime" of this address is Emerson's insistence that God speaks not primarily though the scripture but through every individual. As we shall see, that heresy is also the source of great attraction to Kaplan.

The prayer inspired by Emerson's thinking needs to be unpacked carefully for us to understand the Emersonian aspect of Kaplan's mind. We must first note the specific ways in which Kaplan changed Emerson's language. Kaplan's prayer, though it uses the language of Emerson's essay, is not simply a word-for-word quotation. From the beginning of the prayer, we see that Kaplan sharpens the thoughts and lifts the rhetoric (if indeed we can talk about improving Emerson's revelatory prose). For example, Emerson writes, "That which shows God out of me makes me a wart and a wen. There is no longer a necessary reason for my being. Already the long shadows of untimely oblivion creep over me, and I shall decease forever." Kaplan sharpens and simplifies to "He who hides God from me destroys the reason for my being." There are some points where Kaplan's additions reflect his Jewish consciousness. Thus, "The divine bards are the friends of my virtue, of my intellect, of my strength" becomes in Kaplan "The divine prophets, bards and *lawgivers* are friends of my virtue, of my intellect, of my strength." Kaplan, though, also ignores some of Emerson's most potent ideas, for reasons not entirely clear. The beautiful statement "Men have come to speak of the revelation as somewhat long ago given and done, as if God were dead" becomes in Kaplan, "Let us not speak of revelations as something long ago given and done."[24] It might be that the phrase "as if God were dead" was just too much for Kaplan to articulate; no matter his persistent forays with heresy, some ideas about God's demise were simply unpalatable.

"Coming to the God in ourselves" will, of course, lead us into a discussion of self-reliance and of the nature of the self generally. But we must first fully understand the very radical nature of the statement here. To say that God is within is to say that God is not primarily in scripture, nor in past revelations that give rise to scripture. Yet both Emerson and Kaplan, though they believed that the key to the divine lies within, never fully negated the great revelations of the past, and both had a healthy respect for the biblical canon.

Emerson must be read critically to have any meaning. "Coming to the God in ourselves" does not mean we must support individualism in an unqualified way. We all need rules; both Emerson and Kaplan understood this. George Kateb, one of Emerson's most articulate contemporary disciples, simply dismisses lower forms of individualism altogether. In discussing self-reliance, he puts aside any version of individualism that is self-indulgent, self-destructive, or egotistical. All these are excluded from Emerson's (and Kaplan's) discussion of self-reliance and individualism. It does not mean that these are not problems, but simply that, for Kateb, for Emerson, and for Kaplan, this kind of behavior is but the lowest form that individualism may take and, though overcoming our own narcissism is crucial for any religious awareness, transcending mere narcissism is not a sufficient ideal in itself.[25]

Kaplan referred to this base form of individualism as "playing the God," as opposed to his ideal of being Godlike; the conflict between these two extremes of human capacity, he believed, was a major theme of the scriptures. The sin of Adam and Eve, for example, was precisely this pursuit of power, which is the most self-destructive urge in all of us. If we are to survive, we must learn to subject our egotism to higher ends. In Kaplan's words, the truly religious person "can respect his ego only if it is more than an ego, only if it is a soul, a responsible focus for the creative energy of God in bringing about a better world, one in which life is more secure, more abundant and more happy." Such a person "will love God 'with his whole soul,' that is, according to Rabbi Akiba's interpretation, he would be willing to sacrifice his very life itself to the love of God."[26]

The goal of religion is, thus, to help us subject our lower impulses to our higher capacities. When speaking at New York's Ninety-Second Street Y in 1915, Kaplan stated, "I defined it [religion] as being that phase of the life of a collective body or social group which makes for the subjection of the selfish to the unselfish both in the individual and in the group."[27] For both Emerson and Kaplan, a person's real strength resides not in a strong will but in the renunciation of the lower gratifications of power, fame, and self-aggrandizement.[28] What Kaplan seeks is an "impersonal individualism." Similarly, one Emerson scholar uses the image of abandonment: "We ascend by abandonment that is the deliberate struggle against being calculating, against becoming obsessively self furthering."[29] As Stanley Cavell, the Harvard philosopher, put it, being true to oneself does not mean being self-serving.[30]

For Kaplan, the goal is not to give in to our lowest urges and desires and allow them to take control. Need—yes, says Kaplan; greed—no. When I first met Kaplan in 1972, his formulation of the divine included the notion that there was enough in the world to satisfy our *needs*. The world was not abundant enough, however, to satisfy our *greeds*, particularly for power and pleasure. The inevitability of individual need—thus, its necessarily central role in religious thinking—seems to frighten many religious leaders but was not a problem for Kaplan. He was adamant that we could—and must—distinguish between what we need and what we merely want. It is the overindulgence in satisfying that which we do not truly need—that is, our greed—that we must be concerned with. Religion in its pragmatic form, which we shall discuss below, is rightfully concerned with the fulfillment of legitimate needs. Kaplan agreed with Abraham Maslow, the great humanistic psychologist and the primary ideologist of need, that, once we satisfy our legitimate lower needs, we can move on to the higher ones.[31] If we do not satisfy our lower needs we will forever become imprisoned in a lower stage of functioning.

For Emerson and Kaplan, the divine within refers to the "still small voice of conscience." Emersonian religion rests on the belief in an innate moral sense, the conscience, which, in the past was seen as the veritable voice of God in the soul. In his fight against skepticism, the moral sense represented Emerson's Archimedean point and reflected the freedom from mutability that he so earnestly sought.[32] Kaplan's concept of the conscience follows closely. In the following passage, we see that he rejects a social-scientific interpretation of conscience and considers it instead something far more basic:

> That there is an inner drive to be honest and just, independently of all other drives or impulses is not always recognized or admitted. Yet a sufficient number of instances can be adduced to prove the existence of such a drive. The most familiar manifestation of it is conscience. But very often conscience is made out to be a camouflage for some functional impulse. However, there are cases where it is an irreducible ultimate.[33]

In the post-Freudian age, we are painfully aware that conscience may not easily be considered an "irreducible ultimate." Our conscience is always conditioned by a host of factors. But perhaps we should talk about conscience as the human innate capacity for moral judgments, with the strength of that capacity and its content differing from one person to another and from one culture to another. As Richard Rorty explains, "a sense of moral obligation is a matter of conditioning rather than of insight."[34] Producing a strong moral sense is one of the primary goals, as we know, of religious education around the world. Kaplan's lifelong devotion to education put the development of a strong moral sense at its center. Educators talk much about the moral and ethical goals of education, but these values are rarely implemented in the classroom, especially in Jewish religious classrooms.

Though our moral insight may differ from person to person because of our family, our education, and our cultural background, yet there is a sense of moral standards, of basic fairness and justice that we all share. Religious leaders today are so afraid that their followers will fall into the pit of relativism that, when discussing the issue, they call immediately for reliance on some kind of outside supernatural authority. It is God-reliance that will save us, they say, rather than self-reliance. Part of Kaplan's bravery, and part of what made the Orthodox establishment so uncomfortable, is that he demanded that we not fall victim to the false comfort of relying on God. Instead, we must look within. The Orthodox, like religious conservatives of all denominations, fear that relying too much on the self will inevitably lead to moral relativism, which immediately conjures chaos, moral license, and the decay of long-cherished values. The confusion lies in the word *subjective* that refers both to inwardness and the moral relativity that we fear. Kaplan, however, contends that looking within does not necessarily mean that there is no objective standard.

Moral relativism is obviously a very complex matter, and we cannot fully discuss it here; suffice it to say that Kaplan was well aware of the issue and dealt with it at a very early point. At a rabbinic conclave held in Atlantic City in 1914, Kaplan faced head-on the problem of the interiority of values and moral relativism: "Authority may be based upon personal experience and conviction and yet not be subjective. It may possess the highest degree of objectivity, if the experiences and convictions are those which a normally constituted people share."[35]

He believed that looking inward does not mean that every opinion is the same as every other. It would be moral anarchy, and manifestly ridiculous, if we held all moral judgments to be equal. Our sense of moral law obviously comes from the group of which we are a part. Kaplan taught that if we have had a sound moral education, are sensitive to the needs of the other, are sophisticated and decent, looking within will be the best way to make a moral judgment. In other words, when we rise to the highest level in terms of our moral sensibilities, our innermost thoughts will correspond to the universal moral principles that we all recognize. Often we get lured out of that high place by the "truths of the day," by fashion and by convention. But deep underneath lies the moral compass that we must—and can—access. Contemporary ethical theorists assert that the highest stage of ethical judgment is a postconventional type of thinking that judges situations in terms of universal moral principles.[36]

Let us put the matter another way: morality and fundamental values must be taught, but, beneath those essential teachings, we all have the capacity to judge morally, and, in large measure, we all share the same moral principles. Though there is a particularity to each religion that rises out of its unique historical experience, there is also a shared set of moral principles that we see in the major religions. Kaplan firmly believed that all religions have the same ideals. It is only in their particular embodiments, in the process of making these ideals concrete, that they differ. To take one of innumerable examples, I believe in the fundamental Christian goal of "peace on earth, good will toward men"; yet I would never allow my young son to bring a Christmas tree into our house. In particular manifestations, I differ from my Christian brethren, yet, in fundamental principle (the far more important of the two), we agree.

There is, in other words, a commonness of experience, an innate moral capacity that we all share and that gives rise to religious experience. In the future, Kaplan asserted in 1930, a religion will establish its "validity" "by upholding its universal character, by demonstrating wherein it conforms with the universal principles of human experience." The universal principles Kaplan refers to here are principles that we all have the right to expect: concern for the other and justice as fairness.[37]

Emerson goes much further than Kaplan on the reliability of the private moral sense. Of course, the ultimate measure of human achievement is one's moral behavior, but few of us would go as far as Emerson, who states, "To believe your own thought, to believe that what is true for you in your private heart is true for all men—that is genius. Speak your latent conviction, and it shall be the universal sense."[38] Such a statement only makes sense if we assume that our innate moral capability has been developed to its highest capacity. We are, however, fully aware from the Kaplan diary that he was quite skeptical of the moral capacities of those he dealt with.

Despite Kaplan's more subdued faith in the individual, it is clear that both Kaplan and Emerson place great faith—the heart of their faith—in that self. But what, exactly, is the self, and how can it be defined? For both men, the self is not a concrete entity, but rather a process, or a set of processes. Emerson asserts that the self is "the unattained but attainable."[39] The self, in other words, is never a final condition but always a state toward which we are moving. With our inherently limited individual perception, it is easy to believe that our current level of being is our final level, that the self that we inhabit today is our final self; the reality is that no state is final.

Such an evolving sense of self, as we shall see again and again, is inextricably linked to the way Kaplan thinks. Process thinking—a concept that goes all the way back to the Greeks and to Heraclitus and refers to the notion that change and activity are the most fundamental aspects of reality—was an essential aspect of Kaplan's theology. We shall explore this aspect at length when we talk of Kaplan's concept of God. For the moment, we might quote one of Kaplan's many process statements:

> I know very well what I mean by God. God to me is the process that makes for creativity, integration, love and justice. The function of prayer is to render us conscious of that process. I can react with a sense of holiness or momentousness to existence because it is continually being worked upon by this divine process. I am not troubled in the least by the fact that God is not an identifiable being; for that matter neither is my ego an identifiable being.[40]

When Kaplan thinks of prayer, he often voices this sense of self as process. One Friday in January 1930, he was enjoying the prayers from a Protestant collection that he frequently perused.[41] The collection so moved him that he thought of the rabbinic ideal that a man "should pray the whole day."[42] He then transcribes a particular prayer from this collection that just fit his mood that day: "Let me no longer be sad, downcast, despairing, vexed by remorse or depressed by my failures. Take from me my old self. Give me a new self, beautiful, vigorous and joyous."[43] These words hint at the pleasure that Kaplan took, like Emerson before him, in a self perpetually in flux, an identity defined by its evolution.

Admittedly, there are some pitfalls in the concept of the self as process. Emerson articulates a major source of difficulty: "This one fact the world hates, that the soul becomes; for that forever degrades the past, turns all riches to poverty, all reputation to a shame [and] confounds the saint with the rogue."[44] If the soul is really a process and at the same time is a primary source of truth, then we stand on very shaky ground with respect to our values, our religion, and our common assumptions. Most people do not take well to the volatility that is so much a fact of everyday life. In other words, if we truly believe with Emerson that we are to seek the truth in the present and rely mainly on our present intuitions of truth—the inner voice—then the voices of the past fade into insignificance and do not even have a vote concerning the meaning we seek. Though Emerson asserts the primacy of our living in the present and not seeking the truth from those who are dead, I simply do not believe he means what he says. He contradicts himself often on this score. On the one hand, he tells us that we are timid and that we dare not assert our own opinions but must quote some saint or sage. But then there are times when he too quotes those ancient sages. When Emerson wants some "eternal verity" on a given subject, he will most often consult his own mind. But the rest of us, ordinary folk, hardly have such a luxury. We must consult the great minds of the present and the past.

The concept of self-reliance is central to Emerson's thinking, and I believe that it is crucial to Kaplan as well. Kaplan, however, never uses this term, neither in his journal nor in his published writings. Nonetheless, if we understand precisely what Emerson meant by self-reliance, Kaplan turns out to be the most self-reliant Jewish leader of the twentieth century. Self-reliance, it seems to me, was central to his very being as a Jew and as a thinker. Self-reliance—or, "moral perfectionism," the term preferred by Emerson scholar Stanley Cavell—is synonymous with what Kaplan meant by salvation. Emerson famously states that "The virtue in most request is conformity. Self-reliance is its aversion. It loves not realities and creators, but names and customs." Even a brief consideration will help us understand that, for Emerson, conformity is the great difficulty. We need conformity, but we must move beyond it. Emerson understands that the first voice we hear when we confront any situation of conflict, moral or otherwise, is the voice of authority figures—our parents and community, our society and culture. We must conform to these voices of authority; otherwise, there would be no community and no society—only chaos. Society rests, in other words, on the surrender of the self to the needs of the community.

But the surrender is never total. The self-reliant person is the one who stands back and does not make a decision on the basis of the first instinct. That person turns away from the fashions of the day. Self-reliance is ultimately the aversion to conformity. Emerson states, "It is easy in the world to live after the world's opinion; it is easy in solitude to live after our own; but the great man is he who in the midst of the crowd keeps with perfect sweetness the independence of solitude."[45]

If we are to transcend ourselves, we must seek the truth, and truth is never finished. Each person must cultivate a persistent critical stance, both with respect to him- or herself and to the other. In other words, the essence of thinking is to provoke.[46] Stanley Cavell believes that Emerson himself and his prose enact the self-reliant democratic life "because they always seem in dialogue and never come to the point." Being democratic, to quote the old saw, is "not being too sure you are right." Nietzsche, who in so many ways is a child of Emerson, says that "culture is the child of each individual's self-knowledge and dissatisfaction with himself. Anyone who believes in culture is thereby saying: 'I see above me something higher and more human than I am; let everyone help me to attain it, as I help everyone who knows and suffers as I do.'"[47]

The goal of the self-reliant process is "moral perfectionism." Through constant self-criticism, we can transform ourselves. We can transcend ourselves and move closer both to our ideal self and to the divine. There is not one ideal for the self but many. There is not one model that we all ought to strive for but "for each self there is a genius."[48] Such a self, Emerson believed, must be a moral self—hence, the expression "moral perfectionism," which beautifully sums up both Emerson's and Kaplan's system.

Though Kaplan did not use the expression "self-reliance," he lived it. Self-reliance is not a permanent condition of any individual but comes in moments. Kaplan had many self-reliant moments. We need think only briefly to come up with examples of his standing back from his Judaism, of transcending the accepted beliefs of the time to arrive at something that more accurately expressed his ideals. The most outstanding example is his prayer book, which embodies his unspoken but essential belief in self-reliance. It removes the "chosen people" formula from the liturgy, it removes the immortality formulas, and it removes those statements where the liturgy asserts that the Torah was given to Moses on Mount Sinai. Kaplan's excommunication and the fury directed at him by the ultra-Orthodox were precisely in reaction to these self-reliant moments and for his insistence that self-reliance brought him nearer to the divine. There are many Conservative and perhaps even some Reform Jews who still cannot forgive Kaplan for his heresy or his aversive thoughts, to use Emerson's term.

True followers of Kaplan would not necessarily embrace his ideals but will stand back from themselves and from Kaplan and critically examine everything he said so that they might transcend it and, in doing so, transform themselves.[49] Kaplan's daring example shows us that self-transformation is the essence of the religious quest and the only way to come closer to the divine.

THREE

NATIONALISM AND RIGHTEOUSNESS: AHAD HA-AM AND MATTHEW ARNOLD

> I am more convinced than ever that Achad Ha-Am's conception of
> nationality plus [Matthew] Arnold's interpretation of Israel's genius for
> righteousness contains that which could form the positive expression
> of the Jewish spirit. All it wants is definiteness and detail.
>
> —*Mordecai Kaplan, August 1905*

A key aspect of Mordecai Kaplan's talent as a thinker, as we will see again and again, is his ability to combine widely disparate concepts and ideologies into a single coherent whole. He was, for example, a life-long Zionist and, at the same time, a true nephew of his Uncle Sam, even editing a book of prayers and songs for American holidays.[1] It also happened that the Society for the Advancement of Judaism, the congregation that Kaplan founded in 1922, was first housed in a brownstone once occupied by George M. Cohan,[2] the well-known patriotic entertainer, composer, and playwright. Though a mere bit of trivia, such synchronicity is evidence of the many streams of Kaplan's intellectual life, seemingly divergent but nevertheless overlapping.

In 1905, just twenty-four years old, Kaplan summed up his approach to Jewish life in a single journal entry, quoted above: "I am more convinced than ever that Achad Ha-Am's conception of nationality plus [Matthew] Arnold's interpretation of Israel's genius for righteousness contains that which could form the positive expression of the Jewish spirit. All it wants is definiteness and detail."[3] The juxtaposition of Ahad Ha-Am, the cultural Zionist, a descendent of Hasidic rabbis, with an English poet and critic indicates the work of a great historical imagination. Kaplan presents us here with one of the foundational ideas of his system.

It is well known that the people of Israel and their collective consciousness lay at the center of Kaplan's concept of Torah and of Jewish civilization. This emphasis on Jewish peoplehood owes much to the distinguished cultural Zionist Ahad Ha-Am. Preeminent among Zionists, Ahad Ha-Am is the key to understanding the young Kaplan. It has been said that Kaplan was Ahad Ha-Am's most dedicated disciple. While this is true on the whole, Kaplan was also critical of his mentor in very significant ways.

Ahad Ha-Am (Asher Hirsch Ginsberg) was born in the Ukraine in 1856, where he received a traditional Jewish education in the home of his Hasidic father, a wealthy village merchant. The young Ginsberg studied Talmud and medieval philosophy with a private teacher and was deeply influenced by Maimonides's *Guide for the Perplexed*. He also read the literature of the *Haskalah*, the eighteenth-century Jewish Enlightenment. In 1873, he moved to Odessa, an important center of Hebrew culture, where he came into contact with some of the foremost Jewish authors of his day, including Chaim Nahman Bialik, Mendele Mocher Sforim (Sholem Abramovich), and Ze'ev Jabotinsky.[4] In the late 1880s, Asher Ginsberg began publishing under the pseudonym Ahad Ha-Am (One of the People).Though still in his early thirties and unknown, he criticized the existing policy of the Zionist movement, which advocated immediate Jewish settlement in Palestine. Ahad Ha-Am insisted that educational groundwork was a necessary prerequisite, in order for the Jews of Europe to appreciate the unique dilemmas of returning to their ancestral homeland. His influence was considerably enhanced when, in 1896, he founded the Hebrew journal *Ha-shilo-ah,* a post that he held until 1902. Nearly until his death in 1927, he continued to write topical essays that discussed current controversies in light of his own philosophy.

In the long and tumultuous process of Jewish modernization and secularization, Ahad Ha-Am assumed a place both preeminent and unique. For much of the Jewish intelligentsia across the early twentieth century, men and women whose origins were in Eastern Europe, he was the final authority in matters of ethics, the spirit, and literature. Great poets like Bialik dedicated poems to him. Even many non-Orthodox American Jewish Zionists considered him the spiritual leader of the generation. Yet in his day, he was in some ways quite heretical. His approach to Jewish problems was not that of Jewish tradition but of modern thinkers, among them Herbert Spencer, John Stuart Mill, and Charles Darwin. His thinking, in its essence, is evolutionary.[5]

Ahad Ha-Am can only be understood amid the vast confrontation between late nineteenth-century Jewry and the intellectual currents of the day. Secularization challenged traditional Jews on many levels, creating conflicts not only intellectual but existential as well. Like so many of his generation, Ahad Ha-Am felt alienated from the traditional community of the shtetl and its myopic vision of the outside world and simultaneously dazzled by the intellectual attractions of the modern world. He became a spokesman for the young people of his time who could not continue in the ways of their parents but had not yet discovered a new religious and spiritual path.

Ahad Ha-Am helped his contemporaries—more modern, more urban, more curious about the non-Jewish world—move in a new and productive direction. He encouraged a Judaism that was not supernatural. God, for Ahad Ha-Am, is a primitive expression of his people's will to live, a determination that he terms "the life force." Steven Zipperstein, Ahad Ha-Am's biographer, sums up these central issues: "It was precisely Ahad Ha-Am's assumption that the 'national will for survival' could be substituted for Israel's belief in God, that ethics could replace the law, that the history of the Jews (and more importantly, their eternal role in history) could be understood in secular, not supernatural terms—these underscored the power, and limitations, of his ideology."[6]

For Ahad Ha-Am, all aspects of Jewish culture are, at their heart, expressions of the will to live. The primary problem is that the will to live, which he believed present in every ethnic group, has been weakened in the case of the Jews. This will—which Kaplan, in describing the philosophy of Ahad Ha-Am, called "the collective 'We' feeling"—must be strengthened and renewed before any Jewish society can be established. Kaplan would utilize this idea of the weakened will to live to explain his own notion that Jewish culture must be reconstructed.[7]

For Ahad Ha-Am, the social thinker, God becomes a creation of the Jewish people. To be sure, he had a place for Torah and holiness in his system, but they had no connection to the transcendent. He considered Israel's God to be the most original creation of the collective urge for life and, like the Reformers, reduced Judaism to its ethical core. Yet Ahad Ha-Am was fully aware of the centrality of religion in the culture of Israel. Whereas contemporary secular Jewish thinkers like Freud had a very limited understanding of religion, Ahad Ha-Am had a profound grasp of its power. Yet, in Ahad Ha-Am's vision of the Jewish future, the synagogue would not play a major part. He did not dismiss the past; he did not want to sever his relationship with it. For him, the past becomes a mask that is reconstructed in terms of the basic concepts of his system. Ever the modernist, Ahad Ha-Am played contemporary Western philosophical concepts against medieval Jewish ones. Thus, he discovered connections between Maimonides and Nietzsche, for example, as both cherished the ideal of perfectibility.[8]

Ahad Ha-Am led the perplexed of his time to examine Judaism in a new way, no longer stymied within the narrow confines of tradition. The Torah becomes the spiritual creation of the Jewish people rather than the product of divine inspiration. It is the fruit of Israel's genius. Its uniqueness lies in its emphasis on ethical nationhood, Israel's primary contribution to Western civilization. In this fashion, Ahad Ha-Am retains the concept of the chosen people even as he secularizes it.

If the Jewish people are to survive, their consciousness must be transformed. Ahad Ha-Am had very definite ideas about the way in which this must be done. He believed that the Jews of Eastern Europe, the traditional Jews of his time, were enslaved to the word. They ceased to be creative because they lived under the authoritative Judaism of "the Book," rather than from the "Torah of the Heart" and from the wisdom of ordinary experience.[9] The Jews of both Western Europe and America believed they were emancipated, but, in reality, they too were enslaved and paid a very heavy price for their "freedom." They had sold their souls to gain their rights.[10] They were enslaved by the urge to assimilate. Both the Jews of the West and the Jews of the East, he insisted, must be liberated.

Ahad Ha-Am believed that there were two ways for Jews (or any minority) to relate to the host culture. The first he termed "slavish imitation," by which modern Jews assimilated to the point of self-effacement, abandoning their connection to Judaism. The other way of relating to the host culture entailed a much healthier attitude, an attitude of pride that he called "competitive imitation": Jews would appropriate modalities of the host culture but, at the same time, transform them and make them their own. They would, in other words, "judaize" aspects of the dominant culture. Ahad Ha-Am uses the Jews of Alexandria as an example of the latter, taking Greek modes of thought and custom and transforming them in a Jewish mold:

> Long before the Hellenists in Palestine tried to substitute Greek Culture for Judaism [an example of slavish imitation], the Jews of Egypt had come into close contact with the Greeks—with their life, their spirit, and their philosophy—yet we do not find among them any pronounced movement toward assimilation. On the contrary, they employed their Greek knowledge as an instrument for revealing the essential spirit of Judaism, for showing the world its beauty, and vindicating it against the proud philosophy of Greece. That is to say, starting from imitation which had its source in self-effacement before an alien spiritual force, they succeeded, by means of that imitation, in making the force their own, and in passing from self-effacement to competition.[11]

Ahad Ha-Am's recipe for liberation made a deep impression on the Jewish intelligentsia of both Europe and America. Encountering the ways of modern culture was inevitable by the early twentieth century, but Ahad Ha-Am showed thinking Jews the way in which this appropriation could be done with pride and authenticity. He demonstrated to a young Kaplan the way in which American culture could be absorbed and made into American-Jewish culture. One might say that Kaplan's entire enterprise was an effort to Americanize Judaism with intelligence and pride.

Harold Bloom, the literary critic, makes the same point about Jewish history but calls it the attempt to mask the normative. Bloom looks at Jewish history and finds many instances in which foreign ways are taken by the Jews and made into Jewish ways. One available example is the centrality of study in Jewish life. In the Torah, we find no ideal at all of study, yet, in the minds of the rabbis, its importance is equal to all the other commandments put together. What the rabbis did was take the

Greek ideal of "*Philo* (love) *sophos* (of knowledge) and make it the Jewish way. Philosophy was transformed into the Jewish mode of Torah."[12]

Within Ahad Ha-Am's spectrum of assimilation, it is important to note that, while Kaplan was a faithful disciple, he was not slavish in his devotion to his mentor. Ahad Ha-Am, as we have noted above, had little use for traditional theological notions. In the great transformation that he envisions for the Jewish people, moreover, the synagogue plays no part. Indeed, some have called him a secular rabbi. Kaplan, of course, was in a very profound sense a man of the synagogue; this foundational difference would prove a valuable source of growth for Kaplan.

Kaplan's critical stance toward his mentor surfaces by the time he is thirty years old. Writing in 1909 to his brother-in-law, the Conservative rabbi Phineas Israeli, Kaplan says that "Ahad Ha-Am's nationality is a barren and unproductive idea which lacks religious significance."[13] His critical attitude also emerges repeatedly with his close friend Samson Benderly, another staunch devotee of Ahad Ha-Am; Kaplan resented Benderly's secularism and his lack of appreciation for the synagogue as an agent of Jewish survival.[14] In his historical account of Ahad Ha-Am, Kaplan's tone is diplomatic but his frustration is clear: "It is regrettable, that, with all his deep insight into both the national and the ethical aspects of Judaism, Ahad Ha-Am failed to appreciate the aspect which had contributed most to Judaism's survival under the most adverse circumstances—the religious."[15]

In *Judaism as a Civilization*, Kaplan goes beyond criticism concerning religion and focuses on Ahad Ha-Am's lack of appreciation for the individual. Though always a man of the group, as the years passed, Kaplan emphasized the needs of the individual. Commenting directly on Ahad Ha-Am, he wrote, "It is reactionary, to ask the individual to sink back into his former subservience to the group."[16] Additionally, we should note that Kaplan's notion of civilization was much more inclusive than Ahad Ha-Am's notion of culture.

* * *

Kaplan is not in the habit of citing his mentors, so it is not surprising that Matthew Arnold's name does not appear very often. But just as John Dewey is not mentioned often, despite Kaplan's inability to think without "speaking Dewey" and just as Kaplan never uses the term "self-reliance," though Emerson's notion is essential to his sense of the individual, so too does Matthew Arnold occupy a key space in Kaplan's thought.

That Kaplan, a pragmatist and sociological thinker, was deeply influenced by a Victorian poet is striking and tells us much about the nature of Kaplan's mind and his religious commitments. My sense is that Arnold is actually more central in understanding Kaplan's thought than the social scientists usually named. Arnold, who sought to rescue both religion and the Bible for his Victorian audience, rescued Kaplan in the process. Our inquiry here actually involves two Arnolds, since Kaplan's difficulties with the Jewish tradition began with Arnold Ehrlich (1848–1919), an eccentric and idiosyncratic Bible scholar. The second Arnold came along just in time to save Kaplan from the first.

To understand the importance of Arnold Ehrlich, we must return to Kaplan's early days. He entered the Jewish Theological Seminary (JTS) in 1893, in short pants, a mere twelve-and-a-half years of age. The seminary at that time was housed on Lexington Avenue and Fifty-Ninth Street, across from Bloomingdale's department store. Though living in the JTS dorm when starting school, Kaplan moved home a few years later when his parents relocated nearby. This part of New York City was an important Jewish neighborhood at the time. In addition to the Seminary, the Young Men's Hebrew Association (YMHA), which later moved to its current location on Ninety-Second Street, was, in the late 1890s, located just a few blocks away. In addition to the area's many synagogues were the offices of the B'nai B'rith, which housed the Maimonides Library, well used by Kaplan.[17] Living again at home, Kaplan now resumed Talmud study with his father. Because of their regular study, Kaplan came to enjoy the paternal attention he had never received in Europe.

The late 1890s was also the time when Arnold Ehrlich, then an established but controversial Bible scholar, would visit the Kaplan home. In the absence of any concordance to the Talmud, Ehrlich would call on Kaplan's father when he wanted to know how a particular biblical Hebrew word was used in the Talmud. While there, he shared with the whole family the latest ideas in his biblical commentaries. Through Ehrlich, Kaplan became aware of scholars who doubted the Mosaic authorship of the Bible and theorized that the Pentateuch was written long after

Moses's death. Ehrlich believed that the Pentateuch existed first in many versions, which were later edited into the one document that we now possess—an idea shared by many other biblical scholars of the period, but a radical notion for most Americans, let alone for Orthodox Jews.

Kaplan, young and impressionable, internalized the ideas he heard from Ehrlich and presented them to his fellow students at the seminary. The faculty at the seminary struggled with the scientific view of the Bible, and some found it severely undermining of the tradition. Solomon Schechter famously refers to this tradition as higher anti-Semitism, because, if the Pentateuchal books were actually written after Moses and edited from many sources rather than a single author, then the centrality of Moses and the Sinaitic revelation are undermined.[18]

There is no doubt that Kaplan's father had mixed feelings about his frequent guest. Ehrlich, after all, had undergone a youthful conversion to Christianity; the young student even aided the German scholar Franz Delitztsch (1813–90) in his translation of the New Testament into Hebrew, which was made for missionary purposes. As a result, Ehrlich was generally shunned by the Jewish community in New York, despite his American reconversion back to Judaism under the guidance of Rabbi Gustav Gottheil of Temple Emanuel. He found it very difficult to get a job. It is certainly a mark of the tolerant spirit of Kaplan's father that he befriended Ehrlich, met with him on a regular basis, and aided his research.

Sometimes Ehrlich came to the house on Friday nights. A fellow JTS student, Julius Greenstone (1873–1955), describes the scene in his memoir:

> Friday nights, after the usual stroll in the park, most of the [seminary] students went to bed early. In later years, it became a custom for several students to visit the home of Kaplan's parents, who lived in the neighborhood, where they were joined by the late A. B. Ehrlich, the most original Bible commentator of modern days and the most erratic of men. Conversation became very heated at times, usually turning on the question of higher criticism or some theological topic. We were always deeply impressed with the tolerance of old Rabbi Kaplan, who could join the discussion with the heretical Ehrlich.[19]

Kaplan mentions Ehrlich many times in his written biographical sketches; he consistently remarks on Ehrlich's "heretical influence":

Ehrlich was a frequent visitor in my parents' home when I was in my teens, due to his expectation to get from father, who was expert in the knowledge of the Talmud, the sources of certain rabbinic comments. In the course of his conversations with me, he would have occasion to pour scorn upon the traditional commentators or to express some of his heretical views about the Bible. When mother would overhear him, she would, after he left the house, rebuke father for having anything to do with him. It became later an obsession with her that Ehrlich made a heretic of me and ruined my chances of becoming the Chief Rabbi of England.[20] Her resentment apart, Ehrlich was by no means what one would call a pleasant or sociable human being.[21]

Mordecai Kaplan never overtly rebelled against his father in any way, yet the lingering presence of Ehrlich may have launched the son toward his separate sense of identity. Ehrlich and the seminary reinforced each other. The seminary gave young Mordecai a chance to live away from home and to acquire an independent sense of himself without actually rebelling. The curriculum included some lectures on archeology by Cyrus Adler, which offered another untraditional view of the Bible. Kaplan's father obviously approved of the seminary in general but perhaps not all elements in its curriculum. There were many at the seminary who rejected the major tenets of biblical criticism. Talking to his classmates about Ehrlich's ideas intensified Kaplan's quest for other viewpoints.

Over time, though, Kaplan seems to drift further from the seminary and closer to radicals like Ehrlich. The seminary was a caretaking institution, suffused for Kaplan with many pleasant childhood associations. But it was also an institution of authority that stifled him. In Kaplan's later reflections, the warm protective feeling of the seminary alternates with anger because of its imposition of authority. He also felt that his colleagues did not respect him sufficiently or value his ideas about the Jewish people.

Ehrlich began coming to the Kaplan household when Mordecai was still in his teens. By the time he entered Columbia College for his Master's degree in 1900, Kaplan was already having fundamental doubts about the Jewish tradition, its origin, and its value. When a person studies the function of religion in different societies, it is difficult to maintain the conviction that his or her own religion is from God while the religions of others are not. The innovations of Ehrlich served as crucial prompts during this vital period, enabling Kaplan to become more critical of the tradition.[22]

As he studied philosophy, sociology, and anthropology at Columbia, Kaplan also taught and preached at Kehilath Jeshurun, the Orthodox synagogue. His doubts about the tradition deepened, seemingly by the month. By 1905, he realized that he could no longer fulfill his responsibilities to the synagogue and be honest with himself; he would have to resign from Kehilath Jeshurun. Deeply troubled and searching desperately for a new direction—including a possible job at New York Life Insurance Company and even going to law school—he went to Cyrus Adler (1863–1940), a member of the JTS board and later president. "What do you do for recreation?" Adler asked in response to Kaplan's quandary. "I walk around the [Central Park] reservoir," answered the young rabbi. "Well," Adler said, "When I was young I had my doubts too. Go and take another walk around the reservoir."[23]

We learn of Kaplan's inward state, as always, from his diary. He writes on December 31, 1906,

> Why do I stay where I am, you will ask. Well I did send in my resignation and it nearly broke my parents' hearts. Nor would I have yielded even then, had I known that I have sufficient intellectual power and force of character to make my ideas known. The tragedy of my life no one knows or wants to know. The lie which I live is so clear and palpable to me and yet I cannot tear myself loose from it.

Other aspects of his life only exacerbated his depression. He wrote, "of the vast lump of pleasure which exists in this world is there not just one little crumb for me. . . . I have no message to bring which would make others love me and think me in a way indispensable. My life lacks music." He was lonely. "I shall for once conquer my senseless prudishness for which I have to thank M, and say that the void in my life is due to the absence of love."[24] We can only speculate, but my belief is that "M" stands for "mother"; the biting self-pity he feels here is evidence of emotional turmoil. Sometime later he met, and soon thereafter married, Lena Rubin, the daughter of a prominent family in his congregation. New love, however, was not enough. It was at this point that Matthew Arnold helped rescue Kaplan from his religious chaos.

Though rarely read today, Matthew Arnold (1822–88) was all the rage at the turn of the twentieth century. Lionel Trilling referred to him as "the most influential critic of his age" and considered his position within the realm of literary criticism comparable to that of Aristotle in philosophy. At a time when thoughtful people seemed to be abandoning religion in droves, Arnold, though a modern critic, found religion "good and necessary, whether proved or not."[25] By the time of his death, Matthew Arnold was as renowned for his theology as for his literary criticism and poetry. He spent most of his life as a school inspector but became a celebrated poet in his early thirties. He had the honor of teaching poetry at Oxford and was almost elected librarian of the House of Commons.

For both Arnold and Kaplan, the preeminent spiritual threat was the prospect of losing the holy text as a source of values and as a primary inspiration. They were aware of the dangers of modernity to religious faith and applying the criteria of textual criticism to ancient texts. Both men saw how modernity's guises, everything from the theory of evolution to the emerging revelations of archeological digs in the Middle East, endangered the faith of thinking people. Scholars going back to the late eighteenth century began to assert, to cite one of many examples, that Homer was not written by one author but edited from many sources. Robert Browning, the great poet, expressed the genuine grief that so many felt at the realization that there may have been no man named Homer: "No actual Homer, no authentic text / No warrant for the fiction I, as fact had treasured in my heart and soul so long."[26] If there had been no Homer but only an editor, what could that mean about the Pentateuch and Moses?

Arnold, however, was not as concerned as Ehrlich would be by the particulars of who had authored what and when. Brushing aside the question of historical confirmation, Arnold assumed the important task of revalidating the Bible by means of literary criticism. Religion, he maintained, had functioned for so long as "cure and comfort"; though the foundations seemed to be crumbling for many, suffering continued, and comfort was still needed. As Arnold put it, "The millions suffer still, and grieve / And what can helpers heal / With old-world cures men half believe / For woes they wholly feel? / And yet men have such need of joy! / But joy whose grounds are true."[27] The question that Arnold posed to himself, and to us as moderns, is how we can still use religion in our search for joy, comfort, and completeness.[28]

Arnold's theology rests squarely on Spinoza, particularly in Arnold's critical attitude toward the Bible and in his emphasis on salvation and "blessedness" as coming from within rather than from God. As one scholar of Arnold puts it, "to have mastered the thought of Spinoza is to have mastered half of Arnold's teaching."[29] Arnold may well have brought Kaplan to Spinoza and aided him in appreciating the great naturalist.

God, for Arnold, does not exist in the realm of the supernatural; he believed that the supernatural as commonly understood must be discarded. Though he realized the difficulty of this position within nineteenth-century Christianity, Arnold was nevertheless insistent. As he wrote to his wife, "and it is because I am sure that the belief in miracles must go as belief in witches and hobgoblins has gone that I see how terrible will be the blank and bewilderment in England when it has gone."[30] A few decades later, Kaplan certainly understood such sentiments, as they confirmed his understanding of the dilemma posed by the belief in biblical miracles, as well as the growing divide between his life as a rabbi and his life as a scholar.

Arnold understood both Greeks and Hebrews, similarly to Spinoza: "At the bottom [of] both the Greek and the Hebrew notion is the desire, native in man, for reason and the will of God, the feeling after universal order,—in a word, the love of God."[31] Universal order was, for Arnold, the essence of the divine.

We find the same concept of God in Kaplan's early thought. In an encounter with one of his congregants at the Society for the Advancement of Judaism (SAJ), Kaplan explained that his belief centered on God as "the ordered universe" and referred explicitly to Spinoza. For Kaplan, this notion of order was not merely an idea in his mind but part of the universe itself. The order, Kaplan believed, was not only "in here" but also "out there." From the Kaplan diary,

> On asking Miss Garfiel[32] [about a sermon], she said that I did not make clear whether I conceived God as a being or as an idea, i.e., a generalization of the ideals to which we aspire. I explained to her that to me God was not a being, but Reality[33] viewed as an ordered universe. I believe with Spinoza in a *Deus sive Natura* [God under the aspect of nature]. God was as much more than an idea as the ego is more than an idea representing the sum of psychic forces in the

individual. In fact, Deus and Ego are related to each other as the body and apex of a pyramid. In prayer the Ego becomes conscious of God. Through this awareness it sets into operation psychic forces that are otherwise dormant. Hence the value of prayer.[34]

Though Kaplan maintained throughout his life that God was more than an idea or concept, he did often talk about the "idea of God" and about what believing "in the idea of God means." As a result, many misunderstood him and thought that he believed that God was only the sum of our ideals and not a reality apart from our collective beliefs.

The reality of order outside ourselves was for Kaplan an aspect of divinity and a source of inspiration for the way we should conduct our lives. For Kaplan and Arnold, as for Spinoza, the aim or ideal of religion is, therefore, "the universal order which seems to be intended and aimed at in the world, and which it is man's happiness to go along with or his misery to go counter to."[35]

Indirectly pointing to the ordered universe, Arnold states (in a formulation that is pure Spinoza), "I stand still, and marvel; I listen to what subsists yet, I would fain hear what will go on subsisting; in the movement of the forest, in the murmur of the pines, I seek to catch some of the accents of the eternal tongue." Ruth apRoberts, in her very excellent work on Arnold, explicates this passage: "What subsists becomes for Arnold the best definition of God; he will explain it as Moses' *I am,* and it becomes his favorite term for deity, the Eternal."[36]

Another aspect of Arnold's thinking significant for Kaplan was his understanding of the Bible. For Arnold, the Bible was primarily an aid to building character, a guide in the search for moral perfection. The way to the revitalization of religion and biblical thought came through Arnold's concept of culture and *bildung.* These two ideas are fundamental to Kaplan's concept of God and related to his notion of salvation.

We first need to understand that Arnold does not employ the word *culture* to indicate art, literature, and poetry alone. His use of the term is most clearly explained by Trilling: "Arnold's culture, as he was careful to point out, does not signify what the word commonly does, a vague, belletristic gentility; it means many things but nothing less than reason experienced as a kind of grace by each citizen, the conscious effort of each man to come to the realization of his complete humanity."[37]

This concept of culture is very closely related to the German ideal of *bildung* roughly translated as character building. Arnold, like his teacher Johann Wolfgang von Goethe, was profoundly influenced by Johann Gottlob Herder (1744–1803), the great philosopher and theologian of the eighteenth century. Herder believed that each society is unique, as every person is unique. Each society undergoes its own progress, more or less fulfilling its own potential.[38] As Arnold puts it, "the corresponding phenomenon for the individual is *bildung. Bildung* is rather, the willed harmonious development in the individual of all aspects of the human— as distinct from animal—potential, which Herder calls Humanität." Another statement by Herder further explains the relationship between *bildung* and culture: "It is culture alone which binds together the generations which live one after the other as men who see [but] one day, and it is in culture that the solidarity of mankind is to be sought, since in it the striving of all men coincide."[39] In other words, *bildung* is the striving after perfection in the individual; on the societal level, the cumulative effect of this individual striving is called culture. Perfection of the individual must be the goal for each person, and society in general must be set up in such a way as to foster that process for each member of the community.

For Arnold, *bildung* and religion are actually synonymous. The concept of *bildung* is the means by which we can understand his reworking of biblical theology. *Bildung* is, of course, not a mere state of mind but a process through which people attain higher levels of enlightenment and morality. In Arnold's words, "Not a having and a resting but a growing and a becoming, is the character of perfection as culture conceives it; and here too, it coincides with religion."[40]

Kaplan was indubitably aware of the central European traditions that formed the matrix of his intellectual peers at the Jewish Theological Seminary. He surely knew the centrality of *bildung* to nineteenth century German Jews. They were at the time undergoing the process of emancipation from a more traditional, conservative, restricted form of Judaism. *Bildung* was tailor-made as an ideal for them since it concentrated on the individual rather than on the group and crossed class and ethnic lines. Across the long arc of Jewish history, the religious spirit proceeded from revelation; but with the radical ruptures of modernity, that spirit could suddenly be found with *bildung*.[41] For Kaplan and his peers, *bildung* meant education leading to a moral life. The purpose of this inward process was to wean individuals away from superstition, nurture reason and good taste, and bring people to enlightenment. It was no less than the cultivation of the self.[42]

For our purposes, the concept of *bildung* is essential; it helps us understand Kaplan's concept of salvation, so central to his system. *Bildung* comes to Kaplan from several traditions. It can be traced from Herder to Goethe to Arnold to Kaplan. It informed the thought of Emerson, William James, and John Dewey, all of whom were profoundly influenced by Goethe. Kaplan inherited it from them all, but substituted the term *salvation* for *bildung.* Salvation would, thus, be the maximum fulfillment of the human potential in each person.

Unique in his generation, Kaplan's theology is grounded in English as much as in German theological thought. Before Kaplan, nearly all Jewish religious thinkers on the American scene, whether Conservative or Reform, traced their intellectual origins to the *Wissenschaft* tradition of nineteenth-century central European Jewry. Kaplan is a product of this tradition as well, but the fact that he gained insights from Matthew Arnold and Ralph Waldo Emerson and applied them to American Judaism sets him apart from the others. It marks him as a truly American thinker.

The centrality of Goethe to Arnold and to the *bildung* tradition may help us understand another aspect of Kaplan. Goethe, a poet rather than a systematic thinker, moves easily from one frame of mind to another, creating an ambiguity that can be frustrating. Though Kaplan is more systematic thinker than poet, he has this sophisticated pluralistic aspect about his mind. This is a perfect example of his philosophy of mood. Kaplan easily embraces opposites in his thinking, as we have seen. He is the pragmatist who also embraces a thinker like Herman Cohen, the Kantian par excellence. Goethe here comes to mind:

> [W]ith the many divergent tendencies of my being, one mode of thinking is not enough; as a poet and artist I am a polytheist, as a scientist I am a pantheist— one as firmly as the other. If for my personality, as a moral being, I need one god, I can imagine that too. [43]

Kaplan never quoted this statement, and, while he would surely disavow Goethe's easy usage of polytheism, I also believe that, on a fundamental level, he acknowledged his own divergences and embraced multiple modes of thinking.

There are some who find Kaplan's emphasis on salvation or self-fulfillment as the primary goal of religion quite superficial. In their opinion, he gives in to the American narcissistic ethos of self-improvement and the cloying, self-centered obsessions of the self-help genre. Americans always want to be thinner, look younger; Americans always want to know the secrets, and they want to know them now. But as we have just seen, Kaplan's notion of salvation through *bildung* has a long history, traceable through both American and European Romantic literature and philosophy. In Jewish thought, it follows an earlier rationalistic tradition going back to Maimonides and even to Aristotle, who asserted that the primary goal of human activity is moral and intellectual perfection. Such a concept has little to do with the present-day narcissistic preoccupation with self-help and its roots are far deeper.

For Arnold, Israel is the great "poet" and the source of the most profound understanding of religion. One might say, with Arnold, that poetry is religion at its best because poetry articulates our orientation toward the divine, toward a place closer to the truth. Arnold famously proclaimed that "religion is ethics heightened, enkindled, lit up by feeling... morality touched by emotion."[44] The process of lifting us up ethically is the primary fruit of the poetic imagination and, at the same time, the primary purpose of religion. For Arnold, poetry must play a major part in leading to salvation. It is to the poet that we should turn for moral guidance, not to the philosopher. The philosopher can never articulate the finer points of our understanding; only the poet can. The poet has the sensitivity, the multilayered understanding, and the ability to use language to articulate a sense of the divine.[45]

Though Kaplan is not a poet and never pretended to be one, it is to his credit that one of the people he valued most highly was a poet who saw poetry at the center of the religious life. Though he sometimes expressed himself in moving and lofty language, Kaplan never wrote great poetry. Yet his poetic attempts may be useful as prayers. In his 1945 prayer book, Kaplan included a number of poems that he himself had written.[46]

The core of poetic expression is the metaphor, or in Arnold's terminology, the "figure." Religious thinkers over the centuries would all
agree that religious thinking is best expressed through metaphor. Lit-
eralism, to quote Heschel, is the enemy of religious thinking. Metaphor—or figure, to use Arnold's term—is present in every aspect of his
theological formulation. Arnold challenges us with the notion of God
as metaphor. In Arnold's evolving thought, "God is rather a figurative
way of speaking of reason, of something like Milton's 'Right reason' or
German *Vernuft*."[47]

Arnold requires us is to look deep into the Bible, to probe its images for their root meaning and their relationship to experience. The
metaphor, of course, takes an abstract idea and compares it to a common
experience, object, or human quality. The metaphor may be seen as a
projection, but we must remember that it is never to be taken literally. We
say that evil is a snake and that evil tempts us. But did the snake in the
Garden of Eden actually talk? Rashi maintained that the snake stands
for the evil urge, thereby transforming the snake into a metaphor for
evil. Rashi and the midrash upon which he often built his commentaries always help us interpret these images into a language of daily, human
experience. None of us has experienced a snake trying to convince us to
eat a fruit, but all of us have experienced the temptations of "evil."

When we understand an image as metaphor, we realize that we are
projecting ourselves, our human selves, onto the world in order to explain an abstract idea. In the case of the Bible, we must take its anthro-
pomorphisms (concrete human images) and turn them back into expressions of religious experience. Ancient rabbis maintained that the Torah
speaks in the language of human beings; that language is the language
of the concrete human image, of anthropomorphism. As Arnold put it,
"Man never knows how anthropomorphic he is."[48]

Arnold's rescue of Kaplan should by now be clear. The former's use
of theological language and his interpretation of biblical metaphors were
tantalizing to Kaplan's pluralistic mind. Moreover, his ideas countered
the growing volume of those of biblical critics who diminished Israelite
originality. This Christian, by contrast, was less concerned with bur-
geoning investigations of archeological facts and authorship patterns
and instead found in biblical Israel a deep religious consciousness. Read-

ing Arnold had another value as well. Kaplan's unsettling contact with Ehrlich and his Columbia professors, as well as his growing knowledge of Spinoza, convinced him to abandon Judaism's traditional notion of a supernatural God. By 1908, the clash between these new revelations and his Orthodox synagogue nearly unraveled him. Arnold's answer—like all answers for this pluralistic thinker—did not solve Kaplan's quandaries, but Arnold's formulation of God and his generous theology did point Kaplan in a new and original direction.

Arnold understood that the main concern of religion is right conduct. The Bible is more interested in right conduct than anything else. We all know from our own experience that, in so many areas of life, it is easier to understand what to do than actually to do it. Often, we know what the right thing is, but our impulses pull us away from the right and the good. In those moments when we succeed in doing the right thing, we feel satisfaction. Arnold believed that the possibility for doing right was an innate trait of ancient Israel: "No people ever felt so strongly that succeeding, going right, hitting the mark in this great concern was the way of peace, the highest possible satisfaction."[49] In other words, the Israelites were firmly committed to the deep ethical principle that right conduct brings satisfaction: "righteous order, conduct, is for Israel at once the source of all man's happiness and at the same time the very essence of the Eternal."[50]

But Arnold went still further. Not only does doing the right thing bring (or should bring) satisfaction and happiness; he believed that the world of which we are a product is set up so that it does. The universe is constructed such that we who are its products will fulfill the essence of our being by feeling satisfaction at being righteous. Such a conception of purpose brings us back to Kaplan and his fundamental notion of the particular "power that makes for salvation," an expression that has its origin in Arnold.

One statement in particular from Arnold's *Literature and Dogma* had a huge influence on Kaplan's life: "They [the Israelites] had dwelt upon the thought of conduct and right and wrong, till the not ourselves [the universe] which is in us and all around us, became to them adorable eminently and altogether *as a power which makes for righteousness*, which makes for it unchangeably and eternally, and is therefore called the Eternal."[51] In this statement, Arnold hopes to explain what the ancient Israelites meant by the word *God*. Our central theological problem, Arnold tells us, is that we ordinarily use the word *God* "as if it stood for a perfectly definite and ascertained idea."[52] We interpret it literally rather than metaphorically. But the truth of the matter is that God is neither an object or nor a clear idea. The word itself, Arnold asserts, is a metaphor that stands for the "fact" and the process by which the universe, not ourselves, is constructed so that it makes being good feel good. This aspect of the universe is its essential divinity. God is not a being but a process or series of processes within the universe.

This argument helps explain Kaplan's theological debt to Arnold, acknowledged in the 1905 journal entry that began our discussion. Now we can better appreciate the powerful pairing of Arnold and Ahad Ha-Am in Kaplan's mind. Though these two men did not know each other, their view of Israel's essential character, indeed of the very soul of biblical Israel, is identical—the love and joy of justice and righteousness. Arnold's expression "power not ourselves that makes for righteousness" becomes the basis in Kaplan's later theology for "God as the power that makes for salvation."[53]

Inspired in part by Arnold and by his teachers in sociology, Kaplan chose to dwell on the way God functions in the world, rather than to try to fathom the metaphysical problem of His essence. The pragmatic Kaplan, in his lifelong quest for the meaning of God, always focused on what God helps people do. He repeatedly reformulated his belief in God: "God is that aspect of reality which elicits from us the best that is in us and enables us to bear the worst that can befall us," he wrote in 1933. And then, forty years later, he stated that "God is the assumption that there is enough in the world to meet men's needs but not their greeds for power and pleasure."[54]

Kaplan was not a poet, but sometimes the poetry in his soul is obvious and moving. Soon after he founded the Society for the Advancement of Judaism in 1922, he began to publish a synagogue journal titled *The S.A.J. Review*. During the high holidays in the fall of 1923, he inserted into the review a letter to the children of the congregation, which again illustrates his Arnoldian soul and his deep conviction that doing right and being happy are essentially related.

A Rosh Hashannah Letter from Mordecai Kaplan.

9/11/23

My Dear Boys and Girls:

I wish you all a happy New Year. May the coming year not alone bring you happiness, but also enable you to make others happy, your parents, your relatives and your companions.

Making others happy is no easy matter. It is an art that requires a great deal of study and practice. You probably do not suspect the true name of that art. It is religion. To be sure, a great deal of what people call religion leaves them unhappy, and often helps them to make others miserable. But that is only imitation religion, and not the real thing. All real religion, like the Book of Psalms, begins with *'ashrei,'* which means, "O What happiness," and ends with "Hallelujah," which is a song of rejoicing.

We have established the S.A.J. for the purpose of learning the true Jewish religion, the religion of our fathers. In that way, we expect to learn the art of being happy, and making others happy. May I count upon you to be loyal to this purpose which we have set for ourselves? May I expect that you will help us with your readiness to carry out the little tasks we assign to you? May I hope that you will display a loving interest in all that is truly Jewish, spiritual, and ennobling? Why certainly!

Sincerely yours,

Rabbi Mordecai Kaplan

FOUR

UNIVERSALISM AND PRAGMATISM: FELIX ADLER, WILLIAM JAMES, AND JOHN DEWEY

The question "What is Judaism?" therefore resolves itself into the question "How do these beliefs and practices function?" For the first time we are getting at the very essence of Judaism; for the function of a thing practically constitutes its essence.

—*Mordecai Kaplan, February 1917*

Academics, myself included, are fond of exploring influences, of demonstrating the way in which a key aspect of a person's thought relates to particular sources. It is an attempt to explain through origin. This search for influences, however, should not blind us to the inherent features of a person's mind. In the case of Mordecai Kaplan's universalism and pragmatism, though, such a search is superfluous. We do not need to search for the origin of a particular Kaplanian idea in William James or John Dewey or Felix Adler. Universalism and the pragmatic method were essential parts of Kaplan's mind. Kaplan visited other realms, but he lived in the universal and the pragmatic.

Nonetheless, origins are sometimes helpful. Exploring the roots of a person's thought can yield a deeper understanding or a more incisive formulation of a specific line of reasoning. In the case of Kaplan, a particular concept from James, Dewey, or Adler can act as a kind of midrash, a commentary on his thought that explains or expands his original meaning. Felix Adler, Kaplan's philosophy professor, was far from being a pragmatist, but his universalism fit well into Kaplan's thought universe. Though universalism and pragmatism are not umbilically tied, they are both important features of American intellectual life in the early twentieth century and, therefore, easily available to Kaplan. To understand

Kaplan's relationship to pragmatism and to universalism, we must first understand the circumstances of his early years.

The context of Mordecai Kaplan's thought was framed by the special needs of second-generation Jews in the early decades of the twentieth century, especially in New York City. His appeal and his significance are due to the fact that he spoke to the particular problems of the children of the immigrants who spoke English and were beginning to feel "at home in America."[1] That generation labored under intense pressure to assimilate into American culture, to become authentic Americans. It sought education to succeed in a world familiar yet foreign and enrolled heavily in the New York City's high schools and colleges. With gradual increases in incomes, families moved from the Lower East Side up to the Bronx or out to Brooklyn, but continued to live in Jewish neighborhoods where children attended schools with other Jewish children. The schools were a great socializing force and helped the immigrant children forge a strong, and increasingly secular, Jewish identity.

The road that lay before the second generation was not an easy one. This group struggled with the Depression and also with anti-Semitism, albeit without the virulence of the European strain. There were quotas in colleges and professional schools, and, in many areas of employment, it was difficult for Jews to rise above the lowest levels. To assimilate outright was not easy either. Only a few took this road. Most of these men and women lived poised between two cultures, even two civilizations, often feeling alienated from both. This sense of alienation became the subject for endless movies, novels, and short stories. It also became a primary concern of Jewish leaders and rabbis.[2]

Mordecai Kaplan was unquestionably the central ideologue for a select group of the second generation. He was a spokesman for the minority of the minority, those educated intellectuals, who yearned to be Jewish and American at the same time. He knew their language and understood their problems. Kaplan's ability to speak to committed Jews of the second generation flowed from personal experience. He became an adult during the great migrations of the last decade of the nineteenth and the first decade of the twentieth century, when thousands of Jews arrived from Eastern Europe. By the time the majority of second-generation Jews reached adulthood (in the 1920s), he had already worked out his philosophy and was presenting his views in many different forums. He understood the second generation because he belonged to it. He had matured in America and could provide answers to problems that the generation of the 1920s was only beginning to face.

As a "rabbi" at Kehilath Jeshurun from 1903 to 1909, Kaplan was first confronted by the reality that young Jews even of that era did not find their religion compelling. Their values, their hopes, and even their sense of identity emerged on the whole from the domain of the secular. The children of immigrants found Judaism obscure and oppressive. It was not part of modern life in America. These young Jews saw in America an open society, and, like other ethnic and religious groups, they fully embraced the values of pluralism and toleration. But this very openness, needless to say, also constituted a threat to Jewish identity. The individual Jew, in search of life's meaning, was free to go in almost any direction. Such freedom often threatened to fragment and endanger the Jewish community itself. Some Jews questioned the need for a Jewish community altogether in a society where opportunities seemed unlimited. So many of the functions of the traditional Jewish community had been appropriated by one level or another of government, of neighborhood, and of American culture that it was difficult to see what significance was left in the religion.

Kaplan was very much a creature of his time and place, which, as noted, was both his strength and his weakness. He shared a view of the world common to young, educated American Jews. He was optimistic about the future and believed strongly in America. He lived and thought in the American idiom—the idiom of the pragmatic and the functional. His philosophy was attractive because it so suited the American landscape of change, growth, and opportunity. He embraced the ethics of progress and was focused unapologetically on what could be accomplished. Throughout his life, Kaplan essentially asked himself two basic questions: How could he help the Jewish people survive when the community and the religion seemed to be in a state of rapid disintegration? And, second, how could Jewish thinking and Jewish attitudes regarding religion be transformed so that Judaism would again enable the Jewish people to live more complete lives as individuals and as members of the community? He sought a religion and a God that would make sense to a person living in the twentieth century. Although in many ways a radical, Kaplan, like Janus, always looked in two directions—backward and forward.

* * *

The beginning of Kaplan's religious radicalism is framed by his graduate studies at Columbia and the influence of his teachers. In 1900, he graduated from the City College of New York and enrolled at Columbia University for his Master's. Two years later, he was ordained at the Jewish Theological Seminary.

One of the most profound experiences of Kaplan's early academic life was studying under Felix Adler, the founder of the Ethical Culture Movement. Adler was a prominent personality on the New York intellectual scene and, during this period, taught philosophy at Columbia in addition to directing the Society for Ethical Culture. As we have seen, the clash for Kaplan was between a rigorously traditional family and the areligious inclinations of his graduate studies. Felix Adler added to Kaplan's quandary, but more than anyone also helped him cope with these conflicts. Although Adler was not a follower of William James or of John Dewey, his universalism fit in well with the growing pragmatic temper of the young Kaplan.

Adler was born in 1851, raised in New York City, and eventually attended Columbia University. His secular education opened his eyes to the world of the intellect and undermined his religious commitments. Though his sense of obligation is evident—an 1873 essay, for example, deplores the practice of some Reform Jews who brought trees into their homes at Christmas time—he began to doubt some of the fundamentals of Judaism, doubts that were deepened when he went to Germany to continue his Judaic studies. Even the great German reformer Abraham Geiger, then advanced in years, could not answer Adler's questions.[3]

The primary question that plagued Adler was "Why remain Jewish?" Drawn to prophetic Judaism since his Columbia days, Adler was at the same time drifting away from his Jewish heritage. He believed ethics were universal and opposed the idea that ethics had to be rooted in the experience of a particular people. It was time for Jews to move beyond the narrow confines of their ethnic past, he concluded. He felt that Geiger was too timid to take the next step in the process of modernization. The efforts to divest the Jewish religion of its particularity were only partial and must be taken to their logical conclusion. While Adler was in Berlin, he also studied privately with the young Hermann Cohen, who would soon thereafter become one of the primary liberal Jewish philosophers of the early twentieth century, the founder of the Marburg school of Neo-Kantian philosophy, and a significant influence on Mordecai Kaplan.

By the time Kaplan arrived in Felix Adler's class in February 1903, the Society for Ethical Culture was well established and Adler's ideas had already taken a definitive shape.[4] Ethical Culture under Adler set aside the belief in God as a personal matter and emphasized the centrality of ethics. His understanding of ethics was essentially Kantian and underscored the universalist ideals of the moral life. He prized public works and the use of reason in making ethical decisions. The movement was open to people of all faiths and at its inception included many disenchanted Jews from the fringes of the organized Jewish community.

Kaplan had been taking courses in philosophy for the previous three years and had also read extensively in sociology under Franklin Giddings, the first appointee in sociology at an American university. The doubts Kaplan would express in his journal a few years later were certainly already fomenting. The concerns and the formulations of Adler were precisely what Kaplan needed. Adler wanted to capture the essence of religion to retain its meaningfulness at a time when science, technology, and modernity were relegating it to a smaller and smaller place. Writing in 1905, he sounds very much like the later Kaplan: "There is something in religion besides its doctrines, its symbols and its ceremonies.... That which is everlastingly precious in religion is the conviction that life is worthwhile."[5]

Although throughout his career Kaplan strongly emphasized the interpretation of religion in terms of function and was drawn to the pragmatism of William James and later of John Dewey, Felix Adler and his philosophy are also fundamental to Kaplan's thinking. Despite the fact that Adler did not offer a fully elaborated system, he did spell out many of his basic assumptions and primary concepts. He repeatedly emphasized the primacy of experience in understanding religion, as did many thinkers and students of religion at this time. From Adler, Kaplan absorbed the focus on experience. In Adler's words, "The religion that shall satisfy must be a religion of progress, of evolution, of development, understood not in a scientific sense but in a moral sense. To the question: How can one get religion?, the answer is 'through experience.' We must find in our own inner life the facts which are capable of being interpreted in terms of a religion, the foundations upon which the super-structure of a helpful religion can be built."[6]

Experience here refers, of course, to the life of the individual. It should not surprise us that Adler, coming into his intellectual maturity in the late nineteenth century, was influenced by Ralph Waldo Emerson. Adler read Emerson widely and quoted him often. We have seen how essential Emerson was in molding Kaplan's mind. Kaplan was influenced by Emerson directly but also indirectly through the lectures and books of Adler.[7]

Adler also believed that religion must not violate the scientific understanding of the day and must be based on what people really believe. He spoke directly to the problem of religious conflict when he said, "Let us found religion upon a basis of perfect intellectual honesty. Religion, if it is to mean anything at all, must stand for the highest truth. How then can the cause of truth be served by the sacrifice more or less disguised of one's intellectual convictions." Kaplan was reassured by Adler's primary direction and found such sentiments extremely valuable.[8]

The series of lectures from Felix Adler, which Mordecai Kaplan heard in the spring of 1903, centered on the key problem of justifying the imperative—the "ought" in any ethical system. This primary question, of course, had been asked since the time of Plato; but, in the late nineteenth century, it took on a different cast. Would the course of action required by self-preservation and the course required by morality be the same? If the answer is yes, then those groups that survive would also be the ones that are ethically the most developed.[9] Darwin seemed to believe that altruism and survivability went hand in hand. For us, the important point is not the virtues of Darwin's position but the fact that at every turn the young Kaplan was confronted by the Darwinian revolution and was presented, in this particular case, with the central issue of justifying ethical imperatives.

The strong ethical and humanistic tendency in Kaplan is in evidence from his early years and was undoubtedly influenced by Adler's universalism. Kaplan worried about assimilation, but at the same time he was deeply concerned with all humankind. His universalism and his strong Jewish identification remained in a complex symbiosis from his earliest years. The older Judaism, he explained in 1906, centered its attention on the Jewish people: "The new Judaism moves the center from Israel to Humanity. The Shekhina [presence of God] is in Humanity."[10]

If the presence of God is in humanity, then it must mean, according to the young Kaplan, that no one group has a monopoly on the truth. Although he did not reject the concept of the chosen people until much later, an incipient rejection arose while he was still in his thirties:

> It is just as necessary and inevitable that each should represent the spiritual side of life differently from the other as it is necessary and inevitable that each should have features of his own or speak in a way altogether his own. When we recognize the necessity of varied expression, the sameness and the unity of the underlying essence will stand out more prominently.[11]

Theologically speaking, Adler was clearer than Kaplan. He stated, just like Matthew Arnold, that, when we talk of God, we speak metaphorically because what we say is never literally true; but the metaphor, nonetheless, stands for something real. The gods, including Jehovah, are creations of the imagination, but the eternal is not. His proof derived from morality, and it was very similar to what is found in Kaplan's later works. For example, Adler wrote, "If then, I believe in the ultimate attainment of the moral end, I am forced to assume that there is provision in nature looking to the achievement of that end."[12] Adler's ability to deal with the transcendent certainly made it easier for Kaplan to digest his philosophy as a whole. Despite his emphasis on the ethical, Adler possessed a genuine sense for the transcendent: "the deepest experiences of life have been missed," he tells us, "if we have never been thrilled by the emotions which come from the thought of that vaster life of which ours is a part. It is wonder, evoked by the thought of the vastness, order and beauty of the world that has led men to the idea of God."[13]

According to Adler, it is not only the experience of wonder but the striving after righteousness that leads one to the transcendent. (It was Matthew Arnold's approach that Adler paraphrased.) Speaking of the demand for justice, Adler said, "on the other hand, if the demand for justice is realizable, then in the nature of things there must be provision that it shall be realized; then there must be, as it has been expressed, 'a power that makes for righteousness.'"[14] Adler went on to emphasize God as a power rather than a person.[15] It is clear, then, that the "non-personal God" of Arnold was reinforced in Kaplan's mind by the religious thrust of Adler's thinking. Kaplan's 1905 statement about Ahad Ha-Am and Arnold clearly indicates that the foundations of Kaplan's thought were already firmly in place at this early point, thanks in large part to Adler.

This line of reasoning is also found in Kaplan's *The Meaning of God in Modern Jewish Religion*. Inspired in part by Arnold, Kaplan chose to talk about the way God functions in the world and not about His essence. In his lifelong quest for the meaning of God, he continually focused on what God helps people to do. At the same time, it is well to remember that Kaplan came from a traditional background and was not able completely to supersede it. We sense that background in the following statement: "It is because God is to me the warm personal element in life's inner urge to creativity and self-expression that I can conscientiously employ the name Y H W H when praying."[16]

Kaplan's attraction to Adler was long-lasting but ambivalent. While taking courses with Adler, Kaplan was offered a scholarship by the Ethical Culture Society, which he refused. Kaplan never forgave Adler for leaving the Jewish fold to found the Ethical Culture Movement; he despised him for being a traitor to the Jewish people.[17] He often criticized Adler and was especially distressed when he met members of the university's Menorah Societies who were thinking of joining the Ethical Culture Movement. But contempt was merely the flipside of curiosity; Kaplan himself was attracted to Adler's ethical emphasis and to his universalism. Adler's model promised an ethical ideology that would be open to all and would make no ethnic distinction between different groups. This universalism or cosmopolitanism, as it was sometimes called, was Kaplan's great temptation—his devil, as it were, that plagued him throughout his life. The temptation of many important figures, as we know, is sexual—the proverbial skeleton in the closet. The skeleton in Kaplan's closet was Felix Adler. Despite his disgust with Adler, Kaplan never ceased lusting after the universal.[18]

Kaplan was tempted throughout his life, as we shall see, to move away from the particular—that is, from the Jewish people—and toward a vision of religion and of right conduct that could embrace everyone. No one has been more devoted to the Jewish people than Mordecai Kaplan, yet, paradoxically, the universal and the humanistic were always at the forefront of his consciousness. In his universalism, he was following his mentor, the pragmatist John Dewey, a strong supporter of the universal as evidenced in "The Humanist Manifesto" of the early 1930s that Dewey helped create.[19]

Kaplan's great hopes for the Jewish people were often tempered, as we have seen, by pessimism about the realization of those hopes. In occasional moments of despair, when he felt that Judaism had little chance of surviving, he thought about joining Adler's movement. "Time and again it has occurred to me," he confided in his journal in 1916, "that I ought to join the Ethical Culture Movement."[20] His congregation, the Society for the Advancement of Judaism, was patterned after the Society for Ethical Culture. Indeed, at an early point, he even thought of calling his new congregation "The Society for Jewish Ethical Culture." Until the middle thirties, for example, Kaplan called himself the "leader," as Adler had done, and Ira Eisenstein was the "assistant leader." It was only with the coming of Nazism that Kaplan reverted to the title of rabbi.

Though he stayed within the folds of Jewish tradition, time and again, Kaplan attempted to reinterpret and reconstruct his community in a universalist mode. The goal of fulfillment, both individual and collective, was always on his mind. Desperate to modernize and universalize the Jewish tradition so it would survive the challenges of the twentieth century, Kaplan was attempting to use Adler in the service of the Jewish people in the same way that he had used Spinoza to foster Jewish survival and the same way he had used Ahad Ha-Am to explain Jewish peoplehood. Here, as always, the historical "what ifs" are intriguing: if Adler had been born twenty years later and been exposed to the works of Ahad Ha-Am, where the universal and the particular are united in one direction, he might never have felt the need to establish the Ethical Culture Movement.

Although, as we have seen, the primary thrust of Kaplan's thinking was shaped by Felix Adler, Kaplan was also heavily influenced by his studies in sociology. While at Columbia, Kaplan became immersed in the study of sociology and took every course given by the sociologist Franklin Giddings. Under the influence of Giddings, Kaplan's thinking became heavily sociological, often thinking of problems primarily with reference to the group and the way in which institutions function. Sociologists always distance themselves from institutions, traditions, and ideas as they explore their functions. They are inevitably led to relativize because the study of the traditions of various groups reveals similar, if not identical, functions. Thus, when Kaplan examined behavior, he did so not as a psychologist might, from the point of view of motivation, but rather in terms of its function or consequences.

The most important application of the concept of function was to religion itself. Throughout his career, Kaplan continually reformulated his basic definition of the function of religion. "What we want," he wrote in 1915, "is a religion that will help us to gain our bearings in the world, that will keep down the beast in us and spur us on to worthy endeavors in the field of thought and action."[21] Kaplan repeated often that religion should comfort in times of pain, give hope in difficult times, promote moral development, and provide a sense of order and purpose from day to day.

Kaplan was adamant in his belief that, if religion was to retain its function, it needed to be flexible and progressive. Many Americans, by contrast, viewed the Western monotheistic religions as rigid and dogmatic. A distinction exists, however, between religion as an individual experience and religion as it becomes structured and organized through communal institutions. Viewing religion as experiential emphasizes its perpetual flux, as it constantly grows and changes because the experiences of individuals grow and change. Any particular formulation or creed is only a temporary version of some deeply held insight or profound experience. Further experience and insight will inevitably result in reformulations concerning the ineffable aspects of life.

Kaplan's emphasis on experience is usually understood as flowing from the influence of John Dewey and William James. These men are, of course, basic, as we shall see. It may be, however, that Kaplan's pragmatic thrust is due also to a yet-earlier influence that he encountered while studying at Columbia. His 1902 Master's thesis under Felix Adler dealt with the philosophy of Henry Sidgwick (1838–1900), who was for many years professor of philosophy at Cambridge University and whose book *The Methods of Ethics* is a significant treatise in the Benthamite tradition of utilitarian ethics. Sidgwick criticized both Jeremy Bentham and John Stuart Mill but, nonetheless, remained within the utilitarian school. Kaplan's emphasis on function as well as some of his primary beliefs concerning religion may be derived directly from Sidgwick.[22]

Kaplan's commitment to flexibility is legendary. The challenge of ceaselessly revising creeds the better to reflect our experience is extremely demanding. It would certainly be much easier to retain traditional formulations. But Kaplan knew that, in a profound sense, the experience of the transcendent is always an approximation, as we have seen with Matthew Arnold. There is no way to capture once and for all the numinous aspects of experience. A fixed creed or dogma would inevitably become idolatrous, mistaking that which is transitory and limited for that which is permanent and infinite.

A commitment to the experiential is also a commitment to the pragmatic. Pragmatism by nature rejects whatever is fixed and has an inherent distaste for dogma. It is fact-oriented and scientific in its approach to problems. Kaplan displayed all these qualities but not in a rigorous philosophical sense. He continually focused on the way in which ideas function and their consequences, but, at the same time, he entertained notions (such as the concept of the collective mind) of a highly abstract and almost metaphysical nature.

The pragmatic tradition is intimately linked with the works of John Dewey. It has frequently been maintained that Kaplan's functionalism was decisively influenced by Dewey. The bulk of Dewey's popular work, however, came out in book form only after Kaplan's thinking had already been molded by the sociological tradition. As pragmatists and sociological thinkers have much in common, it is easy to see why Kaplan was drawn to pragmatism. Dewey served to confirm Kaplan's philosophic thrust, rather than to create it. Dewey's work was decisive in helping Kaplan develop and formulate his ideas, but his pragmatic approach was not derived from Dewey.

Dewey was not the only pragmatist who influenced Kaplan. I would argue that William James was also a major influence. Kaplan, for example, was well acquainted with James's famous work *The Varieties of Re-*

ligious Experience. When a group of rabbinical students from the Jewish Theological Seminary requested in 1915 that Kaplan form a study group dealing with religion, he chose works by James as the basis for discussion. The group convened at Kaplan's house every Saturday night to deal with the nature of religious experience.[23]

Pragmatism, a particularly American philosophy, was just coming into its own when Kaplan came into intellectual maturity. William James's *Pragmatism,* published in 1907, developed from a series of lectures that he delivered in Boston at the Lowell Institute and in New York City at Columbia University. Although Kaplan preferred to call himself a functionalist rather than a pragmatist, he operated clearly within the pragmatic frame of mind as defined by James.

"The Pragmatic method," wrote James, "is to try to interpret each notion by tracing its respective practical consequences. What difference would it practically make to anyone if this notion rather than that notion were true?"[24] Even the most rigorous pragmatic thinker does not feel compelled to verify each and every statement that he accepts as true. Nonetheless, the pragmatic thinker passionately believes that all true statements must, at least in principle, be capable of verification through experience. The primacy of experience is found in all pragmatic thinkers. The pragmatist would always believe that our knowledge is partial and that we never have a final or ultimate truth. Pragmatism and the rigid adherence to dogma are, thus, incompatible. In all these ways, we may classify Kaplan as a pragmatist.

Kaplan's clearest direct statement on pragmatism is found in an unpublished manuscript titled "The Meaning of Religion," which he wrote in 1929. The passage is worth quoting in full:

> We do not have to accept pragmatism as a philosophy of life or as a means of getting at the ultimate and metaphysical nature of reality to accept it as a method of knowledge or as the logic of scientific procedure. We make no philosophic or metaphysical commitments when we identify the nature of a thing (for purposes of manipulating it or setting it right when there is something wrong with it) with the manner in which it functions, with the difference it makes in other things. Applying this pragmatic method of getting at the nature of religion we learn as much as there is to be learned about religion for purposes of adjustment and manipulation by having a correct and clear idea of the way in which religion has functioned in the numerous guises which it has assumed in the different civilizations and eras of human development.[25]

A fundamental aspect of Kaplan's thinking is reflected here. His first question about a religious practice or belief was "What function did it originally fulfill?" Then he would ask, "How did this function change throughout Jewish history?" Next, "Does this practice now fulfill the same function that it did in the past?" And, finally, "If it doesn't, what will now take its place and serve the same goal?" These questions were applied by Kaplan to the belief in a supernatural deity, to prayer, to the concept of the chosen people, to the concept of the world to come, and even to many individual *mitzvot*. In each instance, the experience of the individual is key to shaping an answer.

Following this passage, Kaplan elaborates his view of the principal function of religion:

> As a means of faith making man feel at home in the world by inculcating in him a sense of confidence in the inherent tending of the universe to make for man's security and happiness, providing he conform to its nature and controlling agencies.

Within the complex blending that was Kaplan's mind, it is equally likely that the concept of function derived from his sociological studies, from the pragmatic tradition, from his study of ethics and utilitarian philosophy, and from Felix Adler. In any case, the concept of function was central to his view of Judaism and religion in general.

Kaplan emphasized function not only in his writings but in his lectures as well. By 1915, his extensive lecturing throughout the country, at local YMHAs, synagogues, and universities, made him a figure on the national Jewish scene. For example, in 1917, while on a speaking tour of the Midwest, Kaplan lectured at the Menorah convention held at the University of Minnesota.[26] Here he addressed himself to the question "What is Judaism?" and focused on the issue of function. He first chose a number of examples from the tradition that attempted to sum up the essence of Judaism and would allow him to focus on the primary function of Jewish civilization. He cited Deuteronomy 10:12–13: "What does the Lord your God demand of you? Only this: to revere the Lord your God, to walk only in His paths, to love Him and to serve the Lord your God with all your heart and soul, keeping the Lord's commandments and laws, which I enjoin upon you today for your good." He then discussed

Micah 6:8: "He [the Lord] has told you, Oh man, what is good, and what the Lord requires of you: Only to do justice and to love goodness, and to walk modestly with your God." He also called attention to the "Thirteen Principles" of Maimonides, which are enshrined in the daily prayer book.[27] In each case, we need to think about this essence and deliberate as to whether it still functions.

Kaplan then argued that, in the modern world, all these definitions were inadequate. He expanded on the importance of function in defining religion and Judaism:

> With the solvent influence exercised by social environment upon the beliefs and practices associated with the name Judaism, we begin to suspect that Judaism can function only under certain social conditions. The question "What is Judaism?" therefore resolves itself into the question "How do these beliefs and practices function?" For the first time we are getting at the very essence of Judaism; for the function of a thing practically constitutes its essence.

The notion that function constitutes essence is primary to Kaplan's thought and the key to his value system. In his remarks to the Menorah students at the university, Kaplan proceeded to analyze the function of religious beliefs and practices. Ordinarily, we would say that such beliefs and rituals function to make us more aware of the divine or to promote our moral development. And, of course, they do. But, more importantly for Kaplan, religious beliefs and rituals function to connect us with our social group.

* * *

In Kaplan's earliest published writings, his pragmatic emphasis came through as a hard-hitting attack against abstract theology in favor of the experiential: "A condition indispensable to a religion being an active force in human life is that it speaks to men in terms of their own experience. . . . the language of theology might have certain quaintness and charm to the ears of those to whom religion is a kind of dreamy romanticism. But to those who want to find in Judaism a way of life and a higher ambition, it must address itself in the language of concrete and verifiable experience." In his diary in 1914, he noted that the reconstruction of Judaism could only take place "on the basis of natural human experience within the reach of every one of us." Such an emphasis on experience would lead, of course, to considerable diversity of belief and practice in the religious sphere; Kaplan was always willing to accept this diversity as a sign of health.

The doctrine of function enunciated here seems to advocate a kind of anarchy where every man or woman is his or her own religious guide and where there is virtually no uniformity. Kaplan, of course, never endorsed such an idea, but he did believe that modern religion could never achieve uniformity of belief within the ranks. The best traditional faiths could hope for, and the most they should work for, was a unity of commitment along with a diversity of religious belief.

The rationalist is a person who believes that truths endure, whereas the pragmatist believes that only change is permanent—paradoxical as that may seem. "We have to live today by what truth we can get today, and must be ready tomorrow to call it falsehood," William James said.[28] Because Kaplan believed this so strongly, it was not difficult for him to embrace the broader notion of religious truth as constantly evolving.

The implications of this pragmatist position are profound. If there is no ultimate truth because truth is constantly changing, then the identification of God with ultimate truth falls apart. Judaism, Christianity, and Islam alike have long believed that there is an ultimate truth and that each religion possesses it. Medieval religious thinkers in the West inherited from Plato the notion that, beyond the realm of appearances, there is a reality that is eternal and that can be known through one's reason and through Holy Scripture.

For pragmatists, the truth is not the description of any reality, present or ultimate, but a program for action. Neopragmatists like Richard Rorty have helped us understand that we need not be the victims of the Greek distinction between appearance and reality. Philosophically speaking, you might say that, for the pragmatist, "what you see is what you get,"[29] but the only problem—and the great, if terrifying, possibility—is that, in our world, the "what you see" is constantly changing.

Truths might indeed change, but the living energy at the center of Jewish peoplehood does not. Kaplan spoke a great deal about "energy" in talking of the group or the nation or God. Energy is the basic commodity of the modern era and, thus, it is emotionally, intellectually, and spiritually compelling.

The novelty of Kaplan's formulation can only really be appreciated if we set it beside the common approaches of this period. Both Reform and Conservative Jews were eager to show that Judaism embodied a set of beliefs that constituted a rational picture of the universe and not merely a set of rituals and customs. Judaism entailed a whole theology that was embedded in rabbinical dicta. (Thus, the title and the purpose of Solomon Schechter's great work *Some Aspects of Rabbinic Theology*.) Reform and Conservative leaders argued over the relative importance of this or that belief, but no one except Kaplan questioned the notion that Judaism consisted of a series of rational beliefs about the world and the commandments that flowed from them. Kaplan completely redefined Judaism, and, in doing so, he moved the discussion to a different level. His was a paradigm shift.

The question was not which belief to keep and which to throw out in order to strengthen Judaism, but rather how to nurture the life energy of the Jewish people—the physical and spiritual heart that constituted the essence of the people. Just as radical, Kaplan was adamant that the endless dictates of the ancient rabbis were only one source of inspiration. The vital energy is expressed through the collective consciousness of the Jewish people and could be fostered in many different ways: "it may be the Synagogue, the Hebrew Language, the Zionist movement, Jewish education or even student societies," Kaplan wrote to his friend Henry Hurwitz in 1916. But, importantly, Kaplan's revolutionary emphasis is that Judaism is not based on a belief system.

This rejection of dogmatism placed Kaplan within the pragmatic tradition and exhibited the sociological bent of his thinking—the pragmatic person must always be ready to discard a cherished belief if he or she finds evidence that invalidates it. William James offered a guiding principle in the search for truth, with which Kaplan would certainly concur: "If there be any life that it is really better we should lead, and if there be any idea which, if believed in, would help us to lead that life, then it would really be better for us to believe in that idea, unless, indeed, belief in it incidentally clashed with other greater vital benefits."[30]

Additionally, there is in sociology an implicit relativity of truth that sociologists are constrained to accept. Exploring different classes and different cultures, comparing and contrasting their values, describing the social conditions under which certain ideas emerge, it is inevitable that "Truth" comes to be viewed as a more tentative phenomenon. Kaplan's continued exposure to sociology during his education led him to doubt that anyone actually discovered eternal truths. Nevertheless, Kaplan never advocated a relativity of truth with regard to ethical standards. He even went so far as to maintain that "the moral order of the universe, of which man alone happens to be the exponent, is as much an actual reality as the natural order."[31]

* * *

Over the long arc of his intellectual career, Kaplan sought to integrate all the factors we have been discussing: the primacy of function and the naturalistic view of the human being and the universe, the individual and the group. John Dewey was an essential part of this process. He helped Kaplan to combine all his thoughts and to create a new way of approaching religion in general and Judaism in particular. Beginning with *Reconstruction in Philosophy* which was published in 1920, Dewey gained a greater and greater hold on Kaplan's mind. Yet at the same time, it is well to remember that Kaplan developed his philosophy before he started reading Dewey, so that, though Dewey is central, it is more in a confirming sense than in a generative sense. Kaplan is more creative than most realize, both with respect to Dewey and with respect to Emile Dürkheim.

For Kaplan, the philosophy of Emerson—built upon the primacy of the individual—was completed in Dewey. Both for Dewey and Kaplan, the moral perfection of the individual could only take place within the group. Indeed, the purpose of the group was to work for the fulfillment of each of its members. The group for Dewey had mystical connotations, which resonated for Kaplan. In Dewey's words, "When the emotional force, the mystic force one might say, of communication, of the miracle of shared life and shared experience is spontaneously felt, the hardness and crudeness of contemporary life will be bathed in the light that never was on land or sea."[32]

On the importance of Dewey, we hear directly from Kaplan on the occasion of Dewey's passing, though it is well to remember that we often misremember when we consider the long-ago past. There is no doubt a touch of exaggeration here as Kaplan reconstructs his life narrative.

> *Mon. June 2/52* I record with great sorrow the passing of John Dewey. I am indebted to him for the method of thought and world outlook that have enabled me to make sense out of the buzzing confusion of the various modern attempts to fill the vacuum created by the desuetude of tradition. Dewey has helped me arrive at a pragmatic reinterpretation of Bible and Rabbinics. His principle that "an activity which does not have worth enough to be carried on for its own sake cannot be an effective preparation for something else" has encouraged me to conceive of Judaism as a this-worldly civilization. His "Reconstruction of Philosophy" has encouraged me to make Reconstructionism the new key in which to plan for the future of the Jewish people in particular and the forces of education in general. To me he has meant more than Aristotle meant to medieval theologians, because in addition to his thought being a guide, his life and character have been an inspiration to me. If I love America it is because it has produced a John Dewey. That the very university (Chicago) where he developed his revolutionary conceptions of philosophy and education should have repudiated those conceptions and have become the seat of cultural reaction and arrogance should enable me to contemplate with equanimity the way the Seminary is certain to try to squelch Reconstructionist thought as soon as I am gone: To me he is one of the *hasidei umot ha-olam* [righteous among the nations of the world] who find few equals among our own people. Two things I pray for: *ta'hi ahriti kamohu* [may my fate be like his] and *t'n'tz'b'ha* [may his soul be bound up in eternal life].[33]

It was pragmatism and Dewey, more than any other philosophical system, that helped Kaplan reconstruct Judaism so that the Jewish people would survive. Pragmatism represents a complete break with the Western philosophical tradition. For many centuries, but especially since Immanuel Kant, philosophers had been obsessed with the problem of epistemology. This division of philosophy seeks to explore and justify our claims to knowledge. The claim to know is perhaps the most fundamental claim that the mind can make. If we claim to know something, we are asserting, first of all, that it is so, that it is the truth and, hence, certain. In addition, we are claiming that we have good and sufficient reasons for believing it is the case. One of the central problems of epistemology is the limitations of our knowledge. Kant seemed to establish once and for all that our knowledge was limited by our experience and by the concepts of space and time that are part of the mind's way of grasping reality. It is, thus, impossible to know the thing-in-itself, or the *ding-an-sich,* outside the dimensions that the mind gives to what it experiences. This "fact" has plagued philosophers up to the present day. There seemed to be no way in which we could be certain about matters of ultimate importance.

Along came James and Dewey in the early twentieth century, who simply set the epistemological problem aside. They chose to shift the meaning of truth and the goal of knowing. For the pragmatists, and especially for John Dewey, the goal of knowledge was action. To say that we know something is to say we have a program for action. Pragmatism is not to be confused with the practical. The pragmatist is often idealistic and seeks knowledge to improve human welfare. Indeed, the pragmatic thinker emphasizes that, through intelligence, we approach the world and the problems of our life within it. The object of knowledge is not the "world out there" and its essence. Pragmatic thinkers do not deal with essences and eschew thinking about ultimate realities. The critics of William James, for example, never tired of pointing out that he had no metaphysics—thus revealing that they completely missed the central thrust of pragmatism. Kaplan was similarly misunderstood. To experience something for Dewey, for example, is to be engaged in an adventure much like driving a car. When we drive, there is a constant interaction with our environment in which we test what will be the most useful in helping us to attain our goals. This attitude is sometimes called "meliorism."

Simply put, the goal of thought and action for a pragmatist is to improve our lot—a goal at the heart of both Kaplan's ideology and his character. His assumption is that human life can be improved and that we have a responsibility to contribute toward that improvement. In describing the common term for a pragmatic attitude, Kaplan writes, "meliorism is the belief that, though we cannot expect human life or human society ever to be perfect, it can continually improve and the human spirit can continually find fulfillment in an expanding freedom."[34] Such sentiments are pure Dewey. Ours is not the best of all possible worlds, but it can be repaired and redeemed. Kaplan does not see this goal as being utopian. The choices are never between absolute good and absolute evil but greater and lesser good and greater and lesser evils. And we do have the freedom to choose. Kaplan's melioristic emphasis helps us understand the connection between pragmatism and universalism. The fulfillment of the individual and the improvement of society in general are at the heart of Felix Adler's universalism and also central to the thinking of James and Dewey.

Kaplan, like Dewey, has often been accused of a naïve kind of optimism, in accordance with the spirit of a previous era but out of place in a post-Holocaust world. The truth is that Kaplan does have faith, a great deal of faith, but it is not in the inevitability of progress or in the essentially positive nature of human beings. Kaplan's faith is, rather, in the human capacity for renewal; he is a tireless cheerleader for the process (and possibility) of re-creation, an endeavor that we know requires constant encouragement:

> But we must retain our faith that we can learn by our errors, that human nature has been endowed with capacities for self-control and self-improvement, and that, once we identify an evil as such, we can reasonably expect that conscientious efforts to remove that evil will succeed.[35]

Kaplan easily relates his concept of meliorism to Jewish practice. The most obvious example is the Sabbath. On the Sabbath, we celebrate God's creation of the world. We say in the Sabbath liturgy that "God continually renews daily the work of creation." Kaplan interprets this to mean that the urge toward creation is pervasive. Creativity is not only a phenomenon of nature but a human phenomenon. In his words, "By becoming aware of that fact [that is, daily creation], we must gear our own lives to this creative urge in the universe and discover within ourselves unsuspected powers of the spirit."[36]

Indeed, it is not only the Sabbath that calls us to self-renewal but religion in general; the urge toward self-renewal is the root of our faith in the possibility of improvement. "The yearning [for self-regeneration] dies down," Kaplan writes, "unless it is backed by the conviction that there is something which answers to it in the very character of life as a whole. There can hardly be any more important function for religion than to keep alive this yearning for self-renewal and to press it into the service of human progress."[37]

Kaplan's pragmatic and functional method is always to push toward the ideal. He strove throughout his career to rework a concept, a ritual, or a prayer so that it would contribute to moral progress and well-being—in other words, to our collective and individual betterment. Sometimes

Kaplan came across a practice that he felt was beyond reconstruction. For example, he felt the division of Israel into fixed groups on the basis of their ancestry was discriminatory in its essence. Neither the priesthood nor the sacrifices will ever function again, he reasoned, so what is the point of retaining the tripartite division of the Jewish people into priest [*kohane*], Levite, or Israelite. He believed this distinction should be eliminated completely, since there was no way to rehabilitate its function. Another example of his functional method was his continual questioning as to whether a particular *mitzvah* helps us cope. If it moves us toward *shelemut*—completeness or salvation—then we should embrace it with our whole being. If not, then it needs to be reconstructed so that it will function constructively.

In October 1942, Kaplan summed up with great precision the relationship between truth and well-being. "The world has changed," he said. "It used to be that we measured the truth of an idea by the degree to which it conformed to our tradition. Now in the modern world we measure it by the degree to which it helps human beings to make the most of life."[38]

The need for enhancement as a life goal begins, of course, with understanding and awareness. Both Kaplan and Dewey believed above all in the application of intelligence to life's problems. In the 1920s, Kaplan was interviewed about his new congregation by a local Yiddish newspaper. His method, he told the reporter, was to approach life with "spiritualized intelligence." It is well known that, for the pragmatists and especially for Dewey, the use of intelligence in all areas of life was essential to growth and improvement. For intelligence to be spiritualized means to be aware, to be keenly alive to the needs and pains of others.

We cannot fail to mention that pragmatism presents us with some major epistemological difficulties. Namely, if we measure truth by the degree to which it contributes to our well-being, then truth is constantly changing. What we consider true today may be considered false tomorrow. Kaplan and his teachers James and Dewey were willing to accept this dictum. For most of us, this idea is difficult to stomach. We yearn for something permanent to latch on to. Indeed, one might say that essentially the religious quest is the search for the permanent, for the eternal. If the truth is constantly changing, there is nothing that is constant. Kaplan deals with this problem in two ways. First, he points to our ideals as immutable. The fundamental goals of behavior are always there. Moses and the prophets sought righteousness and justice, and we continue to cherish these ideals, or we ought to. The problem of deciding what justice means in a particular situation is always challenging, but those who were inspired by the words of Isaiah and sought to implement the ideals had the same challenge.

The permanent and the absolute for Kaplan lie in the realm of ideals. It is here that he finds constancy:

> To state the matter concretely, the right of every person to the full development of his physical and mental capacities ... The solidarity of the entire human race ... So that we dare not disregard the effect of anything we do ... and the duty of thinking and acting so as to render reality more meaningful and life more worthwhile for every human being ... These are the goals which must be accepted as absolutes.[39]

The ideals are constant, always there propelling us to ever-higher levels. The question is whether the ideals to which we are committed exist only in our minds or whether they have an objective existence. One might even ask whether they have some kind of ontological status. This most interesting question is central to any naturalistic theology.

FIVE

KAPLAN AND PEOPLEHOOD: JUDAISM AS A CIVILIZATION AND ZIONISM

[Emil Fackenheim said that Kaplan represented] "the best side of the American pragmatic genius which refuses to subordinate realities to the requirements of philosophical or theological systems. The other is the indomitable love for *amcha* [the Jewish people] by an indomitable man."

—*Sh'ma, 1972*

Despite our focus on Mordecai Kaplan's individualism and on Ralph Waldo Emerson's influence, Kaplan was primarily a "man of the group." From very early on, he was obsessed with finding a way to ensure the survival of the Jewish people. In his classic work *Judaism as a Civilization*, Kaplan declared that it was only within the group that the individual could find fulfillment: "Only though the interaction with his group can the individual achieve personality and self fulfillment or salvation."[1] The continued existence of the Jews was always his overriding concern. Indeed, he once thought of calling his new approach *Zionist Judaism*. Nothing was more important to him than the fate of the Jewish people.

Not everyone understood Kaplan, including Emil Fackenheim, one of his severest critics throughout the 1950s. Fackenheim eventually came to appreciate Kaplan and wrote a very moving essay in 1974 in celebration of Kaplan's ninetieth birthday. In that essay, he acknowledged that Kaplan's most important quality was his love for Israel and his concern for the fate of world Jewry. Fackenheim never retracted any of his criticisms, even as he recognized the power of Kaplan's devotion to the Jewish people and his pragmatic brilliance as well.[2]

Judaism as a civilization is the concept most associated with Kaplan and is the cornerstone of his system. Many have questioned the use of the term *civilization*. For many years, Rabbi Simon Greenberg (1901–93), a leading Conservative rabbi of his time, would ask me, whenever we met in the Jewish Theological Seminary cafeteria, "Why did Kaplan talk about Judaism as a civilization? The Eskimos have a civilization. Kaplan should have understood that what was distinctive about Jews was their culture. Civilization has to do with knives and forks." Greenberg had a point. Civilization deals with all aspects of the life of a people, and every ethnic group has one; but culture deals with the higher creative aspects of a community. Why didn't Kaplan call his system *Judaism as a culture?*[3]

The most interesting recent explanation for Kaplan's use of the term *civilization* comes from a young academic named Noam Pianko.[4] In the 1920s, when Kaplan began to write his magnum opus, the term *civilization* was quite popular, especially in the works of the Beards and of John Dewey, to describe America.[5] Some also used the term *Christian civilization*. Thus, Kaplan's use of the term fits into the modalities of American thought of the time and may also have been intended to counter an incipient anti-Semitism. In the mid-1920s, there was a rise in American nativism, culminating in restrictive immigration laws. This further motivated Kaplan to emphasize the multicultural nature of American civilization and to maintain that Judaism was also a civilization.

Kaplan's assertion that Jews lived in two civilizations was enormously helpful for the second-generation American Jews for whom Kaplan was a guide. For these children of immigrants, most of whom desperately wanted to be American, Kaplan offered a compelling possibility: yes, he would urge, you can be American, but you can also be Jewish. You can have not one civilization but two. Being a Jew and being an American require adherence to the same values, he argued, so there is no inherent contradiction.[6]

In exploring the concept of civilization, Kaplan turned to a number of writers, one of whom was the British scholar Sir Alfred Zimmern (1879–1957). Zimmern, who taught Greek at Oxford, wrote extensively on political subjects and particularly on the nature of nationalism. He maintained that there were two types of nationalism. One was the civilizational model of nationalism exemplified by Britain; the other was what he called the "*Kultur*" model typified by Germany. Zimmern maintained that, in the British Empire, there were different nations who were members of one civilization. In the German model of nationalism, there was only one culture present, even though the culture might be spread over several nation-states.

Zimmern had strong Zionist leanings and drew many of his ideas from Ahad Ha-Am. He maintained that the German model of civilization, with its emphasis on one group, engenders a deep antipathy toward "the free play of human groupings and discourages all spontaneous or unauthorized associations."[7] Where the German model signified restriction, the British model implied pluralism and toleration of difference. From Zimmern's explication, Kaplan concluded that obviously the best principle for America and for the Jewish people was the British civilizational model of nationalism.

Kaplan's views of the nature of civilization and his pluralistic emphasis were confirmed by the writings of Horace Kallen, who vigorously opposed the notion of a one-dimensional American nationalism. Kallen rejected "the melting pot" ideology, where homogeneity was the goal, and instead opted for the cultural-pluralism model. He preferred the metaphor of an orchestra in which all members maintain their individual identities yet play together in harmony. Kallen, like Kaplan, was a dedicated disciple of John Dewey. He was also a Zionist, albeit a secular one. Kallen's philosophy has been characterized alternately as Hebraism, aesthetic pragmatism, humanism, cultural pluralism, and cooperative individualism.[8]

Both Kaplan and Kallen wanted to "privilege heterogeneity" and insisted on not just the necessity but the benefits of cultural pluralism among Jews. Kaplan, pluralist to the core, throughout his life rejected the idea that there was only one way to be Jewish.

Fitting into American culture, however, was just one of the benefits of the civilization idea. As Kaplan explains in *Judaism as a Civilization*, Jews of this era generally considered Judaism to be a religion. Whether it was given by God (Orthodox) or had evolved over the centuries (Conservative) or was primarily concerned with ethics (Reform), every denomination saw Judaism in religious terms.[9] But for many of the younger generation, religion was simply not relevant to their lives. Unlike what many Jewish leaders of the time believed, dropping this or that belief would not suffice to make Judaism more appealing.

To maintain that Judaism was a civilization, rather than a mere religion, shifted the heart of the discussion about what it meant to be a Jew. Saying from the pulpit that "we have no beliefs that are fixed, no dogmas which may become the center of a new orthodoxy" was an extremely radical statement to make, implying the acceptance of Nietzsche's assertion that God is dead. If Judaism is a living civilization, Kaplan insisted—much to the frustration of the Orthodox—it is constantly evolving, and no one belief or dogma is necessarily permanent. Kaplan believed people must learn to live without absolutes: "We have learned to regard no truth as finished and final. Whatever the teaching be, whoever its authority, it can never be above further research and inquiry. Such an attitude toward truth is entirely unthinkable with regard to any teaching which is believed to come directly from God."[10]

Kaplan's approach to Judaism was revolutionary. He proposed a fresh and original path to Jewish survival. To paraphrase the matter, he was saying that we are all members of particular families and that there is never a need to justify the existence of one's family. It just *is*. The family is a constant, though its particulars are ever-changing, and, as we grow and mature, we should come to understand that family and find fulfillment in it.

The young Jews of the 1920s knew they had little chance of fitting in. They might change their names and their noses but could not escape the fact of being Jews. Kaplan was asking, "Why not accept the fact of one's family, one's group, and one's past—one's biography, if you will—and profit from all it has to offer?" It was obvious that the fundamental values of Jewish civilization were compatible with all that was best in America. Ira Eisenstein summed it up when he attempted to reframe Kaplan's ideas in a more understandable form:

> [Many] talk as though Jews had to be convinced that their family was the best family, for fear they might join another family, as though it were necessary to prove that Judaism is the only true religion in the world, so that Jews might be persuaded to continue to be Jews. This is entirely the wrong approach. Judaism does not have to choose between justifying itself and ceasing to exist. It does have to choose between continuing as a vital force in the lives of Jews and persisting as a source of unhappiness and as a burden to Jews.[11]

Revitalizing Judaism, therefore, means adapting it to a contemporary sensibility; in other words, survival is only possible through reconstruction.

Kaplan's studies at Columbia transformed his thinking.[12] In his ongoing attempt to reconstruct Judaism, he would henceforth always be wedded to the social-science model of knowledge in general and sociology in particular. The social cast of Kaplan's thinking is usually attributed to the eminent sociologist Emile Durkheim. While Durkheim was significant in confirming Kaplan's thought, he was not primary in establishing the fundamental assumptions of Kaplan's system.[13]

Kaplan was much more original in his sociological thinking than he is given credit for. When I originally interviewed Kaplan and asked him about Durkheim, he maintained that Durkheim was primary. "In what language did you read Durkheim?" I asked. He replied that he read Durkheim in English. These details are important because Kaplan wrote a series of articles published in the *Menorah Journal* in 1915 and could not have read Durkheim's work in English before he published his articles.[14] Furthermore, Franklin Giddings, his professor of sociology at Columbia, who was central in molding Kaplan's young mind, had no real theory of the origins of religion. I believe that Kaplan took what he learned from Giddings and applied it to religion, which, in turn, was confirmed by what he read in Durkheim.

Having said this, it is nonetheless instructive to explore Durkheim's thought because it illuminates underlying assumptions of Kaplan's method. We are in effect using Durkheim as a midrash on Kaplan.[15]

David Emile Durkheim was born in Lorraine, France, in 1858. His father was a rabbi, as was his grandfather and great-grandfather. He appeared destined to become a rabbi also, following family tradition, but gave up this course when he was young and eventually severed his ties with Judaism altogether. Instead, he went on to study at the university and became one of the founders of sociology.

Durkheim, in attempting to identify the essence of religion, was struck not so much by its supernatural character as by its obligatory and communal character. He noted that religions exerted enormous pressure on their members, which served to bind them to the common faith. In primitive societies, the shared assumptions of the group usually constituted a major portion of an individual's consciousness. Sociologists call this the collective mind. Durkheim believed that the sacred was a product of this collective mind, in contrast to the profane, which was a product of the individual's private concerns.[16]

Durkheim's notion of the collective mind would quickly become a cornerstone of Kaplan's thinking. Kaplan, like Carl Jung and other theologians, used the term synonymously with collective consciousness, both referring to the beliefs and values that the members of any group hold in common. The collective consciousness establishes the framework within which individuals make their choices. The collective consciousness has a force and power all its own. Kaplan maintained that this collective mind was as real as the individual mind: "Social science is gradually accustoming us to regard human society not merely as an aggregate of individuals but as a psychical entity, as a mind not less but more real than the mind of the individuals who constitute it."[17]

It is helpful to think of the collective mind as analogous to the individual mind. Although philosophers have debated the existence of other minds, in ordinary life we feel no reason to doubt this reality. We take for granted that the individual mind is real, even though we can only observe the functioning of that mind and never the mind itself. In the same way, the collective mind is not a metaphysical entity; it is created by the collective functioning of many individual minds and, like these, is real though unobservable. Kaplan believed that the individual mind had certain qualities that can also be ascribed to the collective mind. The collective mind, for example, has memory, as is illustrated in the case of the Jewish people. The collective mind may also be described as having imagination and problem-solving ability. Kaplan saw these abilities as exhibited by the Jewish collectivity throughout history.

Another way of understanding the collective mind is by comparing it to language. Our language reflects and constitutes the consciousness of the group to which we belong. It is the instrument through which we come to know our world, the glue that holds us together, but also the vehicle of our uniqueness. A particular view of the universe and human nature inheres in our language and gives rise to narratives that help us locate ourselves. We need a story to help make sense of our past and orient us toward the future, to give us hope and a sense of purpose. The scholar Edward Sapir emphasized the significance of language and its foundational aspect in the following terms: "The real world is to a large extent unconsciously built upon the language habits of the group. The worlds in which different societies live are distinct worlds, not merely the same world with different labels attached. We see and hear and otherwise experience very largely as we do because the language habits of our community predispose certain choices of interpretation."[18]

To complete the metaphor, American Jews can speak two languages, the language of American civilization and the language of Jewish civilization. Language as used here does not simply mean vocabulary. It means that, through the study of literature and history, it is possible to understand the spirit and the values of the community and the way in which the community perceives itself. Each language, each culture, carries with it a particular worldview. Jews on the margins—in the 1920s, as in our own day—often ask, "Why be Jewish?" The answer is that speaking two languages is immeasurably richer than speaking one. This understanding is reflected in the fact that our societal ideal has changed from the melting pot to the hyphenated American.

Religion is concerned with values, with morality, and with the perfection (that is, salvation) of the individual. Although William James and many others located the essence of religion within the mind of the individual, Kaplan believed that the community, through the functioning of the collective consciousness, inevitably exerts major influence in determining the nature of the individual's religious beliefs and habits: "Even where the experiences seem most personal and are entirely isolated from the environment, as is the case with visions, trances, and hallucinations, a closer examination will inevitably reveal the operation of social forces generated by the religious life of the group to which the highly sensitized individual belongs."[19]

Not all shared beliefs and values are of equal importance in the religious sphere. Religion reflects primarily the commitments of a spiritual and moral nature. Thus, Kaplan defined religion as that part of the collective consciousness that deals with fundamental and ultimate concerns about the nature of the human, his goals as an individual, and his obligations to his fellow humans: "Religion is the unity of aim which a social group develops whereby each individual in it shall attain the highest degree of perfection."[20] Kaplan emphasized that the perfection of the individual is the sole aim of religion. However, he believed just as adamantly that, since religion is always a group phenomenon, individuals are more likely to perfect themselves within a particular religious community.

People never live in isolation but always in groups, and religion is a way of strengthening and reinforcing the values that hold the group together. The primary Jewish values are, therefore, the expression of the collective consciousness of the Jewish people. In Kaplan's formulation, "The Jewish consciousness is the end whereas the beliefs and practices are the means. The former is life[;] the latter is truth. The immediate function of the beliefs and practices is to integrate the individual into the Jewish consciousness."[21]

To understand the success of a religion—the possibility for perfection in its members—Kaplan emphasized that we need to assess the distinction between the real religion of an individual and his or her professed religion. The distinction is an ancient one. The values that guide our decisions are our real values. We may pay lip service to our religious community's values of altruism, self-sacrifice, honesty, and spirituality; but, if the quest for money, power, status, or pleasure is actually guiding our decisions, then these values constitute our real religion. Religion assumes its highest form when the values of individual perfection become part of our real, as well as our professed, religion.

The converse is equally true: religion becomes ineffective when there is a gap between what is professed and what is real. Kaplan believed that an organized religion confronts a crisis when the religion no longer reflects the collective consciousness of the group, that is, when the real religion of the group is out of line with the professed religion. Another similar crisis occurs when the group ceases to function as a group, and, thus, the collective consciousness is weakened. The fate of any religion is tied inextricably to the quality of life of its members: do a religion's values enhance, sustain, and invigorate the daily lives of its members? Jewish survival depends on the answer to this question. If Judaism consists of an unchanging set of values, then it is extremely vulnerable because these values and ideas may easily be found elsewhere. As Kaplan put it, "If monotheism is the truth, and it is the truth, it is not confined to Judaism. It is not our mission to teach monotheism to the world."[22]

The tormenting question is that, if all truths change, what is our anchor? What is the essence of Judaism? Kaplan addressed the matter rather early on: "We must behold Judaism not in any one doctrine or sum of doctrines but in the innermost life force which has vitalized the Jewish people and has made it the most self-conscious group of any upon the face of the earth."[23] The life force is its own justification, and the values it expresses will be judged to the degree that they contribute to the enhancement of the lives of Jews as individuals and as a group.

The key to Jewish survival, then, becomes the preservation and enhancement of group life and the nurturing of the life force of the Jewish people. There are many ways in which this life force can be nurtured— through synagogue life, through culture and the arts, or through support of the Zionist movement. All efforts to enhance this life force are valuable and contribute to making one a good Jew. Although Kaplan was a synagogue Jew, he was equally devoted to pluralism. Departing fundamentally from the Conservative movement, Kaplan did not see the essence of being Jewish in *halakhah*. Naturally, he hoped that all Jews would recognize the value of observance, but he respected the devotion of nonsynagogue Jews to Jewish causes. The secular Jew fully devoted to Israel was making a valuable contribution to Judaism's collective consciousness, he believed, and might eventually be won over to a more complete Jewish life.

Kaplan has been frequently and strongly criticized for focusing on the communal aspect of religion and neglecting the spiritual side, for equating religion merely with the social life of the group. Kaplan refuted this criticism, insisting that he did not reduce religion to group life but instead that his critics tended to reduce communal life to religion. Religion is important, spirituality is important, but Kaplan was adamant that religion comes only as a consequence of community:

> To expect worship to constitute the principle motive of social togetherness in the same way as professional or business interests, golf or gambling, is to put a strain upon average human nature. To make religion in its commonly accepted sense, the aim of social cooperation is like organizing eating clubs for the purposes of having their members say Grace together. The one unmistakable principle which emerges from the scientific study of religious phenomena is that in order to have religion in common, people must have other interests in common besides religion.[24]

Community precedes religion, or, as the slogan of the Reconstructionist movement says, "belonging is more important than believing." During his tenure at the Ninety-Second Street YMHA, where Kaplan conducted services between 1913 and 1916, some of the members approached him about forming a congregation. In his 1915 Rosh Hashannah sermon to the group, he proclaimed his convictions with clarity and force:

> I have learned from experience that it would be futile to expect you to organize along congregational lines, and to make worship the main purpose of your association. You are not ready for that as yet. You have to know each other better; and it is the problem of how you are to know one another better that you ought first to undertake to meet. You ought to constitute yourselves a neighborhood association, with the only aim of broadening your lives through mutual acquaintances. You ought to take your pleasures together.[25]

Religion comes as a result of group life but does not create it. This emphasis on the primacy of group life is pure Durkheim, so one might say that, even though Kaplan did not derive his foundational principles from Durkheim, he always thought "Durkheimian."

In the years after completing his Master's degree, as Kaplan searched for the right institution to devote himself to, he became painfully aware of the gap between his thinking and much of the New York Jewish community. He was obsessed with the survival of the Jewish people and the notion of the collective consciousness; yet where would he possibly find the appropriate institution for the strengthening of that consciousness? Both the Ninety-Second Street "Y" and Young Israel, two institutions that Kaplan was actively involved in, had severe limitations. The "Y," where Kaplan was employed for nearly three years, had services on a regular basis and also employed a rabbi, but was not a synagogue. Young Israel, an organization that was what we would now call modern Orthodox, in which Kaplan was involved and which he helped create, lacked the recreational facilities of the "Y."[26] Some other kind of institutional setting was needed, one that would be more able to meet the complex religious needs of modern life and to fulfill Kaplan's ideas about community. That institutional setting was to be the Jewish Center.[27]

The Jewish Center, still located on New York's Upper West Side, developed out of a familiar and mundane set of issues. In the years before World War I, there were few synagogues on the West Side. The newly wealthy clothing manufacturers who lived on the West Side yearned for a synagogue that would equal the very impressive Kehilath Jeshurun, just across Central Park on East Eighty-Fifth Street. They turned to Kaplan, already known because of his position at the Jewish Theological Seminary, his services as the rabbi of the "Y,"[28] and his articles in the *Menorah Journal*. Furthermore, he spoke English without an accent and was college educated, two criteria important to the adamantly modern Jewish community of the West Side.

In the spring of 1915, a group of these West Side Jews offered Kaplan a tantalizing possibility. They wanted to build a "fashionable" synagogue for the West Side and turned to Kaplan for help. He wanted an institution that would embody both a synagogue and the social life of a community center. The marriage between Kaplan and the center's founders was providential. The concept of the synagogue center is the logical conclusion of Kaplan's understanding of the relationship between religion and community. As we have seen, Kaplan believed that religions historically grew or declined depending on the vitality of their group life. Although the spiritual search of the individual constitutes the core of the quest for meaning, unless the individual finds himself in some living group, his spiritual creativity will wither and die. There is no way in which religious life can be detached from group life. Even the solitary monk who is living out the ideals of his tradition does so in a community.

It is not surprising, then, that Kaplan was troubled by the "thinness" of contemporary religious life. Traditionally, Jewish life had been bound up with the life of the community as a whole. Since the emancipation,[29] for many Jews religious life had become peripheral or, as Emerson would say, *spectral*. Kaplan was convinced that the survival of Judaism depended on Jews living a life beyond merely praying together. Community precedes religion and gives rise to it. A thriving community will inevitably crave religious expression, he believed, to give form and context to its joys and its pains.

Kaplan had been contemplating the notion of Judaism as a civilization for a while, and it seemed that now everything was falling into place. He was part of the planning of the new institution from the very beginning. The *balabatim*—movers and shakers—of the Upper West Side had searched for a spiritual leader but were unsatisfied with the rabbinical candidates; they prevailed upon Kaplan to accept the post, even though most of them were Orthodox and he was not. Kaplan did not want to be the rabbi due to his heavy work schedule and family obligations but reluctantly accepted the position. The opportunity to test his ideas about revitalizing the group life of Jews, of making a significant contribution toward strengthening the collective consciousness, was just too great to pass up.

Kaplan believed that, just as the institution of the synagogue helped rescue the Jews after the destruction of the Temple in Jerusalem, so the synagogue center would help rescue them now. By embracing all facets of an individual's life, such a center would revitalize Jewish life: "The Jewish Center, in insisting that Judaism must be lived as a civilization, will endeavor to have us work, play, love, and worship as Jews." Kaplan's congregants, for example, would be encouraged to bring their Judaism into the workplace. Rather than voicing pious platitudes about economic justice, the congregants would, it was hoped, engage in ethical living. Kaplan wanted to emphasize "the need for Jews who exercise power in the dominion of industry and traffic to come together in the name of their faith . . . to see what they can do to ameliorate the evils and to improve the relations between employer and employee."[30] Some compromises, however, were necessary; Kaplan agreed to a modified form of separate seating for men and women and to a traditional liturgy, while the synagogue stalwarts—fully aware of Kaplan's growing radicalism—agreed to accept him as rabbi. Kaplan, for his part, promised to be "tactful and circumspect" about his religious views.

At the groundbreaking, which took place in 1917, Kaplan told the crowd that this was not merely a foundation that was being dug, but a "well" that would become "a fountain of new and inexhaustible energy for living the Jewish life." He lifted the very earthly event to a higher plane. Those building the center, he said, were "the tools of a will not their own and higher than their own to perpetuate the life of the Jewish people."[31]

Students of Kaplan may want to speculate about whose will Kaplan was speaking of here. Although he leaned toward a naturalistic theology even during this early period, Kaplan continued to use such expressions as *God's will*. Whether he had in mind God or the Jewish people, we see here a sense of the magnitude of the occasion. We also see a case of Kaplan's inflated rhetoric. He viewed this situation *sub specie aeternitatis*[32] rather than as just another synagogue in New York City. Kaplan's tendency toward hyperbole was both a strength and a weakness.

The "shul with a pool and a school" opened in March 1918. It was a very American institution. With its impressive ten-storey building on West Eighty-Sixth Street, its gymnasium facilities, its pool, and its "cathedral synagogue," there was no place like it anywhere. It attracted visitors from all over the country; even more importantly, synagogue centers began cropping up in other parts of the city.[33] It was the perfect embodiment of Judaism as a civilization: a 24/7 synagogue that catered to the whole range of human needs: intellectual, social, and physical. In addition, it would be a place where young people could socialize and find marriage partners. Kaplan considered the center an experiment in social engineering that would play an essential role in revitalizing the Jewish community.

While the reality of life at the center fell far short of Kaplan's vision, nonetheless, Kaplan did institute an innovative educational program and a meaningful service in the synagogue, although it was not experimental in character. There was a wide range of social and community-oriented activities not usually found in Orthodox synagogues of the time, but the community never achieved the cohesiveness of which he had dreamed. The most accurate description of life at the center is modern Orthodox. In comparison with what had existed in traditional synagogues before this period, the center marked a very significant step toward a bold and innovative American institution.

* * *

With the Jewish Center, Kaplan helped create a means to revitalize the Jewish community on a very local level. But just as the individual was inextricably linked to the social, so too was each local Jewish community linked to the collective consciousness of Judaism. Only working with one or the other was never enough for Kaplan's imagination; so, in the midst of his endless daily commitments to the Jews of New York, there was always looming the emotional tug of Kaplan's much larger commitment: Zionism and the Jewish people. Applying the ideals of Jewish civilization to the Jewish people as a whole was Kaplan's unique way of defining and analyzing Zionism.

Kaplan's devotion to Zionism was profound; we mentioned above that, as a young man, he thought of calling his system "Zionist Judaism." Kaplan, however, was a follower of Ahad Ha-Am and believed that Jewish life in the diaspora would continue as it was but vitalized by a Jewish center in Israel. In the diaspora, the devoted Jew inevitably lived in two civilizations: that of his host country and that of the Jewish people. Such a dual existence, Kaplan believed, could be creative and productive. Kaplan's Zionism was a "soft" Zionism, evidenced by the fact that he lived out his life not in Eretz Yisrael (The Land of Israel) but in New York City.

Why did Kaplan not make *aliyah* and emigrate to Israel as a young man? The answer is a complicated one. He did move to Israel in 1975, when he was ninety-four years old. However, after a few years, his frail health necessitated that he be brought back to the United States where his family could care for him. In the 1920s, many of his friends and colleagues, including Judah Magnes and Henrietta Szold, were already in Jerusalem, as well as some of his students like Alexander Dushkin. Chaim Weizmann, an admirer of Kaplan who visited him every time he was in the United States, wanted Kaplan to direct Jewish education in the *yishuv*, but Kaplan refused. During the 1930s, he spent two years (1937–39) in Jerusalem teaching at the Hebrew University; many wanted him to stay, but again he refused and returned to America. The impending hostilities in Europe were certainly a factor in his decision to return home. Nonetheless, he proposed that he return to Jerusalem every other summer to teach at the Hebrew University. Cyrus Adler, then president of the Jewish Theological Seminary, rejected Kaplan's plan. Kaplan exclaimed that "Adler froze to the occasion."[34]

The choice to remain in America indicates the essential ambivalence of his Zionist vision. While a devoted Zionist, Kaplan was also American to the core. Kaplan said to me once that he loved the climate in Jerusalem but not the climate of opinion. In New York, he hated the weather but loved the climate of freedom and openness; he loved being in the midst of the maelstrom of ideas. Kaplan always found reasons not to make *aliyah,* but the ultimate explanation is one that he never articulated in public. He really did live in two civilizations; as much as he cherished and believed in the idea of the Jewish homeland, he could not live solely in that single civilization. He was fully Jewish and fully American. At the same time, he came to see life in the *yishuv* as a great "religious experiment" and saw its religious potential to be parallel to that of the community in America.[35]

Not surprisingly, Kaplan's vision of Zionism was as distinctive, and complex, as he was. His Zionism was never the Zionism of Herzl. From his years as a young rabbi, Kaplan attempted to distance himself from the European Zionism whose primary emphasis was on gathering all the Jews into the refuge of a Jewish state. He also dismissed the philanthropic Zionism of American Jews, which concentrated on aiding persecuted Jews who settled in the Land of Israel but refused to consider Zion the center of their religious concerns.[36]

Kaplan also rejected the fundamental assumption of classical Zionism, championed by Theodore Herzl and elaborated from the beginning of the Zionist movement until the founding of the State of Israel in 1948. Its central claim—that only a total exodus from the diaspora would ensure Jewish survival—was, for Kaplan, totally unrealistic. Classical Zionism was committed to the notion that Jewish life could be lived to the full only by emigrating to Israel.[37] Ben-Gurion, for example, would deny a Jew the right to call himself a Zionist unless he migrated to Israel.[38] It was obvious to Kaplan and many others that American Jews would never emigrate to Israel en masse. Kaplan viewed the diaspora not only as continuing, but as a permanent feature of Jewish life. He believed that "Zionism has to be redefined so as to assure a permanent place for diaspora Judaism."[39]

In Kaplan's thinking, the regeneration of the Jewish people, not Jewish statehood, is at the heart of Zionism. In his words, "Without a Jewish people regenerated in spirit, no matter how successful the state that it would establish, and how large that population could muster, Zion will continue to be unredeemed." *Regeneration* here is another word for *salvation*. For Kaplan, *salvation* meant to govern one's life according to the prophetic values of justice through laws, and to strive for moral perfection.[40] Kaplan here creates an interesting sense of obligation and reciprocity. While the Jewish state would doubtless be the main embodiment of Jewish civilization, that Jewish state must be governed by the primary values of all the Jewish people. Jewish unity is a prerequisite for redemption. The Jewish state must not only be concerned about itself but about the unity and the welfare of Jewish communities the world over.

Kaplan called his approach "a Greater Zionism" because it moves beyond the ideal of a Jewish state as the sum total of the Zionist vision.[41] It should be noted that Kaplan's concepts of Zionism and of Jewish civilization here goes beyond those of Ahad Ha-Am; he emphasizes not only the culture of the Jewish people but also the organic unity of the cultural, spiritual, economic, and political aspects of Jewish life and the connection of all these to the Land of Israel.[42]

For any Zionist, no matter one's particular commitment, the security of Israel and the vital interests of its people must be at the center of his or her concerns. Nevertheless, for Kaplan, the feasibility of the state is only one element in the total regeneration of the Jewish people. In addition to safety and security, Zionism must be concerned with the unity and health of world Jewry.[43]

Kaplan's "Greater Zionism," therefore, moves beyond the standard Zionist mandate; like so much of his thinking, the focus returns to Jewish peoplehood. Throughout, we have seen the centrality of peoplehood to Kaplan, the notion that the essence of Judaism was devotion to the survival and enhancement of the Jewish people.[44]

Kaplan's attachment to the Jewish people at times assumes an almost mystical form. He is ever the pragmatic rationalist, but when he begins to think about mysticism, his attention moves immediately to the Jewish people. Kaplan, like his mentor William James, studies mysticism from the outside. In attempting to come up with a definition, Kaplan states that the mystical is that "which gives direct personal contact or rapport with what we consider to be ultimate reality."[45] Strange as it sounds, it would seem that, for Kaplan, the Jewish people are an "ultimate reality."

He notes that ordinarily the mystical is associated with nature or with music. But, for him, the Jewish person carries the mystery. In his work *The New Zionism*, he points to the mystical character of the "Mother Church" in Christianity and to the "Community of Believers" in Islam as parallels to the mystical reality of the Jewish people.

It is not only history and experiences of the Jewish people that contain the element of divinity but the ritual system as well. In other words, *mizvot* and prayer for Kaplan always contain a strong identification with the Jewish people, and this identification has a mystical sense about it. Speaking of religious practice and ritual, he writes that "the individual Jew never takes part in them without associating himself with the whole house of Israel . . . [and] this association with the Jewish people is not merely a socio-psychological [phenomenon] but definitely [a] mystical experience."[46]

Kaplan's very emotional attachment to the Jewish people, their land, and their history is illustrated by a diary entry from the early 1930s in which he recalled a visit to Palestine a few years before. "No amount of gazing at the Empire State Building will thrill me," he wrote, "as did the momentary glimpse of the little village of Anatot[47] from the tower in the government building in Jerusalem. Ex-Governor [Al] Smith may be an excellent man but when it comes to eliciting loyalty I much prefer Jeremiah."[48]

A people, any people, requires a homeland, but for Kaplan the nationalism of the Jewish people was not just a matter of having a home and greater security but of helping Jews to lift themselves individually and collectively to a higher moral level. Franz Rosenzweig, for example, believed in landlessness as a spiritual blessing, whereas Kaplan viewed life on the land as a natural basis for its civilization. Yet Kaplan believed that nationalism should be a force for greater humanization among the Jews. He abhorred the narrow self-interest that ordinarily characterizes the actions of the nationalist movements and nation-states.[49] The right to survive, though of course legitimate, must not be construed as an end in itself. One of Kaplan's most outstanding disciples, Rabbi Jack Cohen, z"l, who made *aliyah* in the early 1960s, put it this way: "Kaplan maintained that, without religion, Zionism would produce only another power-ridden society. Without the check upon moral and spiritual arrogance that only an intellectually honest theology calls forth, the Jewish religion would also give rise to a coercive and chauvinistic state." Once again, we see religion as an anchor for a people, which allows individuals to strive toward redemption; without that anchor, many will no doubt still strive but will be distracted by life's base temptation for excessive power.[50]

For Kaplan, one can only have a humane society in a democracy. The basic principles of democratic culture, when applied to Israel internally, imply that that the culture must be free from what Kaplan calls "creedal and clerical authoritarianism."[51] The laws and institutions must be embodiments of justice and confer equality to all citizens. Jewish civilization, whether in a Jewish state or in the diaspora, means the surrender of one's self-interest to the principle of justice through law. Kaplan was fully aware of the inequities in the State of Israel, and abhorred the discrimination against religious and ethnic minorities. The power of the traditionally Orthodox in Israel's internal affairs even in Kaplan's time was all too familiar. Kaplan, a good American, was a believer in the separation of church and state. He was adamant that the Orthodox have the same freedoms as any other group, but they must not dominate or set the agendas, both personal and legal, for other groups. He believed that Conservative and Reform Jews, along with their rabbis and leaders, have the right to function in Israel on an equal basis with the Orthodox.[52] Kaplan never spelled out fully how such separation would work in the Jewish homeland, but, for our purposes, it is only necessary to emphasize his deep commitment to this principle.

Kaplan was ever mindful of the rights of all minorities, both Jewish and non-Jewish, within the State of Israel. His pluralistic commitments and his concern for democracy led him in the 1930s to support the idea of a binational state where Jews and Arabs would have equal rights. This idea was spearheaded, starting in the 1920s, by Martin Buber and a number of other intellectuals.[53] During a visit to Palestine in August 1937, Kaplan noted, "If I had any influence, I would recommend the Jews propose to the Arabs that they participate equally in the government and that the population of the Jews be permanently adjusted to the number of Arabs in the country."[54] It should be noted that Kaplan, like so many others, revised his stand on the question of balanced populations as the situation with Nazi Germany increased the need for a refuge.

Kaplan's commitment to justice through law led him to take rather radical positions on the issue of international law and Israel's obligations in the international arena. For example, Kaplan advocated that the concept of law be applied more rigorously on the international level. He stated explicitly his belief in the ideal of limiting national sovereignty.

Such a limitation would at least mean the strengthening of the United Nations and the International Court at The Hague. It would also mean a serious attempt at disarmament. Here again, religion is synonymous with ethical action: "religion should involve the whole of mankind in the creation of a world society in which all conflicts be resolved not by violence but by negotiation and law." Such thinking sounds unrealistic and sadly utopian to us now, but there is still the argument, made by some well-known legal scholars, that disarmament would actually strengthen international institutions.[55]

Not only in the field of international relations did Kaplan believe that there were special obligations of a Jewish state, but also vis-à-vis world Jewry. Rabbi Jack Cohen, in his analysis of Kaplan's Zionism, has emphasized the very significant implications of Kaplan's affirmation of a permanent diaspora and of Jewish unity: Jews are citizens both in a Jewish state and in their home countries all over the world. In other words, the Jews are a transterritorial people with a center in the Land of Israel. Leaders in Israel must accept the permanence of Jewish life in the diaspora and encourage its creativity. Heretofore, they have only given lip service to their responsibility for Jewish life around the world. Zionists must think not only about the way in which diaspora Jews can help Israel but also about the ways Jews everywhere can live a more creative Jewish life.

For Kaplan's Zionism, the primacy of the Jewish state and the fostering of its interests is not enough. The equally important task must be to strengthen the unity of Jewry around the world and to make the ideal of "righteousness into law" a primary force in the actions of Jews everywhere. Kaplan believed that Jewish unity must assume a concrete form. He called this idea the reconstitution of world Jewry. He became entranced with the notion of the reconstitution of the Jewish people through a Jewish parliament (*kehillah*), and it may be that the early New York Kehillah experiment percolated in his mind over the years as a worthwhile goal in later life. In his last work, *The Religion of Ethical Nationhood*, Kaplan describes how this reconstitution would take shape. "The Zionist movement," he writes,

> should provide for the establishment of three democratically elected and constituted bodies—legislative, judicial and executive—to administer the affairs

of the Jewish people as a whole and of each organic Jewish community outside of Israel. . . . The establishment of a Jewish world parliament would create an authority to speak to and for the entire Jewish people and to maintain a high ethical standard in all human relations and activities.[56]

The Kehillah failed partially due to the complications of Judah Magnes's pacifism during World War I. Though the Kehillah accomplished much in its short life, there were many who never gave it credence. Kaplan, however, seemed entranced with the notion of a Jewish parliament, and it may be that the Kehillah experiment continued to percolate in his mind as a worthwhile goal later in life.

Kaplan's Zionism was, to say the least, outside the usual parameters of the Zionist movement. In his classic work *The New Zionism,* he sums his ideas up in the following terms:

[A]s Zionists, we have to reconstitute our peoplehood, reclaim our ancient homeland and revitalize our Jewish way of life. Each of these three objectives should be pursued with the end in view, both in Israel and in the diaspora, of developing such interpersonal and intergroup relations as are likely to help us become more fully human. That is to be our religion and our mission.[57]

Though Kaplan's greater Zionism seems idealistic, and often impossible, it is nonetheless, then as now, a powerful force in orienting our vision.

*　*　*

Kaplan believed that the Jews were among the first to make a religion of their peoplehood. But he strongly differentiated between the religion of ancient Israel and collective egotism. Loyalty to the Jewish people ideally means accepting the collective ideals of justice and mercy, law and order, and a responsibility to humankind. Loyalty in and of itself can be an admirable quality, but Kaplan knew that, in the case of a collectivity, it is often just another way of talking about self-interest. He believed that Judaism, however, offered a perfect means to overcome the egotism of the self. Judaism projects onto God the ideals of the collective mind; these ideals are then manifested in daily conduct, appearing in Jewish tradition in the form of *mitzvot.* As Kaplan puts it, "The people of Israel, however, did not merely deify their patriotism but subordinated it to a divinity of cosmic proportions. They thereby subordinated it to principles which are coextensive with the cosmos—the principle of law, order and from the standpoint of human functioning, also responsibility to or for mankind."[58]

Yet we naturally wonder how the community relates to the needs and hopes of the individual. Kaplan believed that the community could aid the individual in the search for transcendence, in getting out of the "tiny tub of ourselves," as Philip Roth put it. The community, by making demands, fosters maturity. We internalize the community's standards, which increases our self-control and helps restrain us from our more destructive urges. We need the community, Kaplan tells us, and cannot survive without it, but the community demands a price for all that it gives us. It demands that we live according to its rules. The relationship to the community may be a blood kinship, a political kinship, or, as the Jews also believe, an ethical kinship.

We are never fully human, Kaplan maintains, unless there is a sharing of interests between the self and the other—the community represents that interest. As a result, the community has great value in developing our character. The ideal is for each of us to have loyalties, not only to our family and our immediate community but also to the nation and indeed to all humankind: "Such is the mutuality of human life that none can be saved until all are saved. We are all our brothers' keepers. . . . The categorical imperative of the moral life is: So love your neighbors that you help them to realize their highest potentialities."[59]

In other words, the collective consciousness is not only transcendent and helps us become our best possible selves, but, for Kaplan, it is no less than the *shekhina* herself. Considered by kabbalists to be one of the ten manifestations of the divine presence, translated as the "divine spirit," the *shekhina* is explicitly identified by Kaplan with the collective consciousness. In a 1975 essay, he writes,

> [I]nsofar as the collective mind is shared by every individual member of an organic group as limited as family or, as large as nation, it is identified as a God of salvation, with salvation being the fulfillment of all those needs without which one cannot be fully human. Our God of Israel, the *shekhina,* is none other than the collective consciousness of the Jewish people.[60]

Thus, we have seen that Kaplan's concept of Judaism as a civilization applies equally to the individual, the community, and the people as a whole. Central to his notion of Jewish civilization are the ideals of justice, equality, and the sacredness of the individual. Being a member of the Jewish people means being committed to these ideals. The collective mind of the Jewish people in ancient times first expressed the notion that the Jewish religion was a devotion to these ideals that were personified as the "the will of God." "Justice, Justice shalt ye pursue" we read in scripture. This is a command to the individual and to the people as a whole.

While Kaplan was at times ambivalent about classical Zionism, he was at all times fully devoted to the ethical ideals that he believed were incumbent upon every Jew in every place—and that includes the State of Israel. It was in these ethical ideals, the sum and substance of Jewish peoplehood, that Jewish unity lay and on which Jewish survival depended.

SIX

KAPLAN AND HIS GOD: AN
AMBIVALENT RELATIONSHIP

According to Maimonides, "it is not correct to say that God is living, or that God knows or wills. The truth is that God is life, God is knowledge, and God is will." From the standpoint of knowledge, God is at the same time the known and the process of knowing. Theologically or philosophically speaking, there is little, if any, difference between Maimonides' conception of God and the conception of God that makes for man's salvation.

—*Mordecai Kaplan, "Soterics"*

Some say that Mordecai Kaplan had no theology, while others say that he did not believe in God. Both are mistaken. Kaplan was a courageous man, and if he considered himself an atheist, he would have said so. He was a passionate believer, a naturalist to be sure, but a believer nonetheless. It is quite clear that he would never agree to the derogatory slur that "there is no God and Kaplan is his prophet"; yet, in a certain paradoxical sense, this statement is true.

Though Kaplan dismissed supernaturalism early in life, he was God-obsessed. He thought about God all the time. Nonetheless, he rejected a providential God who concerns Himself with human beings, who directs history, and who lays down laws for us to follow. In a 1905 journal entry, Kaplan rhapsodizes on the infinite, even while emphatically rejecting a "super self" as part of the great beyond: "There is a kind of mysticism which is essential to thought and without which thought is both barren and heartless," Kaplan tells us, "it is of the very essence of literature to embody this sense of the infinite, this longing for the eternal universal beyond. To call this *beyond* a person [however] is meaningless, as [Matthew] Arnold has so well proved."[1]

The rejection of God as a "super self" or a supreme being is consistent throughout Kaplan's writings. In *Questions Jews Ask,* a half century later, Kaplan put it this way: "When, for example, we are told that God is living, we should not take that to mean that God is a being who possesses the attributes of life, which He shares with other living beings, but that He is life itself. God and life are one and the same."[2] If God is not a person, a self, or a mind, then God has no will, can give no laws, and cannot communicate with people in any significant sense. Kaplan does sometimes speak of knowing God, but it is only in a highly metaphorical sense. The problems this image creates for traditional Judaism are numerous.

If God is not a self and has no will, then how can we speak of God as directing history? Yet the first commandment asserts such direction as a truth: "I the Lord am your God who brought you out of the land of Egypt . . . you shall have no other gods beside Me." God's action, the salvation of his people from bondage, is a central tenet of Israelite monotheism. Primary loyalty is due to Him. Even Kaplan noted this when he asserted that the *Shemah* (Deuteronomy 6:4) is not a statement announcing that God is one but rather an oath that we owe allegiance to Him alone.[3]

Some considered Kaplan's beliefs a species of atheism. Rabbi Bernard Drachman, Kaplan's former teacher from his Jewish Theological Seminary days, writing in 1921, put it this way:

> The utterances of Kaplan . . . on some of the fundamental doctrines of religion and his proposals for the Reconstruction of Judaism . . . have come as a great shock to all Jews who believe in the traditional faith of Israel and desire its perpetuation. . . . True Jews, that is to say, believers in a Supreme Being and a genuine Divine Law interpreted by authoritative tradition, cannot look upon such theories and proposals otherwise than with feelings of horror.[4]

Kaplan, however, was utterly emphatic in his rejection of atheism. In an early journal entry that discussed the theological issue of immanence and transcendence, Kaplan makes his position clear and goes so far as to identify belief in immanence with atheism: "The moment God is merely identified with the world and conceived as being immanent but not transcendent, His divinity is denied and He is dissolved into the world. This is the atheism and pantheism which religion so vigorously contends against."[5]

Still, I wonder about a situation where a belief in a Supreme Being is required for membership in an organization. Some time ago, there was an article in the paper about a young man who was denied admission to the Eagle Scouts because he said he did not believe in a Supreme Being. When I read the story, I thought of Kaplan and decided that, were he in this situation, his admission to the scouts would depend on the interviewer's phrasing of the question. If the interviewer asked him about a Supreme Being, Kaplan would have certainly answered in the negative; but, if the person asked merely about belief in God, the situation might have been much more complicated. Kaplan would certainly have given a "yes but . . ." type of answer.

Kaplan, in the candor of his journal, tells us many times about his rejection of the traditional, providential God. "I am not troubled in the least by the fact that God is not an identifiable being," he writes in the journal in 1931, "for that matter neither is my Ego an identifiable being. Nor am I troubled by the fact that God is not perfect. He would have to be static to be perfect. Nothing dynamic can be perfect since to be dynamic implies to be in the state of becoming. But how shall I relate all these ideas to the problem of Jewish religion?"[6]

Colleagues and students who misunderstand Kaplan's theology often call him a humanist. The ordinary use of the term *humanism* means that religion is restricted completely to the human realm. In this sense, Kaplan was definitely not a humanist. Because peoplehood was so central to his concept of religion and because he seemed to equate God with the ideals of the group, many think that he completely dismissed the transcendent and the nonhuman realm. Nothing could be further from the truth.

It might be helpful to distinguish between secular humanism and religious humanism. Secular humanism would see no use or function for religion in furthering the humanist agenda. Religious humanism would see a reconstruction of religion in humanistic terms to be completely compatible with humanistic values. We might describe Kaplan as believing in religion with a decidedly humanistic emphasis, but he was nonetheless a theist.

Kaplan's early dismissals of secular humanism are clear and strong. In January 1934, he gave a talk at the Society for the Advancement of

Judaism entitled "Why Humanism Is Not Enough."[7] A year later, he dealt with the same subject at the seminary. In his class were rabbinic students who thought that his theology obligated him to dismiss the word *God* altogether. They challenged him on the grounds that his use of the word *God* only reinforced the anthropomorphic concept that he rejected. Kaplan defended his usage in the following way:

> In answer to the argument that some of the most worthwhile people are alien-ated from Jewish life and ethical endeavor along Jewish lines because we insist upon using the name of God I replied, first, they are alienated because we do not engage frankly in the task of putting new content into the term God, and secondly it is not the use of the term God that repels them but rather the whole nexus of legends which most of our people insist upon teaching as factual and historical.
>
> In answer to the argument that it is impossible to retain our prayer book if we are to use the term God in the sense in which I suggested, I said that I hold no brief for the prayer book. Why not write new prayers in conformity with the modern conception of God? Why have a prayer book at all? Why not prayers which can be used at discretion and in accordance with actually felt needs?[8]

This journal entry gives us much insight into the theological context in which Kaplan was working. In today's world, few people would be alienated from Jewish life because of the centrality of the belief in God. Indeed, just the opposite may be the case. Many who have been alienated are returning to the synagogue, and God seems to have taken a new lease on life. Nor would they be bothered by Kaplan's radical position on the prayer book. He did not endorse a totally new prayer book. Nevertheless, this statement does reflect his impatience with the traditional liturgy and the fact that, in many ways, it did not work.[9]

In "Why Humanism Is Not Enough," later published in *The Recon-structionist,* Kaplan elaborates his ideas with even greater precision. He points to the various levels of theological understanding that pervaded the ancient and medieval worlds. Kaplan the sociologist helps us to re-member that the conception we have of God changes with the cultural level we have attained: "Thus God may now be understood [not as le-gitimating royal rule] but as the power that endorses what we believe ought to be and that guarantees that it will be."[10] Our faith in God stems from assumptions that underlie our ideals, Kaplan tells us. If we are truly committed to our ideals, then we believe that the world is so conditioned as to make the realization of those ideals possible. Faith in the realization of our ideals is spelled out by Kaplan in the following terms: "Such faith stems from that aspect of the mind which finds expression in the enthusiasm for living, in the passion to surmount limitations, a passion which is uniquely human. Those who possess this enthusiasm, and consequently strive for a better world, are believers in God."[11] Kaplan himself was obviously such a believer and thought that most others shared this conviction, whether they consciously considered themselves believers or atheists.

Religious humanism was quite popular during the 1930s. In 1933, a group of prominent leaders and thinkers, including John Dewey, issued the "Humanist Manifesto," which became the charter of the American Humanist Association.[12] The manifesto seems to echo Kaplan's theology. There were, however, a few key points he would have rejected. He would have agreed with the discarding of supernaturalism but might take issue with the statement that "modern science makes unacceptable any . . . cosmic guarantees of human values." He would also reject the following: "We are convinced that the time has passed for theism, deism, modernism, and the several varieties of 'new thought.'" But considering Kaplan's critical stance toward humanism at this point, it is surprising how much of the manifesto is in harmony with his basic assumptions.[13]

The issue of humanism was still on Kaplan's mind in the 1950s when a biography of Judah Magnes appeared.[14] Kaplan believed that Magnes was a man of "gigantic moral and spiritual stature" and thought Norman Bentwich's biography would rightly place Magnes in the pantheon of Israel's great leaders. However, Bentwich's classification of Kaplan as a humanist, alongside his teacher Felix Adler, caused Kaplan to explode in anger: portraying him as a humanist[15] "evidences a complete ignorance on Bentwich's part of everything I have written. He probably never even heard of my *Meaning of God in Modern Jewish Religion*.[16] What Kaplan was alluding to here is chapter 7 of that work, titled "God as Felt Presence." This chapter is among the most theistic of Kaplan's writings.

Toward the end of his life, Kaplan began to rethink the concept of humanism and eventually became quite comfortable with it. He came to believe that he could work his idea of God into a humanist framework. While there is significant development in Kaplan's use of the concept of humanism, at the same time a common thread runs through all his statements. His theology was never restricted completely to the human realm.

Eventually, Kaplan did use the term *humanism,* but in a reconstructed manner. In his last major work, *The Religion of Ethical Nationhood,* published in 1970 when Kaplan was eighty-nine, he was proud to describe himself as a religious humanist. At the beginning of the book, he explained his use of the term *humanism* to characterize his philosophy:

> When Jewish history and religion are transposed into the key of [religious] humanism, God is conceived as the functioning in nature of the eternally creative process, which by bringing order out of chaos and good out of evil, actuates man to self-fulfillment. Ancient Israel . . . was admonished to follow "God's way of justice and law" (Gen. 18:19). Modern Israel . . . should likewise exemplify ethical nationhood. For all Jews—whether citizens of Israel or of other democratic nations—the Torah should provide inspiration and guidance in consonance with "God's way of justice through law."[17]

Thus, if we understand that there is a humanism that might incorporate a naturalist conception of God, we may rightly call Kaplan a religious humanist.

* * *

Underlying Kaplan's dismissal of supernaturalism was a certain discomfort in the matter of myth, magic, and miracles, which are so often associated with the supernatural. In 1966, he stated the following general principle: "Thus religious humanism, properly understood, does not negate religion as such. It negates only the mythological and metaphysical types of religion."[18]

For the young Kaplan, supernaturalism meant primarily miracle and magic. He never abandoned his dislike of everything magical (or "theurgic," to use his word), though he rightly understood it as part of the human quest for potency. Magic meant for Kaplan any word or action that would bring about the desired effect through the use of supernatural powers. Miracle, of course, refers to events that could not be explained by ordinary or empirical means.

Words were particularly important in the realm of magic. For the traditional or primitive mind, Kaplan believed, "words were . . . not merely symbols that enabled the mind to think, remember and imagine, but actual realities, or forces, that could put other realities or forces into motion."[19]

Magic and miracle insinuate themselves into religion at many points. In terms of biblical religion, one has only to remember Moses before Pharaoh and his many miraculous feats. Or one could point to the unexplainable "power" of the Ark of the Covenant in Israelite history. For Kaplan, magic was equally present in the many rites and rituals of biblical religion: "If [rites and rituals] are supposed to influence directly any supernatural being to extend help, or to withhold from doing harm, they are theurgic."[20] The whole notion of reward and punishment as put forth in the Bible is, in the larger sense, magical for Kaplan. According to the traditional way of thinking, it is assumed that doing the right thing will compel God to reward us. When pain or suffering befalls us, a traditionalist might say it was God's will rather than look to the immediate conditions causing the event. Kaplan hoped that a reconstructed Judaism would move away from the magical aspect of ethical behavior to a more rational view—which we will consider below.

Ours seems to be an age of magic, and I imagine Kaplan would have been uncomfortable with it. Were he alive today, the magic associated with contemporary popular culture in movies and books would have drawn his disdain. He often condemned the primitive belief in prayer as a magical maneuver for bringing about a specific result. He certainly would have agreed with Ralph Waldo Emerson's statement: "Prayer is the contemplation of the facts of life from the highest point of view. . . . prayer as a means to affect a private end is theft and meanness."[21]

We have mentioned that the biblical critic Arnold Ehrlich used to visit the Kaplan household during Kaplan's teenage years.[22] Ehrlich set forth his critical theories about the origins of the Bible and made it clear that magic and miracles made no sense to him. Kaplan used to carry these conversations to his fellow students at the Jewish Theological Seminary, initiating long and heated arguments over the Torah and its nature. The five books of Moses were not taught at the seminary while Kaplan was a rabbinical student, precisely because, at that time, a traditionalist seminary could not endorse contemporary Bible criticism. Kaplan was convinced that Solomon Schechter had instructed Professor Israel Friedlander, Schechter's newly hired Bible professor, not to teach

the Pentateuch because Friedlander had studied with German professors who taught the Bible from a critical perspective.[23]

Kaplan had little patience with the belief in miracles. Thirty years
ago, I experienced this impatience myself. When my son Joshua was
about ten, I took him to see Rabbi Kaplan. Joshua had asked me a very
good question about the plagues, and I wanted to show him off to the
great man. In good Reconstructionist fashion, I had explained that there
were no actual plagues or miracles, but rather they were imagined in
later retellings of the Exodus. "Well," my Joshua asked, "if there were no
plagues, why did Pharaoh let the children of Israel go?" I was stumped.
When I took my son to see Kaplan, I prodded Joshua to ask his question.
I was dumbfounded by Kaplan's answer: "What makes you think that
Moses asked Pharaoh to let the children of Israel go? It was a slave revolt.
They didn't ask permission; they just left." I couldn't hold myself back. I
was incredulous. "What about the confrontation between Pharaoh and
Moses and the plagues?" "Never happened," said Kaplan. "Besides, you
miss the point: the Exodus is not about the miracles and the plagues but
about liberation—about going from slavery to freedom."[24]

Traditional Jews have always accepted a literal belief in the plagues
and in miracles of the Bible. Kaplan maintained that the medieval doctrine of *creatio ex nihilo,* or creation from nothing, was put forward to
allow for the possibility of miracle. If God created all from nothing,
then He was in complete control and could do whatever He wanted. He
was not subject to any preexisting natural laws. Kaplan continued and
explained his own surprise: "While I realized in a general way that the
reason the Jewish philosophers take such pains to emphasize the doctrine of *creatio ex nihilo* is that only such a doctrine is compatible with
the possibility of miracles, the full force of their insistence upon that
doctrine did not strike me until recently."[25]

As a follower of Kaplan, I cannot take the literal existence of supernatural miracles seriously, yet I think that neither Kaplan nor the rest of
us would want to dismiss the belief in miracles of a natural sort. Kaplan
was always aware of the miracles of everyday life. On the occasion of the
birth of his grandchildren, for example, we see his excitement and his
sense of the miraculous. In the following passage from his journal, we
also experience his spiritual side:

Tuesday, December 3, 1935
This morning at 10:38 Hadassah[26] gave birth to a son weighing 7 lbs 14 oz. Mother and child are doing wonderfully. The parturition was perfect. Brother Isador, G. bless him, is the attending physician. May God grant Judith as easy a parturition. He expects her baby sometime in April. God (the sum of those forces that render life worthwhile and significant) has been, to use the conventional parlance, mighty good to me and my family. I feel happy and grateful. Would to God that all human beings had occasion to be as happy and grateful as I am.[27]

Natural miracles, from the birth of a child to the turning of the leaves in the fall, are all around us. One has only to observe the rising of the sun to feel the full force of the miracle. But we must remember that miracle is essentially relational. It begins, of course, with our sense of wonder. Emerson put it well in a lecture he once gave on religion: "In truth, the miracle is always spiritual; always within the man who beholds it,—affecting his senses and his soul. The lover walks in miracles, and the man beside him sees none. Love is magical. It converts a chair, a box, a scrap of a paper or a line carelessly drawn on it, a lock of hair, a faded weed into amulets worth the world's fee."[28] Remarkably, Emerson's point seems to parallel *Midrash Rabbah* where the story of Moses and the burning bush is discussed. We find in the midrash that those who accompanied Moses saw nothing and heard nothing. The miracle is available only to him.[29] Thus, for Emerson and for the midrash alike, the miracle is as much "in us" as it is out there. Kaplan as we remember was a master of midrash and always appreciated its insights.

There was, thus, a whole set of traditional beliefs about God that Kaplan dismissed. God was not in the miracle, nor was God a self who had a will, as we discussed above. In our present mode of speaking, we might say that all the ways of talking about God are metaphors and should not be taken literally as portraying God. The metaphors point and indicate, but they do not describe.[30] They all need to be interpreted carefully or reconstructed; with this awareness of metaphor, however, the traditional God of the Bible does not "look" the same. God would no longer be a supernatural "being."

* * *

We cannot consider belief in God without considering idolatry. Idolatry is, of course, the obverse of belief in God and changes as the concept of

God changes.[31] For the Biblical mind it had to do with images; but by the 12th century—with Maimonides, for example—it was about error or wrong belief. In the words of a contemporary scholar: "In Maimonides' thought, there was a change in the concept of idolatry, and this change was in the direction of internalization . . . The focus of the concept of idolatry was thus transferred from the performance of alien rituals to the harboring of alien beliefs."[32] Kaplan would certainly follow Maimonides on this point.

For Kaplan, the essence of idolatry is the very human tendency to turn the ephemeral into the permanent. Religion in general might be seen as a quest for the permanent, so it is not surprising that we continuously create entities that we consider permanent. We ought to remember John Calvin who famously said, "Every one of us is, even from his mother's womb, a master craftsman of idols." In Kaplan's way of thinking, the primary sin is that we take processes and turn them into things. For Kaplan, both the self and God are processes, but we consistently view them as entities. Kaplan coins the wonderful term *thingify* for this kind of thinking. Commenting on this tendency he says, "Only theologians have a tendency to bring into the field of mature thought the tendency of the immature mind to reify, or thingify, processes, relations and events as though they were identifiable entities."[33]

For Kaplan, like Maimonides and John Calvin, not only objects become idols but beliefs as well. In March 1919, he delivered a sermon at the Jewish Center that dealt with the problem:

> It is not merely the letter of the Second Commandment that is essential to progress in religion. Its spirit is especially necessary today. The spirit of that commandment [against graven images] is that no idea, creed, dogma political belief or institution must assume finality. Every one of our ideas must be held in a state of flux subject to reconstruction upon our acquiring more knowledge of things affected by them.[34]

The epitome of a permanent belief or dogma, in traditional Judaism, is the assertion that God gave the Torah to Moses on Mount Sinai. The divine origin of Judaism's essential laws is fundamental to the religion. Solomon Schechter had this in mind when he referred to higher biblical criticism as higher anti-Semitism. If the Torah is a late document, perhaps even written or edited by Ezra after the Exile, as Arnold Ehrlich and other critics posited, then the revelation at Sinai turns out to be a myth. Moses, the Exodus, all the events of early Israelite history are shrouded in ancient prehistory and cannot be considered to be real historical events in any significant sense. In Kaplan's words, "The modern-minded Jew cannot consider the miraculous events recorded in the Torah and in the rest of the Bible as more than legendary. He, therefore, cannot accept them as evidence of the traditional Jewish doctrine that Israel is God's chosen people."[35] Doubt about the reality of Sinai might, in the minds of some, lead to a cascade of doubts that threaten to undermine Judaism's foundation.

Despite the vast disruptions caused by biblical criticism, Kaplan believed that a middle path was possible. Though Kaplan accepted the assumptions of the biblical critics, he still insisted on the preeminence of the Torah. Indeed, Kaplan believed that the critics did not undermine the significance of the Torah. In a path-breaking article in 1914, he made it clear that, for him, function determined value, not origin. No matter what the origin of the Torah, if it continued to function as the center of Jewish life and belief, then the assumption that it was late does not undermine its holiness.[36]

Nonetheless, Kaplan's challenge to *traditional* beliefs regarding Sinai and revelation were vehement and sustained. In 1943, he confided to his journal:

> The problem of Judaism would not be so acute if the traditional doctrine of revelation were merely obsolete. The trouble is that to cherish that doctrine is as unethical as being guilty of bigamy! To believe that we are in possession of the authentically revealed will of God is incompatible with religious tolerance[,] to say nothing of religious equality.[37]

Kaplan was outraged that Jews thought the divine was revealed only to them. It was intolerant, to say the least, because the implication was that the holy scriptures of all other religions were not as holy as the Hebrew scriptures. Kaplan could not tolerate such a thought because, for him, statements that were holy would naturally be the property of all people of good will.

Kaplan explained the origins of the belief in revelation in the following terms: "The sense of inner compulsion which a highly important truth always carried with it led the ancients to ascribe that truth to a source which belonged to a different dimension of being from that of normal experience. Such a source could only be divine revelation."[38] The ancients had no strong sense of the inner life. Their relentless inner urges were experienced as coming from outside themselves. The ancient Hebrews, untutored in philosophic expression, had the irresistible intuition that their ethical values stemmed from a source other than individual expediency.

Though we are so different in so many ways from the ancients, the revelation at Sinai persists. It is and has been so central to Jewish life, Kaplan knew, that we cannot simply drop it. So the question becomes how the idea of revelation can function in a naturalistic system. Kaplan was not alone in trying to answer this question. Martin Buber, for example, was more traditional than Kaplan on this issue and seems to have felt that Sinai was a definite historical event. In his book *Moses,* he tells us that, even though we cannot know the precise details of the Sinaitic event, it became historical by virtue of the fact that it affected subsequent generations. In Buber's words,

> Whether Sinai was a volcano cannot be determined historically, nor is it historically relevant. But that the tribes gathered at the "burning mountain" comprehended the words of their leader Moses as a message from their God, a message that simultaneously established a covenant between them and a covenant between Him and their community, is essentially a historical process, historical in the deepest sense; it is historical because it derives from historical connections and sets off fresh historical connections.[39]

Ahad Ha-Am, Kaplan's most significant mentor in all matters Jewish, helps us to deal with the historical issue of Sinai in a nonsupernatural way. In his revolutionary essay "Moses," Ahad Ha-Am confronts the historical reality of Moses and his meaning for Jewish life. Kaplan was very moved by the essay and used it to explore his own notion of the divine. The essay will be helpful in explaining Kaplan's stand on Sinai as well.

What, Ahad Ha-Am asks, shall we make of Moses, this hero of the Jewish tradition? Our modern sensibilities tell us that, if he existed at all, he is best described as a very unusual bedouin, a wandering desert leader. Yet he is central to the self-understanding of the Jewish people who have become mostly urban and quite intellectual.

To solve this dissonance, Ahad Ha-Am proposes a distinction (soon fundamental to Kaplan's thinking) between what he called archeological truth and historical truth. The archeological truth is the truth that the detailed evidence of the past reveals to us. The historical truth is that which pervades our minds and our imaginations and influences the collective life of our people. Clearly, Moses, whatever the actual facts of the case, represents the ideals of the Jewish people. Moses is not a warrior or a military leader, though he is represented by the biblical writers as one who can employ effective strategies against Israel's enemies. Rather, he is the prophet, the man of moral strength, the idealist of the ethical. He lives through the ages not as the man he was in his lifetime—whoever that may be—but as a creature of the popular imagination. In the historical truth, we know only the hero who lives in the hearts of the people, the ideal that helps us mold our sense of self.

One might say that the myths or "historical truths" we hold dear tell us more about ourselves and our ideals than the archeological evidence reveals and, in the end, are indubitably more significant morally and religiously. So, Moses, the prophet, the man of the law and of justice, and the leader whose compassionate concern for his people almost never fails, the man who never falls into the egotistical trap of trying to deify himself—that man is the real hero of the Jewish people and reflects their innermost essence. Such was the attitude of Ahad Ha-Am and Mordecai Kaplan.

Kaplan embraced Ahad Ha-Am's distinction between the historical[40] (we might say mythological) and archeological and applied it to the issue of Sinai and revelation. He therefore could see Sinai and revelation as a powerful "historical event" which was central to the self-understanding of the Jewish people.[41]

For Kaplan, it is not important to know the details of what actually happened on Mount Sinai. Indeed, we shall never know. But it was and is a reality in the mind of the Jewish people. We thus cannot ignore Sinai, but rather need to reinterpret this event so it will continue to function for us. Again, Buber comes to our aid. At the end of his seminal work *I and Thou*, Buber refers to his understanding of revelation. He was convinced that Moses's overwhelming experience at the holy mountain did not contain explicit teachings; what it did, rather, was to convince him of the meaningfulness of life.

Kaplan believed that Sinai revealed the soul and mind of the Jewish people. Sinai teaches us that fundamental moral truths are in some way part of the fabric of the universe and that at the root of the Jewish belief is the conviction that morality, justice, and mercy are, therefore, divine. In a poetic and metaphorical—though never literal—sense, these qualities endure as the word of God.

It might be valuable at this point to introduce Heschel's thinking on revelation. Heschel believed that the literal is the enemy of religious thinking. In our day, this attitude is foundational to any liberal or non-Orthodox theology.

The belief that the Torah comes from God presents a problem when we take it literally. Heschel certainly understood that. He tells us, for example, "The nature of revelation, being an event in the realm of the ineffable, is something which words cannot spell, which human language will never be able to portray. . . . as a report about revelation the Bible itself is a *midrash*." In other words, when the Bible says "and God spoke to Moses," it is not describing an actual event—an event that would, by the nature of the ineffable, be impossible to describe. Rather, our anthropomorphic descriptions of God "point to its meaning rather than fully rendering it."

Nevertheless, Heschel's stand on revelation remains problematic. To call the words of God a midrash is to avoid the status of these words and the question of how we should understand them. It seems Heschel still accepts revelation as fact but does not know how to deal with it. Although he tells us that the expression "God spoke" is a metaphor, he nonetheless continues to insist that there was communication of some sort. In Heschel's words, "It was not essential that His will be transmitted as sound; it was essential that it be made known to us."[42] In other words, the events at Sinai, and indeed the whole Torah, are in Heschel's view a communication of the will of God. For Kaplan, on the other hand, since God is not a supernatural being in the first place, the Torah cannot be the communication of God's will in other than a poetic sense. The Torah was and must remain both preeminent and sacred, but it is not the word of God.

For Heschel, because the Torah represents the will of God, the commandments must then come from God. Heschel wants us to take a "leap of action" rather than a "leap of faith" and observe the *mitzvot* without fully understanding the reason why, or without believing completely that the *mitzvot* come directly from God. But perhaps we might suggest that to impute communication to the divine in any sense is an anthropomorphic sin of the highest degree. Kaplan never equivocates on this issue. God does not have a "voice," He does not speak, and He does not formulate any laws (whether those have to do with priestly purity or with the proper place of homosexuals in society or any other laws). Kaplan would say that the notion of God's communicating is simply a reflection of the primitive Israelite mind. One of the steps toward our own intellectual maturity would be to accept the fact that such an expression is entirely poetic and metaphorical.

Heschel famously said that "Revelation is not a long distance telephone call," yet he does, as we see, believe in some kind of communication between a personal God and man.

I would like to report a striking personal episode in connection with the issue of God's communication that is relevant and illuminating. In the early 1970s, I was giving a series of lectures in Rochester, New York, to the leaders of the Jewish community. The feeling was that Jewish leaders ought to know something about Judaism. So I lectured on modern Jewish thought, on Kaplan and Buber and Heschel, among others. Though well attended, and fairly large, the lectures were held in the homes of the participants. On one occasion while discussing Heschel's theory of revelation, I quoted his statement that revelation was not a long-distance telephone call. At that precise moment, the phone rang. The host picked up the phone; the call was for an obstetrician who was in the audience. One of the doctor's patients was ready to deliver her baby. In my mind, the birth of a baby certainly counts as a miracle and a revelation if there ever was one.

Unfortunately, though Kaplan's stand on this issue is crystal clear, he was never was able to act fully on his belief. In his 1945 Sabbath prayer book, we find Kaplan referring to God in a personal sense and using the expression "Blessed art thou" in addressing God. I would suggest that this rather confusing fact, which many have noted, is partially due to his lack of poetic ability rather than any equivocation about God's nature. We also find references to God as the personal ultimate "Thou"[43] in Kaplan's journal. Perhaps the age-old habit of belief in a personal God could not be given up 100 percent. Nonetheless, though Kaplan used the words of the personal address to the divine, it is manifestly clear that his foundational theological commitments are naturalistic and not supernatural. Of that, we can be certain.

This is not the place to speak of Marcia Falk's amazing liturgical work. We shall do that in our discussion of Kaplan and prayer. But it is well to emphasize that her new liturgy powerfully reflects a Kaplanian theology and the effort to make an impersonal God the center of the liturgy. She speaks over and over of the "source of life," for example, rather than God. The Reconstructionist prayer book *Kol Haneshamah*, like Marcia Falk's work, employs such expressions as "the life of the universe" or the "eternal one," instead of the word "God." And both are more Kaplanian than Kaplan's own prayer book![44]

Other questions in connection with revelation remain to be considered. Is it the case that revelation, no matter how we understand it, is a one-time event and does not reoccur? Is it an event, as Heschel maintains, or is it possible that it is part of a process, as Kaplan argues? Revelation does exist in a natural universe in a number of different forms. Midrash keeps the "word of God" alive and thus may be considered a kind of revelation.

In any discussion of naturalistic revelation, we must take poetry into account. The link between revelation and poetry is found in many places in the philosophic literature, particularly in George Santayana and Emerson. Emerson can be helpful here, and, indeed, one might say that Emerson can function as a midrash on Kaplan. As we remember from the Emerson/Kaplan poem, Emerson puts the issue of revelation and God's words in the following terms: "Let the keepers of religion show us that God is, not was. / That He speaketh, not spoke. / And thus cheer our fainting hearts with new hope and new revelation."[45] Anyone, no matter his or her theological inclinations, wants to believe "that God is, not was"; but what shall we do with the next phrase, "that He speaketh, not spoke," if we do not believe that God speaks in the first place? The real question for Kaplan and for the naturalists and for the rest of us is how to keep the divine words alive and vital. Is the issue of inspiration still a live issue though we have moved away from the personal God who speaks? Is revelation still a possibility when now we accept an impersonal divine force in the universe rather than a personal God?

Revelation inspires us and directs our behavior both morally and ritually. The notion of continual revelation is, thus, an important theological issue. Continual revelation might be incorporated into Kaplan's system in the form of classical midrash. Heschel, as we have noted, states that the Torah is a midrash on the word of God. We would like to maintain that the midrash is a reflection of the efforts of the rabbis to keep the word of God alive and vital. Midrash might, thus, be described as continuous with revelation. Kaplan had a lifelong and passionate interest in the midrash. He taught midrash at the Jewish Theological Seminary for thirty years before he began to teach philosophy as a separate subject. Midrash was not available to Emerson, but, if it were, I think he would understand that, in a deep sense, the "voice of God" continues to speak through the midrash. The rabbis certainly believed this and so did Kaplan.

Emerson not only promotes the notion of continual revelation; he also ties the experience of revelation to everyday life. In other words, there is a continuum for Emerson from the great ecstatic experiences of the prophets to our own insights and understandings. I have coined the word *epiphing* for those moments of revelation or epiphany when I have an overwhelming insight that brings a big idea or a big feeling all together. Of course, these "revelations" of mine are very limited in nature and mostly have to do with Mordecai Kaplan; nonetheless, they give me a very small inkling of what the great revelations must have felt like. Even though no mountains moved and no disembodied voice spoke to me out of the cloud, still these moments were still revelations. Emerson's words on continuous revelation are very moving:

> We distinguish the announcements of the soul, its manifestations of its own nature, by the term *Revelation*. These are always attended by the emotion of the sublime. For this communication is an influx of the Divine mind into our mind. It is an ebb of the individual rivulet before the flowing surges of the sea of life. *Every* distinct apprehension of this central commandment agitates men with awe and delight. A thrill passes through all men at the reception of new truth, or at the performance of a great action, which comes out of the heart of nature. In these communications, the power to see is not separated from the will to do, but the insight proceeds from obedience, and the obedience proceeds from

a joyful perception. Every moment when the individual feels himself invaded
by it is memorable. By the necessity of our constitution, a certain enthusiasm
attends the individual's consciousness of that divine presence. The character
and duration of this enthusiasm varies with the state of the individual, from
an ecstasy and trance and prophetic inspiration—which is its rarer appearance—to the faintest glow of virtuous emotion, in which form it warms, like
our household fires, all the families and associations of men, and makes society
possible.[46]

My only difficulty with this astounding passage is the statement "for
this communication is an influx of the Divine mind into our mind." I
am not quite sure how Kaplan would have reacted to this passage. As we
shall see in the next chapter on Kaplan and his theology, when it comes
to God, Kaplan is not the complete naturalist that everyone thinks he is.
His insights move to a higher but intermediate realm, which is not the
supernatural but the "transnatural," as he called it, or the "super-natural,"
as Eisenstein liked to say.

For the naturalist, in addition to midrash, there is another possibility for continual revelation, and that has to do with poetry. We are now
well aware from his reworking of the Emerson and Heschel essays that
Kaplan was alive to the possibilities of new "revelations" coming to us
through contemporary poetry.[47] Kaplan was convinced that the Hebrew
poetry of our own day could be used as liturgical texts just as the Psalms
were of old. The Psalms, of course, were not the direct word of God, but
Kaplan argued that, if there ever were a set of poems that were divine in
content and in style, it would be the book of Psalms.

Kaplan hoped that the writings of Hayim Nahman Bialik and Shaul
Tchernichovsky and the poems he himself created from Emerson and
Heschel would be used for prayer on a regular basis. Many Reconstructionist congregations carry the Kaplan legacy and regularly introduce
new poems, as prayers, into the service. Often these poems might be by
contemporaries such as Yehuda Amichai or even by non-Jews like Rabin-
dranath Tagore. But their presence and function in the Sabbath or festival
service are completely in keeping with Kaplan's purpose.

Kaplan understood that religion and poetry are intimately related
in a number of ways. Some thinkers even go so far as to advocate the
substitution of poetry for religion. Santayana gave voice to this idea, and
Matthew Arnold famously said that "religion was morality touched with

emotion," a statement that could also point to the intimate relationship between poetry and religious truth. Santayana's words on the matter are more direct:

> This idea is that religion and poetry are identical in essence, and differ mainly in the way they are attached to practical affairs. Poetry is called religion when it intervenes in life, and religion, when it merely supervenes upon life, is seen to be nothing but poetry.... The dignity of religion lies precisely in its ideal adequacy, in its fit rendering of the meanings and values of life, in its anticipation of perfection; so that the excellence of religion is due to an idealization of experience which, while making religion noble if treated as poetry, makes it necessarily false if treated as science. Its function is rather to draw from reality materials for an image of that ideal to which reality ought to conform, and to make us citizens, by anticipation, in the world we crave. [48]

But what exactly is the relationship between the fundamental truths that we find in scripture and the words of a poet? Perhaps the possibility of revelation arises from two aspects of poetry. First is the fact that a poet often considers him- or herself the vehicle for the poetry rather than its creator. "We ask not from whence it comes," Nietzsche says, speaking of inspiration. Second, we sometimes have the feeling that the poem existed before—that it did not come into existence at the time of its creation. In Emerson's words, "For poetry was all written before time was, and whenever we are so finely organized that we can penetrate into that region where the air is music, we hear those primal warblings."[49]

In terms of the Jewish tradition and Kaplan, we are reminded of the rabbinic conviction that the Torah existed before creation and that God looked into the Torah when he created the world. Thus, a poet, like a prophet, gives voice to the eternal, and each generation waits for its poet. Kaplan was the "poet" of his generation in the same way that the younger Heschel was the poet of his. Could we not also say that Kaplan and Heschel each in his unique way constitute a new "revelation" and that, in the words of our tradition, "these and these are both the words of the living God."

The poet understands that there is not only his own private soul or source of energy but an additional soul, an extra soul, a *neshama yeteira*, as the tradition refers to our Sabbath self. This added "soul-mind-intellect" allows the poet to understand that there is a great reservoir from which to draw, a great pool of energy that—if he can tap into it—circulates through him and lifts him to prophetic heights. Kaplan voiced the same idea when he stated that "to pray was to commune with the sources of cosmic energy."[50] This notion pervades the writings of Emerson and Rabbi Abraham Isaac Kook, the twentieth-century Jewish mystic. Thus, we might say of a poet and a prophet, both of whom are caught up in the life of the universe, "his speech is thunder and his thought is law."[51]

It is well to remember that a poem is most often the residue of an event. Something happens to the poet, something emotional, something of the sublime, and the poem is his or her way of transporting us back to that experience.

I would also like to suggest that the experience of revelation has to do with the relationship between thought and action, or, as the people of Israel said in reaction to Moses's message, *na-aseh ve'nishma*—we will do it and we will listen. We might reconstruct the moment at the base of Mount Sinai to mean that the pledge to action came even before their understanding was complete. When we have a transcendent insight, we are moved at the same time to action. Indeed, we might say this is a definition of revelation: to hear it is to want to do it—immediately.

Put another way, the holy words are profoundly compelling and move us to action. Yet what was compelling to the Israelites three thousand years ago may not be compelling to us now. For us, as for each generation, other things are compelling, and we must have our own poets and our own prophets.

When we come to matters of the divine and the poetic, the word *sublime* and the concept of the romantic seem the most fitting. Kaplan rarely used such terms and was much more the rationalist than the romantic. We might explain this phenomenon by saying that Kaplan went right from the divine to the ethical without dealing with the sublime, which is in between.

Yet there is a romanticism, a deep sensitive emotionalism, about Kaplan's approach to the divine. This deeper spiritual sense in Kaplan's work will bring us to his appreciation of the numinous, a key concept in matters spiritual.

Romanticism in this context is the typical term attached to the nineteenth-century English poets. The Romantics have given us an enormous range of ways to experience the universe; the standard religious distinction between natural and supernatural is much too restrictive for them. Intuition and imagination, these are the hallmarks of the Romantic—qualities we find much more often in the poet Heschel than in the rationalist Kaplan.

There is, however, a romantic side to Kaplan's mind, though it does not surface often. That Kaplan appreciates the poetical is evident in his creation of new liturgy by turning essays into poetry. In addition to the word *romanticism,* we need another word to characterize the wider range of religious experience of the sublime. We need a word, not a made-up word like *transnatural* (Kaplan's term), which has little emotional clout. That word is *numinous.*

The concept of the numinous may be the beginning of a deeper sense of Kaplan's notion of the divine. This word does not carry the connotation of the supernatural or magical. Following Kaplan, if we do not accept Heschel's supernatural God who seeks man, the God who speaks to the prophets and who gives the law, we still have the mystery, what Heschel calls radical amazement. The poetic, and the numinous, must be available to every person—even the naturalist and the nonbeliever. We, all of us, are amazed not only at the wonders of nature but at the uncanny fact that there is something rather than nothing. In our deepest moments, we wonder about the whole enterprise of existence.

The term *numinous* brings to mind Rudolf Otto. Otto's famous work *The Idea of the Holy,* which defines the term, was published during World War I. There is no doubt that Heschel, studying in Berlin during the 1920s, read and appreciated Otto.[52] Otto's notion of the numinous is so close to Heschel's concept of the ineffable that we can assume a link even without concrete evidence. Where Heschel speaks of the fundamental importance of the mystery, Otto speaks of the *"mysterium tremendum."* At one point, Kaplan himself pondered the connection between Heschel and Otto. "I wonder," he mused, "to what extent Heschel, whose ineffable God is far more to the liking of the Seminary men than God as the power that makes for Salvation, drew on Otto."[53]

Not only did Kaplan think about the connection between Heschel and Otto, but he also read Otto carefully and considered the numinous a necessary element in the religious life. Kaplan insisted that we need religion not only as the social ideal à la Durkheim but also as the numinous of Otto. Kaplan's words here are striking:

> no religious experience is genuine without elements of awe and mystery, provided they do not lead to occultism and supernaturalism. No religious experience is possible without an overwhelming awareness of reality as baffling man's power of comprehension.
>
> According to Emile Durkheim the main content of religious experience stems from the impact of society upon the individual. According to Rudolf Otto, religious experience is the response to the impact of a transcendent presence upon the human mind. Actually these two ways of viewing religious experience supplement each other.[54]

Again it is clear that, though Kaplan did not live in the realm of the numinous or the ineffable, he did visit there from time to time.

* * *

Thus, we see that Kaplan is the naturalist who pushes the boundaries of naturalism to their limits. He is the sociological thinker who is not satisfied with Durkheim but deeply appreciates both Durkheim and Otto. It is almost as if Kaplan had become a follower of Heschel, but not quite. It is evident that Kaplan confronts the mystery as does any sensitive religious thinker, but he never moves beyond the mystery, never posits a supernatural self, never posits a meaning beyond the mystery as Heschel does. Kaplan, in the depths of his religious soul, is yet the dedicated naturalist and humanist.

SEVEN

KAPLAN'S THEOLOGY:
BEYOND SUPERNATURALISM

The eternal is an infinite becoming, and not an actual being. That is why
we should conceive of God as process and not as entity—for God is a
term to designate all those phases of the new direction that life takes on
in man which are indicative of life's infinite possibilities of growth.

—*Mordecai Kaplan, October 1940*

Theologically speaking, we might say that Mordecai Kaplan was caught
between a rock and a hard place. On the one hand, he could not easily
give up the traditional God of his ancestors. On the other hand, he could
not subscribe to the notion of a supernatural, providential deity. His embrace of a naturalistic theology necessitated a rebellion against the father
whom he loved and esteemed. But while he often expressed appreciation
for his father and the religious culture in which he was raised, once he
worked through his new theology, Kaplan never looked back.[1]

* * *

Though Kaplan dismissed the supernatural concept of God and the magic
and miracle so intimately associated with traditional theology, he nonetheless maintained a deep appreciation for the tradition. We must remember that he was brought up in an Orthodox household and that
he had a profound appreciation for the very positive ways in which the
tradition functioned. Let no one say that Kaplan did not cherish Jewish
tradition. Indeed, he believed that, without it, the Jewish people would
be lost. In his words,

> The great value which the religious tradition had for mankind lay not so
> much in the specific beliefs and practices that it prescribed as in the general

orientation that it provided. As a result of such orientation human beings felt at
home in the world. Men struggled and suffered, but they had, so to speak, a roof
over their heads. Nowadays, they no longer have that feeling of being at home
in the world. The sense of homelessness, of forlornness dampens all our joys
and adds torment to our sorrows.[2]

Throughout the modern period, the traditional believer has faced enormous challenges to his faith in God. Some in our own time find no difficulties with the anthropomorphic aspects of time-honored Judaism, yet
for many these images do not work anymore. Abraham Joshua Heschel
speaks very passionately of the God who is in search of the human being,
of the concept of the "divine pathos" where God feels what we feel and
is alive to our suffering. Though Kaplan appreciated such ideas for their
metaphoric power, for Heschel and his followers these are not merely
metaphors but shade off into reality. Heschel's God, as a result, is not
simply congruent with the beliefs of the liberal humanist. The naturalists
among us must find some other way to bring God back into our lives.

Mordecai Kaplan, the most famous naturalist the Jewish people has
ever produced, thought about God and the belief in God almost every day
of his life. Because his thinking was essentially sociological, he would
emphasize function even when it came to theological issues. He wanted
to know how the belief in God functions and why it is so widespread.
For Kaplan, the answer was obvious: the belief in God gives us comfort
when we are afflicted and helps us achieve the best that is in us. As we
have shown above, Kaplan thought that everyone, even dedicated hu-
manists, believed in the divine, though they might not be aware of it.
Kaplan believed that anyone who has faith in a better world and who
works to bring that world into being must assume that the universe is
set up in such a way as to support his or her belief and efforts. Such was
Kaplan's assumption, and for him to assume the world was such a place
was to believe in the divine.

Tradition was vital to Kaplan; his most important task, therefore,
was how to translate—or reconstruct—the traditional Jewish concept
of God into a God that felt authentic to a naturalist. Naturalism, as Kaplan and religious naturalists used the term, rejects the belief solely in
the physical and the empirical and the scientific, to the exclusion of all
else. For us and for Kaplan, the realm of the natural is meant as distinct

from the supernatural, the miraculous, and the magical (or theurgic). All these categories, so ingrained in Judaism for so long, needed to be reinterpreted and reconstructed so they could have meaning for the non-supernaturalist. The religious naturalist would be ready to believe in a spirit or a force or a power that we might experience but at the same time would reject any supersensual realm. It is of transcendent importance to understand that, when we refer to a force or a spirit, we are talking about a process, not an entity. In theological terms, we are using predicate theology to refer to God, not subject theology.[3]

From a theological standpoint, naturalism entails dismissing a personal God who speaks, gives laws, and feels the suffering of His people. At one point in discussing the problem of evil, Kaplan states his conviction that people

> generally assume that God, or Divinity, was a being of infinite power and goodness, meting out rewards to those who obeyed his commands and punishments to those who disobeyed them. The truth is that Divinity is not a being, in the same sense that man is a being. Divinity is *being* or *existence* [itself].[4]

For the naturalist, the natural is not at all a negative category. Rather, it contains the essential components of life; all that we need to organize, experience, and lead us on the path to salvation. As we have seen, salvation in the Kaplanian sense means fulfillment, moral perfection, peace in the social realm, and completeness on the individual level. As a consequence, what drives our metaphysical urge is the concept of predicate theology.

Kaplan used predicate theology to reinterpret his religious system while retaining his belief in God. Of course, there are many who will not go along with him. Almost everyone would call him an atheist; but this would be inaccurate and unfair. As we have mentioned many times, Kaplan completely and absolutely rejected the label of atheist as applied to him. It was as hateful to him as to any traditional believer. Yet his concept of predicate theology, while not completely unknown among liberal rationalists, is quite radical.

Kaplan began to think in terms of predicates early in his career. Put very simply, predicate theology suggests that, instead of talking of God as subject, we talk about God as predicate. Subject theology presents a supreme being—God—who is loving, merciful, and just, whereas predicate theology considers the qualities of love, mercy, and justice to be fundamentally divine. In 1922, Kaplan confided the following to his journal:

> If instead of affirming that God is love, spirit, etc. there were a new religion to proclaim that love is God, that spirit, courage, devotion, etc. are all but aspects of the love that is God, we might have a religion that is in accord with reality as man now knows it to be. Only when the term God will come to have an adjectival force instead of being a substantive, will it exercise a wholesome effect upon human life. . . . [T]hat is to say when people will use the term God for the purpose of emphasizing the supreme importance, or infinite value of certain things, then will religion be operative.[5]

Subject theology, as traditional theology is sometimes called, involves an inherent distortion. It considers a subject to be the actor or the cause, while, for Kaplan, we are referring to a process that is underway. We have noted elsewhere Kaplan's provocative phrase "to thingify" as a way of characterizing our tendency to see subjects where we should see processes. Emerson called it the "tyranny of nouns." Kaplan illustrated this by reference to the process of burning and the expression "fire burns":

> By this time we have learned that there is no independent entity or substance called fire. The predicate "burns" names the process which takes place when we see fire. Likewise when we say God loves, forgives, acts justly, we should understand it to mean that the process of loving, forgiving, and acting justly are divine or God. Perhaps that is what Spinoza understood by the statement "God is," namely that the process of being as such is synonymous with God. Then he went on to say that the process of being manifests itself as thought and extension etc.[6]

The consequences of process are enormous. The most radical predicate statement Kaplan ever made is found in a manuscript from the 1920s about the Torah. Here he carries predicate thinking to its logical conclusion:

> Divine is therefore whatever possesses the quality of furthering man's perfection or salvation. Torah-like is whatever possesses the quality of rendering the Jewish people aware of its function to further the process of man's perfection or salvation. Israel-like is the people that identifies itself with that process.[7]

This radical statement makes clear that God is best understood as a process. If we read it carefully, it also destroys the notion of the Jews as a chosen people. Any people can identify with the process of the divine; therefore, any people can be Israel. In this formulation, the covenant

dissolves. We know from many sources that Kaplan dismissed the notion of the "chosen people," but it is still a surprise to find such a mature
formulation that rejects traditional thinking so early in his life.

If Torah is a process, rather than a particular document, then Torah
can become any literature that inspires and guides the Jewish people;
we can find the divine outside the Hebrew scriptures. Following this
notion, we have noted that many Reconstructionist congregations introduce prayers and readings into the service from a wide variety of
authors and sources, both Jewish and non-Jewish, some of which might
be considered "pagan" in character. Kaplan embraced such ecumenical
uses of source material himself, as we have seen. His was an inclusive
intellectual determination so radical in his time that it helped lead to
his excommunication.

Process is central to Kaplan's thinking, and he is accurately described
as a process philosopher. Though Kaplan does not often cite his sources
by name, he does on occasion refer to the greatest process philosopher
of them all, Alfred North Whitehead. The earliest Kaplan reference to
Whitehead is in the late 1920s. Kaplan had been reading Whitehead's
small volume *The Function of Reason*, which made him aware of the value
of the individual philosopher. Until this time, he tended to think of religion as a group phenomenon. Indeed, when Heschel wants to dismiss
Kaplan's approach to religion, he refers to it as sociological. Nonetheless,
as a consequence of reading Whitehead, Kaplan comes to the conclusion
that perhaps the individual thinker has a role after all. In other words,
though religion may function to strengthen the values of the group, religion must ultimately offer more than group values. Since religion must
also consider the "great out there"—the cosmos as a whole—it is in the
search for answers to life's most baffling questions that people consult
the great philosophers.[8]

In a meeting with alumni of the Jewish Theological Seminary in
1954, Kaplan clarified his thoughts on God and process. It is not surprising that he identifies himself here with Heraclitus and Whitehead rather
than with Plato:

> I had occasion to explain the difference between conceiving God as a being and
> conceiving him as a process. I started out with an explanation of the difference
> between the Parmenides-Platonic notion of being, substance or essence as the

most "generic abstraction," and Heraclitus[9] Whitehead who treat becoming as the most generic abstraction. Those are the two radically opposed conceptions of reality. The reason for my preferring to accept the latter view is that I regard the notion of being or of substance as due to an intrinsic limitation of the human mind, in that it has to freeze a segment of an ongoing process or becoming in order to think about it. What helps to freeze the segments of processes is the use of nouns and verbs, i.e. substantives. These substantives lead the mind to reify the segments, when they are objects and to personify them when they are mental constructs.

Among the mental constructs are the notions of the human person or soul and God. The true nature of both is grasped more in keeping with reality when thought of as process rather than as beings. By habituating ourselves in thinking of reality as becoming we shall find it natural to translate every instance in which either person or God is used as subject into a statement in which they take predicative form, namely "personal" and "divine." The same incidentally applies to the concept "Torah," the unfreezing of which I have been urging.[10]

The concept of "unfreezing the Torah" is also a very useful analogy for a very complex idea. One of Kaplan's great life-long frustrations with traditional Judaism was its rigidity; the religion of his father and ancestors often felt frozen to Kaplan. The use of the predicate, however, enables a theology with almost the fluidity of water.

To elaborate on the ideal of fluidity, referring to the "divine" to explain justice and mercy as divine is really to talk about ourselves and what we must do—that is, be just and be merciful. Indeed, even the most traditional believer would agree that, when we refer to the attributes of God, it is only through human effort that these qualities become operative in the world. In short, there is no justice until we are just, and there is no mercy until we are merciful. Despite the radical implications of predicate theology, in its insistence on the importance of our own individual action, we see an important continuity with Judaism at its most traditional.

In the 1970s, Harold Schulweis, a great rabbi and a devoted disciple of Kaplan, elaborated on the meaning of predicate theology.[11] He asserted that, even in predicate theology, significant problems remain. A philosophical mind might well ask in what or where do the divine qualities inhere. Do they just float freely in the universe? Without a subject, without a controlling God, we are at a loss. Schulweis points out that the question is again a reification. It is as if we make the qualities into things and then ask how and where they exist. However, the qualities we are discussing, like justice and mercy, exist in relation—as Martin Buber so ably taught us. Justice "happens" when we relate to the other justly. In Kaplanian terminology, as we have seen, predicates are a matter of function, an essential part of the goal of our most basic process as humans. When these qualities contribute to the ultimate good, they are divine. Schulweis puts the issue precisely: "Intelligence, compassion, justice and peace are named divine when they serve ends which the community of faith judges to be good."[12]

Another way of formulating predicate theology is to state that religion is primarily about ideals and particularly those ideals that are divine. These ideals are transcendent and have supreme value, even though they do not issue from the "mouth" of a personal, supernatural God. To use Paul Tillich's language, they are matters of ultimate concern.

Certain critics have accused Kaplan of reductiveness. A predicate approach, they argue, reduces religion just to our ideals. Or to put it differently, predicate theology is nothing but ethics. Both Kaplan and Schulweis answer with a resounding "No." In effect, the opposite is happening: through this approach, we lift ethics out of the secular sphere and put it into the realm of the religious.

The predicate approach to theological issues has been used by many thinkers. It is particularly associated with Paul Tillich and his concept of the divine as ultimate concerns. We also find it in the works of other theologians in the twentieth century, particularly Henry Nelson Weiman (1884–1975) of the Chicago school and his associate Edward Ames (1870–1958). In this connection, my colleague Professor Emanuel Goldsmith has done path-breaking work in bringing Kaplan to the attention of Christian scholars.[13] It should also be noted that, in 1943, Kaplan used material written by Ames as the reading for his rabbinical school course in philosophies of religion.

In the realm of predicate theology, John Dewey remains the master. His path-breaking 1934 work *A Common Faith* laid out the fundamental issues of predicate theology. As we have noted, Kaplan had already stated his belief in predicate theology in the early 1920s, but Dewey was more rigorous and complete. Dewey here, like Emerson earlier, can be used as a midrash on Kaplan.[14]

Always thinking in terms of experience, Dewey does not begin by defining religion but by asking how religion functions. For him, a religious experience is one that "brings about a better, deeper and enduring adjustment."[15] It is important to understand that "adjustment" here is not meant in a psychological sense but rather in a cosmological sense. From this perspective, any experience is religious if it connects you to others, to nature, to the world; moves you out of your ego-centered existence; and helps you live on a higher, more transcendent level. The ideal is a total adjustment into a more transcendent realm.

For Dewey, religion is concerned with establishing harmony between the whole self, our ideals, and the universe. We need to understand that such a harmony is beyond what the therapist offers. As one student of Dewey puts it, "The harmonious self is the better self, the unified self, the nearly perfect self."[16] The perfect self is the self that lives according to its ideals.

The concept of the "whole," used in reference to either the self or the universe, is not something that we experience in any direct sort of way. Dewey considers the whole to be a matter of the imagination. We imagine the whole self; we do not know it directly. We act, we remember, but we never experience the whole of ourselves. As Dewey put it, "Neither observation, thought, nor practical activity can attain that complete unification of the self which is called a whole."[17]

For Dewey the naturalist, as for Kaplan, the actual does not encompass all that concerns us. The whole of ourselves or the whole of the universe or the whole of our ideals goes beyond the actual into the possible. To speak of the whole of the universe is not to talk of a physical fact but of an aspect of our metaphysical imagination. In the realm of the moral, the possible whole becomes central, "for all endeavor for the better is moved by faith in what is possible, not by adherence to the actual."[18]

Sometimes in discussing his theology and what it means to be religious, Dewey refers to the "enveloping whole" or, in the eloquent words of a contemporary student of Dewey, "to be religious is to relate to the designed, intentionally coherent totality."[19] Here we have neither the supernatural nor a subject theology but another possibility for a concept of God in the mode of predicate theology. This formulation, though far from being precise or exact, will be valuable in explaining what Kaplan means by the transnatural. It hints at the ultimate, though it does not describe. It helps us understand how the full range of human ideals might fit into a larger whole.

* * *

"Ideals," which are central to Dewey, are the key to Kaplan's naturalism and the bridge to his "supranaturalism," or transnaturalism, as he called it. The transnatural refers to the realm above the natural but still not the supernatural. Here we shall attempt to explain the concept of transnaturalism and the problematics of relating our experience and our ideals to the ways in which they point beyond the ideals to the larger cosmos as a whole, as a "coherent totality."

Though moral and ethical ideals function as the centerpiece of our religious life, they are nonetheless insufficient. The question of the status of the ideals plagues us. "Is there some higher reality?" we want to know. Is it just a matter of our own purposes and feelings that we mean when we as naturalists refer to the divine ideals? As we shall see, Kaplan extends naturalism in many different ways.

The most obvious example is his notion of growth that is as central for him as it was Dewey. Indeed, there is no issue that is as fundamental to both systems. Kaplan is able to take growth one step beyond our own ideals. He puts it this way: "The eternal is an infinite becoming, and not an actual being. That is why we should conceive of God as process and not as entity, for God is a term to designate all those phases of the new direction that life takes on in man which are indicative of life's infinite possibilities of growth."[20] In other words, growth on the human level is the process of becoming on the cosmic level. In our primary goal of life, we are one with the cosmic life process.

For Kaplan, as for so many other religious thinkers, the nature of the divine and ultimate meaning was a lifelong quest. By the 1920s, as he became more conversant in predicate theology, he began to elaborate on his vision of God. Kaplan's later theological writing, starting about 1930, introduces us to the concept of the transnatural.

Terms like "growth" and the "cosmic life process" bring us back to Henri Bergson. Kaplan apparently read Bergson early in life. In 1914, while musing on the matter of God and his relationship to experience, Kaplan states the following:

> Much if not most of the vigor possessed by religious thought of our ancestors
> was due to their imagining God in terms of human experience.... In writing
> this I am reminded of James' treatment of this subject in his book on Pluralism
> which is the best kind of introduction to Bergsonianism. If his contention is
> correct and I am very much inclined to believe it is—we will fare far better as
> the cultivation of the religious sense is concerned not by thinking with Plato
> ideaward but with Bergson lifeward.[21]

In the years after World War I, Henri Bergson was the most popular Continental philosopher; an indication of Bergson's standing is the Nobel Prize for Literature awarded him in 1927. Born of Jewish parentage, he lived the life of an academic philosopher.[22] Early in his life, he became alienated from his Jewish background, but one incident is worthy of note. In the early 1940s, he was considering a conversion to Catholicism. When, however, he was asked by the Nazis to register, he thought it a matter of principle to register himself as a Jew.

Kaplan valued Bergson, and his relationship to the philosopher of the *élan vital* is significant. Bergson illuminates Kaplan and his transnaturalism.

Bergson's thought was especially helpful to Kaplan and that whole generation in dealing with the problem of evolution. Bergson just happened to be born in 1859, the same year that Darwin published *The Origin of Species*. We remember that the notion of evolution both in terms of biology and of society generally was a key aspect of Kaplan's thought. He continually referred to his primary definition of Judaism as an evolving religious civilization.

Kaplan's generation wrestled with Darwin the way that later thinkers wrestle with Freud. Freud undermines faith in our purity of motive. Darwin seemed to undermine everything religious. Evolution seemed to deny God's providence, even His existence. How could a divine hand direct the workings of nature if it all came organically out of itself? Of course, one could say that the whole process was from God, but this is not really satisfying. The Darwinian concept of life seems self-sufficient, and that leaves God out.

Kaplan also understands that, according to Bergson, God is not only identified with the ideals of the collective, but, in the more advanced "dynamic religions," to use Bergson's phrase, God is identified with the life urge or the *élan vital* itself. In Kaplan's summation of Bergson,

Likewise the identification of God not with any of the national church deities, but with the vital impulse itself is not in the direct line of development from the various group religions (which are the outcome of the biological process) but a new creative act....

At all levels and in all forms, the urge to life or the "*élan vital*" is the driving force in the universe Bergson proclaims. The *élan vital* is continuously creative of new forms. Matter inhibits the new forms but the life urge, the life force continuously pushes toward new forms. In dynamic religion, or the higher forms of religion, man or particular people such as the prophets become part of the creative process. Humans become the creators not merely the created. In his later work Bergson substituted an enlightened universalism for his earlier biological naturalism.

The vital impulse permeates the universe and guides the evolutionary process. For Bergson, it is not reason which is primary but intuition. As one student of Bergson puts it, "Intuition is one of the ways in which we commune with the *élan vital,* with the eternally creative source of being which is ultimately God himself."[23]

Bergson was fundamental to Kaplan and his concept of the transnatural. Bergson rescues the notion of divine providence by pointing to intentionality in the universe, the tendency to produce life. For Bergson, the universe moves toward life, toward consciousness, toward morality, toward goodness, toward justice and mercy. All these may be considered as divine within a natural setting.

Bergson's theological perspective fits perfectly into Kaplan's mode of thought. In every case, we must push the natural to its highest point; or, to put it another way, the supernatural is replaced by the natural, as pushed beyond itself. Thus, we enter into the realm of the transnatural, the direction of the universe as set forth by Bergson. Although the issues are complex, Bergson and his *élan vital* are indispensable in explaining Kaplan's theology.

Kaplan found the divine present in our deeds and in our collective striving. He never ceased to believe in the primacy of experience in knowing the divine. Yet, at the same time, he understood that the experience of the divine always points beyond itself. The meaning here is similar to Buber's assertion of the "I-Thou" relationship: if we decide to cultivate another person in depth, then, in any genuine relationship we have to another being, there might always be a hint of the eternal Thou.

Reading Bergson reinforced Kaplan's understanding that the divine is not just a matter of what is most significant in our moral life. The divine cannot be reduced to our collective ideals. The divine must be something more—something transcendent.

Though Kaplan, the master of immanence, often attempts to confine the divine within our own, human lives, he never dismisses the transcendent. His position, as we have seen before, is emphatic: "the moment God is merely identified with the world and conceived as being immanent but not transcendent, His divinity is denied and He is dissolved into the world. This is the atheism and pantheism which religion so vigorously contends against."[24]

Kaplan stated many times that he thought it a grave mistake to reduce the divine to the ideals of the collective. Though he seldom employed Heschelian terms, Kaplan was fully aware of the essential mystery of existence and its centrality to the religious life. Even as he focused on means and ends and human fulfillment, he nevertheless insists that such an emphasis "would in no way detract from the mystery of existence, or in any way lessen our reverence and wonderment in the presence of the unfathomable." We must be careful, Kaplan adds, "not to reduce God to the ethical or the communal."[25]

Students, disciples, and detractors alike have made the mistake of thinking that human fulfillment and moral and ethical ideals were sufficient for Kaplan. The confusion, as we have seen, is understandable: Kaplan so often stressed the idea of God, rather than God Himself, and persistently explored how the belief in God functions, rather than the nature of God Himself [or Herself]. Yet these avenues of thought, like so much of his theology, forced him along a theological tightrope, as he tried to walk a very fine line between immanence and transcendence. As the world watched him walk, slowly, arduously, with the occasional stumble, many people simply did not understand what he was doing up there or, to be more precise, they could not see that he wanted to move beyond the conception of the divine as embodying our highest ideals.

Many journal entries from the 1920s to the 1950s record Kaplan's exasperation at his students' misunderstanding about his basic conceptions of the divine. Over and over again, he shouted his opposition to their theological reductionism, their accusations that he envisioned God solely in human terms of morality and justice. Quite often these misunderstandings surfaced in class discussions at the Jewish Theological

Seminary. More than once his rabbinical students challenged him on his conception of God. They reasoned that, if the traditional notion of the revelation at Sinai were rejected, an idea we will return to again, the only alternative would be for God to symbolize humanity's highest aspirations. The students resisted Kaplan's interpretation that these aspirations represent or imply support in the cosmos. In other words, his students seemed to want either the traditional conception of God or a clear-cut humanist conception—nothing in between. Kaplan, in turn, rejected their rejection.

He described one such session in his journal, asserting the primary theological principle that God is both immanent and transcendent:

> The basic spiritual need of our day is to learn to conceive God as manifesting himself both in human nature and in the cosmos of which we are a part, that is, both as immanent and transcendent. . . . In my reply [to the students], I pointed to the fact that the very conception of objective reality as cosmos or order, or as a universe in which there obtains absolute uniformity of natural law and complete interaction of all its parts is what we should mean by transcendent and cosmic support.[26]

Clearly, Kaplan means to assert his belief in an ordered universe where all the parts are interrelated. That said, we have seen that Kaplan was not the clearest of prose writers. I would not be surprised if the lack of clarity we see in his journals also manifested itself in the classroom. It is easy to imagine a scene in which he does not fully explain himself, while his students try to understand the complexities of his theology. Yet it is clear that Kaplan, in asserting the organic interrelatedness of all the parts of the universe, is pronouncing a great article of faith, for it is never apparent how all the elements of life are related. Yet the oneness is essential to our religious life and our well being.

The significance of order and the interrelatedness of all in the universe stands, in Kaplan's theology, next to the concepts of growth and the driving force of the *élan vital* as fundamental to the transnatural.

In 1943, four of Kaplan's rabbinical students approached him. They were entering the *pardes* (the sacred precinct), one might say.[27] "Can we serve as rabbis without believing in God?" they asked Kaplan. One can almost hear Kaplan shouting at them, pounding on his desk. He describes the moment in the journal:

The purpose of their visit was to air their inner conflicts. They find it difficult to believe in God and yet they want to serve the Jewish people. Can they conscientiously do so as rabbis? They had long ago given up the traditional basis for the belief in the existence of God, namely, revelation. But they have so far found no substitute. What I have been teaching as the alternative to the traditional basis for the belief in God does not convince them. I evidently have not succeeded in communicating to them my own experience of a transcendent correlative to man's will to salvation. They admit the existence of a will to salvation, but they see no need for positing a transcendent correlative of that will. Of course, my contention is not that I intellectually posit it, but that I experience it with the same immediacy as I do my own self. Intellectually I cannot posit the existence of a self, for the little I know of psychology tells me that the self is an illusion. Yet if I were to deny the reality of the existence of self as a center of initiative I would cut the ground from under the element of responsibility, without which human life is inconceivable. The same holds true of otherhood with its element of loyalty and of godhood with its element of piety.

The main question which they must answer for themselves is this: Am I able to take the idea of God as found in the Jewish tradition and transpose it into the key of modern religion? They have been told by Milton Steinberg in the series of lectures on Theology which he is now giving that there are two kinds of religion, theistic and non-theistic. What they would like to be told is that they could be rabbis on the basis of non-theistic religion. This I told them plainly they could not do, since as rabbis their main function was to maintain the identity and continuity of the Jewish tradition. That tradition minus the God belief is like the play of Hamlet without Hamlet.[28]

This unusually clear statement from Kaplan indicates significant movement in his thought from the realm of predicate theology to the transnatural, from the immanent to the transcendent. Kaplan insisted that a religion without God (or a religion where God was merely equivalent to our ideals) was not acceptable for a practicing rabbi. His concept of God was different from that of most people, but he fiercely defended the presence of God. This journal passage laments his failure to make his students understand his basic premise: to state our belief in an ideal and to order our lives around the embodiment of that ideal assume that, in some way, the world, the universe, life itself are set up so that the ideal is achievable. We operate under the assumption of our ability to render the possible actual. Our minds, our ideals, our conscience—all these elements constituting our moral life are also part of the natural world. As Carl Sagan, among others, has stated, "we are the universe come alive, we are the universe made conscious of itself."

The incident with the students illustrates the point that there are several kinds of naturalism. In rebellion against religion in the eighteenth and nineteenth centuries, we find thinkers who believed that everything could be reduced to the physical and that, if something could not, then it did not exist. In reaction against this trend, we find religious naturalism, which, though rejecting a supernatural, supersensual realm, yet posits a force or a spirit that is found everywhere and that embodies the principle of the growth of the spirit that we value so highly. (For example, Ralph Waldo Emerson, George Santayana, and John Dewey are all in this category in different ways.) It was this last kind of naturalism that Kaplan embraces in articulating the "power" that makes for salvation. Thus, there might be a naturalism that, while rejecting supernaturalism, is yet theistic because it involves belief in a divine force or a power.

I do not totally embrace the notion of "the power" here. I think it reifies too much. I would rather say that the universe favors our moral and ethical life and our salvation. Rather than the "power that makes for salvation," I would emphasize the apparent fact that the universe has life, has allowed the development of consciousness, and has given rise to human beings who have the potential for an ethical life.

Kaplan's comments on loyalty and piety are particularly interesting here. In the same journal entry in which Kaplan asserts to the students a strong naturalist theism, he explains (and we repeat the passage for ease of continuity): "the little I know of psychology tells me that the self is an illusion. Yet if I were to deny the reality of the existence of self as a center of initiative I would cut the ground from under the element of responsibility, without which human life is inconceivable. The same holds true of otherhood with its element of loyalty and of godhood with its element of piety."

We praise the virtue of loyalty, but there can be no loyalty without the "other" to whom we are loyal. In the same way, Kaplan tells us that piety necessitates an object, which he calls a "correlative" or an essential pairing. The doughnut is correlative to the hole, the parent to the child, the husband to the wife. Similarly, our feelings of piety are correlative to the divine presence.

In other words, we must progress from the ideal of piety to the object of that emotion. According to Kaplan, there exists in all of us an urge toward salvation or a will toward salvation, and we must ascend from having this urge to contemplating its referent. For Kaplan, the object of piety is not merely a matter of intellect but a matter of direct experience: "They [the students] admit the existence of a will to salvation, but they see no need for positing a transcendent correlative of that will. Of course, my contention is not that I intellectually posit it, but that I experience it with the same immediacy as I do my own self."

The immediacy of God's presence is a recurring theme, perhaps best explained by Kaplan in *The Meaning of God in Modern Jewish Religion:*

> The purpose in the various attempts to reinterpret the God idea is not to dissolve the God idea into ethics. It is to identify those experiences which should represent for us the actual working of what we understand by the conception of God. Without the actual awareness of His presence, experienced as beatitude and inner illumination, we are likely to be content with the humanist interpretation of life. But this interpretation is inadequate, because it fails to express and to foster the feeling that man's ethical aspirations are part of a cosmic urge, by obeying which man makes himself at home in the universe.[29]

It was this passage that Kaplan may have had in mind when he spoke to Martin Buber during a chance encounter in 1938, when Kaplan was teaching at the Hebrew University. The account was another, of the many, misunderstandings of his essential ideas, in this case of the divine as being greater than our societal ideals.

One morning Kaplan met Buber on a bus to Mount Scopus. Not surprisingly, the discussion of the two philosophers centered on Kaplan's perceptions of God. This is Kaplan's journal entry on the encounter:

> Yesterday morning at 10:30 AM meeting of the Faculty Senate took place. As I waited for the bus on Talbieh Street which would take me to the bus that goes to the University Buber came up. This time I decided not to be the one who begins the conversation, as I have been on all the occasions I have met him. He has never asked me anything about myself and I had to goad him into a conversation. The events of the preceding days have upset me so much that they left me no initiative to pull the tongue of anyone, even Buber. But after two or three minutes he began by saying that these days he is reading my book, *The Meaning of God in Modern Jewish Religion*. In the meanwhile the bus came and from that moment on, throughout our ride on both buses we conversed about the idea of

God in my book. He expressed his objection to my approach and said that my God is not a god, because he is entirely immanent. The God of the simple Polish Jew is the God of Israel and the God of the universe.[30] I tried to show him that I devote an entire chapter to the idea that God is a force outside of ourselves. He responded that this idea does not appear as central, but I think that he has not yet gotten to that chapter in my book. He promised me that he would write a review of my book in the form of a letter addressed to me. I cannot say that we thoroughly enjoyed the conversation, but the fact that, at least, Buber behaved himself humanly, taking into consideration the interests of his colleague, pacified me somewhat.[31]

What a disappointment for Kaplan! A major Jewish thinker had misunderstood him and thought that he was only concerned with divine immanence, to the exclusion of transcendence. Adding insult to injury, the promised letter never came.

One last statement on the matter of Kaplan's being misunderstood about transnaturalism should be made. Again it comes from a conversation with the rabbinical students at the Jewish Theological Seminary and is reported in the diary. This time it is October 3, 1939:

The point which I then made [to the students] was that mind, which is the very ground of reality and experience, is experienced as self on the hither end and as God on the end of one's self. This makes self and God correlative terms. The fact is that self has always been a correlative term. What the correlate was, depended upon the cultural and social development of the individual.[32]

I must say that the opening words of the passage completely confound me. Kaplan, the American pragmatist, Kaplan the follower of Durkheim and Dewey, seems to be flying straight up to the lofty realms of the Platonic universe. Yet there is consistency here. His assertion that "mind" is the very ground of reality and experience should be understood in terms of his fundamental rational commitment. Kaplan was not a rigorous philosopher, as we have discussed, and, in his mind, his pragmatism and his rationalism existed comfortably side by side.

Kaplan's assertions here bear a striking resemblance to Emerson's concept of the Oversoul. In pairing Kaplan and Emerson, it might be helpful to recall one of Emerson's key formulations of the Oversoul, in which he emphasizes the connection between the self and the divine: "When the universal soul breathes through a man's intellect, it is genius;

when it breathes through his will, it is virtue; when it flows through his affection, it is love."[33]

In Kaplan's use of the concept of correlative, we also find a hint of Hermann Cohen.[34] Kaplan had a deep and abiding interest in Cohen, even though he was opposed to Cohen's anti-Zionism. In a work published in 1964, Kaplan gives a running commentary on key quotations from Cohen. Of special interest is the following comment by Kaplan on Cohen's notion of revelation:

> Cohen's version of the God idea as a correlative is, no doubt, his most original and important contribution to the vitalization of religion. It inhibits the mind from the tendency to hypostatize, or to personify, Divinity, and turns our attention to the only true source of a genuine understanding of what we should mean by God. That source is, as Cohen reminds us frequently, rational man. By identifying that in man which makes him rational or fully human, Cohen assumes, we arrive at the cosmic idea which spells God.[35]

By using the concept of correlative here, Kaplan, Cohen, and Emerson all want to maintain that the self implies the divine. We shall elaborate the details of this issue below where we consider the self and salvation. We would only remind the reader again of Kaplan's quotation from Joseph Albo cited in a previous chapter: "*Da et naphshekhah ve-tedah et bor'ekha*"—"know your soul and you will come to know your creator." The path to the divine begins with the self and self-knowledge.[36]

This notion of a path from the self to the divine is, of course, central to the theology of Martin Buber. Buber often declares that the I-Thou moment is a glimpse of the eternal Thou. Interestingly enough, there are instances when Kaplan agrees with Buber's thinking. In the 1950s, Kaplan was asked to contribute an article to a volume on Buber's philosophy. In preparing his article, he reread some of Buber's works and found *The Eclipse of God* especially useful. He was surprised himself to find that he identified very much with the central thrust of Buber's existential theology—namely, that God cannot be grasped through abstraction but rather through the "concrete existential reality of personal experience." Moreover, Kaplan believed that his own concept of salvation and the higher unity Buber finds in the I-Thou experience were very much the same:

> I think he [Buber] is virtually trying to say the same thing I have been trying
> to say, namely, that God cannot be known through the medium of abstract
> thought but only through that type of human experience which I identify as
> the yearning for salvation and he as the organic unity of one's personal being.

He then focuses on Buber's use of Spinoza's concept of humanity's love of
God and identifies it with his own concept of the human being's yearning
for salvation. Buber apparently was inspired by Spinoza and believed the
concept of the human love of God was a concrete existential experience.
The Kaplan journal entry includes the following:

> I am quite convinced that what Spinoza speaks of as man's love for God, I refer
> to as man's yearning for salvation, and Spinoza's phrase God's love for man is
> what I refer to in speaking of God as the Power that makes for salvation. I too
> maintain that not through the medium of abstract thinking can we enter into
> actual relation with the real. But instead of assuming that we do so through
> love, I assume that we do so through the yearning for salvation. I confess that
> I have to translate the term "love" as applied to God into some such equivalent
> as "yearning for salvation" to know what I am talking about.[37]

It is almost a mystical moment for Kaplan when he realizes he is much
more like Buber than he (or we) would expect. In this moment of exalta-
tion, he declares, "The yearning for salvation is the yearning for achieving one's unitary being in all the life fullness of which it is capable."

Kaplan was not a great poet, as we have seen, yet in 1936, he crafted a
poem that beautifully expresses his theological commitments and transnaturalism. In its first of several publications, Kaplan called it "*Piyyut* for
the First Benediction of the Evening Prayer."[38] It bears sustained study,
but if we truly understand it, we need not read any further in Kaplan's
oeuvre to comprehend his transnaturalism. In its entirety, the poem
here stands at fifty lines and ranges widely over a variety of theological
themes.[39] Below is the portion most relevant for our purposes:

**The Revelation of God in Nature: A Piyyut for the
First Benediction of the Evening Prayer.**[40]

God is the oneness
That spans the fathomless deeps of space
And the measureless eons of time,
Binding them together in act,
As we do in thought.

He is in the sameness
In the elemental substance of stars and planets

Of this our earthly abode
And of all it holds.

He is in the unity
Of all that is
The uniformity of all that moves,
The rhythm of all things
And the nature of their interaction. . . .

God is in the mystery of life,
Enkindling inert matter
With inner drive and purpose.

He is the creative flame
That transfigures lifeless substance,
Leaping into ever higher realms of being,
Brightening into the radiant glow of feeling,
Till it turn into the white fire of thought.

And though no sign of living thing
Break the eternal silence of the spheres,
We cannot deem this earth,
This tiny speck in the infinitude,
Alone instinct without God.

God is in the faith
By which we overcome
The fear of loneliness, of helplessness,
Of failure and of death.
God is in the hope
Which like a shaft of light,
Cleaves the dark abysms
Of sin, of suffering and of despair.

God is in the love
Which creates, protects, forgives,
He is in the spirit
Which broods upon the chaos men have wrought,
Disturbing its static wrongs,
And stirring into life the formless beginnings
Of the new and better world.

Thou art my portion,
O Eternal;
Thou art my share.
Thou wilt show me the path of life;
Fullness of joy is in Thy presence;
Everlasting happiness does Thou provide.[41]

This prayer suggests—like many of Kaplan's beguiling, and sometimes infuriating, statements—that he did actually believe in a traditional God. Does he not turn to God in the last stanza and cry out, "Thou art my portion, O Eternal"? The personalizing of God here is startling. But it is clear, from all we have stated above, that Kaplan did not seriously believe in a Supreme Being. His lamentations in this poem instead reflect how deep our need is to see God in personal terms.[42]

As we have seen, for Kaplan, statements about God imply beliefs about the world of our experience (immanence) and about the larger universe as a whole and beyond (transcendence). He was convinced that fundamental to the constitution of the universe is an integral relationship between what we believe, our ideals, and the natural processes that surround us. This poem witnesses that same tightrope walk, between immanence and transcendence, savoring both the qualities of our experience and qualities that transcend us.

Order is central to the poem, as it is to transnaturalism. It is apparent that order underlies the notions of "oneness," "sameness," and "unity." Throughout his life, Kaplan insisted on the interrelatedness of all being and the organic quality of the universe where every part has a role and is related to every other part—just as the cells in a living organism are related to the whole. In the *Religion of Ethical Nationhood*, he put it this way: "The cosmic processes of organicity—whereby totalities act upon each of their parts and its parts upon the totalities—is the course of the Godhood or the superpersonal in man. Man articulates his ideas of God and experience or organicity through his consciousness of responsibility. That sense of responsibility emanates—not from nature or the cosmos—but from the organic group to which he belongs."[43]

In terms of the physical universe, Kaplan continued to live throughout his life in the Newtonian world of fixed laws and fixed relationships between physical bodies. The emerging universe of Einstein, with its curved space and relativity of space-time, was as foreign to him as indeed it remains to most of us. Yet Kaplan was not concerned with physics but with theology. When we say there is a "sameness" and a "unity," it is not about the way the universe works in scientific terms. We mean to imply that there is a fundamental unity to all things and that someday all will be one. And let us not forget that Einstein himself was infected with this longing for oneness. Indeed, he spent the last part of his life trying to work out a unified field theory that would bring together all phenomena in the universe into an essential unity—even the messy little quanta that are continuously getting away from us.

It was a lifelong struggle for Kaplan to understand the "sameness and oneness" among all things, but, in this poem, Kaplan outlines his transnaturalism. It is as close as he comes to metaphysics. Spirituality, he claims, is about order and connectedness, about our sameness and our coming together. By contrast, Kaplan believed deeply that those who preach hate are not concerned with religion and God but only with their own passions and their own problems. It is not accidental that the central prayer of the Jewish people states our belief in the oneness of God and by implication the oneness of his world. As my young rabbinic friend Ezra Weinberg likes to put it, spirituality is about connecting the dots.

Scripture begins with God bringing order out of chaos. Jewish tradition commands us to complete that primal work of creation. In a very moving passage, Kaplan sums up the connection between order and the spiritual:

> If I can be sure that the direction in which reality is moving is toward more order, more uniqueness and more love, then I am satisfied that Reality has meaning or pattern. It is that meaning or pattern which gives to Reality the character of godhood and which demands that my life fall in with it. That is what we understand by human life being spiritual.[44]

And let it not be said that Kaplan lacks faith. The belief that the world is moving toward more order, uniqueness, and love is contradicted by our experience every day of the week. Kaplan's basic optimism (or his longing to believe in the unity) is an expression of his faith and his hope. Indeed, for every religious person, the hope for greater order and unity must be at the center of his or her religious life.

Kaplan's theological poem, and his vision of transnaturalism, points to God as the life of the universe, as the underlying order, as the urge toward growth and toward life, as the interrelatedness of all things, and as the fundamental importance of creativity. The essential fact of life is creation. Creativity in this sense defines life. We might say that whatever creates and procreates is by definition alive. The creative principle for Kaplan asserts that God is the creative life of the universe, the sum of all the forces making a cosmos out of chaos.[45]

While contemplating creation, Kaplan cannot quite remove himself from the traditional notion of humanity as created in God's image, with all that this implies. He puts it this way: "the creative principle as far as human life is concerned is incompatible with arrogance, greed and uncontrolled sexual desire and is compatible only with intelligence, courage and good will."[46]

Kaplan goes on to explain that, when we think of the creative principle of the universe, we cannot help but personify it. We, thus, speak of God the Creator. For Kaplan, the implications of believing in God the Creator or in the creative principle are the same. In both cases, we turn to worship in order to bring forth the creative energy. In his words, "the creative principle in human life, especially in the manifestation of intelligence, courage and good will, can best be called into play through that self-conscious act for which there is no better name than worship."[47]

As we shall see below, Kaplan's most important theological work, *The Meaning of God in Modern Jewish Religion,* shows how his predicate theology and his transnaturalism are applicable to the system of *mitzvot.* He believed strongly that ideals are never real unless they are embodied by individuals and by communities. The ritual *mitzvot,* especially communal prayer, help energize us to work toward our ideals. As we encourage others, we are encouraged to pursue our own goals. *The Meaning of God* is organized around the Sabbath and the holidays. It explains to us, for example, how the Sabbath embodies the principle of creativity, how Yom Kippur embodies the principle of moral self-regeneration, and how *Shimini Azeret* embodies our desire for the presence of the divine to extend beyond the Succot festival.[48]

The last element in our detailing of Kaplan's transnaturalism is his concept of energy. Sometimes he compares God to electricity and the forces of energy. In a talk he presented before the leadership of the emerging Jewish Center in 1917, he spoke of God as analogous to lightning and electricity, manifest everywhere and at all times.[49] The notion of energy appears often in Kaplan's early work, more frequently than his later and more famous formulation of "God as the *power* that makes for salvation." Power encourages reification since we tend to see it as a thing, whereas energy keeps us in the realm of process.

The life energy of the universe manifests itself within us both as the will to live and as the will to embody our ideals. This notion is found frequently in Kaplan and is fundamental to his concept of salvation. Kaplan's sense of the cosmic energy and our need to mobilize those energies through prayer finds its earliest formulation in a journal entry from 1905 where he stated that "to pray was to commune with the sources of cosmic energy."[50]

To pray, in other words, is to marshal our highest energies. The thought also occurs in the works of Abraham Isaac Kook. A decade or so ago, one of Kaplan's most important interpreters, Rabbi Jack Cohen, z"l, wrote an important work comparing the thoughts of Kook and Kaplan.[51] In one of Kook's primary works, he gives voice to the point we are making here about energy and the way it relates to our religious life: "One feels the divine life force coursing through the pathways of existence; through all desires, all worlds, all thoughts, all nations, and all creatures."[52]

Never a systematic theologian, Kaplan did not completely spell out his concept of the transnatural. Yet it is now clear that it would be a mistake to limit Kaplan to the Durkheimian concept of God as merely the highest ideals that any society holds forth. What we have found is that, over the course of his life, Kaplan moved into that circle of thinkers who are genuinely religious thinkers, who strive throughout their lives for an understanding not only of the human condition but of the larger universe—what Dewey called "the enveloping whole." The transnatural is, for Kaplan the rationalist, the realm of the thinkable rather than the realm of the ineffable. His movement on the theological plane was asymptotic, which is to say that, throughout his life, he moved closer and closer to the truth of the ultimate, although he never achieved a full understanding.

It is fitting to end this chapter with the familiar admonition from Rabbi Tarfon in the *Ethics of the Fathers:* "The day is short, the task is great, the workers indolent, the reward bountiful, and the Master insistent! You are not obliged to finish the task, neither are you free to neglect it."[53] Kaplan never neglected his quest for the divine, though he never finished it either. Indeed, the quest was the centerpiece of his very being.

EIGHT

SALVATION: THE GOAL
OF RELIGION

Salvation is unhampered freedom in living and helping others to
live a courageous, intelligent, righteous and purposeful life.

—*Mordecai Kaplan, "Soterics"*

Salvation is generally considered a Christian term. Although it appears
in the Hebrew scriptures (*yeshua*), this basic theological concept has
never occupied a central place in rabbinic or in modern Jewish thought.
Nevertheless, as we have seen, it was axiomatic in Kaplan's system from
the very beginning. Though others bristled at the word, Kaplan was quite
comfortable with it. Indeed, we might say that salvation for Kaplan was
as important as God. He cared desperately about salvation and how to
incorporate it into Jewish life. Although he thought about God all the
time, Kaplan was not addicted to metaphysics, as so many theologians
are. When he thought about God, it was in terms of the meaning of God
for the life of the individual and the community; as we shall see, over
his lifetime, Kaplan would offer numerous formulations of this complex
concept, but every one revolved around the creation of meaning, in both
its individual and communal manifestations.

"God as the power that makes for salvation" is arguably the most
fundamental turn of phrase in Kaplan's theological system. The origin
of this idea, Matthew Arnold's aforementioned formulation "God as the
power that makes for righteousness," became a primary trope in Kaplan's
thinking. In essence, he substituted the word "salvation" for "righteousness." So far as we know, this change did not come because of a particular
book or thinker but emerged out of Kaplan's theological development.

For Kaplan, the purpose of religion was to achieve salvation. Salvation is the goal of life, our primary aspiration. We understand that striving toward our primary goal is what gives meaning to our existence. In achieving our goal, we have achieved salvation.

Kaplan never abandoned a belief in God, though he interpreted his belief in naturalistic terms. Though salvation would be central, God would never be relinquished: "By shifting the center of gravity in religion from the God idea to salvation, I am able to retain a strong belief in God as did our ancestors without the necessity of thinking of Him in anthropomorphic terms, and at the same time to concentrate on the problem of human conduct, which really matters, instead of on metaphysics, which is only a mental luxury."[1] We see once again his arduous efforts to move away from the supernatural God of traditional Judaism, a move that he believed would result in a God that would revive twentieth-century Judaism.

By reframing the typical position of God, Kaplan could instead highlight what was even more important. Indeed, Kaplan maintained that, in all religious traditions, the concept of God is determined by the concept of salvation:

> Instead of assuming, as is generally done, that the central element in a religion is the idea of God, we should learn to assign the position of centrality to the idea of salvation. Consequently, whatever constitutes salvation for the group to which we belong determines the idea of God which the religion of that group professes.[2]

Kaplan believed that salvation meant different things at different times. He asserted that, for the ancient Israelites, salvation meant the achievement of a collective well-being; because they were the "people of God," that well-being was inextricably linked with enhancing God's power and glory in the world: "In the Book of Isaiah we read: 'But hear now, O Jacob my servant, Israel whom I have chosen! Thus said the Lord, your maker, Your creator who has helped you since birth; Fear not, My servant Jacob.'"[3] In other words, the national well-being of Israel is connected with God through the covenant. The ancient Israelites assumed an intimate connection between their obedience to God's will and their fate as a people. The God of Israel is a God of history who concerns Himself with the safety of His people. Salvation is national, and *YHWH* is the God of Israel.

Toward the close of the biblical period, however, a sense of the individual emerges. One feels it strongly in the wisdom literature, especially Proverbs, Ecclesiastes, and Job, where the meaning of salvation shifts. With the rise of pharisaism, Kaplan tells us, the national focus of salvation grew more particularized: "The purpose of Jewish existence came to be the salvation of the individual Jew. Salvation was understood specifically as immortality and bliss in the hereafter. . . . 'All Israel are entitled to a share in the world to come,' is a famous statement we read in the *Ethics of the Fathers*."[4] Kaplan notes that this shift meant that the religion of the Jewish people changed from a God-centered religion where the solidarity with God was primarily political to a human-centered rationale, where the Jews were not only a nation but an *Ecclesia*, a "church" or religious congregation. According to traditional thinking, the salvation of the Jews was to be both national (with the coming of the Messiah) and ecclesiastic (with the attainment of bliss in the hereafter). Furthermore, the God of Israel would become the God of all humanity.

The otherworldly meaning of salvation continued to evolve throughout the Middle Ages into the early modern period. Maimonides lists belief in resurrection as a basic principle of faith (the thirteenth), though he refers to it in a very off-handed manner. In his *Guide for the Perplexed*, there is no reference at all to the doctrine. There are one or two stray references to resurrection in Maimonides's Code, the Mishna Torah, but, on the whole, he seems to identify the rabbinic "World to Come" not with the resurrection but with the immortality of the soul. For Kaplan, these stray references to resurrection were less significant than Maimonides's insistence that human perfectibility was a fundamental goal of the *halakhic* system.[5]

With the Enlightenment and the start of a long, slow withering of traditional religion, the Jews emerged into European culture. It was inevitable for Western society as a whole and for the Jews in particular that their sense of the purpose of life would shift from the next world to this world. The children of the Enlightenment followed Rousseau, who believed that human beings through the use of reason could perfect themselves in this life. For modern people, salvation was suddenly a possibility in this life. As Kaplan once put it, "Perhaps if I worked hard enough . . . I might succeed in proving that our salvation lies in learning what to live for in the here and now, whether as Jews or as members of any people."[6] This notion of "learning what to live for" is the goal of Kaplan's system and the center of his existential concern.

The Enlightenment instigated a movement toward a greater humanism. The new emphasis on human beings rather than the divine was central, as we have seen, in Kaplan's *Judaism as a Civilization:* "The denial of the traditional assumptions with regard to nature and [the] means of salvation paved the way for what is generally termed 'the Enlightenment,' which identified man's salvation with his self-realization in this world."[7] This emphasis on self-realization became the key to Kaplan's concept of salvation.

Many years later, Kaplan formulated the same thought in a manner that summarizes his whole ideology of salvation:

> In my opinion salvation is whatever we conceive as maximum fulfillment of the highest possibilities of human nature. It is life at its maximum and optimum. It is a desideratum and not an actual fact. As such it is the object of the most intensive and extensive form of the will to live.[8]

In his fixation on salvation, we can see that Kaplan felt called upon to define this concept and to explain how it worked in this world. Looking across the broad arc of his career, it seems as though he was for the better part of fifty years circling around the idea of salvation, trying to get closer and closer to the exact formulation, to the precise definition. The literal translation of *salvation* in Hebrew is *yeshua,* but Kaplan came up with a more fitting equivalent: the familiar term *shalom,* which broadly means peace. He explains: "The Biblical term that corresponds most naturally to the notion of salvation or life abundant undoubtedly is *shalom.* The equivalent of the concept of God as the Power that Makes for Salvation is *ata shalom ve-shimkha shalom,* which translates from the Hebrew as "You are peace and your name is peace."[9] God's name in classical Hebrew refers to his essence; here, God's essence is peace.

Kaplan does not elaborate upon *shalom* as the equivalent of salvation, but we find it obviously pregnant with meaning. The root *sh'l'm* appears a number of times in the Hebrew scriptures. For us, the most noteworthy instance is its usage in *levav shalem,* "a whole heart" (I Kings 15:14—"Asa was *wholehearted* with the Lord his God all his life").[10] The rabbis used it to mean complete or perfect, as when they refer to a man who is *shalem* "in his body, in his property and in his learning."[11] Thus, we can say that to be *shalem* is to be whole or fully realized, with all of one's powers working harmoniously together.

Shalom as salvation refers to the social aspect; *shelemut,* or perfection, refers to the individual. The ideal of perfection is familiar from the ancient Greeks where Aristotle uses the term to mean the harmonious realization of all our faculties. In the Talmud, the ideal of perfection alludes to the service of God through the *mitzvot,* the many required acts of daily life that facilitate the harmonious functioning of the individual. Maimonides uses the term *shelemut* frequently to refer to the system of *mitzvot* along with reason, both as leading to perfection. For Maimonides, moral perfection and intellectual perfection are the goals of human life.

Perfection for Kaplan is always a moral category. Perfection can certainly apply to piano playing, for example, or a whole host of other achievements, but the physical strata of human life are obviously outside Kaplan's intention. To be perfect or to strive toward perfection is to be empowered ethically, as we have seen in our discussion of self-reliance. Perfection implies self-transcendence: "The tradition represents the attempt and hope that man is destined to transform himself into a higher type of being—that is the permanent core of the meaning of the tradition." If Heschel referred to the core religious impulse as the move toward self-transformation, Kaplan spelled out precisely what that self-transformation entailed: "Salvation is unhampered freedom in living and helping others to live a courageous, intelligent, righteous and purposeful life."[12]

Kaplan believed that religion, in helping us to work toward salvation, must "render life assuring or free from fear, interesting or free from boredom and fulfilling or free from frustration." He also reminds us that Spinoza identified God with necessity; thus, salvation as a moral category would be submission to that necessity.[13]

When Kaplan thought about salvation, the notion that most frequently came to mind was "being fully human." Indeed, during a conversation in December 1950 with Ira Eisenstein, Kaplan, in musing about his accomplishments, lists the equivalence of "salvation" and "becoming fully human" as one of his primary achievements.[14] Although liberal

Christian theologians emphasized this equivalence, Jewish thinkers before Kaplan never did.

As we have seen throughout our exploration, Kaplan's persistent emphasis on the individual can be surprising. We are used to associating him with Judaism as a civilization; when we do think about Kaplan, he seems inextricably linked with, and defined by, the group, the community, the people of Israel. These are indeed the pillars of Kaplan's thought, but, in discussing his theology, it is imperative to point out that, for him, salvation, no matter what its meaning, comes down ultimately to the individual. To put it another way, fulfillment, or becoming fully human or living the life abundant, is a state that only the individual can achieve, but he or she can achieve it only in the context of the group. John Dewey, Kaplan's primary mentor, always stressed that the object of the group was to work for the benefit—that is, fulfillment—of each of its members.

Dewey, the pragmatist, and an important influence on Kaplan's thinking, regarded growth as a fundamental objective. Growth figured prominently in Dewey's theory of knowledge and his ethics. For Kaplan, too, growth is a category of all life. He added a religious dimension to Dewey's thought, insisting that God is the power that makes for growth.

Such growth can be seen across human history, as Western societies have moved from the absolute to the democratic. Because our values and our way of life have changed, Kaplan argued, religion—even its most basic elements—must change with it. Growth, therefore, is an essential aspect of religion and salvation:

> The very fact that we have outgrown a conception and method of salvation that served mankind in the past implies that growth itself is a prerequisite to making the most out of life, for growth is the progressive realization of the potentialities latent in us, potentialities physical, mental, social and spiritual. Growth is thus a prerequisite to finding life worthwhile.[15]

Kaplan once analyzed his philosophy in terms of a series of equivalencies: "Salvation = life abundant = security and growth = living up to one's potentialities and enjoying what life has to offer = vitality and expansiveness = enjoyment and achievement."[16] And lest it be thought that Kaplan, in his quest for the meaning of salvation, forgot the social aspect or the many ramifications of peace, at an earlier point he emphasized that "justice calls for the kind of world in which all persons and peoples are permitted to attain the maximum growth to which their capacities entitle them. In such a world there can be no room for either falsehood or aggression."[17] In another statement, we find one of Kaplan's basic formulations of the meaning of salvation: "Man's basic fulfillment consists in being effective both as an end in himself and as a means to the other or not self."[18]

Kaplan teaches that when we think about these idealistic terms, the ideals toward which we strive help us lay out a map that will guide our actions. Without a map and a sense of the goals, we will never understand how to proceed.

In order not to reify God—to make God into an object—we should remember that growth itself in Kaplan's view is the essence of godhood or divinity. Kaplan goes even further and considers growth to be noumenal, part of the universe outside anything we experience. *Becoming* for Kaplan, the process thinker, is a basic aspect of the universe. He explains his position in biological terms:

> Salvation is related to growth as species to genus. It is the special form of growth which pertains to man. The differentia is both qualitative and quantitative. Self-awareness accounts for that differentia.
>
> Accordingly, God is the power that makes for growth. If we divide growth into noumenal and phenomenal aspects . . . we might say God is the noumenal aspect of growth and salvation the phenomenal aspect.[19]

Kaplan, naturally, defined salvation in pragmatic terms. Though his terminology can be bewildering in its variety, at its heart the idea is surprisingly straightforward. To move toward salvation simply means to become more and more effective. Personally, this means that I want to be effective as a man, as a father, as a husband, as a Jew and in general as a human being. The process is applicable for each of us, in all facets of our lives. In each role, we seek effectiveness.

Kaplan believed that being effective is part of the human urge to live. Kaplan here disputed with Aristotle, whose *Metaphysics* opens with the statement, "All men by nature desire to know." Kaplan would say that all men by nature desire to be effective. Our desire to understand connects us to the world, but our desire to be effective leads us toward fulfillment, toward "life abundant," toward the full use of ourselves in every aspect.

With the shift away from mere survival and toward effectiveness, we begin to fulfill our destiny to remake ourselves, to move toward the full realization of our ideas and our potentialities.[20]

In Kaplan's analysis, human effectiveness entails the full use of one's abilities; to put it a different way, effectiveness can be sought through all aspects of life, through everything we do. From this sense of the totality of salvation, we are reminded of how far Kaplan has come from the traditional Judaism. In the early 1950s, Kaplan quotes Carl Jung on the issue of work and play. According to Jung, we all have a drive to new activity and new experience and being effective includes this drive toward the novel, according to Jung [as quoted by Kaplan]: "This urge," Jung states, "functions when the other urges are satisfied and indeed it is perhaps only called into being after this has occurred. Under the concept of activity, we find wanderlust, love of change, restlessness and the play instinct."[21] In other words, the whole goal of life has to do with satisfaction or with what Kaplan called "life abundant."

Consider one of Kaplan's most joyous expressions for salvation: "life abundant." Here again we have one of Kaplan's fundamental explanatory expressions for salvation. He seemed to go through phases in terms of his explanations. For years, salvation meant to become fully human; for a long time, it was growth; and, later in his life, it became "life abundant." Living the life abundant means looking at the self as a totality without denying any aspect of our interests or our goals. In Kaplan's words, "Salvation as life abundant is realized by the human being through vocation, progeny, and the utilization of excess in play, art and worship."[22] It is no surprise that Kaplan seemed heretical to the ultra-Orthodox, among others. His brazen beliefs must have seemed terrifying, a fundamental upset to the traditional hierarchy of proper religious expression. Imagine what the world would look like if every human activity, if everything from our jobs to our children to our play, held the potential for spiritual fulfillment.

Here we have Kaplan's central concept of Judaism as a civilization. As we have discussed, Kaplan sought to embody this concept in a very American institution—the Jewish Center. This "shul with a pool and a school," with a synagogue on its first floor and a basketball court and a swimming pool on the upper floors, insisted on the simultaneous value of worship and celebration, of the mind and the body. In this seven-day synagogue, you could develop the physical after you had finished with the spiritual.[23]

For Kaplan, it is our divine obligation to develop ourselves fully, to find our unique talents and use them in the service of the divine. In this way, we begin to live up to our origins, to the fact that we are created in the image of God. Ralph Waldo Emerson raised the concept of "life abundant" to a transcendent level. In his essay "Spiritual Laws," Emerson discusses the concept of vocation or calling. Although this notion is much more common in Christian thinking than among Jews, since it nourished Kaplan's thinking, it can be helpful here. Emerson said, "Each man has his own vocation. The talent is the call. There is one direction in which all space is open to him." In other words, each of us has a talent or genius where we do things well and it is easy for us. Such talents, when they do not violate the moral law, imply the full use of all our powers and potentialities, thus fulfilling our purpose to embody the divine.

* * *

Kaplan's notion of salvation implies a movable self. We cannot develop fully unless we change, unless we are constantly in a state of becoming. As we have seen, the self—like God—is not an entity but a process. The self is a "nextness," as Henry David Thoreau would put it, or in Emerson's words, it is "the unattained but attainable self" that we seek.[24] Mordecai Kaplan absorbed both of these ideals into his own thinking and insisted throughout his life on the journey as the most important action of all. Particularly as he got older, he stressed the centrality of growth and self-fulfillment. Starting in the 1930s, he grew more and more uncompromising on the centrality of the self, and, while he maintained that the self is only fulfilled within community, the growth of the individual as the goal of religion became foundational to his thinking.

The sense of self as process is sometimes manifested in Kaplan in the most moving way. We do not ordinarily think of Kaplan as a pious person, but it is through process that we glimpse his own particular kind of piety—idiosyncratic and very much of the naturalistic kind. In the selection below, we see the earnestness of a deeply felt, passionate prayer that Kaplan identified with because it expressed his most private yearning. The prayer has to do with the transcendence of the self to a higher level. How many of us in moments of despair have not felt this emotion and would not join him in this prayer? It is also worth noting that Kaplan cannot remain long thinking about himself but moves immediately from the "self" to the soul of the Jewish people:

Friday, January 10, 1930

When I take up a book of prayers like that of Orchard's or McComb's I feel as though I could go on praying for hours and hours *halevai*[25] *yitpallel adam kol ha-yom* . . . [Oh that a man should pray the whole day . . . —*T.B. Berakhot* 21a] doesn't seem in the least absurd though of course extremely uneconomical. Petitions like the following just fit my mood and needs: "Still every passion, rebuke every doubt, strengthen every element of good within me, that nothing may hinder the outflow of Thy life and power. . . . Transform me by the breath of Thy regenerating power. . . . Let me no longer be sad, downcast, despairing, vexed by remorse or depressed by my failures. Take from me my old self. Give me a new self, beautiful, vigorous and joyous."

How much I am in need of this new self is sufficiently attested by the contents of this journal. But it isn't altogether my own limitations that worry me. To a far larger degree it is the apparent hopelessness of the Jewish situation which as something of a spiritual teacher and leader I am supposed and expected to improve. From the standpoint of that situation I feel "like a polar bear on an ice floe that is drifting into warmer zones as he watches with growling impotence the steady dwindling of his home."[26]

As we have seen, Kaplan, the Emersonian, sought the divine by looking within. Since we recognize the divine partially in the moral and ethical ideals that we seek and since the ideals are discovered through our moral imagination, it follows that the divine lodges within our minds and our hearts. Kaplan went so far as to advocate that, when we come across the name of God, *YHWH*, in our prayers we should have in mind the power manifest in the "spiritual aspirations of Israel as making for self fulfillment."[27]

Because of the identification of self and ideals, it occurred to Kaplan that, in a sense, we do not really know where *we* leave off and the divine begins: "To want to know where the self ends and God begins is like wanting to know where the musician ends and the music begins."[28]

We have cited above Kaplan's concept of God and self as correlatives. In a correlative, one concept implies the other, as parent implies the child or the doughnut implies the hole. Kaplan believed that God and self are correlative terms—that one implies the other. "The point which I then made," he wrote in his journal in the fall of 1939, describing a discussion with his rabbinical students, "was that mind, which is the very ground of reality and experience, is experienced as self on the hither end and as God on the end of one's self. This makes self and God correlative terms. The fact is that self has always been a correlative term. What the correlate was, depended upon the cultural and social development of the individual."[29]

To understand the self as correlative, we must begin with the matter of the self and choice. Indeed, choice is the most characteristic activity of the self. We are what we choose, and there is no self outside what we choose. For Dewey and Kaplan, freedom equals intelligent choice, and intelligent choice is identical with moral and practical freedom. When we make the right choices, we transcend our lower selves; only then can the divine become present. In Kaplan's description, "Divinity is not in us but through us": through our choices we create a self that the divine can inhabit.[30]

To put the matter another way, according to Kaplan, we become a self through the ideals that we strive for. Our ideals define us, and, for Kaplan, our ideals also imply the divine. So, in this sense, the self implies God. But there is more, as we have seen in our discussion of the transnatural. For Kaplan, it is not just that we as individuals have purpose and that each of us strives for ideals; rather, this striving is built into the way in which *all* human beings function. Therefore, our ideals must be considered part of human nature and, thus, part of the natural world. The universe supports our sense of purpose. To paraphrase Oliver Wendell Holmes, whose thought Kaplan embraced, "It is enough for us that it [the universe] has intelligence and significance inside of it, for it has produced us."[31] Our ideals are, thus, analogous to self-preservation. All human beings by nature desire to preserve themselves; self-preservation is an innate human instinct. Kaplan insisted that our instincts included not just this base level of survival but also the fulfillment of our highest ideals.

If we accept aspiration as the bedrock of human nature, we can glimpse the way that the self implies God. The obverse of this equation, how God implies the self, is even more complex for the religious naturalist. The tradition tells us that God cannot be God without the Jewish people. Sociologically and religiously speaking, it is always the case that a God is God of some people or of some group. In their day, even the prophets of Israel sensed this. The writer responsible for Second Isaiah proclaims, in God's name, "Before Me no God was formed, and after Me none shall exist—None but me, the Lord; Beside Me, none can grant triumph. I alone foretold the triumph and I brought it to pass; I announced it, And no strange god was among you. So you are My witnesses—declares the Lord—and I am God." This last phrase has been interpreted to mean "if you are my witnesses, then I am your God" (Isaiah 43:10–12). The transition from the beginning of this statement to the end is radical—from a God who seems self-evident to a God whose existence is contingent on the existence of people who will witness Him.

The whole biblical saga has been interpreted as "God in search of man." Abraham Joshua Heschel expresses this thought in many different ways. He ponders the quotation from Psalms 36:10, "In Thy light we shall see light," and concludes, "There is a divine light in every soul, it is dormant and eclipsed by the follies of this world. We must first awaken this light, then the upper light will come upon us. In Thy light which is within us will we see light."[32] In other words, God has created in each person a capacity to relate to the divine.

Perhaps we should remember at this point the old idea that the God of Abraham, Isaac, and Jacob is not the God of the philosophers. The God of the philosophers is omnipotent and omniscient and not in need of anyone or anything. The God in the Bible and the religious tradition is not this self-subsisting, perfect God, but a God who needs man.

The possibility of linking the individual to his ideals and through his ideals to the divine occurred to Kaplan at a very early point. Kaplan understood that individuality could be used in the service of a higher transcendent goal. Courageously, he did not refrain from embracing this new concept, even though he would be labeled heretical, a relativist who advocated religious and spiritual leniency. For him, it was obvious that there were lower kinds of individualism, not worthy of consideration. He simply bypassed these lower forms, which we would call narcissism, on his way to a more transcendent concept of individuality. It is certainly possible that people might get trapped in the more primitive kind of narcissistic behavior; Kaplan understood this danger but did not dismiss the potential of religious individualism simply because people might abuse or misuse it.

In 1903, when he was only twenty-two years old, Kaplan gave a very moving sermon that dealt with individuality. In the previous year, he had been ordained at the Jewish Theological Seminary at the same time that Solomon Schechter arrived in New York to become its president. It was also in the spring of 1903 that Kaplan became a student of Felix Adler, the founder of the Ethical Culture Movement, who was then teaching in the Philosophy Department at Columbia. Kaplan did not yet have a congregation and preached from time to time in synagogues around the city. The sermons were in English, intended for Americanized audiences. The particular sermon that interests us was delivered on the Sabbath before Washington's birthday. In an attempt to connect democratic ideals with faithfulness to Judaism, Kaplan employed the notion of individuality, which, he insisted, was a shared value.

"Thou shall not follow the multitude to do evil" (Exodus 23:2) was the biblical verse Kaplan used to anchor his message. To persuade his audience to become better Jews, he sought recourse in the ideal of individuality. Sometimes it is necessary to follow the multitudes, he reasoned, for without such behavior, we would never form communities. But more often it is necessary to be independent of the behavior of the masses. He says, "You can be better than the multitude, you can be your own guide, you can be your own man or woman, in short you can be yourself."[33]

Kaplan sounds almost Nietzschean here when he declares that to "Be yourself [is] the teaching of religion." The notion that we must remain independent of popular thought is "peculiar to religion and most of all of Judaism."[34] Kaplan declares: "Being independent requires constant practice; with each custom or mode of behavior that is part of the general trend, we must ask ourselves whether it is right to do this particular thing. We must not simply act mindlessly and do as others do." He continues:

> Individuality is a joy to oneself, a duty to humanity and a duty to God . . . So that even if the joy be far distant, even if we have to fight singlehanded, "be yourself." It is a duty we owe to God who gave us a soul and a life which are His and which is our duty to make grow and develop even as we take care of a plant or a bird that some friend has given us. It is God's soul and we have no right to disable it, to weaken it, to deaden it, which we are certainly doing if we blindly follow in the evil ways of our companions.[35]

Kaplan then applies this line of thought to the Jewish people. We have a history of nonconformity, he reminds the congregation, going all the way back to Elijah and the priests of Baal. In our own day, he says, this nonconformity means to be a nation apart and not to follow those who follow the path to assimilation. We must not "surrender ourselves to the false judgments and prejudices of the multitudes, by forgetting that we are Jews and as Jews must live for the object of fighting against evil in any form whatever."

In such instances, we find the clearest contours of Kaplan's mind. For him, the basic American democratic value of individuality is a given. When he looked into the Torah, it was inevitable that he would see democratic values. It was obvious to him that the concept of individualism can and must be used in the service of the redemption of the Jewish people. One of the great opportunities of twentieth-century Jews—our great "potentiality," as he would say—is that we can find salvation in our individual lives, using the strength of the community.

The individual must always be considered within the context of the community. Martin Buber has helped us understand that the self exists only in relation to the other. In our own time, we find the same emphasis on the other in the works of Emmanuel Levinas.[36] Kaplan did not know of Levinas but was certainly familiar with Buber and was influenced by him. Kaplan had read Buber though we are not sure when this began and how thoroughly he immersed himself in Buber's philosophy. We find what might be considered to be traces of Buber's influence in some journal remarks. In a discussion about theological issues with seminary graduates in the early 1950s, the matter of how to approach God came up. Relationship was central to the discussion: "the moment we transcend our own egos and identify ourselves with one other person we are on the way toward God. God is thus the reality experienced as we-consciousness, in the same way as the self or soul is the reality experienced as I- or self-consciousness."[37]

We can only transcend ourselves when we relate to the other, Kaplan maintained. Through association with others, we acquire our individuality; through this association, we exercise it. The realization of the individual and the realization of the community go hand in hand. John Dewey expressed the thought in the 1890s: "In the realization of individuality there is found also the needed realization of some community of persons of which the individual is a member; and, conversely, the agent who duly satisfies the community in which he shares, by that same conduct satisfies himself."[38] For Kaplan, this reciprocal relationship of self and community was fundamental.

For Kaplan, the interplay between the communal and individual (or the public and private) aspects of religion were necessary and continuous. He commented on Alfred North Whitehead's famous statement—that religion is "what the individual does with his solitariness"—and on the relationship between public (or formal, or organized) religion and the solitary religion of the individual in the following terms: "The truth is that public religion is as much a prerequisite to personal religion as conversation is to individual thought. We would hardly suggest doing away with conversation because it is marked by confusion of ideas and inadequate expression. Public religion . . . is the matrix of the most exalted and inspired achievements in individual religion."[39]

The personal is of the essence in the area of religion, yet it can hardly exist without the formal religion of which it is a part. Regardless of the flaws in organized religion, we need it. Kaplan understood that, though the religious experience may begin in solitude, it inevitably moves into the public space. The power of a private thought or experience increases exponentially when it is shared with others.

* * *

Kaplan's emphasis on individualism as the key element in his salvational theology implies a special place in his system for democratic individualism and democratic culture. To put the matter simply, a democratic society is the place where individuals are most likely to achieve fulfillment and, thus, salvation. Democracy, he believed, is friendlier to individualism than any other system.

Yet his total acceptance of democracy was slow in coming. In his younger years, he often regarded democracy as a threat to the integrity of the Jewish community. Like so many Jewish leaders of his era, and even today, he feared that American freedom would encourage Jews to assimilate into American culture. America has always given Jews the freedom not to be Jews. The young Kaplan feared that Jewish culture would become a thing of the past with only a few fanatical holdouts. With the passage of time, however, his feelings about democracy began to change, his understanding deepened, and he came to realize that democracy could be harnessed in the fight for Jewish survival.

Democracy for Kaplan meant far more than majority rule, but rather a whole culture built upon the encouragement of certain values and certain kinds of behavior, which were, in Kaplan's view, basic to an ethical life. Though the list of such values and behaviors is long—indeed, nearly any aspect of life can have a "democratic" component—of primary importance for him was the proper attitude toward authority, the rule of law, and pluralism. Democracy, therefore, was no mere political system; it was a way of life that—if successful—penetrated the inner core of one's being, one's entire consciousness.

The individualism most threatening to Judaism, and religion in general, was the self-indulgent kind; this was not what Kaplan had in mind when he advocated the value of democratic individualism. "Willful individualism," as he sometimes called it, was the great temptation that Jews and all Americans face; it must be transcended. That was the first step, in journeys spiritual or political, individual or societal. But once we move beyond our base urges, the democratic framework holds great possibility. He referred to this "lower" type of individualism in different ways, but the point was always the same. Individualism is a concept that no one supports without qualification. As one political scientist argues, "Democratic individuality is not boundlessly subjectivist or self-seeking individualism." Democratic culture is by its nature pluralistic, but it need not be "infinitely permissive."[40] The advantages here are numerous. Democratic individualism, Kaplan came to believe, can help us achieve both self-fulfillment and also a more just world. Just as important, for his life-long reclamation project, this higher kind of individualism could be used in encouraging Jews to assert the value of their ethnic identity against those who opted for the melting pot of general American culture.

For Kaplan, this particular brand of democratic individualism meant that each of us ought to have the freedom to make a life for ourselves. America's foundational rights—to life, liberty, and the pursuit of happiness—he writes, "can no longer be regarded as a proclamation of laissez-faire and rugged individualism," in other words, an assertive individualism that dismisses the interests of others. At the same time, "That right still entails the duty of society to make the necessary legal provisions for providing every human being with opportunities to make the most of his life and to achieve salvation."[41] Not self-indulgence but self-fulfillment; not concern only for the self, but rather the use of our self-awareness to promote concern for the other. Unless individualism entailed respect for the dignity and individualism of the other—who could be anyone from our neighbor to those people a world apart—Kaplan was certain that it would turn into evil destructiveness.

Sometimes Kaplan explains salvation and individualism as "making the most out of life" or "permitting every human being to attain the maximum of which he is capable." These "opportunities to make the most of his life" exist on a number of different levels where different sets of values operate. If person is to achieve salvation, these values must be fully integrated and function organically. The integration and coordination of the several levels are the primary function of religion. Kaplan spells out the several different levels rather specifically in the following way:

A. The welfare values are safety, health, word [language], play, beauty = the what of life.
B. The rational values are truth and justice = the how of life.
C. The spiritual values are selfhood, humanity, and godhood = the wherefore of life.

In other words, the essential elements that we strive for daily—health, beauty, self-expression—create the content of our lives; but the way we achieve these elements—the "how"—is through methods that are truthful and just. But these first two values remain unfinished without the third. Here we have the goals of the higher values that transcend our immediate individual welfare: of selfhood, or becoming fully human; of humanity, which means assuring that others also have opportunities to become fully human; and of godhood, the awareness that these two are both related to the ultimate realities of the universe.

Kaplan applies the above system to his understanding of history. In feudal times, the matters of the spirit and of safety were paramount; thus, the Catholic Church, along with the warrior and noble classes, wielded the most power. The commercial revolution allowed the other welfare values, beyond mere safety, to achieve more prominence. Eventually, there emerged a class of experts in the law; lawyers and judges then became the chief agents of government, and the rational values gained preeminence. The Communist and Fascist revolutions of the first half of the twentieth century assumed that all spiritual values were merely reflections of welfare or rational values. What Kaplan meant to show by this historical survey was that there has been an imbalance in the different levels of values and that it is the function of religion to keep them all in an organic relationship with one another.[42]

Kaplan came to believe by the middle 1930s that Jewish values and democratic values were identical. Though American democracy has always been supported by rhetoric that was explicitly Christian, he was adamant that the triptych of welfare, rational and spiritual values were equally applicable. Kaplan's supporters praise his political theory as original, while critics have often tarred Kaplanism as privileging Americanism over Judaism. They decry his philosophy as a reduction and falsification of the fundamental values of the Jewish tradition. His penchant for grand statements—and the equally common difficulty he had in fully articulating his complex ideas—did not always help his cause. Indeed, Kaplan once described Judaism as the "religion of democracy," which surely must have caused some Orthodox Jews, already anxious about the creeping influence of America, to cringe.[43]

But his effort to merge Judaism with American democracy is, like much of his thinking, more complex than his supporters and detractors commonly allow. To understand Kaplan's belief that democracy and Judaism support equivalent values, let us consider his understanding of the core message of the Torah. He often wondered which verse he would choose if he had to reduce the whole Torah to one statement. Most of us would likely go with the rabbis and choose some form of "Love thy neighbor as thyself." Kaplan chose rather to go with Zachariah's statement "Not by might nor by power but by my spirit saith the Lord of Hosts" (Zachariah 4:6). He explains the verse and its equivalence with democracy:

> That motto means that the criterion of human good, of that which renders life worthwhile should not be power, bigness, but the extent to which it expresses the spirit of God. Democracy begins with the refusal to bow before might, to

glorify and worship mere force. The only thing that deserves respect, admiration, is that which has in it a spark of the divine spirit and to the extent that it has it. This sense of values has revolutionized human life and converted it from a more powerful and cunning pursuit of sub-human drives to the creation of a world in which other purposes and achievements than those of amassing wealth and wielding rule over others counts as all important. . . .

It is against the deification of power with its consequences in injustice, cruelty and misery that the wrath of all the prophets and sages spends itself.[44]

The above notion of the deification of power—which Kaplan saw as the essence of evil—was written in 1942 and, like his historical perspective on values, is charged by the spread of Fascism and Communism. Beyond fear and rage, the Nazi onslaught also provoked an elaboration of his thinking about power, democracy, and religion. The only way to defeat Hitler, he believed, was in the triumph of democracy. The triumph of democracy meant the defeat of the law of the jungle. For Kaplan, victory could only be achieved with "peace not on any terms or peace on my terms but peace on terms of justice to all."[45] Only the triumph of a global justice, a sense of right conduct applicable to all humankind, could limit unrestrained power and, thus, provide safety for the Jewish people.

To continue the thoughts embodied in Zachariah's statement, appropriate limits on power would lead to a world in which the spirit of God as justice and loving-kindness would be embodied in all institutions and social relationships. As Kaplan explains, "Justice is fidelity to covenants (Israel's loyalty to her God), equality before the law and the distribution of power (by preventing concentration of wealth) with a view to its maximum service. Mercy is the defense of the weak, the helpless and the stranger [and includes] sensitiveness to suffering."[46]

For Kaplan, these philosophical concepts are not only applicable to a general vision of democracy; they are also intimately Jewish. He reminds us that the only way these very idealistic notions can be put into practice is through the commandments. "'The rest is commentary, now go and learn,'" he writes, citing the foundational rabbinic dictum. "This means that the most exalted professions of the good life are bound to remain mere wishful thinking unless translated into Torah. The equivalent is law plus education."[47] Here again, we see Kaplan's insistence on process. It is only through the daily effort at self-fulfillment that we find salvation; it is only through the daily application of justice and mercy that our world becomes whole. In both instances, only process turns ideals into more than just ideas.

For Kaplan, there is thus a paradigm shift in the religious life from God to the salvation of the individual. We see that salvation—the process of self-fulfillment, or becoming fully human—is central to his thinking on the individual, the community, and the national level. We cannot hope to succeed as human beings—we cannot hope to find individual salvation—unless we understand that all people have the right to a life that is complete, that is full, and that we must strive not only for our own rights but for the rights and the dignity of the other. These ideals, Kaplan insisted throughout his life, are the essence not only of democracy and of religion in general, but also of Judaism in particular. One of his great theological innovations was to push the ancient concept of salvation into a very modern frame, to argue that we can find salvation daily, through our individual selves and our community.

NINE

SALVATION EMBODIED:
THE VEHICLE OF *MITZVOT*

Let every prayer we recite, every song we sing, every teaching we listen to set the current of Israel's life coursing through our whole being, challenge us to test the ever living truth of what Israel has learned concerning man's task on earth, and reveal to us the God who always stands at the door of our heart waiting as it were to be admitted. In this spirit let us pray: "May the words of my mouth and the meditations of my heart be acceptable to Thee O God, my strength and my redeemer."

—*Kaplan diaries, October 3, 1942*

One of the primary differences between religion and philosophy is that religion is always embodied, while philosophy is not. For every religion, there is a series of particular behaviors which the religious person should observe. Primary among these are rituals, especially prayers and holidays. In Judaism, we find the *halakhah,* or Jewish law, which concerns every aspect of a person's life. In explaining Kaplan's approach to Judaism and religion in general, we must first show how his concept of salvation is embodied in the ritual or *mitzvah* system of the Jewish people, and especially in prayer. Our consideration of *halakhah* itself will come later.

Kaplan believed that religion must retain its novelty. When it is new, it affects us deeply and involves us totally. Martin Buber famously said that all religions are true at the beginning. Kaplan's notion of reconstruction asks us to employ practices to ensure that our Judaism is always a fresh and exciting experience.

According to Kaplan, the *mitzvah* system must be reinterpreted in terms of modern concepts; it only has lasting value, like any elements of religion, if it can be brought into line with our contemporary understanding of religion. Kaplan's methodology, as we have seen again and again, uses the concept of function as a primary organizing principle. When considering a particular ritual, we must ask ourselves what its function was in its original setting and evaluate whether that concept or ritual can retain that function in the modern world. If that function is no longer possible or no longer useful, we need to decide if that practice should be reinterpreted and, if not, whether the practice should be dropped.

For example, Kaplan believed in doing away with ancient distinctions between priest, Levite, and the great mass of the people of Israel. Eliminating these distinctions would have meant dispensing with the privileged access of descendents of the ancient priestly class (*kohanim*) to honors in the synagogue and to blessing the congregation (*duchanen*). It would also mean dropping the redemption of the first born (*pidyon ha-ben*), which is tied to ancient laws concerning the priests.[1] For Kaplan, such a disturbance would be minor compared to the potential gains. He saw these distinctions as rooted in ancient "racial" distinctions and contradicting the twentieth-century understanding of equality.

Any and all such evaluations were for Kaplan at the heart of the process of reconstruction. Reconstruction is ongoing and is the means by which a religion retains its vital essence, its relevance to the hearts and minds of its followers. In turn, all aspects of *halakhah*, including rituals, prayers, and other *mitzvot*, need to be reevaluated continually. When we consider Kaplan's influence, we need to ask ourselves how closely we follow the tenets of his system, just as he constantly asked how closely he should follow the tenets of traditional Judaism. Those who follow Kaplan more closely label themselves classical Reconstructionists, while others may be more liberal in their interpretation of Kaplan's thought. In the area of prayer, for example, some prayers that were meaningful to Kaplan no longer make sense for a twenty-first-century believer; in turn, Kaplan dropped other prayers that some believe worthy of restoration. As with any internecine struggle, these debates have at moments become particularly contentious among various strains of Reconstructionists. My hope is to remain apart from this partisan bickering and instead try to clarify how Kaplan's concept of salvation might be embodied in our daily lives. In other words, how the *mitzvah* system may be viewed as a concretization of salvation.

For traditional Jews, the Sabbath is the most holy day, outside of Yom Kippur; the weekly day of rest is intended as a "taste of the world to come." For traditionalists, "the world to come" (*Olam Ha-bah*) will have no death, no toil, no food, not even the begetting of children—life would sustain itself, a self-contained entity.[2] In other words, life would return to the way it was in the Garden of Eden when the world was perfect as God had first created it. But Kaplan, as we know, was far less concerned with "the world to come" than he was with what was happening right here, right now. To create a Judaism that referred to *this* world and the possibility of perfection in *this* life, the idea and practice of the Sabbath needed to be reconstructed. If we do not believe "in the world to come," he asked, but strive to live completely within this world, what is the meaning of the Sabbath, and how might we observe it?

Through his discussions of the Sabbath and the other Jewish holidays, Kaplan laid out an explication of his theology and his concept of salvation. The Sabbath has both personal and social aspects. The cessation from work and the holiness we seek on this day are meant to lift the individual and the group out of the day-to-day existence and focus on the ideals of life. Traditional Jews have long talked of the goal of life as the striving for perfection, a concept that appears in Maimonides and many other medieval thinkers, both Jewish and otherwise. But for these thinkers, the goal of perfection was to be achieved only "in the world to come."[3]

As we know, for Kaplan the striving after perfection was synonymous with salvation. But such striving was not in the pursuit of a delayed, next-life gratification; Kaplan's salvation could be found here, now, embedded within one's own community. In *The Meaning of God in Modern Jewish Religion*, published in 1937 and considered by many to be Kaplan's most important work, he identifies the means to salvation with the notion of integration. The pursuit of an integrated personality, though not discussed by other Jewish thinkers, is, in fact, a key element of how we find meaning in the Sabbath. On the Sabbath, above all else, we strive for integration.

He explains integration in terms of need. Humans have different levels of needs: we have our physical needs (which include sustenance, health, diversion, sexuality), our psychosocial needs (love, cooperation, help, influence), and our spiritual needs (selfhood, humanity, godhood, control of aggression).[4] The ideal is to integrate these levels in an organic way so that each has its appropriate place and one type of need does not dominate the others. This notion of personality integration, as Kaplan calls it, is central to his theology. When one level of need dominates in an individual's life, that person will suffer. For example, in the area of physical needs, domination of one need might lead to overeating or hypersexuality; in the psychosocial area, domination of one need might lead to a desire for influence that causes an exploitation of others; in the area of the spiritual, domination could lead to an overemphasis on the development of the self—a devotion to the spiritual at the expense of the physical or a devotion to the ideal of humanity at the expense of one's own people.

The measure of our self-fulfillment—our integration as individuals and as a society—is the extent to which we incorporate valid ideals. Each need-fulfillment represents an ideal, and the ideals are the key to our self-realization.

The Sabbath symbolizes the full integration of our needs. While actual integration is by no means guaranteed on the Sabbath, we are constantly reminded of the goal, and we have an opportunity to experience a taste of such integration. As we step back from the demands of the world, we are not asked to make any of the moral and ethical compromises that are necessary to keep the world going. While such compromises are always the price of making our way in the world, on the Sabbath, we simply *are*; we do not strive, so we do not have to make the compromises. The peace that we experience on the Sabbath is not incompatible with the striving after perfection that characterizes our actions during the rest of the week.

The weekly observance of the Sabbath reminds us of the full gamut of our needs and reminds us of the possibilities for integrating those needs. Indeed, the Sabbath is built around integration. By eating a good meal, resting, and making love to the person we love,[5] we fulfill our basic needs; by being with our family and our community, we fulfill our psychosocial needs. We study and pray, thus fulfilling our spiritual needs, and, perhaps because we are not working and thus more rested, we treat people more decently (ethical needs). The prayers remind us of the work we must do during the week to correct the abuses and viola-tions that we experience and that we perpetrate.[6] Nahman of Bratzlav famously prayed that the spirit of the Sabbath would carry over into the days of the week.

Kaplan's emphasis on integration, however, seems to miss a central element of the holy day: after all, the Sabbath is not only about holiness, but about remembering and celebrating God's creation. Here we need to keep in mind that Kaplan was a process philosopher. As such, the meaning of a concept may be arrived at through considering how it af-fects human experience. The tradition understands the Sabbath as the celebration of the creation of the world and the rest that came to God on the seventh day. For Kaplan, the emphasis is not so much on the events of creation but the process of creativity. Creativity means novelty; because the world was created out of nothing, its creation asserts a vast sense of possibility. As expressed in the Jewish liturgy, God renews the work of creation every day, and so the work of the spirit is constantly to renew ourselves and our world. Kaplan is not a Kabbalist by any stretch of the imagination, but his philosophy has much in common with the Jewish renewal movement, founded by Rabbi Zalman Schachter-Shalomi. Juda-ism has a very specific meaning for members of the renewal movement, and its practice may include Eastern religious elements, yoga, breathing, and all the esoteric concepts of the Zohar. All these are absent from Kap-lan. But Kaplan's notion of creativity certainly encompasses the notion of renewal in a very broad sense. In his words, "there can hardly be any more important function for religion than to keep alive this yearning for self-renewal and to press it into the service of human progress."[7] For Kaplan, the Sabbath gains its symbolic potency as a reminder of the pos-sibility of integration, but our own individual integration only gains its true power, and true meaning, when placed in the service of the wider world.

The Sabbath, thus, reminds us of the ideals that should guide our life. While our goals are not fully realized on the Sabbath, the Sabbath keeps them in the forefront of our consciousness. The weekly practice of the Sabbath, we trust, will help bring us closer to the fulfillment of our ideals.

In this way, Jewish practice serves as an energizer. Our labors on the other days of the week serve as an opportunity to practice the ideal embodied in the Sabbath, the integration of our many needs and ideals. And then the Sabbath allows us to forgo the busyness necessary in daily life, so that we may consider each day's symbolic manifestation of fulfillment and perfection. Kaplan, like many Jewish thinkers, reminded us that when we focus merely on the opportunity for rest and relaxation that the Sabbath provides, we diminish the potential of Sabbath observance. To further the experience of integration, Kaplan encouraged creative activities that may not have been in accordance with all the parameters of traditional *halakhah* but served to enhance the Sabbath experience. For example, Kaplan asserted that as long as the attendance at services is in place, musical performance is acceptable both within and outside the synagogue. Similarly, he encouraged visits to museums on the Sabbath, as they give an opportunity to experience the fullness of human potential.

The sense of personal enhancement at the center of the Sabbath is described in traditional sources as "having an extra soul" or *neshama yeteira*. In this connection, Kaplan mentions Emerson's essay "The Oversoul," in which Emerson states that "our faith comes in moments, our vice is habitual. Yet there is a depth to those brief moments which constrains us to ascribe more reality to them than to all other experiences." The Sabbath may indeed be habitual, but it also partakes of the transcendent moments that Emerson had in mind.[8]

The Sabbath is associated with a number of other key concepts, including the Exodus and the Covenant. The celebration of the Exodus from Egypt symbolized the movement from slavery into freedom. Kaplan devotes an entire chapter to Passover in *The Meaning of God*, in which he forcefully spells out the connection between the Exodus and divinity as the power that makes for liberation.

The Torah and Jewish liturgy make it clear that God gave Israel the Sabbath as a special sign of the Covenant. As Exodus 31:17 states, "The Children of Israel shall keep the Sabbath and it shall be for them an eternal covenant. It is an eternal sign between me and the Children of Israel that in six days the Lord made the heaven and earth and on the seventh day he rested and was refreshed."

The Covenant is, thus, a reminder of God's place in history and of the special relationship between God and Israel. Traditionally, the Covenant between God and Israel obligated the Jewish people to conform to the law of God and binds God to maintain and protect Israel.[9] The principle of the substitution of righteousness for force, according to Kaplan, is the essence of Israel's biblical faith and the center of its covenantal commitment to the divine. In this way, the law of God shall be the guide in all human behavior. In Kaplan's words, "if we regard God as the life of the universe, the power that evokes personality in men and in nations [,] . . . then we have the responsibility to God to contribute creatively to the welfare of the human race."[10]

The Covenant is an expression of the unity of the Jewish people in the service of the divine. Kaplan believed, of course, that salvation could only take place within a community, thus, Jewish survival was fundamental for him on many levels. Jewish unity was more important to him than any other aspect of Jewish existence. He believed that survival would not be possible without a fundamental unity. For Kaplan, the unity was a unity of purpose and goal, not a uniformity of belief.

In a number of different contexts over the last years of his life, Kaplan called for a kind of constitutional convention of the Jewish people in which Jewish unity would be reasserted. He also called for a renewed dedication to the universal unity of all humankind, which for Kaplan was the essence of the biblical notion of godhood and the Covenant. In 1950, Kaplan proposed to the Rabbinical Assembly that a special agency be designated to work toward the reconstitution of the Jewish people. Jewish unity in the service of world unity was Kaplan's passion. However, nothing ever came of this idea, one of Kaplan's many proposals that was never taken up by his disciples or by the movement.[11]

As previously mentioned, Kaplan devotes a considerable amount of space to the High Holidays in *The Meaning of God*. He notes that though these holy days loom large in the life of contemporary Jewry, the Days of Awe (*Yamim Nora'im*) are not given much attention in the Torah. Kaplan believes that these holidays were not solidly established before the time of the Exile.[12]

One of the central concepts of this season is "kingship" or *malkhuyot*. Kaplan explores the root meaning of this metaphor. Proclaiming God as king arises out of the need ancient Israelites felt "of superhuman support and sanction for their wars, their laws and their routine transactions."[13] But God can only be king so long as men obey His law. The proclamation of his sovereignty and power is primary in the Rosh Hashannah liturgy. As the psalmist says, "He cometh to judge the earth. He will judge the world with righteousness and the peoples in His faithfulness" (Psalm 96:13). Implied in the notion of kingship is the assumption that kingship will only be fully established when "all superstition would disappear, righteousness prevail and salvation be universal."

But sovereignty, Kaplan argues, is not merely about following the dictates of a higher power. Sovereignty, he explains, implies that we should be governed in our behavior by the desire to conform to "God's will," which by definition embraces humanity's highest ideals. We must willingly and joyfully submit to the power within that leads us to be decent and righteous. Divinity is, thus, evidenced when we act according to conscience and knowledge of what is right.

In other words, sovereignty does not exist solely in the province of an all-powerful deity but resides within the human spirit, in our conscience, our minds, and our hearts. Sovereignty is not transcendent but immanent. We still must submit ourselves, to be sure, but sovereignty is only fully embodied through the act of our submission. We make sovereignty, and thus the divine, possible. In turn, the submission of our self-interests to our higher ideals is also what makes possible the betterment of the welfare of the whole. We must harmonize what is best for us individually with what is best for the society generally. Human beings are extremely individuated, Kaplan shows us over and over again, yet we are also very dependent on each other.

The reinterpretation of sovereignty that Kaplan advocates is illustrated in a sermon that he gave on the Rosh Hashannah in 1952.[14] He reports on it as follows:

> The sermon today on "The Quest for Universal Peace" was highly successful. There were not two opinions about it. In the introduction I pointed out that of all the holidays in our calendar Rosh Hashannah is the only that is not designated in the liturgy by the same name as in common parlance. In the liturgy it is called *Yom Ha-zikaron* as it is in the Torah where the term Rosh Hashannah is not to be found. Originally the *Yom Ha-zikaron* was celebrated not as marking the beginning of a new year but as the beginning of the seventh month. Seven seemed to connote for our ancestors completion or fulfillment. The fulfillment in question was that of God's power in the world. The term *zikaron* is therefore

not to be understood as "memorial" or "remembrance" but as "proclamation." God is to be proclaimed king by means of the shofar. The *Yom Ha-zikaron* is thus the equivalent of "I am an American day." It means "I am a world-citizen day," "I am a subject of God's Kingdom" day. That's the kind of a notion that delights me and gives propulsive power to the talk that I gave. This is especially the case when I hit upon the notion shortly before I give the talk. If premeditated too far ahead of time it loses its "kick."

Kaplan's statement here is an essentially religious statement. The core meaning of religion is to lift us out of the "tiny tub of ourselves" and make us see our lives *sub speciae aeternitatis,* as Spinoza declared,[15] under the aspect of eternity. Through his reinterpretation of the notion of sovereignty as embodied in Rosh Hashannah, we move toward perfecting ourselves and perfecting our world.

Continuing this potent, two-way relationship with the divine, another of Kaplan's chapters, on *Shemini Azeret,* is titled "God as Felt Presence." *Shemini Azeret,* the last day of the Sukkot festival, is not considered a major holy day, but Kaplan uses this holiday to make a major statement about his theology. The title itself suggests that this is risky territory for him. How can he argue for the "felt presence" of God when his work has reinterpreted the divine to refer to the details of this world and to focus on individual and communal ideals? The notion of "felt presence"— which might be taken as a translation of the mystical presence known as *shekhina*—has a strongly traditional, and unapologetically supernatural feel about it.

Kaplan begins this chapter with the following statement: "God must not merely be held as an idea; He must be felt as a presence, if we want not only to know about God but to know God. 'Taste and see that the Lord is good.' [Psalms 34:9] says the Psalmist."[16] God is not just an idea but a reality. We have discussed the nature of that reality in previous chapters;[17] here Kaplan asks how we might commune with God through the vehicle of prayer.

To Kaplan, Judaism is more than humanism. In his chapter on *Shemini Azeret,* he urges us "not to dissolve the God idea into ethics. . . . Without the actual awareness of His presence, experienced as beatitude and inner illumination, we are likely to be content with the humanistic interpretation of life."

Shemini Azeret is called the Day of Solemn Assembly, and it can be understood as a festival reserved exclusively for communion with God for its own sake. For the many people who have doubted Kaplan's deeply religious nature, this chapter is essential reading; Kaplan states that ethical living would remain cold and would be lacking all dynamic power "without the emotional intuition of an inner harmony between human nature and universal nature."[18] In the Jewish tradition, the spirit or presence of God, also known as the *shekhina,* is particularly associated with public worship. It is not only in the tabernacle of old that the presence dwelt but any time that ten individuals gather for prayer.[19] Understanding the way in which we share in each other's lives gives concrete expression to our commitment to community. In Kaplan's words, "Realizing that others share our needs, our hopes, our fears and our ideals, we no longer feel dependent entirely on our own efforts for our salvation."[20] His comments on *Shemini Azeret* represent again Kaplan's theology of mood.

We desperately want to transcend the confining walls of the ego, and public worship helps us achieve this goal. "The sense of common consecration to ideals inherited from the past and projected into a remote future means that we have in a sense made ourselves immortal."[21] Even more eloquently, Kaplan tells us that the individual "knows his life to be part of a larger life, a wave of an ocean of being. This is first-hand experience of that large life which is God."[22] The feeling of togetherness which one feels in a crowd is the raw material of religion. This sense of belonging can be a very powerful force, for good and for evil alike. If this group force moves us toward the ethical, we are moving toward religion. If it moves toward the mere assertion of the power of the group, then we devolve into fascism and violence.

Kaplan does acknowledge that there are difficulties with emphasizing worship in its public form. While it may crush individuality, Kaplan states that "no individuality is possible except through the medium of association." When public worship does not work, it is the liturgy that is at fault, according to Kaplan. A religious community is a "community of the heart rather than a community of the mind."[23] People are drawn together, above all else, through their shared fears and hopes and yearnings.

Kaplan is alive to the mystery[24] that we experience in public worship. In Kaplan's mind, for those "less cultured," the mystery takes the form of the superhuman. For those "more cultured," "the mystery is the poetic apprehension of the phenomenon as representative and symbolical of the power behind all life and experience."[25] In other words, the universe does not end at the natural. He believes there is more than the empirical. The path to truth is not only through the mind but through the heart and the spirit.

In attempting to articulate the life of the spirit, Kaplan returns to Emerson's concept of the Oversoul. His quotation from Emerson reads as if it could be a commentary on the *Shema* and its meaning: "We live in succession, in division, in parts, in particles. Meantime within man is the soul of the whole; the wise silence; the universal beauty, to which every part and particle is equally related; the eternal one." Kaplan adds the coda: "But Emerson was apparently unaware of the extent to which communion with God is dependent on the social experience of community worship." For Kaplan, the individual is never complete unless he or she is in community.[26]

Prayer is central to the life of any religious community. The nagging question that we face is why prayer is so difficult. For many Jews across the twentieth century and even today, the experience of synagogue prayer is "dull habit," to use the term for ritual coined by William James. In considering Kaplan's early career, it would seem that, if he had his way, he would do away with the synagogue altogether. He never says so explicitly, but, in his discussion about the synagogue versus the community center in *Judaism as a Civilization,* he writes, "The synagogue should not be displaced by, but it should evolve into the *Bet Am,* or Jewish neighborhood center."[27] The *Bet Am* would be the center of the action, as one might say. The *Bet Am* is where one would work and play as a Jew, where education in its best and broadest sense would be a major component of the program. It would foster music, art, and poetry and offer highly developed recreational activities. Those readers who know Manhattan will immediately recognize that the Ninety-Second Street YMHA and the Jewish Community Center are perfect embodiments of Kaplan's ideal. We could say the same of many community centers around the country. Kaplan seems to assume, as early as 1915, that the synagogue has outlived its usefulness and that we need a more "American" type of institution. But it should be noted that Kaplan lived out his life not as the director of a community center but as the rabbi of a synagogue.[28]

When Kaplan writes about prayer, he has in mind public prayer within the synagogue. The recreational and educational elements of the community center remained essential for him, but the traditional venue for prayer did as well. As stated previously, for Kaplan, religion is primarily the expression of the collective consciousness. It arises out of the need of every society to reinforce common goals and ideals or, in Emile Durkheim's phrase, "to strengthen the collective mind."[29] The synagogue was the place where the collective mind was harnessed, where the collective consciousness was cultivated and attuned to the human being's highest purpose.

In considering the place of prayer, we must consider the concept of God. The nature and content of a people's prayers depend on their concept of God. There is an ambiguity in Kaplan's treatment of God, which can be confusing. Most often, he will talk about the belief in God and less often about the concept of God. In dealing with the belief, Kaplan's sociological self considers function as the primary foundation of belief. Kaplan asks how a belief in God works itself into our lived experience. He analyzes how belief in God functions in various instances, but his strongest formulation is that belief in God should help us when we are afflicted and raise us to the highest level of which we are capable.

Here he veers away from the traditional theology of all three Abrahamic religions, which typically invokes a personal God as the object of our prayers. Indeed, most believers accept a supernatural deity whose will they seek to follow and whose mercy they hope to obtain. Because the God of traditional religion is concerned about His creatures, Christian and Jewish and Muslim alike, it is implied that God hears their prayers. Indeed, in times of stress and tragedy, even the most hardened skeptic may want to turn to God in prayer.

Kaplan did not believe in a personal God, and some of his most astute critics have pointed out that this aspect of his theology is the essential weakness in his system. In the early 1970s, his former student Arthur Cohen had a series of conversations with Kaplan, which were eventually published in book form. In a very moving passage, Cohen explains how

Kaplan's system was flawed because it did not account for a personal God to whom one could turn in times of need. Cohen addressed Kaplan with the following words:

> I am terribly concerned, as you can imagine, with the fact that if I am a person, the law of my nature must be not only a law but must be a person as well. That is to say, my argument with you has always been that you make God an idea which is contingent to the requirement of the collective consciousness rather than as I would insist, a reality who exists in transactional relationship with me. The divine-human continuum extends between persons. There is a modus of mutual address in which my aspiration is raised up to a person who hears, cares, is concerned, and in consequence seeks to energize the destiny of the historical.[30]

The answer to Cohen is found below in our exposition of Kaplan's philosophy of prayer. I hope we have made it clear in our discussion above on God that Kaplan did not in any way want to reduce God to an idea. Cohen, in arguing that Kaplan wanted to reduce God to an idea, is giving an incomplete characterization of Kaplan's belief. Cohen here is simplifying Kaplan. Cohen is correct, however, in his lament that Kaplan's theology lacks the emotional comforts of a personal God. Part of the price we must pay in a naturalist system is that there is no one listening to us when we pray.

Eugene Borowitz, the well-known theologian of the Reform movement, goes even further than Cohen in presenting a traditional position diametrically opposed to Kaplan's theology of impersonalism: "An ideal of God that will not let men speak to Him or let Him be of help . . . in meeting the varied experiences of life, is not an idea for the Jews."[31] Borowitz attacks Kaplan for his belief in a finite God and maintains that Kaplan's system is based upon "simple humanism, in which we put our real trust in people and their goodness, a confidence made dubious by the Holocaust and much else in human conduct."[32]

Though Kaplan is comfortable with being called a humanist, his humanism is not the colorless religion that Borowitz seems to assign to him. Nor is it a theology that merely identifies with the focus on the human being's ideal nature. Kaplan had a strong sense, as we have seen again and again, of the numinous and the spiritual.

As we attempt to make sense of Kaplan's strident ideas and the equally strident criticisms of his critics, I would like to add two more voices to the chorus: Emmanuel Levinas is right, I believe, in calling for an "adult religion," and the Christian theologian Dietrich Bonhoeffer is right in demanding that we grow up in terms of our religious understanding. It is, of course, a fundamental comfort to think that there is a "super self" who hears us when we are in pain and who will have mercy on us when we have sinned; but, as far as Kaplan is concerned, such comfort is simply not enough. The individual, personal, attentive God was one stage in the religious development of humankind. In the modern period, when so many do not believe, we must turn to a more naturalist and less anthropomorphic conception of the divine. Kaplan, as we have indicated above, fully understands the myriad functions of the belief in God and, in turn, demands of us that we find a more rational way to fulfill those functions.[33]

Additionally, it should be emphasized that, for Kaplan the pragmatist, the basic issue of religion is less about God and more focused on personal and communal salvation, fulfillment, and a striving toward perfection. The transformation of our lives is at issue for Kaplan, not whether we have faith in God. We all desire to transcend our limited and lower selves, and religion and the belief in God should help us in this quest.

* * *

In Judaism, there are three types of prayers: supplication (*bakasha*), praise (*shevah*), and thanksgiving (*todah*). The first, supplication, is what most people think of when they think of prayer, an expression of one's own entreaties. Yet supplication is also the lowest, most direct kind of prayer, and it flows more from personal desperation in times of need, rather than from the higher place of our rational understanding. Do we really want to believe that the ultimate power of the universe is concerned with our individual life and our petty needs? Incredibly, the answer for millions of people is yes, that God is concerned with the ups and downs of their daily lives. To put it in the most reductive terms, we want God to be our own personal cosmic bellhop.[34]

As we know, Kaplan had little patience for such a limiting, slavish view of God. The alternative, however, is far less clear. Even the most dedicated follower of Kaplan may still at times wonder to whom she is praying. To put it in the popular formulation, do Reconstructionists really address their prayers "to whom it may concern"? If we are careful, however, we will realize that it does not make any sense to talk of Kaplan or the Reconstructionists addressing their prayers to a specific person or entity. For Kaplan, there is no personal God, so prayer is not an address in any sense.

But how does one pray if no one is listening? Though he rarely spelled out a detailed philosophy of prayer, Kaplan gave much thought to the topic, and we can find ways in which he offers insights into the nature of prayer itself. To begin with, Kaplan states that, for him, prayer is a form of thinking or a particular form of consciousness: "To say 'I believe in praying' sounds to me as absurd as to say 'I believe in thinking.' The question whether prayer is effective is only a special form of the question whether thought is effective."[35] To understand prayer, we must become aware of the different kinds of thinking that it involves. The word "thinking" is used here in its widest sense and should not be construed as referring to merely the rational rather than the emotional. It includes all these modes, which together make up the spiritual.

When we pray, we must stand back and look at ourselves from a transcendent vantage point. The Hebrew for praying is *lehitpallel,* which means not to be in a stance of supplication but to judge oneself. To judge oneself, an individual should distance himself from his life. To stand back—to step outside our egotistical selves—is to begin the process of change and transformation. When we stand back, we can more effectively see the whole: the whole of our lives, of our people, of our nation, and of the universe. Experiencing the whole of anything is not a direct experience but one that flows from the imagination. We do not experience the whole; we imagine it. Thus, the imagination is the most important mental capacity used in the quest for the spiritual.

To pray is to call into existence our highest faculties. As Kaplan put it in discussing the matter of creativity,

> The creative principle in human life, especially in the manifestation of intelligence, courage and good will, can best be called into play through that self-conscious act for which there can be no better name than worship. The worth of man derives from the fact that he possesses the creative principle to a far greater degree than any other being. This is the reason for describing him as godlike or as being made in the image of God.[36]

In other words, prayer is the energizing of our higher creative selves. It is a continuous effort to "raise our consciousness," as the women's movement would have it. Prayer is the calling into existence of the image of God that lies within each of us. It is the public statement of our covenant with ourselves and the willingness to commit ourselves to those ideals that we believe should govern our lives.

Public prayer is primarily concerned with the ethical. As Kaplan put it, "Public worship should concern itself mainly with the improvement of character in the individual and in society."[37] In other words, by making us more conscious of our ideals, we hope that prayer will bring us closer to perfection.

From the commitment implied by prayer, we glimpse the vast—but not unbridgeable—gulf between the actual and the potential. Our potential "operates as truth, when, as reason, it elicits from man the knowledge of reality. It operates as goodness, when, as conscience, it elicits love."[38] For Kaplan, the entire personality is active when engaged in prayer: the actual in terms of our reasoning power and the potential in terms of our imaginative power. Through an increased awareness of the forces in the cosmos that help us realize our fullest potential, we move further along on the road to transformation: "We cannot help being aware of our dependence on the process which we identify as God, namely on all that makes for goodness, truth, and beauty in the world, for our success in achieving a mature, effective, and well-adjusted personality, and we naturally articulate that need in prayer."[39]

Though Kaplan frequently became impatient with his congregants when they prayed, he must be viewed as a pious person who found praying very meaningful. Many have noted the fervor with which he prayed (*davened*) when he stood on the pulpit at the Society for the Advancement of Judaism. How is it possible for an individual to call up such passion when he does not believe in a God who is there to hear his prayers? There may be no one listening, but for Kaplan, it is just as meaningful when the act of praying moves him to become aware of the larger universe and his place in it. There are many prayers that do this. A primary prayer in this regard is the Kaddish, where we speak about God and holiness but do not address God. The Kaddish became for Kaplan a primary metaphor for a prayer that helps us situate ourselves in the universe rather than one that addresses a personal God. Kaplan spoke on matter in his diary:

> Once in a while I get into a kind of praying mood. It is usually the result of my coming across some well-formulated modern prayers. It is never the result of my reading the Book of Psalms. The Psalmist's enemies are not my enemies and he shouts so loud about his troubles that I can't make out what they are.... But I would speak of God in the third and not in the second person, Buber to the contrary notwithstanding. I regard the style, of *"Yitgadal ve-yitkadash"* as much more fitting for my conception of God than that of *"Baruch ata adonai."*[40]

* * *

When Kaplan discussed prayer and why praying does not work for most people, he put forward his deep conviction that praying meaningfully was a matter of *nusach* or the language of prayer. Kaplan more than any other thinker maintained that what people believed and what they said in prayer must fit closely together. Alan Miller, who was rabbi of the Society for the Advancement of Judaism in the 1960s and '70s, makes a relevant distinction between prayer as quotation and prayer as affirmation. In other words, while praying, we say a great deal that we do not believe in. At one time in our lives, these prayers might have been meaningful, but they often no longer are. We are merely quoting the ancient sources. But there are some moments where we do believe strongly in what we say—at those times, we are affirming rather than quoting.[41]

We can see Kaplan's insistence, similarly, as the attempt to move as much as possible from quotation to affirmation. That attempt means not just renewing our relationship with the ancient sources but also changing the language of our prayers so that we can believe and affirm what we are saying. If we do this, according to Kaplan's reasoning, our praying will be much more meaningful. There are no shortcuts here, however; meaningful prayer is a long and difficult pursuit.

Toward the end of his life, Rabbi Ira Eisenstein, who was so important in Kaplan's life-long arduous revision of the language of the liturgy, despaired of the whole process. In an interview dated June 25, 1993, Eisenstein explained:

> I've become ... less concerned with the actual language of prayer.... If you change this word and that word it doesn't solve the problem.... I would treat the traditional prayer book as an exercise in reminiscence. We come together

and for a few minutes we put ourselves into the world of our ancestors, the world of our fathers and see how it feels, how it sounds, that's all. And now if you want to pray—there 's a difference between *davenning* and praying, I make that distinction—pray from our own inside, how we feel, what we'd like to say, if we can use some traditional language fine, otherwise make up your own prayers and they can be gender-free, and not supernatural and all the rest of it. But you can't make over a text like that. It was an awful decision that I came to after all these years.[42]

Kaplan himself never seemed to tire of working on the liturgy. He began this strand of his rabbinical work in the 1920s, with the hope of radically changing the prayer book. He continued revising the sacred texts for many years. Throughout, his goal was simple: to bring the liturgy more in line with what he thought Jews actually believe; here we find the clearest expression of his theological radicalism.

Professor Eric Caplan, of McGill University, has written about the specifics of Kaplan's liturgical innovations. His study of Kaplan is certainly the definitive account not only of Kaplan and the liturgy but of the evolution of Reconstructionist prayer. Some of Caplan's analyses follow.

For all of Kaplan's talk of the "power that makes for salvation" and his theology of an impersonal God, Kaplan still uses the traditional expression "Blessed art thou" throughout his prayer books.[43] How is this possible? More than once Kaplan addressed himself directly to the question. In one of his most informative books, *Questions Jews Ask,* he gives the following answer:

Prayer aims at deriving, from the Process that constitutes God, the power that would strengthen the forces and relationships by which we fulfill ourselves as persons. We cannot help being aware of our dependence on the Process which we identify as God, namely on all that makes for goodness, truth and beauty in the world, for our success in achieving a mature, effective and well adjusted personality, and we naturally articulate that need in prayer. But in what terms can we address God? We cannot do so in terms of scientific or philosophical abstractions, like process or energy, any more than we ordinarily use such terms in thinking about ourselves. Nobody would think of saying: Those processes in relation to my body which make for my personality are hungry. One would say quite simply: I am hungry. Similarly one would not address one's neighbor in terms of all the processes which make him the person that he is; one would address him as you. For similar reasons, we address God in prayer as Thou.[44]

Though Kaplan sheds some light here, he has not succeeded in solving the problem. He explains in a provocative and interesting way what the situation of address means to a person who does not believe in a supernatural, personal God. Unfortunately, his attitude in praying is an "as-if" mode of thinking. We know there is no "Thou" to whom we can pray.[45]

Kaplan's explanation seems to be unsatisfactory; the problem of address remains. In her path-breaking liturgical work, by contrast, Marcia Falk begins with the assumption that there is no super-self out there listening to each one of us and that, when we pray, we speak only of the impersonal forces that have an impact on us. Her liturgy, published in 1996, is, thus, very much in line with Kaplan's theology. Falk, for example, translates the *shemah* as "Hear O Israel—The divine abounds everywhere / and dwells in everything; / the many are one." The second paragraph of the *shemah* begins as follows: "Loving life / and its mysterious source / with all our heart / and all our spirit, / and all our senses and strength, we take upon ourselves / and into ourselves / these promises: to care for the earth / and those upon it, / to pursue justice and peace, / to love kindness and compassion. . . ."[46]

The new Reconstructionist prayer book, *Kol Haneshamah*, uses alternate expressions for God throughout the liturgy. For example, the *Shemah* reads as the following: "Listen, Israel: The Eternal is our God, / The Eternal One alone!"[47] Reconstructionists have, thus, obviously moved beyond Kaplan's limitations.

Kaplan was not a poet and was, for all his radicalism, very much tied to tradition. He initiated the process of liturgical revision but, I believe, did not go far enough; fortunately, his revisions have been completed by Marcia Falk and others. Falk solves the problem of address by using expressions more in line with a naturalist theology. If Kaplan had had the courage of his convictions and were a real poet, he would have morphed into Marcia Falk and composed such prayers as the above.[48]

* * *

The publication of the Sabbath prayer book in 1945 was a landmark event for the followers of Mordecai Kaplan and for the rabbis who excommunicated him. Because its publication was followed within a month by

Kaplan's excommunication, the prayer book became a matter of note in the Jewish community. A number of the senior members of the Jewish Theological Seminary faculty, men who had known Kaplan well and who for decades had shared their academic lives with him, attacked him viciously. When, four years earlier, Kaplan had published *The New Haggadah*, the faculty felt similarly outraged, but the members did not go public with their complaints. Indeed, most of them were aware of the changes that Kaplan made in the liturgy as far back as the early 1920s, but as long as his innovations were confined to his congregation, they were able to control their outrage. However, with the appearance of a new prayer book, looking much like the traditional *siddur* and containing a host of changes in the language of ancient prayers, they could not hold themselves back.[49]

The essential changes that Kaplan instituted in his Sabbath prayer book related to the following concepts: the chosen people, the resurrection of the dead, the doctrine of a personal Messiah, the sacrificial cult, the doctrine of retribution, and, most importantly, the doctrine of revelation. Kaplan's senior colleagues strongly criticized him not only for his shameful omissions or alterations but for changing the language of some of the central prayers of the Sabbath service.[50] For example, Kaplan introduced changes in the well-known Friday evening hymn, *Lekha dodi,* and also added at the end of the service the prayer "Thirteen Wants," which he authored in the 1920s, as a substitution for the traditionally used thirteen articles of faith of Maimonides.[51]

Outrage spread far beyond Kaplan's colleagues. As we mentioned, Kaplan's *siddur* was burned by an ultra-Orthodox organization, the *Agudat Ha-rabbanim* of the United States and Canada, in a ceremony at the McAlpin Hotel on June 15, 1945. It was no accident that this group chose the week when *parshat Korach,* the section from the Torah containing the story of the great rebellion against Moses in the desert, was read in synagogue.

A few months later, three senior members of the seminary faculty offered their own reaction to Kaplan's prayer book in a public letter to the somewhat obscure Hebrew periodical *Ha-Do'ar.* Perhaps in choosing an outlet available only to a very limited audience, they were unconsciously muting their attack. They begin their long public diatribe by divorcing themselves absolutely and completely from the public burning of the book in June 1945 and from Kaplan's excommunication.

Though excommunication was one of the most powerful weapons the Jewish community employed during the Middle Ages, the authors explain, it is completely inappropriate in the twentieth century. Rather, they recommend that the Orthodox rabbis should have condemned the prayer book in the strongest possible terms but not excommunicated Kaplan. The rabbis should have focused attention on Kaplan's contempt for the tradition because of his omission of traditional prayers and primary phrases from the prayer book.[52]

In a subsequent volume of *Ha-Do'ar*, Kaplan attempted to answer some of the charges leveled against him. He charged the ultra-Orthodox rabbis with completely disregarding the needs of the contemporary Jewish community. He asked rhetorically, "would they really be satisfied for our nation to remain the single nation that does not recognize the human rights which have been accepted by all cultured nations as the basis for social life? Could they really want us to make peace with the order of a 'state' where it would be forbidden to express religious opinions which are different from the accepted ones?" Kaplan implored the traditionalists to make peace with the fact that we live in the modern world and argued that Judaism will survive only if there is room to make adjustments to that world.[53]

Among the many critics of the prayer book, one of the most interesting was the Canadian Jewish poet A. M. Klein (1909–72). Klein found fault more with the language of the prayer book than the changes themselves. "The true failing of the book," he wrote in 1945, "lies in the fact that its editors approached their work with metaphysics instead of with imagination." Klein ended his review with a rather beautiful thought from the Baal Shem Tov. In Klein's words, "the Baal Shem Tov said that it was immaterial to the Lord whether the Hebrew of His worshippers was syntactically or even phonetically correct for the Lord sat above, and caught the ascending letters of the alphabet and Himself arranged them according to the desire of the heart whence they issued."[54]

The 1945 prayer book begins with a tantalizing introduction, including a section titled "Experiencing the Reality of God." This section is one of the most forthright theological declarations within all the literature associated with Kaplan. The statement, which is surprisingly traditional, begins, "If prayer is to be genuine and not merely a recital of words, the worshipper must believe in God. He must be able to sense the reality of God vividly, as an intense personal experience." The editors explain that, because the modern views of the cosmos and nature have changed, it is inevitable that our views of God would change. Nonetheless, the introduction states clearly, "What we think of as a coherent universe or cosmos is more than nature; it is nature with a soul. That soul is God."

As we know, Kaplan was one of the three editors of the 1945 prayer book. We know his influence was decisive over much of the book and that he authored many of the new prayers; after all, he was the only editor excommunicated as a result of its publication. But with the introduction's unusual theological statement, its authorship becomes highly significant. Is this really Mordecai Kaplan speaking here? The issue is not at all clear. Eric Caplan, scholar of the Kaplan liturgy, writes of a conversation with Rabbi Ira Eisenstein in which Eisenstein states that Milton Steinberg—a leading Conservative rabbi and Kaplan's most outstanding disciple—was the editor of the introduction.[55] On the other hand, Kaplan himself writes in the diary, "I have also rewritten the introduction to the prayer book."[56] He does not say he composed this key theological statement but that he "rewrote it." It may be that Steinberg composed the introduction, which was then reworked by Kaplan. We will never know the truth of the matter.

The introduction speaks of God as the "soul of the universe" but from a naturalistic point of view. This would seem to be Steinberg's phrase. Steinberg stops short of embracing a complete supernaturalism but does go far beyond Kaplan. One of Steinberg's most moving declarations of faith can be found in his book *A Believing Jew*, edited and published posthumously. In the section on God, Steinberg states,

> The entire universe, as I see it, is an outward manifestation of Mind-Energy, or Spirit, or to use the older and better word, of God. God is then the essential Being of all beings, though all beings in their totality do not exhaust Him. It is His reason which expresses itself in the rationality of nature, in the fact that all things behave in conformity with intelligible forms, in the fact, in brief, that the world is cosmos and not chaos. His power moves in the dynamisms of

physical reality. His will is the impulse behind the upsurge of life on this planet. Individualized He is the soul of man whose thought processes are infinitesimal sparks of his infinite power, whose moral aspirations are fragments of His vast purpose, whose yearning to create is but an echo of His cosmic creativity.[57]

Steinberg's eloquent theological declaration is far from Kaplan's naturalism, yet it resonates with the introduction to the prayer book. And it remains telling that, while Kaplan may not have composed the prayer initially, he certainly approved of its content and left in the key phrases. In reconciling the issue of how to address God in the prayer book, the editors of the introduction write,

> As each cell in the body depends for its health and proper functioning upon the whole body, so each of us depends upon God. Were each cell in us capable of being aware of its dependence upon the whole of us, and were it to express that awareness, such expression would, for it, constitute worship.
>
> Each time we hail and glorify the "Thou" in "Blessed be Thou, O Lord, our God, King of the universe," we enter, in however infinitesimal a degree, into communion with the Spirit that maintains the unity of life and directs that unity toward our salvation. Such communion should normally elevate our will to God's will. Our will is to make the most of life; God's will is that we utilize all life's possibilities for our salvation. This is the nearest we can get to translating the belief in God into living experience.[58]

Again, the theistic nature of the introduction leaves room for ambiguity when considering what Kaplan really believed about God. Though Kaplan and Steinberg disagreed on matters of theology, the introduction reveals that Kaplan acceded to Steinberg's view and allowed him to refer to God as "the soul of the universe." This introduction, reworked by Kaplan, goes far beyond the belief in God as the expression of communal and ethical ideals.

As previously stated, Kaplan was not a rigorous philosopher, so theologically, he moved between a nontheistic and a theistic position. Elsewhere in this book, we have proposed the concept of a theology of mood rather than a rigorous and coherent theology. Kaplan was plainly inconsistent, and, while his writings reveal a variety of theological positions, it is clear that he was not completely uncomfortable with a theistic position. God as the "soul of the universe" must have made sense to him. We should, nonetheless, also emphasize again that, whatever his theological position at any given moment, he never accepted the notion of a supernatural God. To put the matter plainly, to speak of God as "the soul of the universe" is still not to speak of a supernatural God, a super-self, who rewards, punishes, and watches over His people.

Perhaps the most controversial change introduced in the Sabbath prayer book has to do with the concept of the chosen people.[59] The notion that "God chose us from among the nations" is found throughout the prayer book. It is a staple of traditional Judaic belief; even today, many Jews take it very seriously. There is evidence that Kaplan dismissed the notion of the chosen people as early as the 1920s. He had made it clear that he could not accept the traditional concept of revelation. If the belief that God revealed Himself to Israel had to be discarded, then so did the belief that God chose Israel from among the nations to be His people and His special concern.[60] More importantly for Kaplan, the context of chosenness changed with the advent of modernity and the belief in democracy. In a traditional premodern world, it was widely believed that the earth was the center of the universe, and for Jews, the tradition preached that the Jewish people were at the center of the human drama. Kaplan felt that the concept of "chosen people" relied on Israel's notion of itself as a distinct and unique people. In a democratic world of many nations and many peoples, a belief in Israel's privileged status was no longer tenable.

Kaplan was fully aware that violence and expulsion were regular features of the Jewish historical experience. The notion of chosenness in the past served an important salvific function and aided in Jewish survival. Though outwardly Jews may have been repeatedly victimized, in their own eyes, they were still God's favorite.[61] This belief, Kaplan insisted, had become outmoded in light of current democratic realities.

In Kaplan's shift away from chosenness, he makes another very important point that goes to the heart of his religious philosophy. For him, the basic truths of religion—the ethical guidelines and the theological pronouncements—are not the possession of one group but belong to all humankind. He writes, "the role of religion in human life is to humanize men by enabling them to transcend the limits of present human nature. It [religion] emphasizes that which differentiates man from the beast; it identifies the divine element in that which man can make out of himself. . . . to the extent that any civilization contributes to this end, it is religious. That is what we mean when we speak of Judaism as a religious civilization."[62] In other words, the ideals and the function of religion are universal. The particular mode of expression within each religion—its "sancta"—to use Kaplan's phrase, is unique to that religion, but the ideology of the moral life and the unity of humankind are the possession of all religions.

We find a similar sentiment expressed by the contemporary philosopher Emmanuel Levinas. In speaking about Israel's particularism and the concept of chosenness, Levinas asserts that Israel's embrace of chosenness "is a particularism that conditions universality, and it is a moral category rather than a historical fact to do with Israel." In other words, because the commandment flowing from chosenness is to carry out the will of God through the obligations to the "other," it applies equally to all people. In this discussion, Levinas cites an interesting Talmudic principle that points toward universality: "The rabbis say: a pagan who knows the Torah is the equal of the High Priest. This indicates the degree to which the notion of Israel can be separated, in the Talmud, from any historical, national, local or racial notion."[63]

Kaplan realized that a theological and emotional substitute for chosenness must be found. Starting in 1948, with the publication of *The Future of the American Jew,* he offered the concept of vocation or "calling." Familiar to us from the realm of Christian thought, this notion implies that each of us has a calling to perform a special kind of service in this world. Kaplan maintains that the notion of a calling is found in Talmudic literature. He cites the following: "A familiar saying in the mouth of the Sages of *Yavneh* was this: 'I (who study Torah) am a creature (of God); my work is in the city, his in the field; I rise early to my work, he rises early to his. Just as he cannot excel in my work, so I cannot excel in his.' Perhaps you will say: I do much and he does little (for the Torah). But we have learned, 'He who offers much and he who offers little are equal, provided that each direct his heart to heaven.'"[64] In other words, we all serve the divine—we all follow the fundamental human "calling"—when we use our capabilities to the fullest.

Kaplan advocated that this concept of vocation be applied to the Jewish people and substituted for the chosen people concept. As such, it would follow that "no nation is chosen, or elected or superior to any other, but every nation should discover its vocation or calling, as a source of religious experience, and as a medium of salvation to those who share its life."[65] I believe Kaplan would agree that our "calling" should reflect not only our particular talents as a people but also our shared experience. Thus, we who have survived the Holocaust should be especially concerned with genocide and ethnic cleansing in any and every circumstance. In a post-Holocaust world, it is our duty as Jews to be ever vigilant for ethnic violence wherever it occurs.[66]

The language Kaplan most frequently substituted for the chosenness formula in the *Sabbath Prayer Book* is found in the Torah blessings, among other places. Instead of reading "who has chosen us from among the nations," Kaplan would have us read "Who has drawn us near to thy service" (*asher kervanu la'avodato*). It is instructive, and indicative of Kaplan's approach to innovation, that the formula that he substitutes here is itself taken from elsewhere in the liturgy.[67]

In the early 1960s, Leslie Brisman, now a professor at Yale University and then a congregant at the Society for the Advancement of Judaism, experienced Kaplan's liturgical innovation first-hand. As he went up to the pulpit for a Torah honor, Brisman approached Kaplan and asked whether he might further change the Torah blessing. Instead of saying "who has drawn us near to thy service," Brisman wanted to say "who has drawn us near *in* thy service" (*asher kervanu ba'avodato*). In Brisman's recollection,

> I can't recall the exact words I used (as I approached the pulpit) but in essence I began by acknowledging that I knew that *kervanu la'avodato* was chosen because the phrase was already in the liturgy. But still, I urged, if the phrase were *kervanu ba'avodato*, we would be more clearly distancing ourselves from the idea of divine agency in privileging the Jews. *Kervanu ba'avodato* would mean that we found we were, as a community, drawn closer together, closer to one another, in our common worship of godliness. This phrase would most clearly indicate that we, not a supernatural God, [were] the agent of our transformation.
>
> I was startled by how quickly and positively Kaplan responded. He looked up at me with those wonderful eyes, kissed me on the lips, and answered "*od lo, od lo*"[not yet, not yet]. He said he hoped I would live to see a Reconstructionism that could substitute *kervanu ba'avodato* ... But the time was not ripe for that, he said; *ba'avodato* would be too radical a break with the past, and the more ambiguous *la'avodato*, especially because it was already liturgical and thus beyond question, was the way to start.[68]

Once again, we see that Kaplan's willingness to change the tradition is vast, but with clear limits.

The other changes that Kaplan introduced to the Sabbath service are no less controversial than the revision of chosenness. As previously stated, Kaplan's purpose embodied the notion of moving from quotation to affirmation. Most Jews today, for example, do not believe in the resurrection of the dead; the traditional prayer book, however, asserts this belief many times. So Kaplan changed the language concerning resurrection. For the words bringing "the dead back to life," the Kaplan prayer book substitutes "God . . . who in love rememberest thy creatures unto life."[69] Throughout his changes, he strove for language that would be meaningful to the contemporary reality of his congregants, words that would not merely be repeated but would be felt. The introduction to the Sabbath Prayerbook makes it clear that all effort was made to retain the phrases that refer to the immortality of the soul.

The language referring to the belief in a personal Messiah is also changed. The introduction voices the hope that, while we may still look forward to a time of universal redemption, this will not come from the advent of a personal Messiah but rather through the "struggles, hopes, vision and will of all good men."

Once again, when Kaplan drops "outmoded" phrases, he always substitutes traditional language that he sees as more fitting. Thus, when lifting up the Torah, we can no longer say, "This is the Torah that Moses set before the people Israel: the Torah given by God through Moses" because we know that the Torah is post-Mosaic and came to be canonized after Moses's time. Kaplan's substitution reaches back into the tradition and makes use of a well-known phrase: "This is the Torah—it is a tree of life to those that grasp it."

The introduction to the Sabbath Prayerbook also asserts the fundamental principle of the unity of the Jewish people. Thus, the primacy of Hebrew is retained in the Kaplan prayer book, adhering to traditional norms. However, the divergences from the traditional liturgy introduced a paradox. After all, how could the unity of the Jewish people be maintained when this prayer book differs in significant ways from all other prayer books? To this day, Reconstructionists who are unfamiliar with the traditional prayer book often note the strangeness of the "traditional" language used in the services at non-Reconstructionist synagogues. Such would particularly be the case with the blessings before reading the Torah, which, in the traditional form, contain the chosenness formula that Reconstructionists have dropped.

In this way, Kaplan's willingness to change the text of the prayers that are supposed to unite the Jewish people introduces a problem. He obviously felt that the loyalty to the land, the culture, and the language of Israel was crucial in unifying Israel as an international people. Yet his own initiatives contradicted this notion.

The problem is illustrated by a controversy involving the *Kol Nidre* prayer from the High Holiday liturgy. In 1925, Kaplan introduced a controversy at the Society for the Advancement of Judaism when he replaced the words of the *Kol Nidre* with those of the 130th Psalm. The recitation of *Kol Nidre* on Yom Kippur eve is perhaps the most moving moment in the Jewish liturgical year. Though the prayer was composed in the ninth century, it remains central to Yom Kippur, the Day of Atonement. Yet the language of the prayer is legalistic and arcane. In 1925, in a rebellious moment, Kaplan decided to eliminate it from the service, without warning his congregation. In place of *Kol Nidre,* he had the cantor chant the very moving words of the 130th Psalm, using the traditional *Kol Nidre* melody. The words of Psalm 130 read in part:

> Out of the depths I call You, O Lord.
> O Lord, listen to my cry:
> Let Your ears be attentive
> To my plea for mercy.
> If you keep accounts of sins, O Lord,
> Lord, who will survive?
>
> Yours is the power to forgive
> So that You may be held in awe.

Though congregants were surprised, they voiced little opposition to the change. Over the years, however, they called for the reinstatement of the traditional *Kol Nidre*. Perhaps they felt strongly about being united with all Jews on this most holy day of the Jewish year.

Kaplan eventually reinstituted the *Kol Nidre,* not because of congregational pressure but as a result of an exchange of letters with a very learned Jew who also happened to be Ira Eisenstein's grandfather.[70]

* * *

It is fitting that we should end with a prayer from Kaplan, a prayer that sounds much more like Heschel than Kaplan. In the darkest days of 1942, he wrote,

> Let every prayer we recite, every song we sing, every teaching we listen to set the current of Israel's life coursing through our whole being, challenge us to test the ever living truth of what Israel has learned concerning man's task on earth, and reveal to us the God who always stands at the door of our heart waiting as it were to be admitted. In this spirit let us pray: "May the words of my mouth and the meditations of my heart be acceptable to Thee O God, my strength and my redeemer."[71]

TEN

MORDECAI THE PIOUS:
KAPLAN AND HESCHEL

The only way in which man is actually delivered from the sinister use
of high principles is through the grace of God. Of that grace he is the
beneficiary so long as he experiences humility or piety, an experience
which means awareness of a transcendent power in the cosmos—a
universal consciousness or spirit—that seeks to direct humanity into
the path of salvation.

—*Mordecai M. Kaplan, October 1943*

The relationship between Kaplan and Abraham Joshua Heschel—like all
of Kaplan's relationships—is complex and multilayered, both personally
and philosophically.[1] Philosophically, there are areas of agreement as
well as contention. It will be extremely fruitful to explore the ideologies
of these two men, as well as their personal relationship, in greater depth.
The dramatic arc of their relationship—from curious correspondents to
hopeful colleagues to jealous rivals—tells us a great deal, not only about
them as individuals but also about the difficulty of bringing the rational
and the mystical into some kind of unity.

As a follower of Kaplan, I come primarily to rescue Heschel, not to
criticize him. One might ask whether Heschel really needs to be rescued, considering how popular he is. There are, however, many who
find it difficult to relate to Heschel's very personalistic concept of God.
In addition, his deep commitment to *halakhah* and to the precise details of Jewish law, creates a distance between himself and many liberal
Jews. Yet there is much in Heschel of great value even to the most liberal
Jew. Comparing Heschel and Kaplan, we find not only common concerns but common formulations. At times, the formulations of Kaplan

and Heschel are so similar that the vast differences between them seem irrelevant. Heschel frequently functions as part of Kaplan's project of reconstruction. Following the title of Kaplan's book *Judaism without Supernaturalism,* we can think of our exploration as "Heschel without Supernaturalism." And from the opposite perspective, looking at Kaplan through the lens of Heschel, we gain a unique perspective on "Mordecai the Pious." Kaplan, whom we can describe as the sociologist-become-theologian, the radical thinker who often sounds more like John Dewey than Dewey himself, was also the child of a very traditional home, a graduate of the Jewish Theological Seminary, and a rabbi who, for all his "heresy," struggled with the same problems as other Conservative rabbis in twentieth-century America.

As we gain access to Kaplan's expansive mind through his voluminous diary, we see that Kaplan was a man of deep spirituality—an idiosyncratic kind of spirituality that we might term "naturalistic piety." This term seems like an oxymoron because it appears to involve a contradiction. But it does not. Kaplan's naturalistic piety is abundantly displayed, not only in his writings and sermons but more importantly in the way he conducted his own religious life.

Yet, for all their similarities, these two giants were very different, and they often stand in stark opposition. I believe that they did not read each other very carefully and, consequently, that their opinions of each other were distorted and not based on solid knowledge.

Kaplan's students at the seminary always felt that he asked the right questions. Not all agreed with what he said, but the issues he raised were relevant and fundamental. A highly respected professor at the seminary recently told me that many of today's seminary students consider Kaplan to be the most important modern Jewish thinker. In disbelief, I asked, "Not Buber? Not Heschel?" "No," he said, "the students seem to understand intuitively that Kaplan faced the most difficult issues head-on. Heschel was not an American and never really related to the unique problems of the Jew in America." He went on to explain that Heschel understood Jewish life in terms of the traditional European model where Jews lived an isolated, ghettoized life. Heschel expounded the tradition with an unmatched poetic grace but did not always address the most pressing questions.

To consider the relationship between Kaplan and Heschel is to address the fundamental religious issues confronting American Jewry. In the present chapter, we shall consider the personal relationship between these two men, and, in addition, we shall learn of Kaplan's appreciation of Heschel's understanding of Jewish piety.

Abraham Joshua Heschel was brought to Cincinnati's Hebrew Union College in 1940 as part of the effort of American Jews to rescue rabbis and scholars from the Nazi onslaught. He was then thirty-three years old. It was no surprise that Heschel, the scion of a great Hasidic dynasty, was not comfortable among the Reform Jews of Cincinnati. They may have respected his scholarship and even envied his piety, but they practiced a fundamentally different kind of Judaism. They did not even have a kosher kitchen at the college. From the beginning, Heschel considered Hebrew Union College only as his port of entry into the United States.[2] He had his eye on the Jewish Theological Seminary from the time he arrived.[3]

While waiting to be admitted to the United States, Heschel lived for nine months in England. Such was his linguistic ability that he mastered the written, if not the spoken, language during that short time. Upon arrival in this country, he immediately set about teaching and writing in English.

In the spring of 1942, the young Heschel wrote a very fine essay in English, "An Analysis of Piety," that appeared in *The Review of Religion*.[4] The essay caught Kaplan's eye. Kaplan had been contemplating the ontological issue of whether the rational and the spiritual were reducible to the psychological or whether these realms of our thought actually exist beyond the bounds of our brains. In other words, are our ideas merely mental constructs, or do they reflect an outside reality? His concern could be formulated in what medieval philosophers called the nominalist-realist problem—are the particulars or the universals the most real? Do our concepts merely name a group of particulars, they asked, or does the name itself stand for something, independent of the particulars? Kaplan was reassured that Heschel shared his belief in the independent reality of the spiritual or, as he put it, "the need of viewing the spiritual dimension apart from the other two dimensions of experience." Kaplan's diary entry reads as follows:

Mon. Apr.6/1942. . . . The following from Abraham Heschel's "An Analysis of Piety" (*The Review of Religion* March /1942) is in line with the need of viewing the spiritual dimension apart from the other two dimensions of experience: "[Ideas are not to be confused with the psychical setting in which they appear. It is fallacious to identify knowledge with the process of its acquisition or realization.][5] The spiritual content is not identical with the act itself, nor are concepts tantamount to functions of the mind. The spiritual objective content is universal, and should be distinguished from subjective psychical function. Piety is an objective spiritual entity. [There have been times in which piety was as common as knowledge of the multiplication table is today.]"

Kaplan's concern with the spiritual comes to us as a surprise. We tend to think of him as concerned primarily with community and with "Judaism as a Civilization." Yet there is another side to Kaplan that centers on the spiritual and its expression. His religiosity is complex, and, as we have seen again and again, it is a mistake to believe that his thought can be reduced to the naturalistic and the pragmatic. Though a thoroughgoing rationalist, Kaplan valued piety. I would go so far as to say, amid the numerous accusations of heresy and blasphemy waged against him, Kaplan was a pious man.

Kaplan had always believed that one way to compose new liturgy was to take an inspiring essay and turn it into a prayer. After reading Heschel's essay on piety, Kaplan composed a prayer based on Heschel's thoughts and a few years later inserted it into his 1945 prayer book. It is a skillful transformation of an essay into a poem. Not a simple translation, nor a cut-and-paste job, the poem illustrates Kaplan's keen spiritual sense and the clarity of his thought.

Below is the first half of Kaplan's poem/prayer. Nearly all the words are taken directly from Heschel's essay, though Kaplan has inserted a few key changes of his own. Readers of Heschel will feel the familiar cadences of his prose:

The Pious Man

What is piety? Is it abandonment of the world?
Is it scrupulous performance of rites or fanatic zeal?
Let us observe the pious man and probe into his soul.
We shall discover in it that which transcends man,
That which surmounts the visible and available,
Steadily preventing him from immersing himself in sensation
    or ambition,

From yielding to passion or slaving for a career.
For him life takes place amid horizons beyond the span of years.

He senses the significant in small things, he is alive
    to the sublime in common acts and simple thoughts.

He feels the warmth of good beneath the thick
    crust of evil.
In the rush of the passing, he notes the stillness of the eternal.
He complies with destiny; He is at peace with life.
Every experience opens to him the door into a temple of
    light, though the vestibule be dark and dismal.
His responsibility to God is the scaffold, on which he stands,
    as daily he builds his life.

He serves family, friend, community and nation. . . .

Engrossed in the beauty of what he worships, he shuns
    self display.
The wise man, master of himself, oft deems himself author
    of his mastery;
Not so the pious who, no less master of himself, administers
    his life in God's name.
The wise man seeks to penetrate into the soul of the sacred;
The pious man ever strives to be penetrated by it.

Faith engages a man's mind;
Piety, his entire life.

Faith precedes piety; Piety is faith's achievement;
Faith desires to meet God; Piety to abide by Him;
Faith strives to know His will; Piety, to do it;
Faith yearns to hear His voice; Piety, to respond to it.

The pious man is never alone, for God is within reach
    of his heart.

In affliction, though desolate for a moment, he need but
    turn his eyes,
To discover his grief outflanked by God's compassion.
Having achieved understanding, he believes;
Having acquired, he gives away;
Having lived, he knows how to die.

He craves not vainly for the endless rotation of his own
    life's wheel.
He is content to merge his being into that of the God he loves.

[September 19, 1942]

The context of this diary entry is revealing. Kaplan had been thinking about an upcoming course on the ideology of the ancient rabbis: he wanted to begin with a presentation of rabbinic thought, with no attempt to modernize. Only after a very honest look at the rabbis as they understood themselves would he move on to a modern reinterpretation. Kaplan was convinced that modern interpretations of rabbinic thought, such as Solomon Schechter's *Some Aspects of Rabbinic Theology* (1909) distorted the rabbis by updating them without acknowledging our modern very different perspective. As Kaplan put it, "It is highly important that the men [that is, rabbinical students] should learn the complete truth about our tradition so they might realize how necessary it is for us to go on creating new values." Without missing a step, the diary moves from the need for a modern reinterpretation to the new poem: "the course would [then] consist in translating the rabbinic concepts into the modern universe of discourse. Last Thursday, I worked out the following adaptation from 'Analysis of Piety' by Abraham Heschel."[6]

Heschel's notion of piety seamlessly became part of Kaplan's reconstruction of rabbinic thought. With Kaplan's absorption and then restatement of Heschel, it is as if Kaplan were recovering a lost part of himself. As one contemporary scholar puts it, "Reading is a form of self-recovery. We discover in our reading portions of our self that would otherwise have remained subliminal." To consider Kaplan's transformation of Heschel's poetic prose into liturgical poetry is to recognize Heschel as a part of Kaplan's subconscious. The Kaplan-Heschel prayer retrieves a lost part of Kaplan. Or to put the thought in Emersonian language, "other men are lenses through which we read our own minds."[7]

Kaplan, a devoted rationalist, was a deeply religious man, though his piety was strikingly idiosyncratic. Some years ago, I asked Rabbi Ira Eisenstein, Kaplan's son-in-law and most devoted disciple, how long Kaplan continued the practice of *davenning* (praying) in the morning. I had evidence from the diary that Kaplan prayed in the morning on a regular basis into the 1920s and even concluded by studying a *blatt gemorah*, a folio page of the Talmud, thus following a custom of the most traditional Jews even as his thinking diverged ever more sharply from that tradition. But I did not know how long this practice continued.

Eisenstein explained that he had not lived with Kaplan, so he did not know Kaplan's daily regimen. But, in the summer of 1942, Eisenstein and his wife, Judith, spent the vacation months at the New Jersey shore with Mordecai and Lena Kaplan. During that time, Eisenstein observed Kaplan praying daily, although sometimes he seemed to use texts other than the *siddur,* the standard prayer book. His other favorites, not surprisingly, were works by Ahad Ha-Am and John Dewey. The contrast is remarkable: a deeply committed Jew who would a few years later be excommunicated, a man donning his *tallis* and *tefillin,* the prayer shawl and phylacteries (ritual boxes wrapped around arm and head) of the most devout Jews, and then *davenning* from Dewey.

Kaplan, in his radicalism, poses difficult questions for us. Is there a "holy" text that we should pray from, in addition to our traditional prayers from the *siddur?* Where is the truth to be found that is worthy of becoming our mantra? Kaplan is the model—not because we automatically adopt the texts that he found holy but because his actions pose a model and raise compelling questions.

From Cincinnati, the young Heschel kept in touch with Kaplan. While enjoying a Sabbath in New York during the winter of 1943, Heschel visited Kaplan. Apparently, they discussed the *siddur* that Kaplan was working on. The more traditional Heschel disliked Kaplan's vision for radical changes. After returning to Cincinnati, Heschel wrote to Kaplan: "It is not so much a matter of *nusach* [the language of the prayers] what we need is a community of *kavannah.*"[8]

In 1945, Heschel left the Hebrew Union College and joined the faculty of the Jewish Theological Seminary in New York. That spring was a time of momentous events. The war in Europe ended, and, a few weeks before Germany's surrender, President Roosevelt died. The American people and the Jewish community in particular grieved deeply over Roosevelt's passing. To mark the event, Kaplan held services at his synagogue, the Society for the Advancement of Judaism, and spoke at the Jewish Theological Seminary. In his journal, he expressed his feelings about the end of the war in Europe:

> *May 8/45* I am entirely unequal to giving anything like adequate expression to the feelings that well up in my heart at the thought that the war in Europe is at an end. If only it were like waking up from a terrible nightmare! But unfortunately

the unspeakable atrocities committed by the insane murderers are too real to
disappear with the break of the dawn, and the living victims of the war are too
much part of our own lives to be forgotten. And worst of all, the chances that
human beings have learned anything from the war that would render them more
human are very slim, indeed.

Kaplan had recommended Heschel to the seminary for a faculty appointment. It became apparent in the spring of 1945 that Heschel would
be hired to teach in the seminary's Teachers Institute and in the rabbinical school.[9] Kaplan was happy about the appointment and hoped that
Heschel would take over his courses in religion at the Teachers Institute.
Kaplan had instituted these courses a few years after the institute was
founded. They subsequently became a vehicle for the exploration of his
philosophy. For many years, Kaplan had been very popular with the students, but, in the early 1940s, he began to feel his popularity was slipping.

Kaplan looked forward to turning over these classes to Heschel.
However, when Heschel began teaching in the fall, Kaplan was rather
quick to judge his young colleague, as the following journal entry about
Heschel's handling of his courses in religion indicates:

> November 9, 1945: I cannot say, however, I am altogether happy with the solu-
> tion. He is all I would want him to be both as a teacher and as an inspirational
> influence for an affirmative Judaism. But he is not of the type to confront prob-
> lems and difficulties. As a romantic-mystic, he shies away from facts and tries to
> build his universe of discourse entirely with values. I visited one of his classes in
> religion. Despite my having asked him to preface his evaluational interpretation
> of Jewish religion with a factual description of its evolution and its different
> stages, he completely disregarded my advice. In the interview I had with him he
> gave as an excuse that [Abraham] Halkin was teaching them the evolution of
> Jewish religion.

Although Kaplan was quick to judge Heschel as a pedagogue, his judgment did have some merit. Kaplan himself never entered class unpre-
pared. Heschel, on the other hand, was an indifferent pedagogue and
probably resented the fact that his primary teaching responsibilities were
in the Teachers Institute rather than the rabbinical school.[10]

Although he cut down on his teaching duties, Kaplan retained his
deanship of the Teachers Institute. Teaching, formerly a compelling challenge, now became an enervating struggle. His message in years past had
seemed profoundly relevant to the children of the immigrants who came

from religious homes, many of them harboring religious doubts and experiencing conflicts between loyalty to their religious heritage and the
temptations of American culture. For them, the concept of "living in
two civilizations" provided a crucial means to bridge what could seem
an impassable gulf. After World War II, Kaplan confronted students who
no longer had the same doubts and ceased to appreciate his message.
What Heschel had to say, by contrast, seemed much more appealing to
the postwar generation.

Thus, a despairing Kaplan wrote on June 3, 1946,

> With virtually no students in any of those classes in any way troubled by reli-
> gious doubts, and with all of them blinded by a passionate chauvinism, I was un-
> able to make any headway in my attempt to reorient them into an evolutionary
> conception of the Jewish religion. That it was which led me to turn my courses
> over to Abraham Heschel. It did not take me long to realize that he would only
> confirm the students in their obscurantist views. Consequently, I saw there was
> no sense to my pretending to be Dean, since there was nothing left for me to do.

In 1946, Kaplan resigned his position as dean of the Teachers Institute.

Kaplan and Heschel remained colleagues and had many casual contacts over the next two decades. The following entry from Kaplan's diary
describes a typical encounter:

> June 19, 1947. As I was entering the Seminary building last Sunday, I met
> Heschel. He invited me to his new study on the sixth floor. There I got to talking
> with him about Hasidim—he is working up a new collection of Hasidic litera-
> ture; the one he had in Europe has been destroyed. He seemed to be intrigued
> by my comment that Hasidism was in a large measure a reaction against the
> new trend toward the westernization of Judaism. I believe that in addition to
> Hasidism's being an attempt to become reconciled to *Galut* [exile], its contribu-
> tion consists in producing unique personalities of a religio-ethical type.

On another typical occasion, the Kaplans paid the Heschels a social
visit. Kaplan recorded the event in his journal: "Last night Lena and
I visited with the Heschels. We spent a pleasant evening. [Gershom]
Scholem who is in this country had promised to come, but didn't show
up." Kaplan also noted that they discussed the relative contributions of
German and Polish Jewry to Jewish scholarship. Heschel contended that
German Jews had contributed more than Polish Jews, whereas Kaplan
emphasized the centrality of Yiddish literature to the contributions of
East European Jewry.

Sometimes these social occasions had a positive impact. After one such occasion when the Heschels came over for dinner, Kaplan noted, "I felt very much relaxed and managed to get rid of some of the 'gremlins' in my attitude toward Heschel. He and I seemed to be reaching out toward each other across a bridgeable chasm."[11]

After he resigned from the Teachers Institute, Kaplan continued teaching in the rabbinical school. As time went on, he sensed more and more students gravitating away from him and toward Heschel. The following journal entry, from January 1950, recorded an incident during class in which Kaplan lost his temper. The candor is remarkable; such class discussions were certainly rare at the seminary:

> Then followed the period on Philosophies of Religion. I noticed that two of the men who had been there before did not come back to this period. . . . I suspect that they absented themselves deliberately because they cannot endure what to them are my heretical views—and [those] are heretical views. I refused to go on with what I had intended to lecture on because I did not want the eight men who were absent to miss the ideas that I had expected to expound. Instead I tried to get from the students some explanation for the state of affairs which permitted the kind of laxity shown by the class. Before I knew it I realized that I had started a hornet's nest. I was stung more than once by some of the remarks of the students. A battle royal broke out between the rightists and the leftists and between all of them and the Seminary as a whole as represented at the moment by myself. For the most part, the scuffle was a restoration of what breaks out in a class ever since I can remember every time I open the lid: complaints that the members of the faculty take no interest in the students, that they are intellectually dishonest, that the Seminary does not permit the teaching of the Pentateuch and that the text courses have no relation to the problems they will encounter in the rabbinate. What was new was the complaint of the "rightist" students that they are disillusioned in not getting the spiritual warmth and inspiration they had expected. They referred particularly to my course. That hurt me keenly, because I know that their attitude is entirely the result of the efforts of men like [Simon] Greenberg, [Moshe] Davis & [Bernard] Mandelbaum to foster a yarmulke and minyan kind of piety in the institution and of Prof. Abraham Heschel to counteract my influence by making my position out to be merely that of sociology and psychology without any understanding of the meaning of religion. He stuffs [students] with the specious kind of buberized hasidism [sic].[12]

As the discussion heated up, Kaplan became more and more angry but could not stop himself. He regretted his outburst during the class and later noted that he "made a complete ass of himself."

The process of alienation between Kaplan and Heschel was a slow one; thus, even while competition between the two was growing and Heschel was gradually replacing Kaplan as a rabbinical student favorite, Kaplan fondly remembered his first contacts with Heschel. He noted, "I recall how Heschel, who is now being built up as an antidote to Kaplan, while he was still in the HUC, would call me and we would engage in long and interesting conversations. All that has ceased especially during the last three years."[13]

Yet, often Kaplan's paranoia seemed to get the best of him. It is well to remember that Heschel was some twenty-six years younger than Kaplan, so the relationship between them may have had shades of an Oedipal struggle. It was obviously easier for Heschel than for Kaplan; it is never comfortable for the "father" who is being outdone by his son. Kaplan's fears of being overtaken even led him to imagine that applicants to the seminary rabbinical school were being asked whether they had read any Kaplan. "Evidently," Kaplan surmised, "that is a way of screening the students who show a tendency toward independent thinking. All this indicates what a stuffy climate of opinion we are living in these days. I wish I knew of some way of clearing the atmosphere of the humbug and self-deceit which prevail in our institutions of higher learning."[14]

History is nothing if not juicy, and with a diary, it is especially so. Kaplan's honesty about himself in the above selection is profoundly moving. He holds back nothing from the diary. His feelings of anger and of being hurt get the best of him. He is riled up in a fit of emotion yet capable of much insight.

In 1953, as their relationship further deteriorated, the two men were scheduled to participate in a series of lectures at the Institute for Social and Religious Studies, dealing with "The Future of Religious Symbolism."[15] Kaplan wanted to be sure that they did not repeat each other. Summarizing the content of their phone conversation, which lasted twenty minutes, Kaplan characterized Heschel's central thrust as "mainly polemical against the Christian tendency to identify God with a visible symbol." Kaplan then characterized Heschel's thinking in general: "his is a metaphysical-mystical mind that spider-like issues from itself verbal filaments which go into the weaving of iridescent webs for catching unwary flies."[16]

This is a brilliant, if somewhat mocking, description of the elusiveness of Heschel's writing. The mystic, when he is as eloquent as Heschel, ensnares us in the beauty of his prose, but concrete meaning often eludes us. Kaplan makes it clear that the reader may be impressed, overwhelmed, and "stuck" all at the same time. Kaplan, ever the rationalist, believed to the depths of his soul that "it was only on the basis of clarified thought that the Jewish people would remake itself."[17] Such faith in the power of rational thinking may be misplaced, but the statement does reveal the depth of Kaplan's rational commitment. The journal here reflects not merely Kaplan's theological and aesthetic judgments but also his fear that Heschel was replacing him and that his own ideas were losing their appeal.

Nearly a decade later, the situation had barely changed. Though Kaplan was less concerned about his declining popularity with students, the gulf between Heschel and Kaplan grew wider:

> I may be reading some prejudice of mine into his attitude toward those who disagree with him [Heschel], but I cannot help feeling that it is one that is insinuatingly patronizing and sanctimonious. As if to say: "Now listen to me, my friend, you really should be pitied for being such a benighted fool. But as a scion of famous Hasidic dynasties, I am endowed with the divine grace that enables me not only to see through you, but to be of help to you, if you only wouldn't be so pigheaded and listen to what I am telling you."[18]

Not surprisingly, we are often most critical in others of the things that we most fear about ourselves. Though Kaplan's family was solid rabbinic stock, although by no means a dynasty, nearly all of this description could be said about Kaplan himself.

To complete this stormy circle, we need to mention some of Heschel's characterizations of Kaplan. Heschel was giving a speech to the Rabbinical Assembly around 1953, for example, and discussed those who are in "error" about what they advocate for Jewish life. He never mentions Kaplan by name, but evidently he has Kaplan in mind when he says, "The strange thing about many of our contemporaries is that their life is nobler than their ideology, that their faith is deep and their views are shallow, that their souls are suppressed and their slogans are proclaimed. We must not cherish a theory because we embraced it forty years ago."[19]

Another example, perhaps more direct but still without the use of Kaplan's name, occurred in 1955. Heschel gave a series of lectures in Denver and, in an interview to the *Intermountain Jewish News,* made the following statement: "The positivist Jew made an effort to eliminate mystery and spirituality from the world. He attempted to reduce the spiritual to the reasonable, the holy to the social, and the unique to the conventional. That is why he has an understanding of social problems but no understanding of Torah, for the sanctity of the Sabbath, for the grandeur of the Day of Atonement." Kaplan records this statement in his journal, and says "All this is definitely intended to be a thrust at 'The Meaning of God in Modern Jewish Religion.'"[20]

Kaplan was indeed frequently criticized for being too rational but, in the following journal entry, gives a very nuanced response to the Heschelian charge:

> April 28, 1956. God as the Power that makes for salvation is not intended to be a "rational" *explanation* of what we mean by "God." It is meant to be a rational method of indicating where to look for that "inexpressible, indescribable and incomprehensible mystery we name God." All that it is intended to do is to have us realize that we should not look for that mystery in the astronomical or physical conception of the universe, nor to miracles which are only myths, but to that striving in man, by which, when he is at his best, he aims to transcend or metamorphose himself. That is the striving for salvation.

Kaplan was undeniably a rationalist, but, as he points out here, he does understand the limits of reason. He knows that reason does not necessarily give us definitive answers but only points us in the right direction. He clearly wants us to know that he values "the mystery" but differs on where we are to look for it. Kaplan, thus, would begin the search for the divine by looking within the soul of the individual.

* * *

By exploring Kaplan and Heschel more deeply, we come to understand the full extent of Kaplan's spirituality. We shall first discuss those aspects of Heschel with which Kaplan might feel completely comfortable, including some statements where Heschel even sounds like Kaplan. Finally and most importantly, we shall delineate the romantic-pious side of Kaplan's nature, where we see the full complexity of this deeply religious man.

To begin with, there are significant areas where Kaplan and Heschel share religious commitments, though Kaplan tends to be much more circumspect than Heschel. For example, Kaplan fully understands that "the power that holds humanity together through the drive to salvation is a power that transcends humanity." But being Kaplan, he then adds, "How far it transcends it we do not care to say right now. But it transcends humanity sufficiently to render the use of the term 'God' perfectly legitimate."[21] Heschel would have no problem in moving from the universal urge to perfection to the God that commands that perfection.

Kaplan the naturalist is fully aware that naturalism is not sufficient for an ethical and theological understanding. Particularly in the case of piety and holiness, Kaplan believed that a naturalistic understanding is insufficient. Naturalism does not negate these values, but neither does it recommend them, according to Kaplan. The secular or nonreligious person might mistakenly think that these values are not worthy of attention. Yet, as Kaplan put it, "It is quite evident that a person in whose character there is no place for holiness, humility, gratitude and faith is ill-equipped to play his part as a full-fledged human being."[22]

Both Heschel and Kaplan share a love for the Jewish people and agonize over the threats posed by modernity. They both understand the ways that science and the secular life undermine religion. They are both devoted to religion as a mode of personal transformation. Heschel particularizes this goal when he says of the Jewish people, "We never suffer as many others do from a fear of roaming about in the emptiness of time."[23] Kaplan would dissent from Heschel's possible focus here on the Jewish people as having a monopoly on collective purpose—if indeed that was Heschel's intent. They both believe that people are plagued by a sense of purposelessness and that the image of "roaming around in the emptiness of time" most powerfully describes too many of us.

We must be careful not to distort Heschel by making him sound like Kaplan. Nonetheless, they are so close so often. Here, for example, is Heschel talking about the Jewish connection to the past in a way that Kaplan would certainly find most comfortable: "Without solidarity with our fathers, the solidarity with our brothers would remain feeble. The vertical unity of Israel is essential to our horizontal unity with *Klal Yisrael*."[24] Kaplan expresses such feelings often but always adds the caveat that we must not be shackled to the past, either, and that *halakhah* tends to do this. Heschel would never go so far as to say the past deserves a vote but not a veto.[25] Kaplan would certainly agree with Heschel's belief that "Our life must remain to some degree intelligible to Isaiah and Rabbi Yochanon Ben Zakkai, to Maimonides and to the Baal Shem."[26]

There is much in Heschel that will appeal to all religious people, and this includes Kaplan. For Heschel, the root of religion is in the wonder and the amazement with which we respond to our experiences, if our sensitivities are sufficiently attuned to the "mystery." A good definition of religion focuses not only on our sense of the ineffable, to use a favorite term of Heschel's, but on how we embody it in our lives. What do we do with our sense of wonder and mystery? How do we incorporate it into our daily routines? How do we open ourselves ethically and morally to the transcendent? As Heschel often said, the end of our isolation begins with a consciousness that something is asked of us.

Both the traditionalist and the liberal have the same problem in revitalizing religion. How can a sense of piety be recaptured? The sense of the holy has been weakened, yet its retrieval is possible—certainly within a traditional mode, as Heschel emphasized, and even in a naturalistic system, as Kaplan insisted for the better part of his life. When Kaplan prays and is thankful for the energy and purpose of the day, he is beginning to live under the aspect of eternity or, as Spinoza would have put it, *sub specie aeternitatis.* "Are we alone in the wilderness of the self," Heschel asks, "alone in this silent universe of which we are a part and in which we feel like strangers? It is such a situation that makes us ready to search for the voice of God in the world of man." Who would not want to join Heschel in the search for the voice of God? It is not an actual voice that we search for, Kaplan insists over and over again; and, despite his penchant for mysticism, Heschel understands that. Furthermore, Heschel's search for "the voice of God" is nearly identical to Kaplan's "quest for salvation." Kaplan's language sounds very different from Heschel's, but it is still the transcendent that they both seek. If Heschel had a deeper understanding of Kaplan's concept of salvation, I do not think he would consider it a violation of his meaning.[27]

Both men ultimately hungered for holiness in a scientific, technological civilization that values the profane. All religious thinkers want to lift us above that base level in which so many of us live our days. Kaplan has an early diary entry that affords us a wonderful example of the way in which piety works in his naturalistic world. In the late 1920s, Kaplan records his feelings about the simple matter of walking home after teaching his class and having lunch. As he sits down to eat, he is very much moved by the larger context of his experience and records it:

> The lunch I found at home was the ideal one for the appetite I had worked up on the walk, oatmeal porridge prepared at my suggestion, asparagus tips on toast in an ocean of cream sauce and a cup of coffee with the dried crumbs of chocolate cake.
>
> As I sat alone and ate the lunch I said to me, "This is a fair quid pro quo." I gave the world three hours of homiletics and the world gave me back a nourishing lunch. I can never cease marveling at the miracle of exchange of goods and services. Not all the Ten Plagues of Egypt with the dividing of the Red Sea thrown into the bargain can compare in marvelousness with the miracle of exchange that makes it possible for me to get asparagus on toast in exchange for the homiletic interpretation of a few paragraphs of *Leviticus Rabba*. It is for this marvel of marvels that I thank God whenever I say grace, and I say it quite often with cap on or without a cap.[28]

Most of us spend our time on the level of "What's for lunch?" We live in a routinized world, absorbed with the banal. Perhaps that is inevitable. We cannot live at the top of the mountain all the time. So how do we move from the level of "What's for lunch?" to a higher consciousness? Kaplan shows us the way. Here is the pious man who lives on the level of the sacred, even when he is just having lunch. It is a kind of mini-revelation that Kaplan is having here; his deeply Jewish soul ties it up with saying the grace after meals.

Kaplan "the pious" writes that he says grace with a cap or without a cap. Perhaps this is his protest against what he once called "*yarmulke* piety." He was protesting the religious upsurge at the seminary in the 1940s that focused more on the wearing of the yarmulke than on its meaning. Perhaps in an ironic way, Kaplan's disgust with "*yarmulke* piety" is analogous to Heschel's attack on the "religious behaviorism" of the orthodox. Heschel often decried the mechanical spirituality of the super-Orthodox and called it "religious behaviorism." From their divergent perspectives, Kaplan and Heschel both condemned the observance of "pious" acts when they remained empty, when they lacked real intention.

There are times when Kaplan writes in the traditional mode to such a degree that what we have is "Kaplan as Heschel." One rather startling example appears in the midst of World War II:

> Oct 12, 1943. The only way in which man is actually delivered from the sinister use of high principles is through the grace of God. Of that grace he is the beneficiary so long as he experiences humility or piety, an experience which means awareness of a transcendent power in the cosmos—a universal consciousness or spirit—that seeks to direct humanity into the path of salvation.
>
> It is not only in the rational interests that man needs God to direct him to such use as will lead to maximum life but also in the spiritual interests. The spiritual interests of personality can be synthesized with those of society only through the exercise of humility. That humility only the awareness of God can evoke from man. That humility is, in fact, itself the awareness of God as pride is the denial of God.

Here we see Kaplan commenting on the ways in which reason, conscience, religion, love, and other high ideals can be used for sinister purposes. Considering the date of the entry, we do not have to ask what he is referring to. He goes on to say that the only way to be delivered from a sinister interpretation of such ideals is by the grace of God. It is only through such grace that one can have a moral understanding of ideals. The denial of God brings one to disaster. Only the awareness of God gives us the humility upon which all spiritual life depends.

The concept of grace is quite traditional, both in Judaism and Christianity. Though I do not think Kaplan had anything supernatural in mind here, his language is startling. He probably means that the "gift" of humility and the awareness of a transcendent power are a necessary element in religious consciousness. But his language and choice of words are traditional and conventionally religious.

While Kaplan is theologically radical, nonetheless, he cannot get the voice of the traditional God out of his head. The God of Abraham, Isaac, and Jacob is still with him. This seeming paradox confuses us, since most of us are unaware of Kaplan's deep ties to the tradition. The result is that we gain, and perpetuate, only a partial understanding of his work, unable to appreciate fully the spiritual bounty that he has to offer us.

In Kaplan's published writing, he often edited out the traditional. If we have read Kaplan at all, we have read those published works, and thus, have a distorted, and often stilted, impression of him. But once we explore Kaplan's journal/diary, we find a much larger world of words. We see his own origins, brought up on the words of his father—an Orthodox *rav*—and on scripture. So it should not surprise us that Kaplan, like Janus, looks back as well as forward. The centuries-old collective consciousness of the Jewish people is part of his psyche. There are layers here from the past, and, like all of us, he carried with him the traces of previous generations. It is a mistake—one that he himself encouraged in his published writings—to see him as living and working in the narrow space of American pragmatism and sociology. Rather, like all great religious thinkers, his ideas range across a wide spectrum, always cognizant of the weight of the past as well as the possibilities of the present day.

It is with prayer that we see most vividly the commonalities and contrasts between Heschel and Kaplan. In the aforementioned Rabbinical Assembly speech in 1953, Heschel launched a frontal attack on Kaplan without ever mentioning his name. The attack was emotional and moving: "Now, if the Torah is nothing but the national literature of the Jewish people, if the mystery of revelation is discarded as superstition, then prayer is hardly more than a soliloquy."[29]

In response to this criticism, we might point out that even a soliloquy, when it rises to a passionate pouring forth of the soul, can have a spiritual dimension and create a sense of the numinous. Furthermore, it is not a small thing to call the Torah the national literature of the Jewish people, thus bestowing tremendous value on it. Heschel, however, clearly lays down the gauntlet when he says that "the issue of prayer is not about prayer; the issue is about God. . . . unless God desires our prayer, how ludicrous is all my praying."

Heschel's protest against naturalist theology is vigorous, almost pained: "If God is a *what*, a power, the sum total of values, how can we pray to it? An 'I' does not pray to an 'it.' Unless, therefore, God is at least as real as my own self; unless I am sure that God has at least as much life as I do, how could I pray?"[30] The language here is highly anthropomorphic and, therefore, suspect for the naturalist. There are many ways to respond, and some come from Heschel himself. For example, he often talks of prayer not as supplication but as a preparation for prayer. Prayer is not always about asking for something.

Are we to be forever chained to the notion of God as the cosmic ear who hears our laments? Who can deny the value of many of our prayers, which have nothing to do with appealing to God in a moment of difficulty? Take the *Mode Ani* prayer that observant Jews are commanded to say upon awakening in the morning. It is a simple expression of gratitude for being "resurrected" from sleep back into life—a call to begin the day with a shout to the universe that we are happy to be alive. It is the joy of feeling our life energy, of just being alive; that is the key. Such a declaration of joy does not require that someone is listening. In the words of the poet Rainer Maria Rilke, "praise emerges as the truest and most creative use of consciousness." And, of course, most of our prayers are hymns of praise and thanksgiving.[31]

Heschel also attacks Kaplan's central emphasis on the social. He criticizes those who would revitalize the synagogue by converting it into a community center. Probably Heschel is referring here to centers that do not also house synagogues as part of their on-going activities. More importantly, he also dismisses prayer as the "identification of the worshipper with the people of Israel."[32] At a later point in the same 1953 speech, Heschel says, seemingly in direct opposition to Kaplan's theology, "the purpose of prayer is not to promote Jewish unity." Although Kaplan never sees social identification as the sole purpose of prayer, he strongly believes that communal bonding is an important consequence of prayer, no matter what our religious philosophy may be. He believes that such social identification would help ensure Jewish survival and promote devotion to social change.

It is interesting that Heschel, in dismissing the social, points to the work of Edward Ames, a Protestant theologian who follows Emile Durkheim and defines religion as embodying and reinforcing the ideals of a given society. As we have already noted, Kaplan assigned readings from Ames to his students at the seminary, though he was unhappy when they concluded that it was sufficient to follow Ames and accept God as the sum of the highest ideals of our society.[33] Kaplan demanded more of them, thus coming closer to Heschel's point of view.

Heschel, in attacking the notion of what he calls the "sociological fallacy," certainly seems to have Kaplan in mind. According to Heschel's version of this kind of thinking, "the individual has no reality except as a carrier of ideas and attitudes that are derived from group existence."[34] If Heschel was thinking about Kaplan here, then this certainly would be a fundamental distortion. Let us put it another way. Whether Heschel is talking about Ames or about Kaplan, neither one would have maintained that the individual is totally constructed from the social reality of his or her environment. In Kaplan's case, with his emphasis on salvation, it is clear that he views religious values as derived from the life of the individual as much as from the group.

Kaplan resented being classified as a sociological thinker rather than as a religious thinker. This sensitivity surfaced during an outburst in class against the irrelevance of rabbinical studies at the seminary that we noted above. Some of the students complained that that they were "disillusioned in not getting the spiritual warmth and inspiration they had expected" and referred specifically to their studies with Kaplan. The attack, as we have seen, hurt him "keenly." Kaplan attributed their feelings to Heschel's encouragement, who wanted to "counteract my influence by making my position out to be merely that of sociology and psychology without any understanding of the meaning of religion."

The truth is always more complex than we imagine. We have seen that, from the beginning, Kaplan had a deep appreciation of Heschel and was instrumental in bringing him to the seminary. Kaplan was aware that the overpowering magnetism of Heschel's mystical piety drew the students away from him. Nevertheless, we, the readers of Kaplan's journal, are drawn to him and his candor as he faced the changing mood of the seminary students. Kaplan was indeed a rationalist, but he valued the mystical side of Judaism as represented by Heschel. Perhaps it was with some hesitancy in the end, but the two giants of twentieth-century American Jewish thought did appreciate each other.

ELEVEN

THE LAW: *HALAKHAH* AND ETHICS

What we need is a regimen of observance which shall be affirmative and inspiring. But if this requirement is to be met, it can be only on the acceptance of diversity in regimens as normal and legitimate. All that is necessary is that they help to intensify the Jewish consciousness of their observers, and help to channel that consciousness in the direction of salvation.

—*Mordecai Kaplan, December 1942*

To understand fully Mordecai Kaplan's approach to *halakhah* and *mitzvot,* we need to examine the seminal influence of growing up in a traditionally rabbinic household in New York City. Rabbi Israel Kaplan, Mordecai's father, had *smikhah* (rabbinical ordination) from some of the most famous European rabbis of his time. The family came to New York in 1889 so that Rabbi Kaplan could serve on the rabbinical court of the newly appointed chief rabbi of New York, Jacob Joseph. Israel Kaplan was a "*musarnik,*" as Mordecai Kaplan used to say, devoted to studying and practicing *Mussar,* which is a part of the Jewish tradition marked by its focus on the perfection of one's moral sensibilities and sense of obligation to others.

The habits and mores of Kaplan's Orthodox upbringing were deeply ingrained in the young man; all aspects of observance, in turn, were defined by the emotional closeness he had with his father. In one of his earliest diaries, a twenty-year-old Mordecai Kaplan recounts how he was alone and feeling depressed in his room when his father invited him to join him in studying Talmud. An hour later, the young Kaplan was revived and refreshed, ready to proceed with his own studying. The family home was strictly kosher, and Mordecai kept kosher throughout his life, albeit in an open way, trusting his hosts when he was away from home.

In emotion and by habit, Kaplan was an Orthodox Jew. However, his personal ritual regimen became more liberal over the years, and his observance was typical of most Conservative rabbis in the early twentieth century. It was marked by a natural assumption of traditional practice, yet favored a liberal sensibility over adherence to strict halakhic parameters. In *A Guide to Jewish Ritual*, a forty-eight-page pamphlet published in 1962, Kaplan outlines specific guidelines for observing the central *mitzvot* of the Sabbath and holidays and the practices of eating *kashrut*.[1] Kaplan's personal observance is not reflected in the strictures he outlines in the pamphlet; for example, while the *Guide* states that one could be less strict about *kashrut* when eating away from home, Kaplan himself did not eat meat outside his home.[2] The *Guide* states that, in any case, even outside the home, "foods consisting wholly, or in the main of biblically forbidden meat or sea food should not be eaten. . . . Communal institutions must adhere to the strictest traditional standards."[3] Kaplan's ambivalent perspective on *kashrut* is revealing. Obviously, he felt more comfortable eating kosher food both in and outside his home. Yet he still needed to question the issue and consider it from a point of view informed by his own philosophic stance regarding *halakhah*. In 1922, he wrote,

> I realize that if it were not for the environment in which I move, I would probably have given it up (*kashrut*) as an obsolete institution. But then again might I not have given up more besides. Is it, after all, so wrong to be the product of one's environment? Of course, if the traditional belief or institution is socially harmful it . . . would be my duty to urge its abrogation. But I cannot see wherein I am less broadminded or universal in my outlook because I have all my life abstained from 'trefa' [nonkosher] food. It seems to me that with the present lack of Jewish content nothing could be more fatal than to break down the principal fence against assimilation.[4]

With respect to the Sabbath, Kaplan lived within walking distance of the Society for the Advancement of Judaism and did not usually ride on the Sabbath. When he was on the lecture circuit, however, he would ride to synagogue, if necessary. Throughout his life, Kaplan continued to observe the Sabbath prohibitions, even though he did take certain liberties, albeit minor ones. For example, he was inconsistent about writing on the Sabbath. He noted in his diary in December 1928 that, while taking a walk on the Sabbath, he had some thoughts about the place of Palestine in Jewish life but out of "regard for the traditional prohibition," he did not write them down. He thought, nonetheless, "what a senseless thing this prohibition of writing on the Sabbath! How much more sensible it would have been to prohibit preaching on the Sabbath."

Kaplan's ambivalence was clearly evident. He often prepared his sermons late on Friday night, and sometimes he wrote down his thoughts. In his journal, he noted that, one Friday evening, his daughter Selma walked into his study while he was working on his sermon. Kaplan hastily put down his pen and started rustling papers, hoping that she had not seen him writing. After she left, he finished working on the sermon and then—in another example of the revelatory nature of his journal—he wrote up the whole incident.[5]

Kaplan considered that what one did in private and what one did in public were separate issues, and he understood that traditional sources supported him on this matter:

> I do not see how it is possible to continue the prohibition of handling the pen on the Sabbath. Although I have abrogated for myself that prohibition I handle the pen only when unseen [*betzniah*, in private]. Incidentally, it is an interesting fact that Jewish ritual law makes a distinction between flagrant and secret transgression, regarding the former as far more reprehensible.[6] I suppose it is the tendency of all law to lay stress on outward conformity rather than on inner consent. Sumptuary laws are not bothered by the moral evil of hypocrisy. On the other hand, insofar as they frankly differentiate between flagrant and secret transgression they remove the very quality of hypocrisy from secret transgression.[7]

The rules laid down by the *Guide* are general in nature but quite precise, and the book's language is not particularly legalistic in tone. Indeed, there are clear indications that Kaplan had little patience with the minutiae of the *halakhah*. However, he believed in maximal observance. Kaplan states that optimum observance of the Sabbath requires "a cessation from all vocational activities" but not from "pursuits engaged in purely as forms of self expression" or those that give one joy. But if one's occupation required work on the Sabbath, the individual should attend synagogue if at all possible and then go to work. Play and creative cultural activities are to be encouraged but only after attending synagogue services. Refraining from turning lights on and off or using a "shabbos goy"—a non-Jew who performs forbidden activities on the Sabbath— add nothing to the spirit of the day, Kaplan insisted; thus, such elements seemed inauthentic to him at best and harmful at worst. The *Guide* recommends that travel be restricted to trips to the synagogue and to activities that would strengthen family ties. It also recommends not smoking in synagogue on the Sabbath but says nothing about smoking in general.[8]

Regarding smoking on the Sabbath, there was an interesting confrontation in the 1930s between Kaplan and his daughters. While on an ocean voyage, one of his daughters lit up a cigarette on the Sabbath, Kaplan admonished his daughter to put out the cigarette because it was the Sabbath. She responded defiantly, "You make your rules, and we make ours."[9]

The *Guide* contains a long section on Sabbath observance in the home that deals with lighting candles and eating a traditional Sabbath meal, including the rituals of *kiddush* (sanctification of the wine), recitation of *hamotzi* (blessing for breaking bread) over the *hallot* (special Sabbath bread), and recitation of *birkat hamazon* (grace after the meal) and *zemirot* (special Sabbath songs). Among Kaplan's innovative suggestions was what he called a Sabbath seder. On Friday night, in addition to the traditional rituals, Kaplan advocated a discussion before the meal of some appropriate traditional text. Kaplan considered the seder a uniquely Jewish educational ritual; he wanted to see it practiced not only on Passover but every Friday night.

While steeped in tradition, Kaplan's thinking was marked by a pragmatic frame of mind; he realized that, in the context of a democratic America, one cannot legislate religious behavior.[10] The *Guide* emphasized the performance of positive acts and did not focus on the prohibitions. Kaplan believed that, while the prohibitions have a religious and moral function, they too often weigh us down and cause us to lose sight of the goal of the ritual.[11]

In addition to laying out specifics in the *Guide*, Kaplan also spelled out general principles that might help the individual or the congregation navigate the uncharted waters of ritual innovation. First and foremost was the principle that, although there should be unity of purpose, there need not be uniformity of practice. As Kaplan stated, "Uniformity of observance is neither attainable nor desirable." In evaluating rituals, Kaplan acknowledged that there was a hierarchy depending on the form and the content of the ritual. Some are valuable in both form and content (public Torah reading, for example), some arbitrary in form but significant in content (*tefillin* or the *mezuzah*), some are arbitrary in form and convey no clear meaning (like certain aspects of the kosher laws). "None of these can be dispensed with as completely lacking in value however."[12] In other words, in Kaplan's evaluation, those rituals that were valuable in form and content were the most precious, and those with an arbitrary form have much less value; but, despite the hierarchy, he recommends caution in dispensing with any *mitzvah*.

Kaplan's greatest area of innovation was with liturgy, as we have explored elsewhere. When most people think of Kaplan and innovation, they think of the institution of the Bat Mitzvah. While Jewish boys had taken part in a Bar Mitzvah ceremony on their thirteenth birthdays for millennia, Kaplan was one of the first rabbis to push for the practice with a girl. The first Bat Mitzvah in the United States was held on March 18, 1922 (18 Adar 5682), at the Society for the Advancement of Judaism. Kaplan always said that he had four reasons for instituting the Bat Mitzvah: his four daughters. Although he had thought about the issue long before, the preparations for his daughter Judith's Bat Mitzvah were minimal. It is quite clear that she already knew the blessings, so there was no need for preparation on that score. Only a week before the event, Kaplan reviewed the blessings and the Torah portion with Judith. Apparently, she read the Torah, while Kaplan himself read the portion from the prophets. The Society for the Advancement of Judaism had just recently been established, and men and women sat separately, following the custom of their previous synagogue, the Jewish Center. Judith noted in a conversation with this author that she felt very nervous and painfully aware that her mother and sisters were sitting far away in the back of the congregation. Despite this difficulty, the Bat Mitzvah was born, and as Judith put it, "no thunder sounded, no lightning struck . . . and the rest of the day was all rejoicing."[13]

Although there was little opposition from the congregation, the institution of the Bat Mitzvah had a strange coda. Once a girl had become

Bat Mitzvah, she was not ordinarily called up to the Torah for an honor again. This situation did not change at the Society for the Advancement of Judaism until the late 1940s or early '50s.[14] It seems evident that the congregation was ready for the Bat Mitzvah ritual but not for women regularly appearing on the pulpit. Kaplan himself was ready for women to read Torah, but since the congregation was not, he chose not to oppose them on this matter.[15] It is clear that social realities lag behind ideology.[16]

It is well known that Kaplan was a fierce advocate of women's rights throughout his life. His concern for women may be traced partially to his biography. Sophie Kaplan Israeli, his sister, older by four years, taught him when they were children. Rabbi Israel Kaplan felt strongly that girls ought to be educated, so he sent his daughter to *heder*, though such a practice was uncommon in the small shtetl where they lived.

The earliest evidence of Kaplan's concern for the place of women in Jewish life surfaced during his tenure as rabbi at the Jewish Center, between 1918 and 1922. The raging issue of the day was whether women ought to have the right to vote.[17] The Center seemed reasonably progressive insofar as women were concerned. Statements in the *Center Journal* strongly supported women's rights. Wherever possible, women were included in important ceremonies. As part of the dedication of the Center, a *Sefer Torah* (Torah scroll) was finished by each congregant inscribing a letter. The *Center Journal* noted proudly that "all the women as well as the men participated in the ceremony."[18]

Nevertheless, the synagogue was Orthodox. Seating was separate though equal, and there was never any question of altering the synagogue ritual to include women.[19] In his preaching, Kaplan went beyond mere support of their right to vote, which he took for granted; he advocated, loudly, for the full emancipation of women, by which he meant full participation in all aspects of public and political life. Yet he did not suggest changing any rituals to include women.

In the fall of 1918, Kaplan used the Torah portion *"Haye Sarah"* to deal with the issue of women's rights. Preparing the way for the sermon, that week's *Center Journal* published the following question: "Shall the emancipation of women be merely a duplication of men?" On Shabbat morning, Kaplan pulled no punches: "Judaism of the *Galuth* [Diaspora] has said nothing and done nothing to lay claim to any share in the Emancipation of women." The major religions, moreover, have always lagged behind when it came to movements for social betterment. He asserted that, by contrast, "the movement to emancipate women was nothing more than the logical extension of democracy."

Since Judaism in general offered little help on the issue of emancipation, Kaplan suggested looking to the Bible for guidance. He pointed out that there are many strong holy women in the Bible, including Deborah, Miriam, and Rebecca, who was the focus of the week's portion. If Genesis presented us with the matriarchs, however, it also presented us with the curses of Eden. The curse on Eve reads, "Toward your husband shall be your lust, yet he will rule over you" (Genesis 3:16). Kaplan maintained that women are destined to be redeemed from this curse in the time to come, just as man will be redeemed from his curse. We know this because Genesis also tells us that God said, "Let us make humankind in our image, according to our likeness! Let *them* have dominion over the fish of the sea." The key word here, Kaplan explained, is *Veyirdu*, which means "they"—both male and female, in other words, shall rule the earth together. He believed that the ideal is that men and women were meant to be equal and the world is a fall from that ideal.

Kaplan looked closely at Rebecca and used her as a model.[20] Women must be emancipated not for power but for service. Just as Rebecca went the extra measure in her service to Abraham's servant in not only giving him water but in also watering his camels, so must women do the same. It is almost as if Kaplan were talking about women in the same terms that Jews in general have always talked about themselves—as the chosen people. The Jews alone are the only ones who have known God, says the prophet; therefore, they have a higher standard to follow. If women were really free, said Kaplan, they would revolutionize the political sphere by lifting it to a higher level. The chosenness of women, he believed, made them more humane: "Women will purify politics, make industry more humane and make justice to the consumer instead of profits to the producer the standard of the market." Emancipation is not aimed at power, "neither her own particular power, nor that masculine power which has contributed so much to the destruction of the world." As Hannah so eloquently put it in her hymn of thanksgiving to God, "for not by strength [power] shall man prevail."[21]

The social context of the time with respect to women is well known and does not need iteration here. A great many of the recent immigrants were poor, and it was perhaps inevitable that some of their daughters would end up as prostitutes.[22] Women were exploited both sexually and economically.

Kaplan was particularly sensitive to the economic plight of women. At one point, he thought of giving up the rabbinate and visited his brother-in-law's silk mill in Paterson, New Jersey. He was visibly disturbed by the conditions that he found and singled out particularly the circumstances of women at work.[23] In *Judaism as a Civilization,* he called for the emancipation of women and noted that "In 1931 there were at least 10,000 cases of Jewish women in Eastern Europe whose husbands had abandoned them, had journeyed to other countries and had remarried. . . . The existence of such a condition contributes largely to the spread of prostitution and white slavery."[24]

For Kaplan, as for any socially aware person, it was obvious that equality for women must begin in the workplace. If women were made to work for substandard wages, they were only a few steps away from slavery. So, when a New York State Court of Appeals declared unconstitutional a law providing minimum wages for women, *The Reconstructionist,* a magazine that Kaplan edited, published a strong protest. There already existed a minimum wage law, which, unbelievable as it seems, did not include women. The 1936 editorial points out that employers sometimes paid their female workers as little as $6 a week.[25]

Interestingly enough, it was not only a sense of justice that led Kaplan to support the minimum wage generally; it was also a matter of religious conviction. In the words of the editorial,

> if Jews are to be serious about reconstructing their life as Jews, about reviving their culture and re-creating their tradition, they must needs make the emancipation from the shackles of economic insecurity and the fretfulness of an uncertain existence an integral part of their efforts at reconstruction.

Here again, we see Kaplan's insistence on an equality of purpose across gender; only when man and woman can live a life without economic insecurity is reconstruction possible.

Though Kaplan dealt with the status of women in Judaism in his 1934 magnum opus, it was in later writings that he developed his ideas more fully. For example, a 1936 article, "The Status of the Jewish Woman," contained a hard-hitting challenge to the traditional place of women in Jewish life.[26] From the opening words, Kaplan was unapologetic in his criticism: "Few aspects of Jewish life and thought so strikingly illustrate the need for transformation and reconstructing as the status of women."[27] His was a clarion call for fundamental change in the status of the Jewish woman. It is not only that she has the right to equality, Kaplan asserted, but that this equality will bring out the "latent powers of creativity which can only benefit her and the Jewish community."

Though the tradition contains positive images of Jewish women, he declared in this 1936 article (in contrast to his sermon of 1918) that women must not be fooled by the citing of examples from the past where women were held in high esteem. From the matriarchs up to the famous women of the rabbinic period, women like Beruriah, wife of Rabbi Meir, and Rachel, wife of Rabbi Akiba, received much praise. They were extolled for their intelligence, their virtue, and their wisdom; but Kaplan cautions us that we should not be misled: "It is, therefore incorrect to infer from the renown enjoyed by the few exceptional women of Israel that the woman was accepted as the equal of man, or that she even enjoyed what we now consider the inalienable rights of a human being."[28]

Kaplan does admit that the lot of Jewish women was often better than her legal status, but cautions that it is a mistake to confuse the lot of women with her status. Often men treat their wives quite decently in traditional society, but this should not "mitigate the evil of inferior status." Whatever her lot, Kaplan tells us, "traditional Jewish law undoubtedly treated her as a lower type of human being than a man."[29] In Jewish law, he points out, women are on the same level as minors, slaves, and people of unsound mind.

Kaplan's call for equality, however, must be seen in the context of developments in Reform Judaism, some of which preceded him by almost a century. At the rabbinic conference of 1846 in Breslau, a commission was appointed to reevaluate the role of women in Jewish life. It recommended that "the rabbinical conference declare women to be entitled to the same religious rights and subject to the same religious duties as man."[30] Mixed seating was introduced by Reform leader Isaac Meyer Wise in 1851, and, in his prayer book *Minhag America,* Wise went so far as to assert that the *minyan,* the quorum necessary for public worship, consisted of "ten adults, males or females."[31]

Kaplan asserted that a woman is made to feel her inequality in a myriad of ways. She is exempt from such *mitzvot* as *tefillin* (phylacteries), *tzitzit* (fringes of the prayer shawl), and *shofar,* the implication being that she should not be exempt and should rather feel obligated in these matters. She is not considered worthy of being included in the *mezuman,* the blessings after a meal (and she should be). A father has no obligation to teach his daughter Torah (and he should). A woman is unqualified to act as a judge or to serve as a witness in a Jewish court (and she should be considered qualified). The implication also, though Kaplan never says as much, is that women should be given the opportunity to serve as rabbis. We remember that, when the Reconstructionist Rabbinical College opened in 1968, Kaplan was a member of the faculty that trained women as well as men to be rabbis.

As we see so often in religious life, social change lags behind ideological change. Liberal rabbis in 1846 called for equality for women, but we do not see women rabbis until late in the twentieth century. Sally Preisand was ordained by Hebrew Union College-Jewish Institute of Religion in 1972, Sandy Eisenberg Sasso by the Reconstructionist Rabbinical College in 1974, and Amy Eilberg by the Jewish Theological Seminary in 1985.[32]

In conclusion, we see that Kaplan was deeply sensitive to the inequalities that women suffered in Jewish life, but that he never carried out the full implications of this position. Kaplan never anticipated all the ways in which the creativity of Jewish women has emerged in our own time, but he certainly would give wholehearted support to the vast array of changes that women have brought into the religious life of the Jewish community: from baby-naming ceremonies to new gender-sensitive liturgy to feminist theology to a feminist interpretation of the Torah and the prophets.

* * *

Let us return to the matter of *halakhah* generally. Kaplan was strongly committed to the belief that the ritual life ought to be maximal but innovative at the same time. This principle of maximalism was quite important to him. In his diary, he wrote in 1945 about how, in contrast to premodern Jews whose lives were suffused with Jewish practice and precepts, our modern lives are more fragmented. When considering how Jews are to modify their approach to ritual, Kaplan argued that *mitzvot* must suffuse one's life in a manner he referred to as "plenitude":

> Being a Jew to the maximum means refraining from the tendency to reduce Judaism to a way of speaking without acting. It has been proposed to meet the danger of Judaism's being crowded out by spiritualizing it into abstract doc-trines about God and man to a point where it no longer occupies any space. But that proposal ends up in spiriting Judaism away altogether. The position taken by the Seminary has always been that Judaism must be lived with all the senses and not only with our common sense. It must be audible and visible, tangible. Hence the maximum of ritual observance is advocated not so much because of authoritative rule as because of the feeling that Jewish life to have saving quality must be abundant and not thin and ghostlike.[33]

We have seen that Kaplan insisted on constantly evaluating all aspects of religious practice to ensure that they continue to contribute to the well-being of the group and the enhancement of the individual. But of equal importance, in this process, was his reliance on the traditional. We see again that, though revolutionary in his ritual innovation, Kaplan never forgot his roots. He was, after all, brought up in a very traditional home. In this regard, he writes, "presumption with regard to Jewish us-age should always be in favor of the traditional procedure."[34]

We are right to wonder whether such a stance is possible: can one be traditional in observance and still be a Reconstructionist? His "favor of the traditional" seems like a contradiction, especially alongside his career-long efforts at change. But here, again, we see his devotion, above all else, to the health and survival of the Jewish people. As hinted at in the chapter's epigraph, Kaplan insisted that we support the diversity of Judaism, which meant that the community needed to accept the tradi-tionalism of those who followed the tenets of time-honored observance, just as it needed to accept the innovations of people like himself. He cer-tainly would have liked the congregation in a small community named *Katef* in Israel that has three seating sections, one for only women, one for only men, and mixed seating in the middle.

Kaplan's devotion to diversity is illustrated by an interchange he had with Rabbi Israel Levinthal (1888–1982), a friend and a well-known

Conservative rabbi who was quite traditional in his observance. In this exchange, Kaplan stressed that, as long as the Reconstructionist movement accepts diversity, one could be traditional in observance and still be a Reconstructionist. Levinthal thought he would have to give up his devotion to *halakhah* if he were to become a Reconstructionist. However, Kaplan made it clear that innovation in *mitzvot* would only be proposed for those who could no longer accept traditional *mitzvot*:

> Here is Israel Levinthal who heads one of the largest Conservative congregations in the country. He himself is, I am sure, in sympathy with the general purpose of the movement to arouse interest in Judaism, though he regards our antinomian approach to ritual practices as entirely unsatisfactory. Why not try to convince him that R. [Reconstructionism] as such is not committed to the antinomian attitude? It merely happens to provide a type of adjustment for those who find themselves incapable of subscribing to the legalistic approach in matters of ritual practice.[35]

Kaplan states the issue clearly and emphatically:

> What we need is a regimen of observance which shall be affirmative and inspiring. But if this requirement is to be met, it can be only on the acceptance of diversity in regimens as normal and legitimate. All that is necessary is that they help to intensify the Jewish consciousness of their observers, and help to channel that consciousness in the direction of salvation.[36]

When it came to ritual innovation, Kaplan believed in change, but he also believed that the freedom that leads to change could be threatening. His ambivalence was marked by a traditional belief that the freedom that comes with modernity weakens as it fragments. The secularization rampant across the twentieth century—the very forces that made Kaplan a lodestar for his students prior to World War II—meant that Jews could just walk away from Judaism with no ill effects on their daily lives. As we have seen, he spent much of his life figuring out ways to prevent his people from just walking away from their faith. But unlike some of his contemporaries, even as he struggled to compete with the forces of modernity, he remained appreciative of all that modernity offered. He was committed to finding a way to forge Jewish unity under conditions of freedom and democracy. While unity of purpose was essential, he believed, the vast diversity of the American landscape in the twentieth century meant that a uniformity of practice and behavior was not possible and not even desirable. Kaplan's understanding of the notion of individual fulfillment and the diversity that it implies is a very American concept, as we have seen, and is at the center of his religious ideology.

While Judaism is more than just Jewish law, Kaplan knew that *halakhah* has always been primary in the religious life of the traditional Jew. Because of Jewish autonomy, *halakhah* had a quasi-legal status, with the community consensus being a powerful force in compelling obedience. As Jews were emancipated across Europe and the Americas in the late eighteenth century and early nineteenth century, every aspect of Jewish life was impacted. The *halakhah* ceased to be law in a strict sense. As Jews became citizens, they were required to obey the law of their respective countries and were denied an independent law of their own. Nonetheless, the authority of the *halakhah* continued, as did the authority of the community consensus that underlies it. Both of these, however, have become progressively weakened in the course of the modern era. The growth of science, both physical and social, undermines religion on many fronts. Religion appears more and more to be the product of people's search for meaning rather than the absolute truth as revealed by God. The domain of the secular continues to grow.

Mordecai Kaplan, needless to say, is very much a product of these developments and his own approach to *halakhah* needs to be examined in the context of the Conservative movement, which begins in the nineteenth century and which seeks to find a proper fit between the truths of tradition and the forces of modern culture. According to Kaplan, the Conservative movement made a number of significant contributions regarding the status of Jewish law. Conservative leaders and thinkers generally assume that the law is binding because it is an expression of the "religious spirit of the Jewish people," but at the same time, regard the law as human and fallible and the product of its historical context.[37] In all denominations, including Conservative Judaism, traditionalists still believe that the *halakhah* has its origin in the Torah, which is assumed to be divine in its origin. Traditionalists support the validity of Jewish law, regardless of its status.

Kaplan's arch theological rival at the Jewish Theological Seminary, Louis Ginzberg, stated the Conservative traditionalist position in the following terms: Rabbis throughout the generations have "always believed that changes [in the *halakhah*] were implicit in the written law. Those who advocated a deliberate break with the past are undermining the very existence of Judaism." Even more bluntly, during the 1927 annual Rabbinical Assembly convention, Ginzberg roared at the gathered rabbis, "to you I say: hands off the Law."[38]

Kaplan, needless to say, dissented from the traditionalist position on many fronts. He advocated a position of greater flexibility and emphasized the damage that could be caused by the rigidity of people like Ginzberg: "The notion of Jewish law as inherently valid, regardless of the extent to which it is ignored by Jews, is not only untrue but harmful."[39] He held that the scripture and all the laws are not the word of God in any meaningful sense. They may, however, yet be considered divine. Kaplan states,

> The alternative to regarding Judaism as a specific tradition which consists of supernaturally revealed laws and teachings is to regard Judaism as a civilization which is both the product and the incentive of the will to live as a people.... the Torah may still be considered as a divine revelation in the sense that it testifies to the reality of God as the spirit that promotes righteousness in the world. To assert this is not, however, to affirm what our fathers meant when they spoke of *Torah min hashamayim* [Torah from Heaven]. It affirms that the Torah reveals God, not that God revealed the Torah.[40]

If the *mitzvot* do not come from God, are they still commands that must be obeyed? Why should we obey them if they are not the commands of God? The secularist might say that we should dispense with them altogether. This would be fatal for Judaism and for the Jewish people. As Kaplan states, "to resort to the secularist solution of abolishing the *mitzvot* altogether is to perform a surgical operation that might kill the patient."[41]

A more reasonable solution to the problem of *mitzvot* would be to consider them as customs issuing from the spirit of the Jewish people. The *mitzvot* and the *halakhah* are relevant to our spiritual needs because they are the product of our people's search for meaning over the last three millennia: "This concept places the basis of Jewish unity not in an authoritative traditional creed or code but in the common purpose of Jews to raise the moral and spiritual level of their group life."[42] Kaplan believed that there is only one standard by which to judge the *mitzvot*:

"they are divine only to the extent that they actually do express principles which help men to live well."[43]

In his classic work *Judaism as a Civilization,* Kaplan proposed that we use the Hebrew word *minhagim* (customs) instead of *mitzvot* (commands) or *halakhah* (law). The term *minhag* refers to a ritual practice for which there is no basis in the authoritative writings. This ritual practice is, thus, less imperative than the obligatory commandments. Rather, they are folkways, customs that accrue their power over generations of observance. Kaplan explains, "If we were henceforth to designate 'all commandments pertaining to the relations between man and God' as *minhagim* or folkways . . . we would convey the thought that they should not be dealt with in a legalistic spirit, a spirit which gives rise to quibbling and pettifogging. They should be dealt with as the very stuff of Jewish life, which should be experienced with spontaneity and joy."[44]

Kaplan's position can be explained as follows. Law must always deal with specifics. We need only think of any contract or agreement to see how the force of the law is in the details. The classical formulations of Jewish law in the Talmud and its commentaries most frequently ask questions of quantity. In dealing with *kashrut,* for example, the question is how long one should wait after eating meat before one can eat milk or how much milk one must drink for the drink to make a person "dairy."[45] Regarding the Sabbath, the question is how far one may walk before the day ceases to be a day of rest. Traditional Jewish texts can seem, especially to the modern eye, unhealthy, obsessed with the questions of "how much," "how long," etc. These matters of degree can seem far from the life of the spirit. Throughout the Kaplanian corpus, over and over again, we find that he had little patience with the minutiae of the *halakhah*—with the quantities and the degrees of observance. Neither in *A Guide to Jewish Ritual* nor in his personal life is there a deliberate focus on the details of the law. Even though he had been imbued with the minutiae of the law from an early age, his teachings deliberately concentrate on the essence of the *mitzvot,* rather than the intricacies of their practice.[46]

It is important to stress that, in referring to a *mitzvah* as a custom or *minhag,* Kaplan is in no way advocating the abandonment of a sense of obligation or uniformity in religious life. Kaplan knew that customs gain their strength precisely because they are the expression of the collective will and always carry the force of generations of community habit. Customs or habits are deeply bred into our psyches from a young age. Customs are, thus, a means to strengthen Jewish life. Kaplan preached not the commands of God but the educative value of habit: raise your children with Jewish habits, he would say, and you will not have to be concerned with the issue of whether a particular ritual is commanded by God.

As a Conservative rabbi—revolutionary in thought and traditional in background—Kaplan does assume that the committed Jew must have a sound sense of obligation. Referring to the *halakhah* as custom rather than law, as Kaplan did early on in his career, does not mean that each of us can do anything we want. According to Justice Oliver Wendell Holmes, whom Kaplan greatly admired, duty was more fundamental than rights in the common law. Holmes believed that duty flows from the notion of obligation to care. In other words, if you own a house you have the obligation to care for it. The whole area of torts or damages flows from this obligation of concern. If you are a parent, you have an obligation to care for your child. Such obligations are not legislated but are part of the common law, the tradition of public practice in Western Europe for centuries. In the same way, being a Jew carries with it certain long-held obligations, habits, and concerns. Judaism has always carried with it the habit of life-long learning, for example, and being a Jew makes little sense without this commitment. This habit has been strong among the Jewish people for centuries, and we still feel the obligation, even though the command does not come from God.

There has recently been a resurgence of interest among some Reconstructionists in the matter of obligation in Kaplan.[47] Going back to *A Guide to Jewish Ritual,* if we read it carefully, we see that Kaplan expected a minimum of commitment to the *mitzvot* of the Sabbath and *kashrut.* Although there is great latitude in the way one might spend the Sabbath, he made it absolutely clear that synagogue observance must be a feature of the Sabbath if it is to remain the Sabbath. As we noted above, Kaplan felt there was little reason to dispense with *kashrut* in the home, though there was greater freedom when one was not at home. Still, he was insistent that one should not eat nonkosher food under any conditions.

Nonetheless, he was tolerant and accepting of those who dissented from his own commitments and the minimum that he prescribed. As we have emphasized over and over again, Kaplan was a pluralist. For him, there were many different ways of being Jewish, all of which were legitimate. He was also aware that Reconstructionism's innovative approach to ritual excluded some Jews from his community. Critics often failed to grasp his essential pluralism, which allowed many different levels of ritual observance, including the traditional.

In the wake of Kaplan's lifetime, we have witnessed myriad innovations in the Reconstructionist and Renewal movements that have influenced even the more staid Conservative congregations. We need to adopt what works, and that means there will be many different kinds of ritual practice. On the other hand, those who are more traditional might ask whether Reconstructionism emancipated its followers from *mitzvot* altogether. Kaplan would certainly stand firmly with those who hoped that a meaningful if innovative, maximal ritual system would be the norm even among the most liberal Jews. With respect to innovation, one could always cross over the line, but there was significant latitude.

Looking at the varieties of Judaism today, I do not think Kaplan would have preferred many of the new customs of the Renewal movement, with its meditations and dancing and its devotion to the structure of the classical Jewish Kabbalah. But, at the same time, I think he would support the notion of "renewal." Because of my research on Kaplan, people often ask how Kaplan would have felt about one or another specific contemporary innovation. Kaplan, of course, tells us nothing in his writings about contemporary issues such as gay and lesbian rights, but we must imagine him responding not as he was, having been born in the late Victorian era, but as if he were a young man today, yet still holding his general approach and his fundamental values. Just as he did in his own lifetime, he would today embrace the unity of the Jewish people without being afraid of change and innovation. Let's remember what he did with the prayer book and the concept of chosenness. I have no doubts that he would see the current direction of the Reconstructionist and even the Renewal movements as reasonable alternatives for strengthening the civilization of the Jewish people. Though some may be more comfortable with "classic Reconstructionism," there is no necessity to stay with that position. As the rabbis would say, "These and these are the words of the living God." Kaplan championed the sometimes contradictory values of diversity and community. For him, communal religious life in the modern world must remain "voluntarist, democratic and quasi-contractual."[48]

In an amazing discussion of the way in which a democratic Jewish polity might work, confronting the twin challenges of religious pluralism and obligation, Kaplan describes in *The Future of the American Jew* a reconstituted Jewish community in which dues-paying membership is available to those who agree to a minimum of requirements (including, for example, not marrying outside the faith and giving one's children a Jewish education). It has never ceased to amaze me that, in Kaplan's vision of a reconstituted Jewish polity, the Jewish community would have the right to eject members who did not conform to the minimum requirements. Thus, Kaplan, the most famous excommunicant of the twentieth century, would for all intents and purposes reintroduce excommunication.

Congregations within the community would be formed of like-minded members, with each group having the right to formulate its own specific additional membership requirements.[49] For example, an Orthodox-leaning group might want to impose very stringent requirements, while a very liberal group might have very few. The ideal for Kaplan would be one founded on freedom and diversity, with all groups within the Jewish community dedicated to a shared goal of individual fulfillment. And, most importantly, each group would be devoted in its own way to the survival of the Jewish people as a religious civilization.

* * *

The *halakhah* legislates for every conceivable aspect of human life, including the most personal and intimate. The rabbis were as much concerned with purity laws and menstruation as they were with property damage and the structure of daily prayer. But more than any other aspect of life, the ethical and the moral were at the center of their religious concerns, or, to put it another way, "morality is the soul of the *halakhah*."[50]

Ethics and morals were a primary preoccupation for Kaplan from very early on. Given his father's devotion to *Mussar*, the pursuit of the ethical, Kaplan was familiar with its concepts and was undoubtedly raised in a home devoted to one's moral improvement. *Mussar* is an ancient concern, with outstanding ethicists throughout Jewish history devoting themselves to the clarification of the moral life. Bahya Ibn Pakuda, with his *Duties of the Heart,* and Moshe Hayim Luzzatto, with *The Path of the Righteous,* are the best-known of these thinkers. In the late nineteenth century, Israel Salanter (*né* Israel Lipkin, 1810–83) founded the *Mussar* movement to which Kaplan's father was dedicated. Salanter believed that the only way to fight the new trend toward enlightenment was to supplement Talmud study with a new devotion to ethical literature to ensure a higher level of ethical behavior and discipline among traditional Jews.

Salanter attempted to understand the primary ethical dilemmas. As one scholar of *Mussar* states, "Salanter sought to explore the composition of the human soul and provide a series of techniques to help minimize the 'disconnect' so often experienced between our actions and our ideals."[51] Understanding the "disconnect" is the key to moral behavior. The methodology consisted in the creation of *Mussar* groups in which individuals would criticize each other's behavior and try to help them find the wherewithal to overcome their weaknesses. Right action required continuous self-examination (*heshbon ha-nefesh*), through the study of specific ethical texts that would help the student to attain a higher level of ethical behavior. Each person must have a clear recognition of his or her evil inclination, the *yetzer ha-rah* (or the id, one might say) and should be vigilant about gaining self-control through self-criticism and meditation. This continuous introspection would reform the person's character so that acting ethically would become second nature. The goal was moral perfection, which, for Kaplan, was the essence of salvation.

Mordecai Kaplan had a special relationship not only to the *Mussar* movement but to one of its classic texts. Luzzatto's *The Path of the Righteous (Messilat Yesharim)*, written in the eighteenth century and used extensively by Salanter, was extremely popular among traditional Jews across Eastern Europe during the nineteenth century. In 1915, Solomon Schechter, president of the Jewish Theological Seminary, gave Kaplan the assignment of translating and critically editing this most important ethical work.[52]

In his introduction to the book, Kaplan situates this work within the context of its time but also points out the ways in which it is relevant to our time. With its emphasis on *shelemut,* meaning completeness or fulfillment, the work dovetails beautifully with Kaplan's ideal of salvation. While the law controls conduct, certain behaviors are beyond the law and cannot be controlled by the law. Kaplan suggests that this realm, where there is no strict compulsion, is the realm of the ethical. He points out that there are some who think of Judaism as primarily concerned only with outward control, but for Luzzatto and for Kaplan, inwardness is the key to moral behavior. The purpose of ethics is to persuade the individual to do his duty of his own free will. The rabbis offered the "word of God" as the incentive to obey, but today we are exhorted to use our powers of reason in guiding moral behavior.

Many of Kaplan's colleagues were aware of his involvement with ethical issues. In the 1940s, for example, when Louis Finkelstein, president of the seminary, was organizing his massive volumes on the history and culture of the Jewish people, he turned to Kaplan to write the chapter on Jewish ethics.[53] In a long and informed essay titled "A Philosophy of Jewish Ethics," Kaplan detailed the history and development of Jewish ethics, going all the way back to biblical times.

In this essay, Kaplan begins by discussing the ethics of Aristotle and Plato and their opposition to the Sophists' contention that values are merely masks for power. For both Plato and Aristotle, values such as justice were distinctive, independent, and accessible through reason. The Stoics, who came later, stressed duty as an imperative of reason, but these ideas were not widespread among the masses in Greece and Rome and did not take hold on a popular level. Pagan civilization, Kaplan believed, never embodied the moral insights of the philosophers in societal habits, rituals, and daily customs. The Stoics remained the chaplains of the well-to-do. It was, rather, through Judaism and through Judaism's daughter, Christianity, that the ethical energy spread over the world. The Jewish contribution to Western civilization, thus, consisted in the fact that the Jewish people "restored confidence in the original and underived character of ethical values and their independence of the considerations of expediency and self-interest." Kaplan asserted that the essence of Judaism is the affirmation of the objective character of the ethical and, as such, attempts to place the moral and ethical into the habits and customs of everyday life. Were it not for Judaism, the ethical notions of the philosophers might have remained the property of the intellectual few. Judaism helped make popular the principle that the "moral standards were part of the very nature of reality, and that to function as human beings, we must always strive to approximate them in all our relations with one another."[54]

In his essay for Finkelstein, Kaplan points to the centrality of Kant in asserting the rational foundation for ethics. The ethical must be observed for its own sake, not for the sake of happiness or any other good:

> This fact which Kant points out as true of the moral law, is what human beings normally experience in the form of intuition, and what the Jewish people with its tradition, which it regarded as divinely revealed, helped to conserve for Western Civilization. But what the Jewish people accomplished no individual thinker or school or philosophers could have accomplished.[55]

Thus, the Jews preserved the Kantian notion, even though they did not discover it. Ethically speaking, the Kantian understanding implies that one cannot simply act out of self-interest but must live in accordance with a higher principle to measure behavior. Jacob Agus, a prominent Conservative rabbi and admirer of Kaplan, goes so far as to maintain that the categorical imperative is the main substance of revelation. For Agus, the awareness of the divine mystery and the awareness of the objective moral law are transformed by the pious individual into acceptance of the will of God: "Organized religion safeguards these insights of the few for the enlightenment of the many. While God speaks through all things, we comprehend His word only through the channels of conscience, whole-souled dedication and the deepest truthfulness."[56]

Kaplan's interest in Kant goes back to his days as a graduate student when he studied philosophy.[57] His fascination with Kant, like his preoccupation with ethics, is illustrated by his interest and devotion to Hermann Cohen. Hermann Cohen (1842–1918), the son of a cantor, was born and raised in Germany, attended the Jewish Theological Seminary in Breslau, and studied with Heinrich Graetz, its most famous teacher. While this was a creative Jewish community, Cohen was not engaged with Judaism; rather, he spent more than forty years teaching at the university at Marburg and became celebrated as the founder of the Neo-

Kantian school of philosophy. However, Cohen never completely severed his ties with the Jewish community. In the early 1880s when the German historian Heinrich von Treitschke launched an attack on Judaism and denied Judaism's spiritual significance, Cohen asserted in response that German Protestantism and liberal Judaism were essentially alike.[58]

Though there were fundamental differences between them, Kaplan's interest and indeed admiration for Cohen are understandable. Kaplan tells us that there were few works that could surpass Cohen's rational religion in defining the meaning of Jewish existence in a naturalistic way.[59] Yet, at the same time, Kaplan is very open about his criticism of Cohen. The great rationalist failed to understand the part that the historic Jewish community, or the notion of Jewish peoplehood, plays in the development and meaning of religion and ethics. According to Kaplan, Cohen denied that social forces were significant in creating religion. Such forces were accidental and secondary to the formative powers of reason. In his comment on this issue, Kaplan explains that religion is not only the product of individual experience but of the social as well. In Kaplan's words, "To Cohen, religion is essentially an individual experience [but] from the standpoint of functional rationalism [Kaplan's name for his own system] religion is the product of society as well as the expression of personal experience and reflection."[60]

* * *

In Kaplan's naturalistic universe, we have given up the great "commander on high." If our subservience to God is no longer the reason for living an ethical life, we are left with enormous problems. Once we have given up the commander, it is only the ideal and its attraction that we can hold before us. Kaplan understood that we must make people want to be good. This is our greatest challenge and the heart of the ethical problem. In Kaplan's purple prose, it is the "integration of the urge to selfhood and the urge to mutuality." Being good is not a matter of conforming to the will of someone else but conforming to the ideal. We must create the good life as a work of art.[61] For Kaplan, the ideal of self-fulfillment is part of living a moral life or what we have called moral perfectionism.

Kaplan subscribes to the notion that religion's central purpose is to build character. Or to put it another way, the primary function of religion is to create virtuous men and women. In contemporary America, people are much more concerned with the mystical than the ethical, but these two ideals of holiness are not inherently incompatible.

For Kaplan, the most exalted ideal of holiness is what he calls redemptive love. His ideal of redemptive love is the highest that we can strive for and is none other than the selfless love that is also at the heart of Christianity:

> In contrast with man's cardinal sin, which consists in playing the god, man's cardinal virtue consists in being Godlike. To be Godlike is to exercise that redemptive love which expresses itself as forgiveness in such a way as to elicit penitence from the sinner.
>
> Redemptive love has nothing in common either with erotic love or with possessive love. It not only calls forth the best in others as well as in ourselves, when the love is mutual and no grievance of any kind mars it; it can also break down the wall of evil and wrongdoing that divides men, and reestablish happy and wholesome relations among them.[62]

Kaplan always maintained that all Western religions are essentially the same, though the ethical ideals are embodied in different ways. He had no problem embracing the notion of an idealized ethical sphere, a notion essentially identified with Christianity. At the same time, he never abandoned the centrality of the halakhic ideals of righteousness and justice. Here again, Kaplan shows himself to be the true pluralist, concerned with Jewish survival but understanding that survival as synonymous with the welfare of all humankind.

TWELVE

KAPLAN AND THE PROBLEM OF EVIL: CUTTING THE GORDIAN KNOT

Where in this conception of God is the place of evil? It is not in necessity but in the creativity of God. Evil is not (as I formerly believed) mere chance or negation, but something very real. It would not be evil if it were mere negation of being. All evil may be reduced either to the destruction or lowering of life. It is the antithesis of life, and in man, of salvation. The first is physical; the latter is moral evil.... What we have to assume with reference to God in order that we may accept His godhood is not that He is without evil, but that He is struggling to free Himself of the evil in His being. The evolutionary process whereby life rises to self-knowledge and to the evaluation of evil is an expression of this divine struggle to overcome the evil it has generated.... In man's efforts to achieve salvation it is also God who seeks to exercise his creative power for good and achieves as it were His own salvation.

—*Mordecai Kaplan, July 24, 1940*

The problem of evil and the issue of theodicy have always been among the most difficult aspects of traditional religion. If God is good and merciful and if God controls what happens in the world, how can He inflict so much needless suffering? Many thousands of volumes have been written to try to answer this question.

When considering the problem of evil in theological terms, our exploration is two-pronged. We need to look at the challenge that Mordecai Kaplan, and every other theologian, must face: how does one understand the existence of evil and suffering in the world? And at the same time, we need to apply such analysis to find a way to cope with the inevitable suffering that we experience. In our consideration of Kaplan's approach to the problem of evil, we shall move back and forth between these two, considering Kaplan's efforts at helping us cope with suffering and considering his explanation for evil.

Many believe that Kaplan had no theory of evil and takes no account of human pain and suffering.[1] It is widely held that his notion of theology and his notion of salvation consist only of his belief that the universe is so constituted as to aid us in our search for salvation. If such is the case, what happens to the reality of evil? Kaplan, for example, published almost nothing about the Holocaust.

Always the pragmatist, Kaplan's goal was to understand the evil that causes suffering and to consider how to cope in an imperfect world. The result, far from skirting the issue, is a courageous optimism. He is convinced, for example, that we should not grow complacent or accept these problems in our midst. "Man to be fully human must never make peace with evil," Kaplan tells us. He admonishes us that we must have an "unreconciled heart"—a term that we very much associate with Henry David Thoreau.[2] Of course, the "unreconciled heart" is really that of a revolutionary who refuses to accept society's evils. Let us remember that it was the one night in jail for refusal to pay taxes that made Thoreau famous in his time and in ours. The revolutionary drive for change and transformation always appealed strongly to Kaplan.

When he was rabbi at the Jewish Center in the early twentieth century, Kaplan was accused of being a Bolshevik because of his fiery sermons dealing with economics. Kaplan responded by asserting that he was really two people, Mordecai the Capitalist and Menachem the Bolshevik.[3] In a later analysis, Kaplan made the distinction between ascetics and revolutionaries: "The ascetic tries to sever his connection with the world, the revolutionary to overturn it." It is obvious that Kaplan identifies more with the revolutionaries than with the ascetics. Dissent held a great allure for him; he asserts that "there is often more godliness in protest than in easily achieved faith."[4]

Kaplan is fully aware of the doubts that suffering arouses in our religious beliefs. "Why me?" is a question we have all asked at one time or another. The challenge of making sense of suffering, both individual and collective, is always with us. Kaplan addresses himself to the question of religious doubt by emphasizing that we need to focus on the good at the same time that we do not deny the evil. When we have doubts, he explains, our

> will must be directed not to negating the doubt, for that would be suppression, but to reaffirming the faith which the doubt challenges; not to denying the reality of evil but to admitting the reality of good and to focusing our attention upon it. This is neither to suppress doubt nor to resolve it, but to transcend it. ... Evil is not overlooked or pronounced as unreal, but neither is it permitted to become a bogey that paralyzes our will to live and to achieve.[5]

In the Kaplanian naturalist universe, chance or randomness occupies a central place. In an early entry in his diary (from 1926), Kaplan uses this concept of chance in clarifying his general theological position on God and the problem of evil:

> I find myself at present believing in God as the Living Universe. The evil in the world is due to chance which is as necessary to reality as the negative is necessary to the positive. Is God finite or infinite? The question is either meaningless or irrelevant. God is all that there is.[6]

We are all subject to the inevitability of randomness or chance. Both in the case of natural disaster and in the case of intentional human evil, being in the wrong place at the wrong time is often the context of suffering. But the problem of evil has not ceased because we recognize the role of accident. The problem has just shifted. In the case of moral evil, it is imperative for us to cope with human cruelty and the pervasiveness of violence that plagues our world.[7] There is perhaps little we can do about the natural evils from which we suffer. But, in either case, the suffering, according to Kaplan, does not come to us as the consequence of "the will of God." Suffering frequently, but not always, comes to us as a result of chance or accident.[8]

Chance or accident cannot be eliminated, but it is possible to chip away at it. Kaplan believed that we should not deny evil, either moral or natural, but that we must seek to do what we can to minimize it. This is the attitude of the person of action. Kaplan would say, let us work toward the elimination of cancer, or let us try to find ways to at least predict natural disasters or have early warnings so we may flee from the disaster to safety. In the effort to maximize our safety and our health, we embody the divine, according to Kaplan. In his words, "When the human being invents a lightning rod he robs chance of an infinite number of opportunities to combine its path with the path of human beings. Such chance combinations that bring evil can be and are being averted more and more. This is the functioning of godhood through man."[9]

It will never be possible to remove all the events that cause suffering. The factors we cannot remove Kaplan refers to as "inexorable." He distinguishes between the inexorables of life and the evils of life. He maintains that the inexorables, like death, are not evil—they just "are." Anything that comes into being and is alive must die. Thus, death is inexorable but not evil.

Evils like sicknesses and poverty, though, can and should be reduced, according to Kaplan. Such evils are not inexorable and, therefore, may in principle be reduced or eliminated in time. Not surprisingly, Kaplan the pragmatist focuses on what may be overcome. Yet he would fully admit that there are evils that we can never eradicate. In such moments, we need to maintain our focus, summon our courage, and continue to move ahead.

How was Kaplan's twinned emphasis—on acknowledging evil but not becoming paralyzed by it—put into practice? We have an instructive example from 1927, when the twenty-four-year-old son of one of the leaders of the Society for the Advancement of Judaism died by drowning.[10] It is difficult to imagine a more devastating event for a parent than the loss of a child. Kaplan, naturally, was called upon to speak at the funeral and chose to use the occasion to deal with *Tsidduk ha-din,* a prayer that is a traditional part of the burial liturgy and that translates roughly as acknowledgement of divine justice. Later that day, he noted in his journal that, although his remarks were completely "subversive of the traditional notion of *Tsidduk ha-din* [because he proclaimed the absence of any justice], I even received some compliments from the more traditional members attending."[11]

The journal entry, which contains the essence of the eulogy Kaplan delivered that day, centers on the issue of vindication and how the mourners might be comforted. His hope is that he might comfort the mourners by pointing to those long-established notions that portray God as participating in our suffering. We need to have the courage to carry on, he insists, finding inspiration from the traditional belief that God participates in our pain:

> This is the idea I developed: Vindicating the ways of God as a means of taking up life's task in spite of the catastrophe which has occurred cannot take place in the traditional way of regarding calamities as punishment for sins. We must learn to vindicate God by conceiving Him as the general who orders the vast army of the living in its combat against blind chance and the unconscious cruelties of nature. When our beloved falls at our side the thought that there is a God who is a *Mefaked Tzevah Milhamah* [a military officer] who is leading us on in this warfare against the evils of mere chance should hearten us to keep on fighting. As such [a] leader of the forces of life, God grieves with us over those who perish through no fault of theirs. Even over those who die for and through their sins, God is said to mourn *kalani me-roshi kalani me-zero'i* ["My head hurts, my arm hurts," from *Mishna Sanhedrin* 6:5][12]; all the more over those who pay with their life for their courage and virtue, *yakar be-eiynei adonai* [Psalms 116:15, "The death of His faithful ones is grievous in the Lord's sight."]

Kaplan's use of a blatantly personified God here is astonishing, yet it is a good example of the traditional Judaic concepts that were embedded deep within him and the fact that he had no difficulty in using these time-honored metaphors when they were called for. He was, after all, ever the pragmatist. Despite the surprising supernatural elements, the focus here is clear: we must carry on; we must not give up. When in the throes of pain, we see no hope, yet when we look at the larger picture, we see ourselves *sub speciae aeternitatis.*

This is the message of God to Job: cease being preoccupied with your own suffering; instead, look at the world and yourself from the vantage point of the transcendent. Though the tone may seem harsh—as Kaplan's lack of embellishment often did—at the heart of his message is hope. More than anything else, Kaplan the pragmatist wants to help us carry on despite our pain and anguish.

If God is our captain in fighting back the forces of the night, then Kaplan is certainly one of His lieutenants. There are many who think that human nature is evil and depraved and who mock those who see the human urge to goodness as more basic. In our day, in the wake of the Holocaust, such optimism can appear shallow and superficial. Kaplan, however, complicates this reductive pessimist/optimist binary. He believes that there is a basic will to live that is inherent in all life and that the will to live is more fundamental than any other. In human beings, he calls this principle the will to be effective: "When that will is frustrated by want, misery, pain, then individuals are not able to avail themselves of whatever potential they have for being effective. It is then that they lash out and become vicious and dissipate, gamble, overwork, or go off on wild adventures, killing others or themselves."[13]

Kaplan seemed to think that his eulogy was not in line with traditional thinking. For us, his comments on his own heresy that follow the journal eulogy are more important than examining whether he was in fact heretical. After summarizing his remarks, he writes the following:

> This conception of God is undoubtedly heretical from the standpoint of Jewish thinkers of the past. But the fear of being guilty of heresy does not affect me in the least. I am chiefly interested in having a conception of the universe and of God which can give me courage to go on fighting against the terrible odds of unwarranted suffering and meaningless death. I prefer God without perfection than perfection without God. The God of philosophy is perfection with a capital P, cold, impersonal, immovable, infinitely negative.
>
> It is because God is to me the warm personal element in Life's inner urge to creativity and self-expression that I can conscientiously employ the name YHWH when praying.[14]

Before we leave this 1927 statement, it is worthwhile noting that Kaplan moves here from one conception of God that is quite traditional (the commanding general in the battle against evil) to a much more limited sense of the divine (the warm, personal element in life's inner urge to creativity). Kaplan was not a rigorous philosopher, as we have seen, but a rabbi. He had no trouble in advocating theological concepts that were diametrically opposed to one another. Here we see that movement within the same journal entry.

We should emphasize that, in a Kaplanian universe, comfort comes not from any theological or metaphysical belief but from the members of our community. When we are sick or in mourning, it is from our fellow congregational members that we must draw consolation and solace. Kaplan tells us that, when we comfort, we become agents of the divine.

* * *

Let us now turn to the issue of how Kaplan explains the problem of evil and suffering. In a set of articles Kaplan wrote in the early 1960s, he addresses himself in general terms to the problem of evil. He first reviews the way evil and suffering have been dealt with in the Jewish tradition. He traces the well-known assumption of biblical theodicy, in which suffering is considered a punishment for sinful living. He then points out the vehement protest against this view found in Psalms,[15] Job, Jeremiah, and Ecclesiastes. Kaplan quotes the stirring words of the prophet: "Thou art always in the right, Eternal one, when I complain to Thee, yet I would argue this with Thee: why do the wicked prosper, why are the scoundrels secure and serene? Thou plantest them and they bear fruit. Thou art always on their lips and far from their hearts."[16] In discussing Job, Kaplan notes the conventional interpretation of the last chapters and "Voice of the Whirlwind" as counseling acceptance. In the face of suffering, Kaplan tells us, resignation has been the primary counsel of traditional religion throughout history.

Later in the essay just quoted, however, Kaplan asserts that this attitude of resignation has contributed to the worsening of the human condition:

> We should be troubled mainly by the fact that the attitude of resignation which religion has been recommending to the victims of man's inhumanity is certain to play into the hands of those who practice inhumanity. Animal man is parasitic and pugnacious. Human man is just and peace-loving. Religion's function is to make man more human. Instead, it has been indirectly and inadvertently suborning his inhumanity.[17]

Kaplan ends the essay by agreeing with the famous statement from Karl Marx: "Religion teaches all who toil in poverty all their lives to be resigned and patient in this world, and consoles them with the hope of reward in heaven. . . . Religion is the opiate of the people, a sort of spiritual liquor, meant to make slaves of capitalism which drowns humanity and their desires for a decent existence."[18]

For Kaplan, the most significant aspect of theodicy is that it may lead us not only to question the meaning of God as a "person" (for example, God's cruelty) but perhaps even the very existence of God.[19]

Overcoming the resignation of traditional religious thinking, however, was not sufficient. Kaplan advocated going much further, as he himself had done decades earlier, discarding the notion of a personal God. In his young mind, as we have seen, the difficulty of accepting the biblical miracles aroused doubts that led him to dismiss the supernatural basis of the tradition. In the course of time, the problem of evil reinforced his dismissal of a providential God:

> What has been wrong, therefore, with the various attempts which account for the existence of evil in the world has been the fact that they all started out with the erroneous premise concerning God. They generally assume that God, or Divinity, was a being of infinite power and goodness, meting out rewards to those who obeyed his commands and punishments to those who disobeyed them. The truth is that Divinity is not a being, in the same sense that man is a being. Divinity is *being* or *existence* [itself] insofar as it is a correlate of whatever man does to improve himself and his world, or insofar as he so lives as to leave the world better and happier for his having lived. That is the way of conscience.[20]

In other words, the whole theology of reward and punishment, which is so central to traditional religion, flows from the belief in God as a "person." If we see the divine as encompassing all reality, as infusing all being, then the problem of theodicy does not exist in the same way, for there is no deity that rewards or punishes. The traditional concept of reward and punishment also assumes a God who is omnipotent, a God of "infinite power," as Kaplan puts it. For Kaplan, it is clear that "Godhood should not be made synonymous with omnipotence, omniscience or any other attribute implying infinitude."[21]

There are some scholars who have no use for a Kaplanian God, who is a power or a process and not a person, and therefore cannot come to our aid in times of need. Neil Gillman, professor of philosophy at the Jewish Theological. Seminary, among others, has criticized Kaplan on this score.[22] There is, in a sense, a mixture of metaphors here. If God is not a being for Kaplan, then the issue of whether He is omnipotent or limited is irrelevant. It may be that Kaplan's critics have never understood that, in a naturalistic universe, the problem in its classical formulation does not make sense.

Among liberal theologians, Rabbi Richard Rubenstein is one of Kaplan's most significant critics.[23] Many years ago he wrote a very provocative essay on Kaplan and the problem of evil. Though Rubenstein accepts Kaplan's naturalistic theology, he dissents from Kaplan's "optimistic humanism." Like Kaplan, Rubenstein views evil as undermining traditional theological assumptions: "The real objections against a personal or theistic God come from the irreconcilability of the claim of God's perfection with the hideous human evil tolerated by such a God. ... A God who tolerates the suffering of even one innocent child is either infinitely cruel or hopelessly indifferent."[24]

Rubinstein is critical of Kaplan's belief that the universe aids in our fulfillment. It is significant that, when people criticize Kaplan on the problem of evil, they invariably point to his optimism and his belief that the universe is set up in such a way as to help us achieve salvation. Rubinstein puts it this way: "The optimism of religious liberalism and of Reconstructionism was their weakest plank, and it has been this unwarranted optimism about man and human possibilities which has given both traditional religious forces and existentialists their greatest weapon against liberalism." Rubenstein counters the Kaplanian optimism with his assertion that "Man has proven capable of irredeemable evil."[25]

Rubenstein's discussion of Kaplan is indicative of the weakness of the Kaplan critics. They resent the Kaplanian optimism that seems to be so out of line with our experiences of the twentieth century. Yet it should be clear that we need the Kaplanian hope in countering the evils that we face. Indeed, Kaplan never denies the evils of the twentieth century.

Rubenstein moves almost imperceptibly at the end of his analysis from dealing with Kaplan to a comment on John Dewey, Kaplan's most important philosophical mentor. "The Twentieth Century is the century of Freud," writes Rubenstein, "not of Dewey." Freud tells of the darker side; Dewey is the optimist. Rubenstein seems to want to criticize Kaplan by criticizing Dewey. In any case, Rubenstein emphatically rejects the notion that we should act as if the world wants to aid us in fulfilling ourselves. He rejects what he considers to be the unwarranted optimism of Dewey and Kaplan.

He tells us, nonetheless, that, even if we are not unduly optimistic but recognize the evils of the world for what they are, we can still work on improving our lot. Unwittingly, he seems very Kaplanian here. He counsels us that we can and should face reality in our attempt to cope with suffering. In his words, "There is something morally and psychologically satisfying in making the very best one can of a limited and tragic existence." Rubenstein goes on to give his own naturalistic and more "realistic" theology, but that need not detain us.[26]

With regard to Kaplan's optimism, Rabbi Richard Hirsh, director of the Reconstructionist Rabbinical Association, rightly points out that Kaplan is most often what Hirsh calls an "if-ist" rather than inveterate optimist: "Kaplan is an if-ist; if we act in a responsible manner there is the possibility of real progress. Conversely if we act irresponsibly, we reverse that progress we have made, making our task twice as difficult." Or, as Kaplan put the matter in another context, "The character of life should not be judged by the actual but by the possible."[27]

Kaplan's beliefs on the issue of theodicy present us with a number of problems. First, we must admit that he is sometimes guilty of the uncritical optimism of which he is accused. Kaplan's optimism is often frustrating, especially when we think about the human evils of the Holocaust and the natural evils of the latest tsunami or earthquake. In 1930, Kaplan wrote,

> If you want to know whether the good counterbalances the evil, ask yourself, Can human life be improved and enhanced despite all that we know of the evil that exists in the world? Is it possible for man to escape the dire consequences of such evil disasters as earthquakes and hurricanes? There is no question of his ability to overcome all man-made evil. There is equally little doubt that with the application of intelligence there is no natural catastrophe against which he cannot protect himself.[28]

One of Kaplan's most astute traditional critics, Eliezer Berkovits (1908–92), a modern Orthodox scholar and theologian, criticizes Kaplan's assertions of the essential unreality of evil. In Berkovits's words, "We read [in Kaplan], for instance, that earthquakes and volcanic eruptions, devastating storms and floods, famines and plagues, noxious plants and animals, 'are simply that phase of the universe which has not yet been completely penetrated by godhood.'"[29]

If we want to understand Kaplan, we must realize that the above statements do not exhaust his position on the matter of the problem of evil. Although Berkovits is more or less correct in his analysis here, Kaplan also expresses beliefs almost directly opposite to the one just cited. In his diary in 1944, Kaplan laments, "I cannot reconcile myself to his [Milton Steinberg's] assumption that *all* evil is found in the end to prove to have served some good."[30]

For Kaplan the optimist, divinity is purposive and directed toward life and the worthwhile. Chaos is, then, the absence of divinity. But this does not mean that Kaplan denies the existence of evil, either moral or natural, as Berkovits and Rubenstein seem to argue.

The problem is that Kaplan, in a characteristic way, stands on both sides of the issue of evil. Often we find the optimism we have just noted, but, at other times, we find him asserting the reality of evil as a characteristic of human interaction and of the universe.

In the first place, we must understand that Kaplan is not merely an inveterate optimist or a naïve pollyanna but is fully aware of the world's evil and suffering.[31] He wrote often in his diary about Nazism and Hitler and the suffering of the Jews, yet these sentiments never found their way into his later published writings. As a consequence, it is easy to think that he had nothing to say about the Holocaust and its meaning (or lack thereof). But he obviously felt the pain of those who suffered under the Nazi onslaught.

> These are days of unprecedented tragedy for our people who have fallen into the grasp of the Nazi beast. It is questionable whether one has a right to be happy, even if one is fortunate enough to be placed as I am, safe from all harm, and to have such joy as came to me the last few days.[32]

Kaplan's intense identification is reflected frequently in his reaction to significant events as they happen. For example, a few days after Hitler invaded Poland, he wrote,

> On Friday, the supreme madman of the world started the great conflagration. God knows what the outcome will be. The mind simply refuses to contemplate the dread possibilities. Yesterday England and France declared war on Germany. After their long record of criminal selfishness and stupidity which converted the German nation into a maddened herd, I was afraid that they might have become so corrupt as to permit this horrible creation of theirs to have its way. So dreadful has life become that one has to find relief in two such empires—or shall I say vampires—declaring war on a rattlesnake like Hitler.[33]

Kaplan was among the many American Jews who felt that the Allies were not doing enough to save Europe's Jews. In the midst of the Warsaw Ghetto Uprising in 1943, he noted,

> It is futile to discuss the Nazi brand of anti-Semitism which is no longer content with re-enslaving the Jews. It is determined to annihilate them. The only power to have halted this most ghastly crime resides in the united nations now fighting the Axis nations. But the [u]nited nations themselves are not so free of anti-Semitism as to feel in the least impelled to take special action in behalf of the Jews.[34]

Yet withal, it is quite surprising that nowhere in Kaplan's published corpus do we find a sustained discussion of the Holocaust or of Nazism. It is well to remember, however, that the liberation of the concentration camps in 1945, which revealed the full extent of the atrocities of Nazism, was not immediately followed by philosophical or religious discussions. Indeed, it was not until Elie Wiesel's book *Night* appeared in 1960 that a sustained discussion began. In 1960, Mordecai Kaplan was seventy-nine years old.

Nevertheless, Kaplan's concern was not limited to the suffering of the Jews. He was equally concerned with the ideology that gave rise to that suffering. Whereas our concern with the Holocaust is to attempt to cope with its enormity, Kaplan confronted the German onslaught by attempting to deal with the way that Nazism related to his own beliefs. He frequently agonized over the issue of nationalism and how to differentiate this most destructive form of national pride from the Zionist ideology that he embraced. The moral aspects of nationalist movements drew his most sustained attention. In Kaplan's analysis, we find that nationalism has a number of elements and that these elements typically are present in different degrees in any nationalist movement. There is first the political element that gives rise to the nation-state. There is also what he calls the "racial-theological" element in which the self-centered or egotistical aspect of nationalism is raised to its greatest intensity. Nazism, of course, falls under this category. Third and finally, there is the creative aspect of nationalism where the cultural uniqueness of a given people or nationality is expressed.[35]

In a long and provocative discussion of the racial-theological aspect of nationalism, Kaplan concludes with a rather startling assertion: nationalist chauvinism, which has become so destructive in the twentieth century, is also found within the Jewish tradition itself in the concept of the "chosen people." In February 1939, he writes that, within certain kinds of nationalism, an individual is more likely to insist that his nation be regarded

> as not only unique but as superior to all other nations, as fulfilling more adequately the meaning of humanity than any other nation. One's nation must be regarded as divinely chosen, as enjoying a greater share of the divine spirit than any other. Its language must be regarded as the most beautiful, its laws

as the most sacred, its history as the one most divinely guided, its morals as
the most just and its folkways as the most humanizing. "My nation can do no
wrong," must be the motto for each citizen. Whatever adventures it enters upon
to extend its dominion or to improve its will on others are a manifestation of its
superior energy and will and a means of bringing other peoples within the circle
of its bliss. It is not hard to recognize in all this the type of nationalism preached
by Chauvinists and now emphatically avowed by Germany, Italy and Japan.[36]

In considering this brand of chauvinism, suddenly roiling the world into
war, Kaplan then realizes that these qualities apply also to the Jewish
people. He continues the above analysis:

> Merely to state what this type of nationalism means is to make evident its im-
> moral character to those who take for granted that a doctrine which implies that
> any one group of human beings is alone entitled to the distinction of humanity,
> whereas all other groups represent lower types of humanity cannot be consid-
> ered moral.
>
> What then shall we make of our own tradition which apparently conforms
> to this type of nationalism, in that it would have the Jew regard his people as
> divinely chosen, its Torah or civilization the most perfect and only those who
> become proselyted and accept its authority as eligible for the life of bliss in
> the hereafter? To be sure there are stray passages in rabbinic literature which
> sound a universal note, and it is possible to offset R. Judah ha-Levi's conception
> of Israel as being as much superior to the rest of mankind as the latter is to the
> animal world, with Maimonides' contention that all human beings are eligible to
> eternal life. But the main burden of Jewish tradition is undoubtedly inclined to
> be strongly nationalistic, in the sense of this second type of nationalism.

It is quite astounding that Kaplan goes to such lengths in rejecting this
kind of chauvinistic nationalism. As early as the mid-1920s he had discarded the concept of the chosen people. His analysis of this concept
and its rejection are spelled out at length in *Judaism as a Civilization*.[37]

In the above analysis of nationalism, Kaplan favors what he calls
the cultural or civilizational aspect of nationalism. In Kaplan's brand of
nationalism, a strong universalism is wedded to his national commitment. Every people or nation, Kaplan maintains, has a sense of its own
unique contribution to the world at large, in such areas as music, art, and
literature. This aspect of group life should assume a primary place in any
national movement. Destruction and violence results from the other aspects of nationalism, Kaplan asserts, but never from the cultural aspect.

Kaplan's most moving analysis of the problem of evil is found in
reaction to a British white paper of 1939, which declared a restriction on

Jewish immigration.[38] At this time, Kaplan was in Jerusalem teaching at the Hebrew University. He thus felt the full impact of the restriction on Jewish immigration by the British mandatory power, which came in the spring of 1939.

> Tonight the substance of the "White Paper" will be broadcast. Its contents are sufficiently known by this time. The *yishuv* [the Jewish community in Palestine] is like a seething cauldron. A general strike and demonstrations have been accounted for tomorrow. God knows what the outcome will be. I simply find it impossible to grasp the implications of this perfidious act of England by which she hands us over to the mercies of the savage Arab hordes....
>
> I still believe that before all else we Jews ought to answer ourselves the question To what end? What are we Jews for? Without some kind of a satisfying answer, our condition ceases to be even tragic, and becomes completely meaningless. There can be no evil greater than meaningless suffering.
>
> I say that we must redeem this suffering of its meaninglessness and I don't think it is so difficult. The existence of mankind as a whole, bound up as it is with every conceivable evil, would appear nothing less than a cosmic error, if we were not to attach significance to consciousness, spirit, mind, reason, a significance that all the infinite universe of dead matter cannot destroy. If man thus dares affirm his right to existence in the face of a vast universe that woke him to life only to crush him with its infinite ponderousness, why should not the Jew have the courage to defy the savage element of mankind that seeks to annihilate him? It is man's function to assert the right of the mind to exist. So it is the Jew's function to assert the right of human individuality, which is the most important expression of the mind. The minority status to which Jews seem to be condemned is the opportunity which the Jews must exploit to affirm the right of the human being to be something else besides being a creature of the herd, to be himself. This human dignity, which it has fallen upon the Jew to defend, is what the Jew should live for as a Jew.[39]

Here, in a nutshell, is Kaplan's most articulate response to the problem of evil. In a paradigmatically pragmatic response, Kaplan eschews metaphysical explanations in favor of pragmatic strategies for dealing with and overcoming meaninglessness. He asserts that the way for humans to cope with radical evil is to summon the courage to assert the right of the mind and the spirit to exist and to function freely. Only through the focus on the transcendent aspects of our nature in the face of radical evil can we overcome meaninglessness and suffering. Just as it is every human being's duty to assert the right of the mind to exist, so it is the Jew's duty to assert the rights of the individual. The Jews must exploit their minority status and affirm the right of all people to resist being part of the herd. This is the destiny of the Jewish people and the meaning of their existence.[40]

In Kaplan's analysis of evil, the human propensity to dominate is primary. He has no doubt that the lust to dominate has been always with us; the biblical injunction against it goes to the heart of the matter. The prophet cries out, "Not by might nor by strength but by my Spirit, said the Lord of Hosts."[41] This verse was one of Kaplan's favorites and, for him, summarized the moral thrust of the Torah against violence and domination.[42]

However, it was not only the urge to dominate that explains the Nazi hatred of the Jews but the fact that the Jews symbolized for Hitler, as they have for so many anti-Semites in the past, the essentially alien, the archetypal other. In Kaplan's words, "When nationalism reached its frenzied climactic [sic] in Nazism, it needed an opportunity to symbolize its ruthlessness against the right to be other. It found that opportunity in the Jew, who vis à vis the rest of the world is the very embodiment of the right to be other."[43]

Beside the urge to dominate, there are other explanations that are not from Kaplan but are related to this most primitive of all compulsions. The most interesting alternative theodicy comes, not surprisingly, from Milton Steinberg, Kaplan's most outstanding intellectual disciple. In a path-breaking article now buried in the obscurity of the early volumes of The Reconstructionist, Steinberg gives us a brilliant naturalist alternative to Kaplan's attitude toward evil.

Steinberg begins by reminding us that our understanding of evil and its ultimate origins depends on our concept of God. Steinberg is a Kaplanian but also a theist, which means that, although he dismisses the concept of a supernatural being, he is comfortable with such theological expressions as the "mind energy, or Spirit of the universe." In a stirring passage, Steinberg spells out what he means:

> His [God's] power moves in the dynamisms of physical reality. His will is the impulse behind the upsurge of life on this planet. Individualized, He is the soul of man whose thought processes are infinitesimal sparks of His infinite fire, whose moral aspirations are fragments of His vast purpose, whose yearning to create is but an echo of His cosmic creativity.[44]

But even if God is more than and other than the mere "power that makes for salvation," how does this help us with the problem of evil? Steinberg uses an evolutionary model in considering the problem of evil. We have obviously evolved from the lower forms and, of course, share much with them. We are a "near relative to the plant and, in consequence, exposed to bacterial attack, hunger and thirst." But, more importantly for our problem, we are also "blood brother to animals and, like them, engaged in competitive struggle, like them capable of rage, hatred and bloodlust." Steinberg also reminds us that we share much with the divine, for "As God is the reason in all things, so man is capable of thought and of the knowledge of the truth. As He is freedom, creativity, a resident in all souls and the source of all goodness, so His mortal individualizations yearn after freedom, [the] will to create, [and] strive after insights into other hearts and aspire after ideal ends." Thus, even though the divine resides in our higher selves, we never fully transcend our lower selves. The urge to dominate that is so omnipresent in the lower animals finds its place in us: "though the vegetable has transcended the mineral, or it would have remained inorganic, the animal the plant. As for man, the heritage of the beast is still powerful in him."

For Steinberg, we are the creations and the progressive incarnation of a cosmic "Thought Will." Our present level of life is not the last one; rather, as one level emerges from the previous level, the previous falls away. But that takes time. "God as He mounts from level to level is, like an embryo bursting forth from the womb, still stained and flecked with the stuff of His immersion." Evil, then, becomes "the unremoved scaffolding of the edifice of God's creativity." Of course, we would prefer that it were otherwise, and we become impatient and angry with ourselves and with those who inflict themselves upon us; but, as Steinberg points out, we have no choice but to deal with the reality that we have been given.

Though we have here the beginnings of an alternative model of understanding evil, the question of comfort still remains. For Steinberg, our insight into the nature of evil is itself part of the comfort: "understanding can be a great strength provided that it is the understanding not only of the how but of the why. Men can bear up under agony, they can even elect to undergo it, if they feel that some purpose is served thereby.

What they find more intolerable than pain itself is pain that is point-less." If we have faith that we are part of the emergence of a better world, Steinberg believes, our suffering during the course of that emergence may become easier to bear.

In thinking about this matter of the emergence of a better world, Steinberg does not hesitate to use the word "faith," though he prefers the term "hypothesis." And it is well to remember that the Steinberg article was written in 1943, in the midst of the Nazi onslaught. His hypothesis, or his faith, is formulated in the following terms: the believer "does not fight alone, nor in human company only, nor with his heart torn by doubts over the outcome. Behind him, in him, beside him and before him, works that Power that drives the universe which is also a power that makes for righteousness."

In Kaplan's 1945 prayer book, as we discussed earlier, we find a very theistic statement about God as the "soul of the universe." If Kaplan understood the full implications of that statement with respect to the problem of evil, he might have emerged with an analysis very similar to the one we have here.[45]

* * *

It is fair to say that Kaplan believed he had been released from the ago-nies that the problem of evil presented. He explains his "solution" in a magnificently illuminating journal passage from the early 1950s dealing with Judah Magnes. Magnes (1877–1948) was an outstanding American rabbi and the first president of the Hebrew University. Kaplan believed that Magnes found the problem of evil a theological stumbling block and, in his search, resorted to the "easy" solution of asserting that mys-tery was the essence of religion. For Kaplan, however, such a solution was no solution. Contrasting himself with Magnes,[46] Kaplan declared,

> I, on the other hand, am satisfied to cut the Gordian knot, and to identify as God only those aspects of reality which contribute to man's self-fulfillment or self-transcendence. As for the evil in the world, I recognize it entirely for what it is, not as something to be reconciled with God, but as something God and man or God through man ever strives to overcome, as does the light that penetrates ever further into the darkness and overcomes it. As for mystery, I don't have to go in search of it among the complexities of sin and suffering. It is so unfathomable to me in the transcribing of thought on paper as in the millions of constellations reported to exist in the Milky Way.

For Kaplan, the primary issues are how we overcome and how we cope with suffering. How do we transcend it? When we face tragedy, what we need is the hope that we will find a way to get through it. We need hope because hope transforms and energizes and allows us to go on.

It is fitting that we end our consideration of Kaplan and evil with some words from Walt Whitman, who more than anyone else was the prophet of hope and the poet of the positive. Kaplan admired Whitman as he admired Emerson.

In the midst of the Civil War, Whitman learned that his brother was wounded and lay in a hospital in Washington, D.C. He travelled to the capital looking for his brother but could not find him. Instead, Whitman focused his attention on the other wounded soldiers. He returned to the soldiers again and again and devoted himself to their care and feeding. Whitman looked into the face of suffering and tragedy and saw hope. Through his actions, Whitman tells us that the most humane of responses is in our concern for each other in a time of tragedy. Such a response, in Kaplan's terms, expresses the essence of the divine.

In a book about this phase of his life, Roy Morris quotes from one of Whitman's great declarations of hope:

> To anyone dying, thither I speed and twist the knob of the door,
> Turn the bed-clothes toward the foot of the bed,
> Let the physician and the priest go home.
>
> I seize the descending man and raise him with resistless will,
> O despairer, here is my neck,
> By God, you shall not go down! hang your whole weight upon me.
>
> I dilate you with tremendous breath, I buoy you up,
> Every room of the house do I fill with an armed force,
> Lovers of me, bafflers of graves.
>
> Sleep—I and they keep guard all night,
> Not doubt, not decease shall dare to lay finger upon you,
> I have embraced you, and henceforth possess you to myself,
> And when you rise in the morning you will find what I tell you is so.[47]

CONCLUSION

I have been thinking about Mordecai Kaplan for the better part of the last forty years. I have for a time avoided this conclusion—but, in the final analysis, we must admit that Kaplan really is a heretic. The word is an uncomfortable one, especially with the image it conjures of a roomful of rabbis burning his prayer book. Indeed, it is a word that caused Kaplan himself terrible discomfort for the last four decades of his life; the decree of the ultra-Orthodox haunted him. Yet *heretic* is the word I keep returning to. It is the only word I can find that conveys the full force of his radicalism. Kaplan often stands outside the conventional parameters of Judaism either traditional or modern.

People frequently want to know where to place Reconstructionism on the spectrum from Orthodoxy to Reform. Most Reconstructionists place their denomination between Conservative Judaism and Reform. But, in many essential ways, Reconstructionism is far to the left of Reform Judaism. If Reconstructionists understood the full implications of Kaplan's Judaism, the movement would be the most revolutionary and radical of all the denominations.

We have characterized Kaplan's thought as a theology of mood. He was a man of enormous, challenging ideas but was frequently ambivalent about the details of his ideas; he could not, or did not want to, remember all the inconsistencies in his reasoning. The traditional and the contemporary were always at war in his mind. Arthur Hertzberg put it well in his introduction to *Judaism as a Civilization:* "It is to the merit of Kaplan and his historic importance that in him authentic Judaism, the learning and temperament of a Lithuanian Rav, encountered the dominant philosophy in America of his day, the pragmatism of John Dewey."[1] He cherished both the burden of the Jewish tradition, passed down from his father, and the possibilities of new thinking from so many new and varied sources.

Kaplan's inconsistency or ambivalence is perhaps best illustrated by his conflicted attitude to the centrality of the Jewish people. He once called his system of thought "Zionist Judaism." At the same time, he was "seduced" by the universal. Deeply influenced by Felix Adler, the founder of the Ethical Culture Movement, Kaplan always had the universal and humanistic in the forefront of his consciousness. Kaplan's big secret was not sexual. The skeleton in his closet was Felix Adler, with his relentless emphasis on the ethical and the universal.

Kaplan's deeply ingrained universalism took a very radical form with reference to the Jewish tradition. He was among the very few who dismissed the notion of the chosen people. American Jews, in his time as in ours, attempt to rationalize their beliefs, insisting that being the chosen people does not mean Jews are superior. It just means that we have more obligations. But feeling that we have more obligations certainly reflects a sense of superiority. Living in and embracing democratic culture as we do, it simply makes no sense to believe in the Jews as the chosen people. Throughout our history, this central dogma of the Jewish tradition served to aid in Jewish survival. Now it no longer does. Kaplan was outraged at the irrationality of the belief that the powers that rule the universe would be revealed only or primarily to one group. How intolerant and egotistical, he thought. Kaplan stated that the belief in the special revelation to the Jewish people was as unethical as bigamy and completely incompatible with religious tolerance and equality.

The dismissal of chosenness, however, is religiously and Jewishly cataclysmic; by implication, the Covenant between God and Israel is dissolved. There is no more fundamental belief in all forms of Judaism than the Covenant—the special commitment of God to the children of Abraham and of Israel to its God.

But for Kaplan, as we have seen, such cataclysm has a solution. For Kaplan, our fatal flaw as thinking beings is that we tend to perceive entities where there are in fact processes. We "thingify," as he liked to say. To correct this flaw, we need to think in terms of predicates. Kaplan used the terms "God-like or divine," "Torah-like" and "Israel-like." With his predicate lens, God becomes the divine aspect of our lives; Torah becomes any scripture that aids in one's search for the divine and shows one the way to moral completeness; Israel becomes the group that dedicates itself to this quest.

Kaplan could not simply discard the Covenant. He had to reconstruct it. The Covenant should represent for the Jewish people their commitment to the eternal ideals of justice and righteousness. The Covenant is an expression of Jewish unity in service to the divine. Prayers become a public statement of our dedication and our willingness to commit ourselves to our ideals. Within this reconstructed Covenant, his theology of mood emerges again and again; there are times when Kaplan slips back into traditional ways of thinking and speaking. He loved his father very much and internalized much of his thinking. Kaplan's radicalism is balanced by the burden of his father's mind. We just need to read the dedication of *Judaism as a Civilization* for a reminder: "To the memory of my father and teacher, Rabbi Israel Kaplan, a man of crisp mind and noble spirit who guided me in my wanderings through the wilderness of doubt and confusion." Israel Kaplan, who died in 1917, would have been quite upset with his son's magnum opus, but his son's dedication remains.

Kaplan was at the center of the twentieth century's transformation and Americanization of Judaism. We might call his approach the democratization of Judaism. Rather early in his career, Kaplan saw America's democracy as a great threat. Its unbounded freedom, so wonderful and so novel, also allowed the recent immigrants and their children simply to walk away from Jewish life. Yet in time, Kaplan came to appreciate what might be called "democratic culture." The democratization of Judaism does not mean that we decide all issues by majority vote. That would be silly. Democracy stands for the rule of law. It stands for the primacy of law in the life of the individual, for the nation, and among nations; for continual suspicion of authority, for the right to free expression, and for the right to be critical. But if the right to be critical is at the center of the democratic consciousness, it follows we must be ever critical of our own beliefs. Kaplan urged us to incorporate these democratic values into the Torah and the reconstruction of tradition. He once referred to Torah as life-long moral education. To be a Reconstructionist and a religious extremist would be a contradiction in terms.

Given Kaplan's open mind and dedication to religious pluralism, it is not surprising that many consider him the patron saint of the most innovative experiments of contemporary Jewry. These include not only Reconstructionism but also the Jewish Renewal movement, the Havurah movement, *Eilat Hayim,* and Humanistic Judaism. If we consider Kaplan's basic principles, we see a direct line to those groups that are at the forefront of liberal experimentation. The foundation of his principles was a fierce functionalism and an equally strong determination to eliminate dogma that he felt no longer contributed to the survival and vitality of the Jewish people.

Kaplan, pluralist to the core, rejects the idea that there is only one way to be Jewish. He asserts plainly and forcefully that "No uniform pattern of Jewish life can meet the needs of different Jewries any longer."[2] In other words, the more individual choice there is for Jews the better. He often asserted that our Judaism, whatever its form, must be a full-bodied Judaism, not a skeletal Judaism. In favoring variety over uniformity and traditionalism, Kaplan would be heartened by the astonishing range in the "Judaisms" of our time.

Our Judaism, however we understand it, must be embodied in our lives on a regular basis. For the Jewish people, this means the *mitzvah* system. Though he lived a life similar to any Conservative rabbi of his day, Kaplan was not a halakhic Jew. He stated many times that, though not halakhic, he was a maximalist, believing that the religious regimen should fill our days and our years. He was the ritual innovator: from the Bat Mitzvah to the radical recasting of the liturgy, he was ready to reconstruct in order to make ritual more meaningful and rescue it from "dull habit."

Kaplan attempted to reinterpret Shabbat, that most central of Jewish inventions, in terms of his ideals. On Friday evening, we leave behind our lower selves, our week-day selves, our week-day worries; in their place, we embrace a more transcendental self, a *neshama yeteirah,* as the rabbis liked to say. The Shabbat should not mean merely abstention but rather the one day in which we move consciously toward perfection, not in the next world but in this world. After we have come together in synagogue, Kaplan would have us each pursue his or her own creative path toward perfection. Such was the democratic spirit of Mordecai Kaplan.

Kaplan frequently used the term "salvation," even though it grated on some ears and is associated more with Christianity than with Judaism. He understood it as the ultimate goal of religious life. In ancient times, it had to do with the safety and security of the Jewish people. In the Middle Ages, the term came to refer to life in the hereafter. For us on this side of the Enlightenment, it has come to mean personal fulfillment or becoming fully human, or personal integration, as Kaplan liked to say. The integration that he so valued was understood in moral terms and had no place for the narcissism or self-indulgence so prevalent in our culture. As we have seen, there is a long and noble history behind Kaplan's notion of the moral perfection of the individual.

However we understand the religious life, its highest aspirations—salvation, perfection, spirituality, an awareness of the divine, all these must take place within community. For Kaplan, the group is central to the fully functioning individual. We need each other. He would certainly agree with Emmanuel Levinas who speaks to us of the suffering of the other, which induces in us a sense of obligation and, therefore, a sense of the divine. Only within the group can the individual achieve the highest degree of perfection. Indeed, the purpose of the group is to set up a context in which each of us has the maximum opportunity to achieve our full humanity.

We are never fully human, Kaplan maintains, unless there is a sharing of interests between the self and the other—the community makes that sharing possible, and Kaplan believed that the community has great value in developing our character. The ideal is for each of us to have loyalties, not only to our family and our immediate community but also to the nation and, indeed, to all humankind. Kaplan wrote, "Such is the mutuality of human life that none can be saved until all are saved. We are all our brother's keepers. . . . The categorical imperative of the moral life is: So love your neighbors that you help them to realize their highest potentialities."[3]

In other words, the collective consciousness is not only transcendent and helps us become our best possible selves but, as a matter of fact, Kaplan understands this as the *shekhina* itself (herself). This central theological expression, translated as the "divine spirit," is explicitly identified by Kaplan with the collective consciousness of the Jewish people. In an essay from the early 1970s, he wrote, "Our God of Israel, the *shekhina,* is none other than the collective consciousness of the Jewish people."[4]

We have seen the centrality of the concept of Jewish peoplehood in the Kaplanian universe. He sometimes spoke of the "Jewish people" in almost mystical terms. It is no surprise that he was a devoted Zionist. For Kaplan, the goal of Zionism has always been the regeneration of the Jewish people, not merely the establishment of a Jewish state. The Jews are unique because of their status as an "international people" as he put it, an "international nation with a home to give them cultural and spiritual unity."[5] Kaplan continued to maintain this special brand of Zionism even after the state was established. Indeed, his final work was titled *The Religion of Ethical Nationhood.*

For Kaplan, piety and community are essentially related. In his words, "If piety is, as Santayana put it, reverence for the source of one's being, then piety demands an attitude of reverence for one's community that is on par with reverence for one's own human person, and in fact an integral part of it."[6] Kaplan quotes his mentor John Dewey, who pointed out that "we live in the universal and the community is a symbol of that." The total quotation is worth noting. "Within the flickering inconsequential acts of separate selves," writes Dewey, "dwells a sense of the whole which claims and dignifies them. In its presence we put off mortality and live in the universal. The life of the community in which we live and have our being is a fit symbol of this relationship."[7]

Kaplan's theology opens up the possibility of a profound spirituality in our very modern era, particularly for those who have rejected religion because of its supernatural foundations. Although, theologically speaking, Kaplan was most comfortable as a naturalist, he also deals with the supra-natural. To deal with the supra-natural, however, is not the same as accepting the supernatural. The supra-natural is the realm of the poet, who feels a heightened sensitivity to the natural world, where as Emerson would say, "all the noise becomes music." Kaplan was not a poet, but he had the sensitivity of one. His own theological poem where he dwells on the unity and the mystery of all existence refers to this realm of the supra-natural. For Kaplan, the supernatural meant the acceptance of a Supreme Being who created the universe and governed it, a Being who was the source of our ancient laws and our highest ideals. After he turned away from the belief in God as a supernatural being, he never looked back.

To be a naturalist means first of all to accept the axiom that the road to truth leads through the rational, the empirical, and the scientific. Kaplan from his earliest years was wedded to the social sciences. He believed that understanding scriptures requires a thorough grounding in history, anthropology, sociology, and archeology. But then, because he was a rabbi, Kaplan would also consult Rashi, the great medieval commentator. The midrash was as much his métier as the pragmatic thrust of his thought.

Dewey and William James, Kaplan's intellectual mentors, dwelled in the same realm as the sociologists. With their embrace of the empirical method, their emphasis on the experimental even in the area of ethics, the philosophers and the sociologists fit beautifully together. Sociology and pragmatism were symbiotic in the mind of Mordecai Kaplan.

Many years ago, I wrote an article titled "The Sociologist as Theologian." I am still convinced that this formulation accurately describes the main principles of Kaplan's method. When he thinks about God (which he did all the time), he moves invariably from a sociological analysis to a theological statement. He tells us, for example, that the concept of God functioned in the same way for the ancients as government does for us: that it was the source of authority, and order and law. Thus, even in a reconstructed theology, the primacy of law must be at the center of our religious beliefs about the fundamental realities of the universe.

But the insight, and the provocation, of Kaplan's sociological mind have also warped our perception of him. To appreciate Kaplan's religious views, we have to go beyond the realm of the sociological; to understand Kaplan only in terms of the sociological would be a grave error. He warned frequently and emphatically that we must not reduce God or the divine to our more easily understandable categories. He believed that religion began as a way of reinforcing the highest values of any society; religion was the glue that held that society together. But, at the same time, he was careful to point out that religion is more than an expression of community and that God is more than the sum of our ideals. The divine is more than the totality of community.

Throughout Kaplan's life, there were individuals, both great and small, who misunderstood his belief in God. Perhaps it was his fault that he spoke too often of what it means to believe in God rather than about God. Our belief in the ideals of justice and righteousness assumes a world and a universe that is set up to support those ideals. It assumes the phenomena of mind and morality and consciousness. Justice Oliver Wendell Holmes seconded Kaplan's assumptions: "It is enough for us that it [the universe] has intelligence and significance inside of it, for it has produced us."[8] For Kaplan, the concept of the human being, the reality of being fully human, implies a greater divine reality that supports that ideal. If our ideal is the unity of the self, that implies a greater unity outside the self.

The most compelling statement on the issue of the divine reality, of the support for the existence of conscience and our ideals, of our moving beyond the natural to the supra-natural (or "transnatural," as Kaplan called it) comes from a published work and is thoroughly familiar to those who read Kaplan religiously. In *The Meaning of God in Modern Jewish Religion*, Kaplan states,

> The purpose in the various attempts to reinterpret the God idea is not to dissolve the God idea into ethics. It is to identify those experiences which should represent for us the actual working of what we understand by the conception of God. Without the actual awareness of His presence, experienced as beatitude and inner illumination, we are likely to be content with the humanist interpretation of life. But this interpretation is inadequate, because it fails to express and to foster the feeling that man's ethical aspirations are part of a cosmic urge, by obeying which man makes himself at home in the universe.[9]

Kaplan's theological transnaturalism points to God as the life of the universe, as the underlying order, as the urge toward growth, as the interrelatedness of all things, and as the fundamental importance of creativity. The creative principle for Kaplan asserts that "God is the creative life of the universe; the sum of all the forces making a cosmos out of chaos."[10]

Kaplan for all his skepticism was yet a man of profound faith. In spite of the chaos in the world, he held that the world is moving toward more order, uniqueness, and love, even though our experience often seems to contradict this. Kaplan's basic optimism is an expression of his faith and hope that, as for most religious people, was at the center of his life.

Arthur Hertzberg, the well-known scholar and Conservative rabbi, in his 1981 introduction to Kaplan's magnum opus, brilliantly and eloquently captured the essence of Kaplan's theology:

> He [Kaplan] is a believer, for even in the most rationalist formulations he has never questioned the intrinsic value of Judaism or his commitment to it. That is as much a given for him as it is for any romantic or mystical Hasid. It is possible to discern a deep current of personal mysticism . . . a sense that one's individual life ultimately belongs, at its best and most creative, to the very web of the universe, to its ongoing createdness and creativeness.[11]

The Jewish people has always survived by adapting themselves, by taking the best in the cultures among whom they lived, and by "judaizing" what they borrowed. *To judaize* here means to incorporate the ideal within the life of the community and to remember that at the top of the list of goals are always justice and righteousness. From this vantage point, Kaplan is the embodiment of this adaptation instinct. His lifelong struggle to breathe new life into the traditional by adapting it to contemporary sensibilities helped conserve Jewish values while drawing in those at risk of assimilation. Now, more than a half century after the burning of his prayer book, it is clear that his ideas are more essential than ever. Rather than undermining Judaism, Mordecai Kaplan's thinking, in its radical embrace of naturalist theology, in fact, reaffirms the heart of Jewish civilization for our time.

APPENDIX:
"THIRTEEN WANTS" OF
MORDECAI KAPLAN RECONSTRUCTED

In 1926, Mordecai Kaplan formulated what he called the "Thirteen Wants" as a way of expressing the fundamentals of his life as a Jew. Perhaps the word *ideal* is more fitting than the word "wants." Kaplan certainly had in mind a reconstruction of Maimonides's "Thirteen Principles of Faith."

I have taken the liberty of reformulating these "wants" in language perhaps more fitting for the present. Kaplan thought of substituting the words "pray" and "hope" in some of the wants. The original "wants" are found in the *Sabbath Prayer Book* (New York: The Jewish Reconstructionist Foundation, Inc., 1945), 562.

Here is Kaplan's own estimation of the "Thirteen Wants" some twenty years later, as recorded in his diary for December 6, 1949:

> This morning, as Lena and I were reading our prayers together at home, I concluded them with the reading of the "Thirteen Wants." I was so impressed as I always am by their relevance and comprehensiveness as well as their aptness in setting forth what a Jew should experience to be a good Jew that I remarked to Lena, "When I am gone, I do not want any eulogies delivered at my funeral. All I would ask is the recital of the 'Thirteen Wants.'" Insofar as a person's wants [ideals] constitute his real self, these "Thirteen Wants" constitute my selfhood as a Jew.

1. We pray that Judaism may help us to find meaning and direction in our lives.

2. We hope that our community may be a source of support in times of trouble.

3. We pray that Judaism may help us to use our blessings for just and righteous ends.

4. We are committed to using our leisure to the best advantage—physically, intellectually and spiritually.

5. We hope that our homes will be a warm safe haven and a stimulating place to live and grow.

6. We pray that our children may flourish morally and spiritually. We want to enable them to accept with joy their heritage as Jews.

7. We pray that our synagogues enable us to worship God in sincerity and truth.

8. We want our religious traditions to be understandable and to be made relevant to our present day needs. We want to find new and creative ways to incorporate Jewish ideals into our daily lives.

9. We are committed to strengthening the State of Israel as the center of the Jewish people and as the expression of the Jewish spirit.

10. We hope that Judaism will find new and compelling expressions in philosophy, literature and the arts.

11. We hope that all Jewish organizations will accomplish their goals within the sphere of the ethical and the spiritual.

12. We hope that all Jews will be ready to help each other in times of need and to cooperate in furthering Jewish life.

13. We want Judaism to advance the cause of justice, freedom and peace.

NOTES

PREFACE

1. The Kaplan papers at the Reconstructionist College are now in the process of being catalogued. For Kaplan's published work, see the complete bibliography in Emanuel S. Goldsmith, Mel Scult, and Robert Seltzer, eds., *The American Judaism of Mordecai M. Kaplan* (New York: New York University Press, 1990), 415–53. There are over four hundred items in that bibliography. There is also Kaplan's diary, discussed throughout this book.

2. On Kaplan and community and his concept of "Judaism as a civilization," see chapter 5.

3. For a very suggestive book on this issue, see George Stack, *Nietzsche and Emerson: An Elective Affinity* (Athens: Ohio University Press, 1992).

4. See chapter 2 on Kaplan and Emerson, which discusses the Kaplan-Emerson prayer.

5. See Chapter 10 on Kaplan and Heschel. That chapter discusses the Kaplan-Heschel prayer mentioned here.

6. For Kaplan's theological views, see chapters 6 and 7. Salvation (discussed in chapter 8) is, of course, a major category in Kaplan's thinking, as important as his beliefs about God. The key to Kaplan's well-known formulation of "God as the power that makes for salvation" comes from Matthew Arnold. See chapter 3 for a discussion on the way this poet influenced Kaplan's thinking.

7. On the Kaplan prayer book and the excommunication that followed it, see chapter 1. That chapter also analyzes Kaplan's attitude toward Spinoza.

8. For Kaplan's views of prayer and of holiness, particularly the Sabbath and holidays, see chapter 9.

9. Milton Steinberg, *The Prophet's Wife* (Springfield, NJ: Behrman House, 2010).

10. The original of the Kaplan diary is housed at the Jewish Theological Seminary in New York City. There is also a photocopy at the Reconstructionist Rabbinical College in Wyncote, Pennsylvania. The seminary has put the diary online, and it can be accessed at www.jtsa.edu/library/digitalcollections/archives/kaplan/html. A number of years ago, I edited a selection from the early diary titled *Communings of the Spirit: The Journals of Mordecai M. Kaplan, Volume 1: 1913–1934*, ed. Mel Scult (Detroit: Wayne State University Press, 2001). Throughout this work where we quote a statement from the diary that is also in that collection, I shall indicate both the location and page number. In terms of

my use of the diary for publication, the first question is whether Kaplan intended the journal to be published. When I first examined the diary in 1972, Kaplan indicated that he had shown the early volumes to other scholars interested in his life and thought. His daughters reported that, from time to time, he read them passages. He noted in his will that the diary should not be published for five years after his death, thereby implying that, after that period, it was permissible to publish the diary.

11. Emerson diary, "Spring?, 1853." *Emerson in His Journals,* ed. Joel Porte (Cambridge, MA: Belknap Press of Harvard University Press, 1982), 446. Porte apparently did not know the exact date of this diary entry.

12. Camp Cejwin was founded in 1919 by Albert and Bertha Schoolman as a way of implementing Mordecai Kaplan's philosophy. The camp was a project of the Central Jewish Institute, created in 1916 "to integrate Judaism with the American way of life" (interview with Albert Schoolman, June 1972). Cejwin was the first of a system of Jewish community camps in the United States. It closed in 1999.

13. A number of years before I met Kaplan, he had a microfilm made of the diary. He allowed me to have a copy of the microfilm, from which I made a positive book-type copy of each volume. I recently gave my microfilm to the Jewish Theological Seminary, and it can be viewed in the general reading area. The original of the diary is in the Rare Books Department.

14. Kaplan diaries, May 14, 1931, Jewish Theological Seminary (hereafter JTS), box 2, vol. 6; *Communings,* 439.

15. *American Hebrew,* October 14, 1927.

1. EXCOMMUNICATIONS

The epigraph is from Kaplan diaries, April 9, 1939, box 3, vol. 8.

1. Steven Nadler, *Spinoza's Heresy: Immortality and the Jewish Mind* (Oxford: Clarendon Press, 2001). The interested reader might also want to look at Heidi M. Ravven and Lenn Goodman, eds., *Jewish Themes in Spinoza's Philosophy* (Albany: State University of New York Press, 2002).

2. For an Orthodox view of Kaplan, see Jeffrey S. Gurock and Jacob J. Schachter, *A Modern Heretic and a Traditional Community: Mordecai Kaplan, Orthodoxy and American Judaism* (New York: Columbia University Press, 1997).

3. The story of Korah and his rebellion against the authority of Moses is found in Numbers 16.

4. Related to the author in an interview with Kaplan, June 1972.

5. The best general work on Jews in New York is still the classic by Moses Rischin, *The Promised City: New York's Jews, 1870–1914* (Cambridge, MA: Harvard University Press, 1964). For a critical evaluation of the condition of traditional Jewry in New York, see the translation of Rabbi Moses Weinberger's 1887 work, *People Walk on Their Heads: Moses Weinberger's Jews and Judaism in New York,* trans. Jonathan Sarna (New York: Holmes & Meier Publishers, Inc., 1982).

On the Chief Rabbi see Abraham J. Karp, "New York Chooses a Chief Rabbi," *American Jewish Historical Quarterly* 44 (March 1955): 129–198. On the Chief Rabbi and the situation of New York Jewry in the 1880's see Jeffrey S. Gurock, *The Men and Women of Yeshiva: Higher Education, Orthodoxy, and American Judaism* (New York: Columbia University Press, 1988), Chapter 2.

6. The details of Kaplan's early life may be found in my biography of Kaplan, *Judaism Faces the Twentieth Century: A Biography of Mordecai M. Kaplan* (Detroit: Wayne State University Press, 1993).

7. Ehrlich is mentioned in every autobiographical piece Kaplan wrote. For a list of these, see the Kaplan bibliography in Emanuel Goldsmith, Mel Scult, Robert Seltzer, eds., *The American Judaism of Mordecai Kaplan* (New York: New York University Press, 1990), 415–52. For a more extensive discussion of Ehrlich, see below chapter 3.

8. For a full discussion of Kaplan and Ahad Ha-Am, see chapter 3.

9. The details of the reorganization are found in this author's account of the seminary under Schechter: "Schechter's Seminary," in *Tradition Renewed: A History of the Jewish Theological Seminary—Volume 1,* ed. Jack Wertheimer (New York: The Jewish Theological Seminary of America, 1997), 43–102.

10. The full details are found in Scult, *Judaism Faces the Twentieth Century,* 67–69.

11. Early Kaplan diary, May 7, 1905. Ira and Judith Kaplan Eisenstein Reconstructionist Archives, Reconstructionist Rabbinical College (hereafter RRC), Wyncote, PA.

12. Early Kaplan diary, August 23, 1905, RRC.

13. See my biography and chapter 5 below for more on the Jewish Center. See also the fine work by David Kaufman, *The Shul with a Pool: The Synagogue Center in American Jewish History* (Hanover, NH: University Press of New England, 1999).

14. See Mordecai Kaplan, "A Program for the Reconstruction of Judaism," *The Menorah Journal* 6, no. 4 (August 1920): 181–196. It should be noted that this rather radical article by Kaplan was published a few years after his father's death.

15. Scult, *Judaism Faces the Twentieth Century,* chapter 6, "The Quest for Community: The Jewish Center." See chapter 7 of my biography for details about the founding and early years at the Society for the Advancement of Judaism (SAJ). See below in this chapter for a key quotation from this article.

16. See the index of Mordecai M. Kaplan, *Judaism as a Civilization: Toward a Reconstruction of American Jewish Life,* with a New Introduction by Mel Scult (Philadelphia: Jewish Publication Society, 2010), for the many references to the chosen people concept. For a full discussion of the publication of this work, see Scult, *Judaism Faces the Twentieth Century,* chapter 13.

17. Kaplan, *Judaism as a Civilization,* 441.

18. See Kaplan diaries, September 25, 1934, JTS, box 2, vol. 8, for further references to the issue of *kashrut.* The Kaplan diary of 1913 is at the Jewish Theological Seminary. See "Selected Bibliography and Note on Sources," section "Kaplan's Diaries," below. See the discussion on Kaplan and Jewish law in chapter 11, for more material on Kaplan's own religious regime.

19. Leo Jung, "Orthodoxy, Reform and Kaplanism," *Jewish Forum* 4 (April 1921): 778–83.

20. We might recall that Moses is not mentioned in the traditional *haggadah* at all. The faculty of the Seminary wrote Kaplan a nine-page letter criticizing him and "calling him on the carpet" for his departure from tradition. For a selection of most of the relevant but not all the documents connected to the publication of *The New Haggadah* (New York: Behrman House, Inc., 1941), see Jack Wertheimer, "Kaplan vs. The Great Do-Nothings: The Inconclusive Battle over *The New Haggadah,* " *Conservative Judaism* 45 (Summer 1993): 20–37. After this whole incident, Ira Eisenstein recommended

that Kaplan leave the seminary. Kaplan was not yet ready. He was sixty years old at the time.

21. See www.ezrastorah.org for pictures and brief biographies of the men on the executive committee.

22. *Ha-pardes* 19, no. 4 (July 1945), 210 The journal may be accessed online in Hebrew at www.Hebrewbooks.org, click on journals, *Ha-pardes*, 1945, July. I am indebted to Dan Cedarbaum, past president of the Jewish Reconstructionist Federation and present executive director of the Kaplan Center for Jewish Peoplehood, for finding the actual text of the *herem* and to David Golumb, Professor Emeritus of the Reconstructionist Rabbinical College, for the translation.

23. For more on the details of *The New Haggadah* and the *siddur,* see chapter 9.

24. See *T.B. Gittin* 45b. The relevant text reads "Rabbi Nahman said, 'We have it on tradition that a scroll of law which has been written by a *min* [heretic] should be burnt.'" I am indebted to my son Rabbi Joshua Scult of Jerusalem for this Talmudic reference.

25. The chief rabbi was Rabbi Herzog. This fact was related to me in an interview with Kaplan. Selma Kaplan Jaffee, one of Kaplan's daughters, showed me a letter of support for Kaplan from Einstein. A group at the SAJ had written to Einstein hoping he would issue a supportive statement, but, though he condemned the excommunication in his return letter, he would not issue a public statement.

26. For a fascinating study of Lieberman and his relationship to the *haredim,* see Marc B. Shapiro, *Saul Lieberman and the Orthodox* (Scranton, PA: University of Scranton Press, 2006). A more comprehensive study is Elijah J. Schochet and Solomon Spiro, *Saul Lieberman—The Man and His Work* (New York: Jewish Theological Seminary, 2005).

27. Kaplan diaries, June 16, 1945, JTS, box 4, vol. 13. We should also mention the article printed in the Hebrew publication *Ha-Do'ar* in the late summer of 1945. It was signed by the three most senior members of the JTS faculty: Saul Lieberman, Alexander Marx, and Louis Ginzberg. The article was cautious but extremely critical of Kaplan and his prayer book. It consists of a long diatribe against Kaplan and the prayer book but stops short of agreeing that Kaplan ought to be excommunicated. We shall detail the contents of this article and Kaplan's response in our discussion of prayer in chapter 9.

See also Zachary James Silver, "The Excommunication of Mordecai Kaplan. How an act of intolerance paved the way toward cultural pluralism in post-war America" (unpublished Honors Thesis, University of Pennsylvania, 2005). For a shorter version of this work, see "The Excommunication of Mordecai Kaplan," *American Jewish Archives* 62:1 (2010):

28. Steven Nadler, *Spinoza: A Life* (Cambridge: Cambridge University Press, 1999), 108–9.

29. Ibid., 105.

30. Ibid., 72.

31. Ibid.

32. Ibid., 153–54.

33. In the early 1940s, Kaplan taught a course at JTS titled "Philosophies of Judaism." It was important to him that it be called "Philosophies of Religion," in the plural, thus making it clear that he was not teaching his own ideology. His notes for this course are among his papers in the Kaplan Archive at the Reconstructionist College. The quotation here comes from these notes in the section on Spinoza.

34. See Gurock and Schachter, *A Modern Heretic and a Traditional Community.*

35. *The Journals and Miscellaneous Notebooks of Ralph Waldo Emerson, Volume VII, 1838–1842,* ed. A.W. Plumstead and Harrison Hayford (Cambridge, MA: Harvard University Press, 1969), 178 (March 19, 1839).

36. Kaplan diaries, January 3, 1940, JTS, box 3, vol. 9.

37. See *Spinoza: Ethics, Part Two,* trans. and ed. G. H. R. Parkinson (New York: Oxford University Press, 2000), 151 (proposition 44).

38. In his introduction, Parkinson states, regarding happiness, "that Spinoza has other terms for this condition, including blessedness (beatitude) and salvation (*salus*)." Ibid., 45.

39. See Kaplan's class notes for his course in "The Philosophies of Religion," Kaplan Archive, RRC.

40. Emmanuel Levinas, *Difficult Freedom: Essays on Judaism,* trans. Sean Hand (Baltimore: Johns Hopkins University Press, 1990), 106.

41. Kaplan Diaries, April 9, 1939, JTS, box 3, vol. 8.

42. This theme occupies a major place in Maimonides, *Guide for the Perplexed,* trans. Shlomo Pines (Chicago: University of Chicago Press, 1963).

43. Kaplan diaries, April 1, 1956, JTS, box 5, vol. 18.

44. On more recent efforts to reclaim or at least reconsider Spinoza's position vis-à-vis the Jewish people, see Steven Nadler's *Spinoza's Heresy,* as well as Ravven and Goodman, eds., *Jewish Themes in Spinoza's Philosophy.* In addition to the Spinoza course at the Jewish Theological Seminary mentioned above, this author also taught a course in Kaplan's philosophy at the Seminary, offered for the first time during the fall semester of 2006.

45. Benedict de Spinoza, *Theological-Political Treatise,* trans. Michael Silverstone and Jonathan Israel (New York: Cambridge University Press, 2007), 9.

46. Spinoza's *Ethics,* as quoted in Matthew Stewart, *The Courtier and the Heretic: Leibniz, Spinoza and the Fate of God in the Modern World* (New York: W.W. Norton & Co., 2006), 101. On the same theme, see Steven B. Smith, *Spinoza, Liberalism and the Question of Jewish Identity* (New Haven, CT: Yale University Press, 1998).

47. For a full discussion of this issue, see Shaul Magid, "The Spinozistic Spirit in Mordecai Kaplan's Revaluation of Judaism," *Modern Judaism* 20, no. 2 (May 2000): 159–80, at 161.

48. Mordecai M. Kaplan, *The Meaning of God in Modern Jewish Religion* (Detroit: Wayne State University Press, 1994), 3.

49. For more on the issue of the primitiveness of biblical religion, see Howard Eilberg-Schwartz, *The Savage in Judaism: An Anthology of Israelite Religion and Ancient Judaism* (Bloomington: Indiana University Press, 1990).

50. For a fuller presentation of this issue, see Leora Batnitzky, "Mordecai Kaplan as Hermeneut: History, Memory and His God Idea," *Jewish Social Studies* 12, no. 2 (Winter 2006): 88–98. This whole issue of *Jewish Social Studies* is devoted to Kaplan and contains papers given at a conference on his ideas at Stanford University in February 2004. The lectures at the conference were recorded and can be obtained from Stanford University Taube Center for Jewish Studies.

51. Kaplan diaries, November 1, 1925, JTS, box 1, vol 3. See also Mordecai Kaplan, *Communings of the Spirit: The Journals of Mordecai M. Kaplan, Volume 1, 1913–1934,* ed. Mel Scult (Detroit: Wayne State University Press, 2001), 215

52. Kaplan diaries, September 10, 1928, JTS, box 1, vol. 4.

53. Kaplan diaries, November 6, 1952, JTS, box 5, vol. 16.

54. The reader will find Kaplan's theology detailed in chapters 6 and 7.

55. For a full discussion of Kaplan and Durkheim, see chapter 5.

56. For a very interesting account of the status of ideals in the thought of John Dewey, see Victor Kestenbaum, *The Grace and Severity of the Ideal: John Dewey and the Transcendent* (Chicago: University of Chicago Press, 2002).

57. For the statement about atheism found in *Communings of the Spirit*, 62, see Kaplan diaries, March 30, 1913, JTS, box 1, vol. 1.

2. SELF-RELIANCE

The epigraph is from Joseph Albo (d. 1444), prominent Spanish Jewish philosopher, author of "The Book of Principles." Quoted in Mordecai M. Kaplan, *Ha-emunah ve-hamusar* [Belief and Morality] (Jerusalem: Rubin Mass, 1954), 12. The translation is my own. Kaplan's volume does not exist in English.

1. See the very suggestive essay by Eugene Borowitz, "The Autonomous Jewish Self," *Modern Judaism* 4, no. 1 (February, 1984): 1–39.

2. Sidney E. Ahlstrom, *A Religious History of the American People* (New Haven, CT: Yale University Press, 1972), 605.

3. See above chapter 1.

4. The Baeck and Emerson prayers discussed here are found in Kaplan's diary entry for August 23, 1942. The Heschel prayer is found in the diary entry for September 19, 1942. See Chapter 10 for a discussion of Kaplan's Heschel poem. The poem Kaplan created based on the work of Leo Baeck is found in *The Sabbath Prayer Book* (New York: The Jewish Reconstructionist Foundation, 1946), 426.

5. I learned of this loose-leaf prayer book some years ago, but it was a deeply emotional experience when I recently discovered a copy among the papers of Ira Eisenstein, z"l, at the Reconstructionist Rabbinical College with the Emerson and Heschel poems side by side. The letters z"l stand for two Hebrew words *zikhrono/a livrakha*, meaning "may his/her memory be for a blessing." It is most often used soon after a person has passed away when the writer or speaker wants to honor that person.

6. For a full discussion of Kaplan and Heschel and the Heschel-Kaplan poem, see chapter 10 below.

7. This term is very much associated with the work of Stanley Cavell. His essays on Emerson have been recently collected into one volume, *Emerson's Transcendental Etudes*, ed. David Justin Hodge (Stanford, CA: Stanford University Press, 2003).

8. Alfred Kazin, *God and the American Writer* (New York: Alfred A. Knopf, 1997), 42.

9. The essay on which Kaplan's poem is based is "The Address before the Harvard Divinity School—1838." For more information, see n. 24 below.

10. This title is Kaplan's.

11. Kaplan was working on the *Musaf* (additional service for the Sabbath) in August 1942, and he states that "one of the following selections should be read." Then follows the Kaplan-Baeck prayer, "Life Is What We Make It," and two Kaplan-Emerson prayers, including "Needed Prophets for Our Day." The obvious implication is that the Emerson prayer was to be part of the *Musaf* service.

12. The remainder of this passage may be found in Mordecai Kaplan, *Communings of the Spirit: The Journals of Mordecai M. Kaplan, Volume 1, 1913–1934,* ed. Mel Scult (Detroit: Wayne State University Press, 2001), 57.

13. In a sense, the present chapter is a meditation on this quotation.

14. The best discussion of Emerson's concept of "self-culture" is his essay "Self-Reliance," found in every edition of his essays. In the edition by Stephen Whicher, it is found together with relevant quotations from the Emerson diary. See *Selections from Ralph Waldo Emerson: An Organic Anthology,* ed. Stephen E. Whicher (Boston: Houghton Mifflin, 1957), 147–68.

15. The concept of *Bildung* has a long and significant history. See my discussion in chapter 3 on Kaplan and Arnold.

16. Kaplan diaries, November 23, 1943, Jewish Theological Seminary (hereafter JTS), box 4, vol. 12.

17. Kaplan diaries, September 6, 1943, JTS, box 4, vol. 12. Kaplan gives the date of Emerson's entry as 1883, which is obviously wrong since Emerson died in 1882. See Emerson's essay "Circles" for the classic exposition of the ideas contained in this passage. I have not been able to locate the exact source of this Emerson statement. However, Emerson frequently revised statements he first made in his journals, and it may be that Kaplan is quoting here from an original journal entry. There is another version of this statement that is found in a lecture Emerson gave at Dartmouth in 1838: "We assume that all thought is already long ago adequately set down in books,—all imaginations in poems; and what we say, we only throw in as confirmatory of this supposed complete body of literature. A very shallow assumption. Say rather, all literature is yet to be written. Poetry has scarce chanted its first song. The perpetual admonition of nature to us, is, 'The world is new, untried. Do not believe the past. I give you the universe a virgin to-day." "An Oration Delivered before the Literary Societies of Dartmouth, July 24, 1838," in *The Collected Works of Ralph Waldo Emerson: Volume I, Nature, Addresses and Lectures,* ed. Alfred R. Ferguson et al. (Cambridge, MA: Belknap Press of Harvard University Press, 1971). It may also be found in *Journals and Miscellaneous Notebooks of Ralph Waldo Emerson,* ed. William H. Gilman (Cambridge, MA: Belknap Press of Harvard University, 1960) 7:17.

18. See the very fine essay by Allan Lazaroff, "Kaplan and John Dewey," in *The American Judaism of Mordecai Kaplan,* ed. Emanuel S. Goldsmith, Mel Scult, and Robert Seltzer (New York: New York University Press, 1990), 173–97.

19. Stephen C. Rockefeller, *John Dewey: Religious Faith and Democratic Humanism* (New York: Columbia University Press, 1991), 444.

20. "Soterics," Reconstructionist Rabbinical College (hereafter RRC), 153, RG1, RS15, Shelf 37.

21. Mordecai Kaplan, *Ha-emunah ve-hamusar* [Belief and Ethics] (Jerusalem: Rubin Mass, 1954), 12. Kaplan's footnote to the passage lists his source in Hebrew as Joseph Albo, *Sefer Ha-ikkarim, ma-amar shlishi, perek vav.* There are many editions of this work. The translation here is my own.

22. *Ralph Waldo Emerson: Selected Journals, 1841–1877,* ed. Lawrence Rosenwald (New York: Literary Classics of America, 2010), 107.

23. "Convers Francis: Remarks on Emerson in 1838, 1855, and 1858," in *Emerson in His Own Time,* ed. Ronald Bosco and Joel Myerson (Iowa City: University of Iowa Press, 2003), 3–6.

24. Emerson's Divinity School Address is found in many collections of his writings. I have used *Selections from Ralph Waldo Emerson: An Organic Anthology,* ed. Stephen E. Whicher (Boston: Houghton Mifflin Company, 1957). This collection is especially useful

because Whicher, a great Emerson scholar, has introduced relevant material from Emerson's journals before and after each essay.

25. See the very illuminating discussion in George Kateb, *The Inner Ocean: Individualism and Democratic Culture* (Ithaca, NY: Cornell University Press, 1992), introduction.

26. Mordecai Kaplan, *The Future of the American Jew* (New York: Macmillan and Company, 1948), 283.

27. Kaplan diaries, February 8, 1915, JTS, box 1, vol. 1; *Communings*, 84.

28. See discussion in George Kateb, *Emerson and Self-Reliance* (New York: Rowman and Littlefield Publishers, Inc., 2002), 32.

29. Ibid., 29.

30. For a discussion of this issue, see Stanley Cavell, *Conditions Handsome and Unhandsome: The Constitution of Emersonian Perfectionism* (Chicago: The University of Chicago Press, 1990). See especially the introduction, where Cavell states this idea—of being true to oneself as being distinct from being self-serving—as fundamental to Emerson's thinking.

31. Abraham Maslow, *Motivation and Personality* (New York: Harper Collins, 1987), passim.

32. For a discussion of conscience in Emerson, see Stephen Whicher, *Freedom and Fate: The Inner Life of Ralph Waldo Emerson* (New York: A.S. Barnes, 1953), especially 33–37. See also Barbara Packer, *Emerson's Fall: A New Interpretation of the Major Essays* (New York: Continuum Publishing, 1982), 137ff.

33. Kaplan diaries, Dec. 25, 1943, JTS, box 4, vol. 12.

34. See Richard Rorty, *Philosophy and Social Hope* (New York: Penguin Books, 1999), 15.

35. Kaplan diaries, August 23, 1914, JTS, box 1, vol. 1; *Communings*, 68. For a very insightful discussion of this issue, see Steven Lukes, *Moral Relativism* (New York: St. Martin's Press, 2008).

36. My thanks to Barbara Gish Scult for her help in formulating this paragraph. Lawrence Kohlberg's six ethical stages are relevant here since the highest stage is a postconventional type of thinking that judges in terms of universal moral principles. See Lawrence Kohlberg, *Moral Stages: A Current Formulation and a Response to Critics* (Farmington, CT: S. Karger, Inc., 1983), passim. These stages can also be found via an Internet search for "Kohlberg moral stages."

37. "The subjective is not necessarily relative": Kaplan diaries, August 23, 1914, JTS, box 1, vol. 1; *Communings*, 70. "Universal character of experience": Kaplan diaries, June 30, 1930, JTS, box 2, vol. 6; *Communings*, 408.

38. Ralph Waldo Emerson, "Self-Reliance," in *Selections from Ralph Waldo Emerson*, 147.

39. See "History," in *Essays: First and Second Series by Ralph Waldo Emerson* (New York: Vintage Books/The New Library of America, 1990), 3. Also discussed by Cavell, "Aversive Thinking: Emersonian Representations in Heidegger and Nietzsche," in *Conditions Handsome and Unhandsome*, 3ff.

40. Kaplan diaries, January 15, 1931, JTS, box 2, vol. 6; *Communings*, 432. Henri Bergson (1859–1941) was the primary process philosopher who influenced Kaplan. He will be discussed below in chapter 7. There are many metaphysical process thinkers including Alfred North Whitehead (1861–1947), who is preeminent, that Kaplan read only from time to time and did not know well.

41. In this entry, he mentions two authors by name. One is Orchard. He is probably referring to the collection by W. E. Orchard, *The Temple: A Book of Prayers* (New York: Dutton, 1918). Kaplan had no problem in using Christian prayer collections. Ira Eisenstein once told me that he and Kaplan introduced Christian prayers into the service at the Society for the Advancement of Judaism after taking out Jesus' name.

42. Found in the Babylonian Talmud, *Berachot* 21a.

43. See Kaplan diaries, January 10, 1930, JTS, box 2, vol. 5; *Communings,* 394.

44. See "Self-Reliance" in *Selections from Ralph Waldo Emerson,* 158.

45. All the quotations in this paragraph are from Emerson's "Self-Reliance."

46. Cavell, *Conditions Handsome,* 38.

47. Cavell, quoting Nietzsche, *Conditions Handsome,* 51. There is a whole host of ways in which Nietzsche and Emerson are related. See the very suggestive study by George Stack, *Nietzsche and Emerson: An Elective Affinity* (Athens: Ohio University Press, 1992).

48. This expression is found Cavell, *Conditions Handsome,* 52; it is not clear whether this sentiment is from Emerson or Nietzsche or Cavell.

49. I am fully aware that there are elements in the Emerson-Kaplan poem that we have not discussed, the most important being continuous revelation. It seemed appropriate to me to include this discussion below in the chapter on God.

3. NATIONALISM AND RIGHTEOUSNESS

The epigraph is from Kaplan diary, August 17, 1905, RRC.

1. Mordecai Kaplan, J. Paul Williams, and Eugene Kohn, eds., *The Faith of America: Readings, Songs, and Prayers for the Celebration of American Holidays* (New York: Henry Schuman, Inc., 1951).

2. Cohan was immortalized by James Cagney in the film *Yankee Doodle Dandy.*

3. Kaplan diary, August 17, 1905, Reconstructionist Rabbinical College Archives (hereafter RRC).

4. For the details of the life of Ahad Ha-Am, see Steven Zipperstein, *Elusive Prophet: Ahad Ha-Am and the Origins of Zionism* (Berkeley: University of California Press, 1993). Many provocative ideas are contained in the collection of essays edited by Jacques Kornberg, *At the Crossroads: Essays on Ahad Ha-am* (Albany: State University of New York Press, 1983). See also the essay by Deborah Dash Moore on the intellectual ambiance at this time: "A New American Judaism," in *Like All the Nations? The Life and Legacy of Judah L. Magnes,* ed. William M. Brinner and Moses Rischin (Albany: The State University of New York Press, 1987), 41–57. See also the very fine vignette of Ahad Ha-Am by Rav Tzair (Chaim Tchernowitz) in his *Book of Memoirs: Portraits and Appraisals, Sages of Odessa* [Hebrew] (New York: The Jubilee Committee, 1945). This work has not been translated into English but should be. It brings the Odessa group to life like no other work.

5. My summation of Ahad Ha-Am here is based on the works already cited and on an essay by Baruch Kurzweil that appears in *Hemshekh u-mahapekha* [Modern Hebrew Literature: Continuity or Revolution] (Tel Aviv: Schocken Press, 1965). This work has not been translated. See also Kaplan himself on Ahad Ha-Am in *The Greater Judaism in the Making: A Study of the Modern Evolution of Judaism* (New York: The Reconstructionist Press, 1960), 415–31. It is also interesting to note that Kaplan dedicated his last book to Ahad Ha-Am; see *The Religion of Ethical Nationhood: Judaism's Contribution to World Peace* (New York: The Macmillan Co., 1970). The dedication reads as follows: "To the

memory of Ahad Ha-Am (Asher Ginzberg) who revealed to me the spiritual reality of the Jewish people, of Solomon Schechter who granted me the opportunity to transmit it to my students and of Louis Dembitz Brandeis, who pleaded for ethical nationhood in American life."

6. Zipperstein, *Elusive Prophet*, 123.

7. See a very fine late expression of this concept in Kaplan, *The Greater Judaism*, 420.

8. Kaplan was, of course, well acquainted with Nietzsche. We have already documented Kaplan's relationship to Emerson. For both Emerson and Nietzsche, the ideal of perfectibility stood at the center of their thought. See the chapter on salvation below, and the excellent book by George Stack, *Nietzsche and Emerson: An Elective Affinity* (Athens: Ohio Unversity Press, 1992).

9. See, for example, the essay *"Torah she'ba'lev,"* in *Kol Kitveh Ahad Ha-Am* [The Complete Writings of Ahad Ha-Am] (Tel Aviv: D'Vir, 1953), 51–64. For the English translation, see "The People of the Book," in *Ahad Ha-Am: Essays Letters and Memoirs,* trans. and ed. Leon Simon (Oxford: East West Library, 1946), 58–65.

10. See *"Avdut Be-Tokh Herut"* [Slavery in the Midst of Freedom], in *Kol Kitveh Ahad Ha-Am,* 64–66. A number of essays by Ahad Ha-Am have been translated in Robert Alter, ed., *Modern Hebrew Literature* (New York: Behrman House, Inc., 1975).

11. See *"Hikkui ve-hitbolelut"* [Imitation and Assimilation] in *Kol Kitve Ahad Ha-Am,* 86–90, or its translation in *Essays, Letters, Memoirs: Ahad Ha-Am,* trans. and ed. Leon Simon (Oxford: East and West Library, 1946), 71–76.

12. My notes record the language of the quotation here but not the exact source for this idea of "masking the normative," as Bloom calls it. I wrote to Bloom for the source of this concept in his work, but he did not know it either.

13. Kaplan's remark is in a letter to Phineas Israeli, dated January 31, 1909. I am grateful to Nathan Israeli, z"l, his son, for permission to quote this letter, which was in his possession.

14. For more on Benderly and Kaplan, see my biography, *Judaism Faces the Twentieth Century: A Biography of Mordecai Kaplan* (Detroit: Wayne State University Press, 1993), especially chapter 4, which deals with the Teachers Institute. Benderly, a dedicated Zionist, was a primary force in Jewish education for many years. Every major figure in Jewish education in the first half of the twentieth century was influenced by him. He served as head of the Board of Jewish Education for many years. In the early years of the twentieth century, the Teachers Institute was located in what we would now call the East Village of Manhattan. The Board of Jewish Education was nearby, and Kaplan and Benderly frequently met for lunch. See also the new biography by Nathan Krasner, *The Benderly Boys and American Jewish Education* (Waltham, MA: Brandeis University Press, 2011).

15. Kaplan, *The Greater Judaism,* 431.

16. Mordecai M. Kaplan, *Judaism as a Civilization: Toward a Reconstruction of American Jewish Life,* with a New Introduction by Mel Scult (Philadelphia: Jewish Publication Society, 2010), 282.

17. I know he used the Maimonides Library because, among his books at the Reconstructionist Rabbinical College, I found a volume with a bookplate from the Maimonides Library that he never returned. Steven Siegel, z"l, the archivist of the Ninety-Second Street Y, brought the matter of the neighborhood to my attention. The location of the B'nai B'rith office is mentioned by Deborah Dash Moore, in *B'nai B'rith and the Challenge of Ethnic Leadership* (Albany: State University of New York Press, 1981). The

early seminary bulletins listed names and addresses of students, so we know where the Kaplan family lived from year to year.

18. In Schechter's more colorful private correspondence, we find the following comments on biblical criticism: "I wish that the Messiah would come who would revive the dead, so that prophets and the rabbis could tell those German dogs of professors to their faces how they disfigured their words and forged them with the purpose of showing the superiority of their God Christ. I am despairing to see justice done to Judaism by the Christians. However, I am boring you with theological nonsense." Solomon Schechter to Mrs. Herbert Bentwich, October 14, 1894, Bentwich papers, Central Zionist Archives, Jerusalem.

19. Ehrlich is mentioned in every autobiographical piece Kaplan ever wrote. The quotation here comes from Julius Greenstone, "Reminiscences of the Old Seminary Days," *United Synagogue Recorder* 6, no. 4 (October, 1926): 9. For Kaplan's biographical pieces, see the Kaplan bibliography in Emanuel Goldsmith, Mel Scult and Robert Seltzer, eds., *The American Judaism of Mordecai Kaplan* (New York: New York University Press, 1990), 415–52.

20. In 1912, Joseph Hertz was elected chief rabbi of the British Empire. Hertz was a JTS graduate. Kaplan's name had also been submitted by Schechter.

21. Kaplan diaries, June 24, 1949, JTS, box 4, vol. 14.

22. We have noted earlier that Kaplan, after graduating from the seminary in 1902, took a pulpit at the East Side Orthodox congregation Kehilath Jeshurun. Although he did not have the title of rabbi, Kaplan had primary responsibility for the synagogue until the well-known traditional scholar Rabbi Moshe Zevulun Margolis (called the *Ramaz*, 1851–1936) was brought on board in 1906. Kaplan later noted that the two got on rather well. See Scult, *Judaism Faces the Twentieth Century* for the story of Kaplan and Kehilath Jeshurun.

23. Interview with Kaplan, June 1972. The Central Park Reservoir was a favorite place for Kaplan's walks. He walked there with Judah Magnes, with Louis Finkelstein, and with Ira Eisenstein. The relationship with Finkelstein is intimately tied to the reservoir. See the full account of the account is in Scult, *Judaism Faces the Twentieth Century*, 229–31. The story is quite unbelievable.

24. "The lie which I live," Kaplan diary, December 31, 1906; "My life lacks music," Kaplan diary, November 25, 1906; "senseless prudishness," Kaplan diary, August 23, 1905. RRC.

25. Lionel Trilling, *Matthew Arnold* (New York: Harcourt Brace Jovanovich, 1939), 191. Arnold's most important essays on religion and culture are "Culture and Anarchy" (1869) and "Literature and Dogma" (1873). We shall also have occasion to refer to some of his other work, especially an essay on Heine and one on Spinoza, which have proved useful.

26. Robert Browning, "Development" (1889), in *The Complete Poetical Works of Robert Browning* (New York: Macmillan, 1915), 1312–14; as quoted in Ruth apRoberts, *Arnold and God* (Berkeley: University of California Press, 1983), 24.

27. Matthew Arnold, "Obermann Once More," in *The Collected Prose Works of Matthew Arnold*, ed. R. H. Super (Ann Arbor: University of Michigan Press, 1960–1977), 5:559. Cited in apRoberts, *Arnold and God*, 156.

28. Trilling, *Matthew Arnold*, 217.

29. apRoberts, *Arnold and God*, 32.

30. Nicholas Murray, *A Life of Matthew Arnold* (New York: St. Martin's Press, 1996), 251.

31. Matthew Arnold, "Hebraism and Hellenism," in *Collected Prose Works of Matthew Arnold,* 5:165, as cited in apRoberts, *Arnold and God,* 148.

32. Evelyn Garfiel (1900–87) was a psychologist, professor at the University of Chicago, and the author of *Service of the Heart: A Guide to Jewish Prayer* (Northvale, NJ: Aronson, 1989). She was active in the Conservative movement and taught at the Jewish Theological Seminary. In 1923, she married Max Kadushin, a devoted disciple of Kaplan. On her relationship with Kaplan, see my biography, *Judaism Faces the Twentieth Century.*

33. Kaplan originally wrote, "God was not a being, but the world viewed as ordered universe." He crossed out "world" and substituted "Reality." As discussed in the previous chapter, Kaplan reviewed the diary and frequently "corrected" what he wrote.

34. See Kaplan diaries, October 13, 1922, JTS, box 1, vol. 2. This selection can be found also in *Communings of the Spirit,* 168.

35. Matthew Arnold, *Culture and Anarchy: An Essay in Political and Social Criticism,* ed. J. Dover Wilson (New York: Macmillan Co., 1875), 46.

36. apRoberts, *Arnold and God,* 155.

37. Trilling, *Matthew Arnold,* 252.

38. See "Herder and the Enlightenment," in Isaiah Berlin, *The Proper Study of Mankind: An Anthology of Essays,* ed. Henry Hardy (New York: Farrar, Straus and Giroux, 1998), 359–436.

39. *The Notebooks of Matthew Arnold,* ed. H. F. Lowry, Karl Young, and W. H. Dunn (London: Oxford University Press, 1952), 48, as cited in apRoberts, *Arnold and God,* 45.

40. Matthew Arnold, "Culture and Anarchy" in *Collected Prose Works,* 5:94, as cited in apRoberts, *Arnold and God,* 143.

41. See, for example, George Mosse, *German Jews: Beyond Judaism* (Bloomington: Indiana University Press, 1985), passim.

42. Ibid., 13.

43. James Simpson, *Matthew Arnold and Goethe* (London: Modern Humanities Research Association, 1979), 139, as cited in apRoberts, *Arnold and God,* 47.

44. Matthew Arnold, "Literature and Dogma," in *Collected Prose Works,* 6:176, as cited in apRoberts, *Arnold and God,* 191.

45. On the relation between poetry and religion, see especially George Santayana, *Interpretations of Poetry and Religion* (Cambridge, MA: MIT Press, 1989).

46. Kaplan's poems are discussed in various chapters in this work: in chapter 2, the poem based on an essay by Emerson; in chapter 10, the poem based on an essay by Heschel; and in chapter 6, "The Supernatural," the poem most clearly expressing Kaplan's theology.

47. apRoberts, *Arnold and God,* 143.

48. Matthew Arnold, *Literature and Dogma* (New York: Macmillan, 1903), 29.

49. Ibid., 23.

50. Ibid., 30.

51. Ibid., 28. The italics are in the original.

52. Ibid.

53. Kaplan's use of the term "salvation" rather than Arnold's "righteousness" will be explained in our discussion of salvation.

54. "The best that is in us," Kaplan diaries, May 28, 1933, JTS, box 3, vol. 7; "Men's needs," interview with Mordecai Kaplan, August 1972.

4. UNIVERSALISM AND PRAGMATISM

The epigraph is from Kaplan Diaries, February 4, 1917, box 1, vol.1; also in *Communings of the Spirit: The Journals of Mordecai M. Kaplan Volume 1913–1934*, ed. Mel Scult, (Detroit: Wayne State University Press, 2001) 112.

1. On the second generation, see Deborah Dash Moore, *At Home in America: Second-Generation New York Jews* (New York: Columbia University Press, 1981), as well as Arnold M. Eisen's fine work on the intellectual history of American Jewry in the second and third generations, *The Chosen People in America* (Bloomington: Indiana University Press, 1983). The best work on Jewish immigrants in New York is still Moses Rischin, *The Promised City: New York's Jews, 1870–1914* (Cambridge, MA: Harvard University Press, 1964).

2. For some interesting parallels to Kaplan (e.g., Horace Kallen, Morris Raphael Cohen, and Lionel Trilling), see Susanne Klingenstein, *Jews in the American Academy, 1900–1940: The Dynamics of Intellectual Assimilation* (New Haven, CT: Yale University Press, 1991).

3. The details of Adler's life, unless otherwise noted, are drawn from the excellent biography by Benny Kraut, z"l, *From Reform to Ethical Culture: The Religious Evolution of Felix Adler* (Cincinnati, OH: Hebrew Union College Press, 1979).

4. John Herman Randall Jr., "The Department of Philosophy," *A History of the Faculty of Philosophy, Columbia University* The Bicentennial History of Columbia University Series (New York: Columbia University Press, 1957), 102–46.

5. Felix Adler, *The Religion of Duty* (New York: McClure Philips & Co., 1905), 4. This book is in Kaplan's library at the Rabbinical Reconstructionist College, as are the following: Felix Adler, *Life and Destiny or Thoughts from the Ethical Lectures of Felix Adler* (New York: McClure Philips & Co., 1903); idem, *The Essentials of Spirituality* (New York: James Pott & Co., 1905); idem, *The Reconstruction of the Spiritual Ideal* (New York: Appleton and Company, 1924); and idem, *The Ethical Philosophy of Life* (New York: D. Appleton and Company, 1927). Again I want to stress that, even though we shall be quoting particular statements, the importance of Adler is in his general approach and not in any one remark that he made.

6. Adler, *The Religion of Duty*, 23; see also Adler, *Life and Destiny*, 25.

7. See Kraut, *From Reform Judaism to Ethical Culture*, 106 and 246.

8. Adler, *Life and Destiny*, 132–33.

9. Columbia University Archives, Felix Adler Papers, box 100–1900E-1904B, folder E, "Lectures for Course at Columbia. February 17, 1903." These lecture notes were typed out by Adler, and each session is dated. The course is Philosophy 18, "Political and Social Ethics," which we know Kaplan took because of his registration book and also from my conversations with Kaplan. On Kaplan's studies at Columbia in general, see Mel Scult, *Judaism Faces the Twentieth Century: A Biography of Mordecai Kaplan* (Detroit: Wayne State University Press, 1993).

10. Kaplan diary, May 8, 1906, Reconstructionist Rabbinical College.

11. Ibid.

12. Adler, *Duty of Religion*, 42.

13. Ibid., 35.

14. Ibid., 37.

15. Ibid., 39, 40.

16. Kaplan diaries, July 20, 1927, Jewish Theological Seminary (hereafter JTS), box 1, vol. 3.

17. Kaplan had never despised Ehrlich because he converted back to Judaism and he was accepted by Kaplan's father. Israel Kaplan would certainly have nothing to do with Felix Adler.

18. Kaplan offered an Ethical Culture scholarship, Kaplan diaries, February 19, 1917, JTS box 1, vol. 1; Kaplan thinking of joining Ethical Culture, Kaplan diaries, July 2, 1916, JTS, box 1, vol. 1. For the opinion of Ira Eisenstein, see, "Ethical Culture Sees It Through," *S.A.J. Review* 8, no. 16 (December 28, 1928): 2. The *S.A.J. Review* preceded *The Reconstructionist*. [The review was Kaplan's synagogue bulletin, the originals of which are found at the Society for the Advancement of Judaism]. Two of Kaplan's daughters attended the Fieldston School, which was run by the Ethical Culture Society.

19. See chapter 8 for a discussion of "The Humanist Manifesto."

20. For a clear expression of Kaplan's ambivalent though largely critical statement on Ethical Culture, see the journal entry for Monday, February 19, 1917, in *Communings of the Spirit: The Journals of Mordecai M. Kaplan, Vol. 1, 1913–1934*, ed. Mel Scult (Detroit, MI; Wayne State University Press, 2001), 112.

21. Mordecai Kaplan, "What is Judaism," *The Menorah Journal* 1, no. 1 (Dec. 1915): 309.

22. The thesis is written in Kaplan's hand and runs to ninety-five pages. "The Ethical System of Henry Sidgwick" was submitted on February 28, 1902. It can be found in the Rare Book Collection of Columbia University's Butler Library. The thesis is referred to in *Columbia University—Master's Essays, 1891–1917, Vol. I* (New York: Columbia University, 1917), 70. For more information on Kaplan's graduate work, see my biography.

23. For examples where scholars ascribe influence to Dewey, see Ira Eisenstein and Eugene Kohn, eds., *Mordecai M. Kaplan: An Evaluation* (New York: Jewish Reconstructionist Foundation, Inc., 1952), 19; articles on Kaplan in the *Encyclopedia Judaica;* and Charles S. Liebman, "Reconstructionism in American Life," in *American Jewish Yearbook 1970* (New York: The American Jewish Committee, 1970), 51. Alan Lazaroff's study of Dewey and Kaplan compares and contrasts the two men but makes no attempt to establish Dewey's influence on Kaplan. See Allan Lazaroff, "John Dewey and Mordecai Kaplan" in *The American Judaism of Mordecai Kaplan*, ed. Emanuel Goldsmith, Mel Scult and Robert Seltzer (New York: New York University Press, 1990), 173–97. "The bulk of Dewey's popular work": e.g., *Democracy and Education* (1916), *Reconstruction in Philosophy* (1920), *Human Nature and Conduct* (1922), and *A Common Faith* (1934). "When a group of rabbinical students," Kaplan diaries, February 1915, JTS, box 1, vol. 1.

24. William James, *Pragmatism and Four Essays from the Meaning of Truth* (New York: Meridian Books, 1955), 27. *Pragmatism* was originally published in 1907.

25. The manuscript titled "The Meaning of Religion" is in Kaplan's own hand and is among his private papers. The comment cited here is on page 3, RRC.

26. The Menorahs were a group of college-age students devoted to the study of Judaism on a more sophisticated level than might be found in the local synagogue. Kaplan published regularly in *The Menorah Journal*.

27. Our discussion here on his lecture at the University of Minnesota is based on his account in the Kaplan diaries, February 4, 1917, JTS, box 1, vol. 1; also in *Communings of the Spirit*, 112. The full meaning of Jewish peoplehood and the collective consciousness will be explored below in chapter 5.

28. William James, *Pragmatism and Four Essays from the Meaning of Truth* (New York: Meridian Books, 1955), 145. The first edition of this work was published in 1907. I know there are many editions. I chose a recent easily available one.

29. Rorty's position is stated in many places. See his essay "Pragmatism as Romantic Polytheism," in Richard Rorty, *The Revival of Pragmatism: New Essays in Social Thought, Law and Culture* (Durham, NC: Duke University Press, 1998); see also Richard Rorty, *Philosophy and Social Hope* (New York: Penguin Books, 1999), 33.

30. "If there be any life," James, *Pragmatism,* 59. "it may be the Synagogue," letter to Henry Hurwitz, March 17, 1916, Kaplan letter file, RRC. See parallel ideas of Israel Friedlaender in the fine work by Baila Shargel, *Practical Dreamer: Israel Friedlander and the Shaping of American Judaism* (New York: Jewish Theological Seminary, 1987), passim.

31. Kaplan diary, December 8, 1905, RRC.

32. John Dewey, *Reconstruction in Philosophy* (Boston: Beacon Press, 1948), 201.

33. The formula often engraved on gravestones and said at funerals. Hebrew letters stand for words in the formula.

34. Mordecai M. Kaplan, *The Future of the American Jew* (New York: Macmillan, 1948), 299.

35. Mordecai M. Kaplan, *Questions Jews Ask: Reconstructionist Answers* (New York: The Reconstructionist Press, 1956), 124.

36. Mordecai M. Kaplan, *The Meaning of God in Modern Jewish Religion* (Detroit, MI: Wayne State University Press, 1994), 62.

37. Ibid., 63.

38. Kaplan diaries, October 12, 1942, JTS, box 4, vol. 11.

39. Kaplan diaries, December 9, 1942, JTS, box 4, vol. 11.

5. KAPLAN AND PEOPLEHOOD

The epigraph is from Emil Fackenheim, "Mordecai Kaplan, a Critic's Tribute," *Sh'ma: A Journal of Jewish Responsibility* 18 (October 1974): 145.

1. Mordecai M. Kaplan, *Judaism as a Civilization: Toward a Reconstruction of American Jewish Life* with a New Introduction by Mel Scult (Philadelphia: Jewish Publication Society, 2010), 335 (original publication: New York: Macmillan and Company, 1934). The fascinating story behind the publication of Kaplan's classic can be found in Mel Scult, *Judaism Faces the Twentieth Century: A Biography of Mordecai Kaplan* (Detroit: Wayne State University Press, 1993), chapter 13, "The Climax: Judaism as a Civilization and After." Readers may be interested to look at the new edition of *Judaism as a Civilization,* published in 2010 by the Jewish Publication Society and Jewish Reconstructionist Federation, with my new introduction. This new edition also contains the introductions of Kaplan himself, of Arthur Hertzberg, and of Arnold Eisen.

2. After the epigraph at the head of this chapter, Fackenheim went on to say, "Now as then, I am baffled by the dilemma of how Reconstructionism, if a mere minimum common denominator, can be nothing less than a philosophy of Judaism, and of how, if more than such a minimum and a genuine philosophy, it can unite orthodox and non-orthodox religious Jews, on the one hand, religious and secularist Jews on the other." Emil Fackenheim, "Mordecai Kaplan, a Critic's Tribute," *Sh'ma: A Journal of Jewish Responsibility* 18 (October 1974): 145. I also have an article in this issue about Kaplan and Matthew Arnold. Kaplan's ninetieth birthday was, of course, in 1971 not in 1974.

3. As a matter of fact, in the Kaplan diary during the 1930s, Kaplan uses the terms "culture" and "civilization" interchangeably, though he seems to favor "civilization."

4. For the published version of this paper, see Noam Pianko, "Reconstructing Judaism, Reconstructing America: The Sources and Functions of Mordecai Kaplan's 'Civilization,'" *Jewish Social Studies* 12, no. 2 (Winter 2006): 39–56. The next few paragraphs of this chapter are based on Pianko. For an expanded view on Kaplan, see also Noam Pianko, *Zionism—The Roads not Taken: Rawidowicz, Kaplan, Kohn* (Bloomington: Indiana University Press, 2010).

5. Reference here is to the preeminent historian Charles Beard and to his wife Mary Ritter Beard. Together they authored *The Beards' Basic History of the United States* (Garden City, NY: Doubleday, Doran & Co., 1944).

6. On the similarities between American civilization and Jewish civilization, see the fine book by Milton Konvitz, *Judaism and the American Idea* (Ithaca, NY: Cornell University Press, 1978).

7. See Alfred Eckhard Zimmern, *Nationality and Government with Other Wartime Essays* (London: Chatto and Windus, 1918), as cited in Pianko, "Reconstructing Judaism." For Kaplan references to Zimmern in *Judaism as a Civilization*, see Pianko, "Reconstructing Judaism, Reconstructing America."

8. See the collection of essays on Kallen, Milton Konvitz, ed., *The Legacy of Horace M. Kallen* (Teaneck, NJ: Fairleigh Dickenson University Press, 1987).

9. For Kaplan's criticisms of the major denominations of his time, see *Judaism as a Civilization*, Part Two, " The Current Versions of Judaism."

10. Mordecai Kaplan, "Is Judaism a Revelation or a Philosophy," a sermon at the Society for the Advancement of Judaism, November 2, 1923, in Reconstructionist Rabbinical College Archives (hereafter RRC).

11. Ira Eisenstein, *Creative Judaism: Based on Judaism as a Civilization* (New York: Behrman's Jewish Book House, 1936), 65. This work is an attempt by Eisenstein to rewrite *Judaism as a Civilization* so that it might be usable for Jewish educators and adult-education groups. It is a model of clarity and simplicity. It should be republished.

12. In this early period, Kaplan's energy was not yet completely absorbed by his duties as rabbi and by his graduate work. He walked around the reservoir in Central Park on a regular basis with his friends and later with his students. During the first three decades of the twentieth century, he records conversations and walks in Central Park with Judah Magnes, Max Kadushin, Louis Finkelstein, and Ira Eisenstein. See the index of Scult, *Judaism Faces the Twentieth Century* on Kaplan and Finkelstein and Central Park. He also swam regularly; see page 295 in the above biography for a photo of Kaplan in a bathing suit at the Jersey shore.

13. Regarding Durkheim, there is an interesting personal anecdote involving Rabbi Jacob Agus (1911–86). I once asked Agus, a great rabbi who had a contentious but respectful relationship with Kaplan for nearly a half century, whether he thought Durkheim was a primary influence. "Well, I will tell you a story," Agus began. "Once, many years ago when I was working on my dissertation, which included a chapter on Kaplan, I approached him and asked him whether Durkheim was a primary influence on his thinking." "Never read him," answered Kaplan. "Ten years later," Agus continued, "Kaplan was saying that Durkheim was the most significant influence on his thinking from the beginning." Apparently, Kaplan was suffering a lapse in memory, as he cites Durkheim many times in *Judaism as a Civilization*.

Agus met Kaplan in the late 1930s, when Agus was a young man and uncertain of his direction. They were friends for many years, though there were many disagreements between them because Agus was much more traditional than Kaplan. In the 1960s, Agus wrote Kaplan a letter in which he said that his conversation with Kaplan three decades earlier lead directly to Agus's going to Harvard and studying Jewish philosophy with Harry Wolfson, the greatest scholar in Jewish philosophy at the time. See the Agus folder in the Kaplan Papers at RRC.

14. Since Durkheim's classic work did not come out in English until 1915, *The Elementary Forms of Religious Life* (London: George Allen & Unwin, 1915), the date of Kaplan's reading is pushed beyond his early graduate years. Kaplan's major series of articles in the *Menorah Journal* appearing in 1915 gives us the general outline of his philosophy before he read Durkheim.

15. For Durkheim in *Judaism as a Civilization,* see index.

16. Steven Lukes, *Emile Durkheim: His Life and Work* (New York: Harper and Row Publishers, 1972), 242.

17. Mordecai M. Kaplan, "What is Judaism," *The Menorah Journal* 1 (December 1915): 316. The phrase "collective mind" does not come to Kaplan from Carl Jung but is found in many other sources, including the writings of his sociology teacher at Columbia, Franklin Giddings.

18. Edward Sapir, "The Status of Linguistics as a Science," *Language* 5, no. 4 (1929): 209. I am indebted to Rabbi Ed Feld for pointing out the primacy of language in understanding Kaplan's notion of civilization.

19. Mordecai Kaplan, "How May Judaism Be Saved," *The Menorah Journal* 2 (February 1916): 43.

20. Kaplan diaries, January 10, 1916, Jewish Theological Seminary (hereafter JTS), box 1, vol. 1.

21. Kaplan diaries, February 4, 1917, JTS, box 1, vol. 1; Mordecai M. Kaplan, *Communings of the Spirit: The Journals of Mordecai M. Kaplan, Vol. 1, 1913–1934,* ed. Mel Scult (Detroit, MI: Wayne State University Press, 2001), 112.

22. Mordecai M. Kaplan, "The Essence of Judaism," an undated speech found in RRC.

23. Kaplan diaries, January 26, 1914, JTS, box 1, vol. 1.

24. Mordecai M. Kaplan, "The Synagogue and the Community," speech dated 1932, Kaplan Papers, at the American Jewish Archives.

25. *Y.M.H.A. Bulletin* 14 (November 1913): 11. This issue records the attendance at the High Holiday Services that Kaplan ran for about six hundred people. All the quotations in the last two paragraphs are from the text of the speech. It has no title but is headed only "Spoken the second day of Rosh Hashannah, September 10, 1915 at the YMHA services" and is found in the Kaplan Papers at RRC.

26. Kaplan participated in the founding of Young Israel but was only involved for a few years. For details see Scult, *Judaism Faces the Twentieth Century,* 137–38. On Young Israel in general, which came into existence in 1912, see Rabbi David Warshaw, *A History of the Young Israel Movement, 1912–1937,* unpublished master's thesis, Bernard Revel Graduate School, Yeshiva University, 1974.

27. The more complete account of Kaplan and the Jewish Center is found in Scult, *Judaism Faces the Twentieth Century,* chapter 6. The standard work on the Jewish Center is David Kaufman, *Shul with a Pool: The Synagogue Center in Jewish Life* (Hanover, NH: University Press of New England, 1999).

28. Kaplan succeeded Judah Magnes as the Ninety-Second Street YMHA rabbi and served for a number of years after he left Kehilath Jeshurun in 1909.

29. Emancipation here, of course, refers to the period of the French Revolution and afterward when the Jews first became citizens and thus were emancipated from their previous restricted status.

30. Kaplan's first major use of the term "civilization" in connection with Judaism was at the dedication of the Jewish Center, March 24, 1918. Excerpts from this speech are found in "Judaism as a Living Civilization," *American Jewish Chronicle* 4 (April 19, 1918): 676–79. We shall discuss the contents of this article below. The quotations in this paragraph are from this article. This article should not be confused with "The Jewish Center," *American Hebrew* 102 (March 22, 1918): 529–31.

31. Kaplan diaries, May 22, 1917, JTS, box 1, vol. 1.

32. "Under the aspect of eternity." A favorite expression of Spinoza that Kaplan used frequently.

33. There were probably more synagogue centers in Brooklyn than anywhere else. Especially noteworthy were the Eastern Parkway Jewish Center and the East Midwood Jewish Center. For a full account of these institutions in the 1920s, see Deborah Dash Moore's fine work, *At Home in America: Second-Generation New York Jews* (New York: Columbia University Press, 1981).

34. Kaplan diary, March 28, 1939, JTS, box 3, vol. 8. The actual diary entry reads as follows: "I received a letter from Cyrus Adler yesterday in reply to Shocken's of Jan. 25. Every one of his official letters reminds me of the phrase "he froze to the occasion." Of course he turned down Shocken's suggestion that I should come to the University for the summer semester once in two years. Devoid as he is of imagination, how could he sense the value of a personal contact between the Seminary and the Hebrew University?"

35. See Mordecai M. Kaplan, *Future of the American Jew* (New York: Macmillan, 1948), 122, for this point.

36. Mordecai Kaplan, *A New Zionism* (New York: The Herzl Press and the Jewish Reconstructionist Press, 1959), 19.

37. Ibid., 75.

38. Mordecai Kaplan, *The Religion of Ethical Nationhood: Judaism's Contribution to World Peace* (New York: The Macmillan Co., 1970), 125.

39. Kaplan, *A New Zionism*, 41.

40. Ibid., 12.

41. I am very deeply indebted to Professor Yossi Turner of the Schechter Institute in Jerusalem, who first enlightened me on the distinction between the Herzlian-Ben Gurion emphasis on the state and its security and the Kaplanian emphasis on regeneration. In addition to a series of lectures Professor Turner gave at Mevakshe Derech in Jerusalem that I attended, I also had the privilege of reading his chapter on Kaplan's Zionism in his as-yet-unpublished work "Zionism and Diasporism in Twentieth-Century Jewish Thought: An Enquiry into the Problems of Jewish Existence" (in Hebrew). The title of the chapter in English would be "Zion and the Diaspora in Mordecai Kaplan's Conception of Judaism as Civilization." This very important work-in-progress by Turner investigates the attitudes of the leading twentieth-century Jewish thinkers regarding their perception of Zion and the diaspora—as a focal point for considering their various understandings of the problems of Jewish existence and their respective visions of pos-

sible solutions. The specifics of the presentation of Zionism in this present chapter are my own, however.

42. For the point about Ben-Gurion Zionism versus Kaplanian Zionism, see Turner manuscript, 10, 27. I think it would make most sense to put the two references together.

43. Kaplan, *Ethical Nationhood*, 120. On this theme of nonstatist Zionisms, see the important work by Pianko, *Zionism*.

44. The details of our brief sketch are found elsewhere. For Kaplan and Ahad Ha-Am, see chapter 3 above. For Kaplan at Kehilath Jeshurun and his studies at Columbia, see my Scult, *Judaism Faces the Twentieth Century*, chapter 2, "Beginnings: Graduate School and the First Pulpit."

45. Kaplan, *A New Zionism*, 115.

46. Ibid.

47. Jeremiah came from Anatot. See Jeremiah 1:1.

48. Kaplan diaries, September 21, 1932, JTS, box 2, vol. 7. Found also in *Communings of the Spirit*, 486.

49. Kaplan diaries, January 14, 1957, JTS, box 5, vol. 17. For a complete discussion of this issue, see Kaplan, *Judaism as a Civilization*, chapter 17, "The Nationhood of Israel." See also Turner manuscript, 28–29, for an analysis of this issue.

50. Jack Cohen, "Reflections on Kaplan's Zionism," in *The American Judaism of Mordecai Kaplan*, ed. Emanuel Goldsmith, Mel Scult, Robert Seltzer (New York: New York University Press, 1985), 401–15, at 408. See also Jack Cohen's more recent work, *Democratizing Judaism* (Brighton, MA: Academic Studies Press, 2010), especially chapters 10, 11, and 12.

51. Kaplan, *The New Zionism*, 27.

52. Kaplan, *Ethical Nationhood*, 125.

53. The idea of a binational state was first proposed by a small group of intellectuals in the 1920s; founders and early supporters included Martin Buber, Henrietta Szold, Albert Einstein, and Judah Magnes. For more on this group, see S. L. Hattis, *The Binational Idea in Palestine during Mandatory Times* (Haifa: Shikmona, 1970), as well as Judah L. Magnes, *Dissenter in Zion: From the Writings of Judah Magnes*, ed. Arthur A. Goren (Cambridge, MA: Harvard University Press, 1982), 272–73. While Kaplan was not a member of Brit Shalom, he did support the concept of binationalism, as the quotation indicates.

54. Kaplan diaries, August 7, 1937, JTS, box 3, vol. 8.

55. On the issue of limiting national sovereignty, see Kaplan, *Ethical Nationhood*, 16, 55.

56. See Kaplan, *Ethical Nationhood*, 133–34. Kaplan had this idea even in the 1950s; see *The New Zionism*, 15.

57. Kaplan, *The New Zionism*, 45.

58. This quotation is from "Soterics," an unpublished manuscript in the Kaplan archives at the RRC (p. 200). See comment on notes at the end of this book.

59. Kaplan, "Soterics," RRC, 239.

60. Mordecai M. Kaplan, "Our God as Our Collective Conscience," *Reconstructionist* 41, no. 1 (February 1975): 15–16. We should mention that, although Kaplan does deal with the matter of conscience, here it is clear from the article that he intends to focus on consciousness. Meir Ben Horin in his seminal work on Kaplan, *Transnature's God: Studies in*

Mordecai Kaplan's Theology (Wilton, CT: Adar Nisan Books, 2004), points out that Kaplan elaborated the rabbinic references where the rabbis refer to God as the *shekhina* and the collective consciousness is obviously implied. See Talmud Bavli, Megilah, 29:b, and Bamidbar Rabbah, 12:4. This notion of God as the collective will be more fully explained in the next chapter.

6. KAPLAN AND HIS GOD

The epigraph comes from Mordecai Kaplan, "Soterics," RRC, 44. RG1, RS15, Shelf 37. "Soterics" is an unpublished manuscript from the 1950s. Kaplan obviously intended to fill in the exact location of the Maimonides quotation but did not.

1. The slur in the previous paragraph was actually made in a review of Kaplan's work *Judaism as a Civilization.* This was related to the author in an interview with Kaplan in 1972.

The quotation mentioning Arnold is from the Kaplan diary, August 21, 1905, Reconstructionist Rabbinical College (hereafter RRC). See chapter 3 above on Matthew Arnold. It was precisely at this time, 1905, when Arnold was most present in Kaplan's mind. Hence, there is not only a reference to him here but also the sense of the importance of literature to theology, which, of course, Arnold emphasized.

2. Mordecai M. Kaplan, *Questions Jews Ask: Reconstructionist Answers* (New York: The Reconstructionist Press, 1956), 102.

3. For Kaplan on the *Shemah,* see Mordecai M. Kaplan, "Rabbinic Ideology," RRC, 21, a manuscript found among Kaplan's papers at RRC that deals with the ideology of rabbinic Judaism. Agreeing with Kaplan on the centrality of God as directing history according to the tradition, we find in Moshe Idel the statement that we worship God not because He is One but because He directs history. See Moshe Idel, "Intellectually We have Become Impoverished: An Interview with Moshe Idel," in *Minds across Israel* [Hebrew] (Jerusalem: The Department of Jewish Zionist Education, The Jewish Agency for Israel, *Yediot Ahronot,* 2005), 55.

4. "Editorial," *Jewish Forum* 4, no. 1 (January 21, 1921): 645–46. This editorial was written in reaction to Kaplan's article, "A Program for the Reconstruction of Judaism," *The Menorah Journal* 6, no. 4 (August 1920): 181–96.

5. Kaplan diaries, March 10, 1913, Jewish Theological Seminary (hereafter JTS), box 1, vol. 1. See also Mordecai M. Kaplan, *Communings of the Spirit: The Journals of Mordecai M. Kaplan, Vol. 1, 1913–1934,* ed. Mel Scult (Detroit: Wayne State University Press, 2001), 62.

6. Kaplan diaries, January 15, 1931, JTS, box 2, vol 6; *Communings of the Spirit,* 432.

7. See Kaplan's article, "Why Humanism Is Not Enough," *The Reconstructionist* 2, no. 7 (May 15, 1936): 12–16.

8. Kaplan diaries, January 29, 1935, JTS, box 2, vol. 7.

9. We shall consider the relationship of God to the liturgy in chapter 9.

10. Kaplan, "Why Humanism Is Not Enough," 14.

11. Ibid., 16.

12. The manifesto may be found online at http://www.americanhumanist.org /Humanism/Humanist_Manifesto_I.

13. The statement regarding theism is the sixth statement in the manifesto. The manifesto was signed by thirty-four men and women, including Anton J. Carlson, John Dewey, John H. Dietrich, and R. Lester Mondale.

14. Norman Bentwich, *For Zion's Sake: A Biography of Judah Magnes* (Philadelphia: Jewish Publication Society, 1954). Bentwich was an English Zionist who settled in Palestine, worked as a lawyer and was quite active in the Yishuv. He and Kaplan became acquainted during Kaplan's years in Israel, 1937–39. Bentwich also wrote a biography of Solomon Schechter, who had been very friendly with his father, Herbert Bentwich. There is a great deal of material on Solomon Schechter in Norman Bentwich's papers at the Central Zionist Archives in Jerusalem. The Bentwich biography is *Solomon Schechter (1847–1915): Scholar, Sage and Visionary* (New York: The Jewish Theological Seminary, 1938).

15. For Kaplan, when the word *humanism* is used alone, it refers to what we have described as secular humanism.

16. Kaplan diaries, March 25, 1951, JTS, box 4, vol. 15.

17. Mordecai M. Kaplan, *The Religion of Ethical Nationhood: Judaism's Contribution to World Peace* (New York: Macmillan Co., 1970), 10.

18. Mordecai M. Kaplan, "Between Two Worlds," in *Varieties of Jewish Belief,* ed. Ira Eisenstein (New York: The Reconstructionist Press, 1966), 140–41.

19. Mordecai M. Kaplan, *Judaism without Supernaturalism: The Only Alternative to Orthodoxy and Secularism* (New York: The Reconstructionist Press, 1958), 38–39.

20. Ibid.

21. Ralph Waldo Emerson, "Self-Reliance," in *Selections from Ralph Waldo Emerson: An Organic Anthology,* ed. Stephen E. Whicher (Boston: Houghton Mifflin Co., 1957), 162. See also Kaplan, *Judaism without Supernaturalism,* 38.

22. See chapter 3, "Nationalism and Righteousness: Ahad Ha-Am and Matthew Arnold."

23. Interview with Mordecai Kaplan, 1972. According to Professor Baila Shargel, Friedlander's biographer, it has never been clear what Friedlander believed about biblical criticism.

24. It is interesting to note that in Kaplan's *The New Haggadah,* which he published in 1941, the plagues are omitted. See *The New Haggadah for the Pesach Seder,* ed. Mordecai M. Kaplan, Eugene Kohn, and Ira Eisenstein (New York: Behrman's Jewish Book House, 1941).

25. The plagues have, however, been restored in the most recent edition: *The New American Haggadah Shel Pesach,* ed. Mordecai M. Kaplan, Eugene Kohn, Gila Gevirtz, Ira Eisenstein, (Springfield, NJ: Behrman House, 1999). Kaplan Diaries, September 10, 1928, box 2, vol. 4; *Communings of the Spirit,* 265.

26. Hadassah was Kaplan's second oldest daughter. The oldest was Judith, the first Bat Mitzvah. "Partruition" means birth.

27. Kaplan diaries, December 3, 1935, JTS, box 3, vol. 8. The child born here is Jeremy Musher, 1935–73. Judith Kaplan Eisenstein's child is Ethan Eisenstein. Ethan passed away in 2003.

28. The lecture was first delivered at the Masonic Temple in Boston on January 22, 1840. See Ralph Waldo Emerson, "Religion," in *The Early Lectures of Ralph Waldo Emerson,* vol. 3, 1838–42, ed. Robert E. Spiller and Wallace E. Williams (Cambridge, MA: The Belknap Press of Harvard University Press, 1972), 278.

29. See *Midrash Rabbah,* Shemot 2:5.

30. Professor Neil Gillman is fond of saying that all statements about God are metaphors. This idea came from one of our many conversations.

31. The standard work on the history of idolatry is Moshe Halbertal and Avishai Margalit, *Idolatry* (Cambridge, MA: Harvard University Press, 1992).

32. Ibid., 109.

33. Mordecai M. Kaplan, "Soterics," RRC, 41.

34. Center Sermons, March 29, 1919, RRC.

35. Mordecai M. Kaplan, *The Future of the American Jew* (New York: Macmillan Co., 1948), 214. We shall consider the issue of Kaplan's attitude toward the chosen people concept in chapter 9 on ritual and prayer.

36. Mordecai M. Kaplan, "The Supremacy of Torah," *Jewish Theological Seminary: Students Annual, 1914* (New York: Jewish Theological Seminary, 1914), 180–92.

37. Kaplan diaries, July 11, 1943, JTS, box 4, vol. 12.

38. Mordecai M. Kaplan, "A Philosophy of Jewish Ethics," in *The Jews, Their History, Culture and Religion,* ed. Louis Finkelstein (Philadelphia: Jewish Publication Society, 1960), 1017.

39. I am grateful to my brother, Professor Allen Scult, for pointing out this passage to me. The passage is found in Martin Buber, *Moses: The Revelation and the Covenant* (New York: Harper and Row, 1958), 16–17.

40. Today, we would most likely call the historical truth a "myth," as in Neil Gillman's use of that term. See, for example, Gillman's *The Death of Death: Resurrection and Immortality in Jewish Thought* (Woodstock, VT: Jewish Lights, 1997), among other places.

41. Needless to say, there are many places in this work where Kaplan spells out the fundamental and enduring values that are expressed through the event of Sinai.

42. The quotations in this and the preceding paragraph are all from Abraham Joshua Heschel, *God in Search of Man: A Philosophy of Judaism* (New York: Farrar, Straus & Cudahy, 1955), 185ff.

43. For an interesting example of Kaplan's use of the personal God image, see below at the beginning of chapter 12, where, in conducting a funeral, he resorts to God in a personal and moving sense.

44. See Marcia Falk, *The Book of Blessings: New Jewish Prayers for Daily Life, the Sabbath, and the New Moon Festivals* (San Francisco: Harper San Francisco, 1996).

45. I fully understand that Emerson cannot be a midrash or commentary on Kaplan. It ought to be the reverse, but I am using "midrash" here in a highly metaphorical sense. For me, Emerson explains and expands the thoughts found in Kaplan, hence Emerson as a midrash on Kaplan. (In the same sense, as discussed elsewhere, I think John Dewey can also be used as a midrash on Kaplan.) In terms of the concept of "keeping the word alive," Emerson's transcendent epigrammatic poetic style comes very close to sounding like contemporary scripture and the "voice of the divine." Surely, the great transcendentalist functioned as scripture for the young men of his generation who marched off to war carrying their collections of Emerson with them.

46. "The Over-Soul," in *The Portable Emerson,* ed. Carl Bode (New York: Penguin Books, 1946), 218.

47. See Kaplan's reworking of Emerson essay into a poem in chapter 2 and his reworking of the Heschel essay into a poem in chapter 10.

48. George Santayana, *Interpretations of Poetry and Religion* (Cambridge, MA: MIT Press, 1989), 3. There are some, Richard Rorty among them, who believe that poetry could perform the same functions as religion but without all the rituals. Indeed, Rorty

seems quite annoyed by ritual. I do not think Dewey would completely agree with his disciple, but he comes close, as we shall see. See particularly Richard Rorty, "Pragmatism and Romantic Polytheism," in *The Revival of Pragmatism: New Essays on Social Thought, Law and Culture,* ed. Morris Dickstein (Durham, NC: Duke University Press, 1998), 21–37.

49. Ralph Waldo Emerson, "The Poet," in *The Portable Emerson,* ed. Carl Bode (New York: Penguin Books USA, 1957), 244. See also Arthur Green, *Seek My Face, Speak My Name: A Contemporary Jewish Theology* (Northvale, NJ: Jason Aronson, Inc., 1992), 107–10.

50. Kaplan diary, December 1905, RRC.

51. Emerson, "The Poet," 255. For the affinities between Kaplan and Kook, see Jack J. Cohen, *Guides for an Age of Confusion: Studies in the Thinking of Abraham Y. Kook and Mordecai M. Kaplan* (New York: Fordham University Press, 1999). I am proud to say that I was able to help in bringing this book to Fordham's attention. It was originally written in Hebrew and was translated by the author himself.

52. See Edward Kaplan and Samuel H. Dresner, *Abraham Joshua Heschel: Prophetic Witness* (New Haven, CT: Yale University Press, 1998), 133. The authors mention Otto as an influence over Heschel but give no specific reference.

53. Kaplan diaries, May 15, 1954, JTS, box 5, vol. 17.

54. Mordecai M. Kaplan, *The Future of the American Jew* (New York: Macmillan Co., 1948), 198.

7. KAPLAN'S THEOLOGY

The epigraph is from Kaplan diaries, October 29, 1940, JTS, box 3, vol. 9.

1. In Kaplan's dedication of *Judaism as a Civilization: Toward a Reconstruction of American Jewish Life,* with a New Introduction by Mel Scult (Philadelphia: Jewish Publication Society, 2010; originally published 1934), he characterizes his father as his guide and teacher during the time of his confusion. The elder Kaplan, of course, would have been very disturbed by the content of *Judaism as a Civilization,* even though it came from a loving son.

2. Kaplan diaries, February 8, 1950, Jewish Theological Seminary (hereafter JTS), box 4, vol. 15. Israel Kaplan died in 1917 while Mordecai Kaplan was in the process of preparing a startling article, "A Program for the Reconstruction of Judaism," which appeared in the *Menorah Journal* 6, no. 4. I do not think that Kaplan would have ever published this article while his father was alive.

3. See the discussion of predicate theology later in this chapter.

4. Mordecai Kaplan, "The Unsolved Problem of Evil Concluded," *The Reconstructionist* 29, no. 8 (1963), 15.

5. Kaplan diaries, September 3, 1922, JTS, box 1, vol. 2. I regret to say that I neglected to include this statement in Mordecai M. Kaplan, *Communings of the Spirit: The Journals of Mordecai M. Kaplan, Vol 1, 1913–1934,* ed. Mel Scult (Detroit: Wayne State University Press, 2001).

6. Kaplan diaries, November 6, 1952, JTS, box 5, vol. 16.

7. Mordecai M. Kaplan, "Torah and Salvation," 30. The manuscript is found in the Kaplan archives at the Reconstructionist Rabbinical College (hereafter RRC). The title is mine. The manuscript has no title. From the paper and the typeface, it is quite clear that this document is from the 1920s.

8. For the Whitehead reference, see Kaplan diaries, November 18, 1929, JTS, box 2, vol. 5; and *Communings of the Spirit*, 376. Kaplan, of course, studied philosophy as an undergraduate and as a graduate student. It is, consequently, surprising that the thought that the individual philosopher has a contribution seems a discovery to him. Many years ago, I came across in Kaplan's papers a recommendation that his philosophy professor, W. H. Sheldon, wrote while Kaplan was studying for his master's at Columbia. It reads in part, "In referring to Mr. Kaplan's work with me (Philosophy 3-Kant) I should like to say that his summaries have been masterpieces of clearness and directness, singling out the most vital points in Kant, and that his criticisms have that quite ideal quality of at once laying their finger on the nerve of the argument. Especially the latter have shown unusual penetration in so difficult a subject as Kant's Transcendental Deduction and are to me indications of a decided philosophic ability which ought to be cultivated."

9. I have chosen never to alter Kaplan's diary text even though it may be awkward or ungrammatical, as it is here.

10. Kaplan diaries, April 2, 1954, JTS, box 5, vol. 17.

11. Harold Schulweis, "From God to Godliness: A Proposal for a Predicate Theology," *The Reconstructionist* 51, no. 1 (February 1975): 16–26.

12. Ibid., 24.

13. For Weiman and Kaplan, see especially Henry Nelson Weiman "Kaplan's Idea of God," in *Mordecai Kaplan: An Evaluation,* ed. Ira Eisenstein and Eugene Kohn (New York: Jewish Reconstructionist Press, 1952), 193–211; in addition, see Emanuel S. Goldsmith, "Kaplan and Henry Nelson Weiman," in *The American Judaism of Mordecai M. Kaplan,* ed. Emanuel S. Goldsmith, Mel Scult, and Robert Seltzer (New York: New York University Press, 1990), 197–221; and also by Goldsmith, " Salvation in the Theologies of Henry Nelson Weiman and Mordecai M. Kaplan, in *New Essays in Religious Naturalism,* ed. W. Creighton Peden and Larry E. Axel (Highlands NC: Highlands Institute for Religious and Philosophical Thought, 1993), 83–98. Goldsmith has been significant in influencing the work of Jerome A. Stone. See especially Stone's *Religious Naturalism Today: The Rebirth of a Forgotten Alternative* (Albany: State University of New York, 2008), 111–19, for a section on Kaplan.

14. See chapter 2 on Emerson for an earlier use of this concept of midrash, as well as an explanation in chapter 6.

15. John Dewey, *A Common Faith* (New Haven, CT: Yale University Press, 1934), 14.

16. Victor Kestenbaum, *The Grace and Severity of the Ideal: John Dewey and the Transcendent* (Chicago: The University of Chicago Press, 2002), 180.

17. Dewey, *A Common Faith,* 18, as quoted in ibid., 181.

18. Dewey, *A Common Faith,* 23.

19. George Kateb, *Emerson and Self-Reliance* (New York: Rowman and Littlefield Publishers Inc., 1995), 65.

20. Kaplan diaries, October 29, 1940, JTS, box 3, vol. 9.

21. The book by William James is *A Pluralistic Universe: Hibbert Lectures at Manchester College on the Present Situation in Philosophy* (London: Longmans, Green, 1909). The quotation from Kaplan's journal is found in January 27, 1914, JTS, box 1, vol. 1; see also *Communings of the Spirit,* 64–65.

22. Three works of his particularly stand out: *Matter and Memory,* published in 1896; *Creative Evolution,* which came out in 1907; and *The Two Sources of Morality and Religion,* originally published in 1932.

23. Leszek Kolakowski, *Bergson* (South Bend, IN: St. Augustine's Press, 2001), 34. Samuel Hugo Bergman, in his book *Contemporary Thinkers* [Hebrew] (Jerusalem: The Hebrew University, 1935), has a chapter on Bergson that has been very useful in our summary.

24. Kaplan diaries, March 30, 1913, JTS, box 1, vol. 1. This statement is also found in *Communings*, 62, and is used a number of times throughout this work.

25. Mordecai M. Kaplan, "Soterics," RRC, 241. See also Mordecai M. Kaplan, *The Meaning of God in Modern Jewish Religion* (Detroit: Wayne State University Press, 1994).

26. Kaplan diaries, November 23, 1955, JTS, box 5, vol. 17.

27. In reading of this incident, I could not help but be reminded of the legend of the four rabbis who entered the *pardes:* Ben Azzai, Ben Zoma, Aher (Elisha Ben Avuya), and Akiba. Ben Azzai looked and died; Ben Zoma looked and went mad; Aher destroyed the plants; Akiba entered in peace and departed in peace. The legend is recorded in the Babylonian Talmud *Hagigah* 14 b. All Kaplan's students, of course, survived this encounter. Kaplan diaries, March 19, 1943, JTS, box 4, vol. 12. Among the students were Jack Cohen, z"l, and Sidney Morgenbesser, z"l.

28. Kaplan diaries, March 19, 1943, JTS, box 4, vol. 12.

29. See chapter 7 "God as Felt Presence," in *The Meaning of God in Modern Jewish Religion*. The quotation here is on page 244.

30. Kaplan might have responded to Buber that the latter's concept of God was also hardly that of the simple shtetl Jew. But, alas, it is always easy to think of the right response after the event.

31. Kaplan diaries, July 9, 1938, JTS, box 3, vol. 8. Kaplan in this passage is referring to the passage in the *Meaning of God* just cited. While he was in Palestine, Kaplan kept his journal in Hebrew. The passage here was translated by the late Professor Nahum Waldman, z"l, a good friend and a fine Hebrew scholar.

32. Kaplan diaries, October 3, 1939, JTS, box 3, vol 9.

33. "The Oversoul," in *The Portable Emerson,* ed. Carl Bode (New York: Viking Penguin, 1946), 212.

34. Hermann Cohen (1842–1918) was a German-Jewish neo-Kantian liberal philosopher.

35. In this relatively neglected work, Kaplan presents a series of quotations from Cohen that he calls an epitome and appends a running commentary. See Mordecai M. Kaplan, *The Purpose and Meaning of Jewish Existence* (Philadelphia: The Jewish Publication Society, 1964), 107.

36. The quotation is from Albo, the medieval philosopher who was quoting Al Gazzali, whose thought, of course, goes back to Aristotle and Plato. It is found in Mordecai Kaplan, *Ha-emunah veha-musar* [Faith and the Ethical] (Jerusalem: Rubin Mass, 1954), 12. Kaplan's footnote to the passage lists his source in Hebrew as Joseph Albo, *Sefer Ha-Ikkarim, ma-amar shlishi, perek vav.* The translation here is my own.

37. All the material here is taken from the Kaplan diaries, February 10, 1957, JTS, box 5, vol. 18. The volume containing Kaplan's essay is *The Philosophy of Martin Buber,* ed. Paul Schilpp (La Salle, IL: Open Court Publishing Co., 1967).

38. *Piyyut* is the medieval Hebrew word for a prayer-poem.

39. The fifty lines here are only part of the entire poem that may be found in Kaplan's Sabbath prayer book, 382 (beginning in Hebrew).

40. The poem is found in Kaplan's 1945 prayer book, 383–91, as "God, the Life of Nature." It is found in a shorter adapted version in *Kol Haneshamah: Shabbat Vehagim* (Wyncote, PA: The Reconstructionist Press, 1996), 757. It was first published in *The Reconstructionist* 1, no. 18 (January 1936): 11–13, as "Revelation of God in Nature: A *Piyyut* for the First Benediction of the Evening Prayer."

41. Psalm 16:5, 11.

42. The reader will find an interesting correlation between the ideas expressed here and the latest book by Arthur Green. My sense is that Green is much more a Kaplanian than he thinks. See Arthur Green, *Radical Judaism: Rethinking God and Tradition* (New Haven, CT: Yale University Press, 2010).

43. Mordecai M. Kaplan, *The Religion of Ethical Nationhood: Judaism's Contribution to World Peace* (New York: Macmillan Co., 1970), 61. See especially chapter 3, "Nature's God as the Source of Moral Law."

44. Kaplan diaries, June 24, 1930, JTS, box 2, vol. 6; also *Communings*, 415.

45. The thought is found many times in Kaplan's *The Meaning of God in Modern Jewish Religion*. It is also found in the Kaplan diaries, February 18, 1926, JTS, box 1, vol. 3. The thought is also found many times in Arthur Green's *Seek My Face, Speak My Name* (Northvale, NJ: Jason Aronson, Inc., 1992); see especially 109ff.

46. Kaplan diaries, December 17, 1929, JTS, box 2, vol. 5; also *Communings*, 388.

47. Ibid.

48. See chapter 12 for a full discussion of the way Kaplan applies his theology to the *mitzvot* and the *halakhah*.

49. The full outline of Kaplan's conversations with the center leadership is found in the Kaplan diaries, August 31, 1917, JTS, box 1, vol. 1; also *Communings*, 120.

50. Kaplan diary, December 1905, RRC. This quotation appears a number of times in this work.

51. Jack Cohen, *Guides for an Age of Confusion: Studies in the Thinking of Abraham Y. Kook and Mordecai M. Kaplan* (New York: Fordham University Press, 1999).

52. Abraham Isaac Kook, *Orot Ha Kodesh* (Jersalem: Mossad Ha-Rav Kook, 1963), 1:269. As quoted in Daniel Matt, *The Essential Kabbalah: The Heart of Jewish Mysticism* (New York: Harper Collins, 1995), 31.

53. The translation here is taken from *A Prayerbook for Shabbat, Festivals and Weekdays*, ed. Rabbi Jules Harlow (New York: The United Synagogue of America, 1985), 619.

8. SALVATION

The epigraph is from Mordecai M. Kaplan, "Soterics," 2, RRC.

1. Kaplan diaries, March 25, 1951, Jewish Theological Seminary (hereafter JTS), box 4, vol. 15.

2. "Soterics," 4, Reconstructionist Rabbinical College (hereafter RRC). RG1, RS15, Shelf 37.

3. The quotations here are, respectively, from Isaiah 43:12 and Isaiah 44:1ff. This section on the meaning of salvation is based on Mordecai M. Kaplan, *The Purpose and Meaning of Jewish Existence* (Philadelphia: The Jewish Publication Society, 1964), 5ff.

4. Ibid., Kaplan quotation. Rabbinic quotation from the *Ethics of the Fathers*, first statement, and also in *Mishna Sanhedrin*, 10:1.

5. For the best introduction to Maimonides's thought, see Micah Goodman, *The Secrets of the Guide for the Perplexed* [Hebrew] (Or Yehudah, Israel: Dvir Publishing

House, 2010), esp. 119–28 on redemption. See also Joel L. Kraemer, *Maimonides: The Life and World of One of Civilizations' Great Minds* (New York: Doubleday, 2008).

6. Kaplan diaries, February 27, 1946, JTS, box 4, vol. 13.

7. Mordecai M. Kaplan, *Judaism as a Civilization: Toward a Reconstruction of American Jewish Life*, with a New Introduction by Mel Scult (Philadelphia: Jewish Publication Society, 2010), 12. This work was first published in 1934. There is also much illuminating material in Mordecai M. Kaplan, *Questions Jews Ask: Reconstructionist Answers* (New York: The Reconstructionist Press, 1956), chapter 2, "God as the Power That Makes for Salvation."

8. Kaplan diaries, October 23, 1953, JTS, box 5, vol. 16. We have also used this quotation above in chapter 3, which discussed Matthew Arnold.

9. This expression will be familiar from the *musaf* (additional) service for festivals. *Amidah, Musaf* [additional] *Service, Siddur Sim Shalom: A Prayerbook for Shabbat, Festivals, and Weekdays,* ed. Rabbi Jules Harlow (New York: The Rabbinical Assembly, 1985), 474.

10. See also Genesis 33:18, where it means safety; or Genesis 34:21, where it means friendly. Or Joshua 8:31, where it refers to stones that are in their original (perfect), unhewn state.

11. *T. B. Tractate Shabbat* 30:b, *"shalem be-gufo, shalem be-mamono shalem be-torato* (perfect in his body, complete in his property, and complete in his learning).

12. "Soterics," 2, RRC.

13. Kaplan diaries, August 5, 1934, JTS, box 2, vol. 7.

14. It is telling that Kaplan lists elements in his philosophy as accomplishments. Kaplan diaries, December 31, 1950, JTS, box 4, vol. 15: "Last Friday Ira came to see me for the purpose of orienting himself for the chapter he wants to write for my Jubilee Book. That gave me a chance to recall some of the seminal ideas which I have contributed to the understanding of Judaism and religion. They are the following: 1) Judaism is an evolving religious civilization; 2) To have religion in common people must have in common other interests in common besides religion; 3) God is the Power that makes for salvation; 4) The identity and continuity of a religion derive from the sameness of its sancta; 5) A religion must have both a folk and an individual appeal; 6) What we want as Jews and not what we believe is a criterion of Jewish loyalty; 7) Salvation means becoming fully human; 8) The creative or artistic approach to the problems of salvation and civilization is bound to be more fruitful than the revelational or the philosophic."

15. Kaplan diaries, December 16, 1942, JTS, box 4, vol. 12.

16. Kaplan diaries, June 1, 1943, JTS, box 4, vol. 12.

17. Kaplan diaries, November 23, 1942, JTS, box 4, vol. 11.

18. "Soterics," 213, RRC.

19. Kaplan diaries, January 12, 1942, JTS, box 3, vol. 10.

20. For Aristotle, see *Metaphysics,* in *The Basic Works of Aristotle,* ed. Richard McKeon (New York: Random House, 1941), 689. I am indebted to my brother, Professor Allen Scult, for pointing out the connection to Aristotle. Material in this paragraph is based on Kaplan, "Soterics."

21. This reference to Jung is from Kaplan's "Soterics," 192, RRC. In mentioning Jung, Kaplan gives no citation as to where in Jung this idea can be found. For our understanding, the mere citation is important since it shows that, in the 1950s, Kaplan was reading the current humanistic literature.

22. Kaplan, *Soterics,* 195, RRC. RG1, RS15, shelf 37.

23. For a full description of the origins and the workings of the Jewish Center, see Mel Scult, *Judaism Faces the Twentieth Century: A Biography of Mordecai Kaplan* (Detroit: Wayne State University Press, 1993), chapter 6, "The Quest for Community: The Jewish Center." For a more complete treatment, see David Kaufman, *The Shul with a Pool: The Synagogue Center in American Jewish History* (Hanover, NH: Brandeis University Press, 1999).

24. See "History" in Emerson, *Essays: First and Second Series by Ralph Waldo Emerson* (New York: Vintage Books/The New Library of America, 1990), 3. Also discussed by Stanley Cavell in "Aversive Thinking: Emersonian Representations in Heidegger and Nietzsche," in *Conditions Handsome and Unhandsome: Constitutions of Emersonian Perfectionism* (Chicago: University of Chicago, 1990), 3ff.

25. Kaplan here uses the more common and colloquial expression, *halevai;* the original Talmudic text reads *u-levai.*

26. Kaplan diaries, January 10, 1930, JTS, box 2, vol. 6; also see Mordecai M. Kaplan, *Communings of the Spirit: The Journals of Mordecai M. Kaplan, Vol. 1, 1913–1934,* ed. Mel Scult (Detroit: Wayne State University Press, 2001), 330. In this passage, Kaplan is referring to an English book of prayers, *The Temple: A Book of Prayers, by the Rev. W. E. Orchard, D.D.* (London: J.M. Dent and Sons, 1913). The Talmudic question at the beginning of this passage is, if one is in doubt that one has said the *Amidah* prayer, should one say it again.

27. Kaplan reminds us that, although keeping in mind the concept of fulfillment when we pray may not be practical, it is no less practical than some of the suggestions made by the rabbis about contemplating the name of God while praying. He refers to the rabbinic notion that the name of God refers to the "seventy-two letters which are meant as a meditation on the name of God," apparently a reference to the belief that the verses in Exodus 14:19, 20, 21 are each one of them an allusion to the name of God. The rabbis thought we should keep the whole verse in mind when we use the tetragrammaton. Each verse consists of seventy-two letters. See *T. B. Sukkah* 45a, Rashi, loc. cit. Others hold that the verse in question is Deuteronomy 4:34. See Judah Theodor's note to page 442 of J. Theodor and C. Albeck's edition of *Midrash Bereshit Rabba* (Jerusalem: Mossad Bialik, 1996) for the full journal entry explaining all of the above. See also *Communings,* 359.

28. Mordecai M. Kaplan, *Not So Random Thoughts: Witty and Profound Observations on Society, Religion and Jewish Life by America's Leading Jewish Thinker* (New York: The Reconstructionist Press, 1966), 148.

29. Kaplan diaries, October 3, 1939, JTS, box 3, vol. 9. This passage is discussed above in chapter 7.

30. Kaplan, *Not So Random Thoughts,* 144.

31. Kaplan diaries, August 3, 1943, JTS, box 4, vol. 12. After having read Max Lerner on Holmes, Kaplan says, "I have come away from Holmes, as have many others, with a feeling of new strength." The quotation cited in the text here is not mentioned in Kaplan's diary but may be found in a letter to Lewis Einstein's daughter, May 6, 1925, in *The Holmes-Einstein Letters: Correspondence of Mr. Justice Holmes and Lewis Einstein 1903–1935,* ed. James Bishop Peabody (New York: St Martin's Press, Inc., 1964). Kaplan started me reading Holmes, which I found very productive.

32. Abraham Joshua Heschel, *God in Search of Man: A Philosophy of Judaism* (New York: Farrar, Straus & Cudahy, 1955), 143.

33. The quotation here is from Mordecai Kaplan, "Individuality—Necessary to Know Our Own Worth." This sermon is contained in a notebook of sermons, one of which is dated for Rosh Hashannah, 1903. The notebook is at RRC. Kaplan was hired as "minister" at Kehilath Jeshurun in the late fall of 1903.

34. Ibid.

35. Ibid.

36. There is no need to document the significance of the other in the works of Martin Buber. For Levinas, we have found the following useful: Samuel Moyn, *Origins of the Other: Emmanuel Levinas between Revelation and Ethics* (Ithaca, NY: Cornell University Press, 2005).

37. Kaplan diaries, October 3, 1951, box 4, vol. 15. The discussion noted here took place during Buber's visit to the United States. He had been invited by the seminary and gave speeches in New York and around the country, a number of which Kaplan attended. On one occasion when Kaplan spoke at Yale, he heard some reactions to Buber who had spoken there a few weeks before: "Buber had given four lectures, but everybody seemed to know that no one understood what he was saying. That is the common report from all the cities where he gave those lectures. Everywhere he spoke the place would be filled to overflowing, and people were spellbound by his charismatic presence, but very few, if any, knew what he was driving at." Kaplan diaries, February 2, 1952, JTS, box 4, vol. 15. Kaplan spoke at the parting ceremony for Buber, along with Paul Tillich, which was held at Carnegie Hall for an audience of about eight hundred. He made some insightful comments on Buber's work in his twenty-five-minute talk and tells us about the experience of coming up with the ideas that occurred to him while he was performing his morning "ablutions" in the bathroom: "The time when such ideas literally leap into the mind is when I dress in the morning, and the place is the bathroom. This morning that experience was repeated. . . . the idea suddenly came to me that Buber's main contribution consists in so reinstating the biblical universe of discourse so that it can function once again as a common thought world for both Jew and Christian as was the case before the modern scientific outlook destroyed the biblical universe of discourse. With that in mind all else I have to say about Buber easily falls into place." Kaplan diaries, April 6, 1952, JTS, box 4, vol. 15.

In 1951, on the occasion of Kaplan's seventieth birthday, Martin Buber sent him the following "birthday card," which I found a long time ago among the Kaplan papers.

For Mordecai Kaplan:

Liberalism and traditionalism are contrasts, liberty and tradition are none. Tradition is true and living only if it renews itself constantly in liberty and the will to preserve brings forth inner transformations. And as to liberty from where shall it take the substance to its work, if not from the depths of tradition. This cooperation manifests itself most strongly in times of a great crisis, when the decisive task is to educate a generation of educators. To the unity of tradition and liberty, to it alone the power is given to call up such a generation and to endow it with regenerative force.

Martin Buber.

38. John Dewey, "Outlines of a Critical Theory of Ethics," in *Early Works: 1882–1898*, Vol. 3, *Essays and Outlines of a Critical Theory of Ethics* (Carbondale, IL: Southern Illinois University Press, 1971), 320–23, as cited in Robert Westbrook, *John Dewey and American*

Democracy (Ithaca, NY: Cornell University Press, 1991), 62. This statement was made by Dewey in 1891.

39. Kaplan, *Not so Random Thoughts,* 131.

40. "Willful individualism," in Kaplan diaries, January 4, 1945, JTS, box 4, vol. 13. The political scientist here is George Kateb, *The Inner Ocean: Individualism and Democratic Culture* (Ithaca, NY: Cornell University Press, 1992), 31. The argument in this paragraph is based on Kateb. We shall take up the matter of pluralism and relativism in the chapter on ethics.

41. "Rugged individualism" in Kaplan diaries, November 25, 1943, JTS, box 4, vol. 12.

42. Kaplan diaries, December 16, 1942, JTS, box 4, vol. 12. The whole system of values spelled out here was part of the ideology contained within Kaplan's theory of soterics. "Soterics" is the name Kaplan gave to his system in the 1940s. The word *soter* comes from the Greek and means to save, and Kaplan intended to say that his system was a scientific system like physics but with the goal of salvation.

43. Kaplan diaries, December 16, 1942, JTS, box 4, vol. 12.

44. Kaplan diaries, December 24, 1942, JTS, box 4, vol. 12.

45. Kaplan diaries, December 16, 1942, JTS, box 4, vol. 12.

46. Ibid.

47. Kaplan diaries, December 24, 1942, JTS, box 4, vol. 12.

9. SALVATION EMBODIED

The epigraph comes from Kaplan diaries, October 3, 1942, JTS, box 3, vol. 11.

1. Kaplan advocated that the ceremony of *pidyon ha-ben,* the redemption of the first-born male child, be eliminated. See Mordecai M. Kaplan, *Questions Jews Ask* (New York: The Jewish Reconstructionist Foundation, 1956), 247. Rabbi Jack Cohen, z"l, advocated a reconstruction of the ceremony that would shift the meaning away from the emphasis on the priests and include the dedication of the child (either male or female) to a life of Torah and good deeds. Conversation with Rabbi Jack Cohen, z"l, 2007.

2. Mordecai M. Kaplan, *The Meaning of God in Modern Jewish Religion* (Detroit: Wayne State University Press, 1994), 47. Original publication, New York: Behrman, 1937.

3. See reference to Maimonides and "the world to come" in ibid., 49–50.

4. For a full explanation of Kaplan's theory of needs, see chapter 11 on ethics. The classification of needs appears many times in Kaplan's work. For me, the issue is especially nostalgic because the first time I met Kaplan, at Camp Cejwin in 1972, I attended a class he conducted with the counselors centered on the issue of needs. (Parenthetically, the issue of feminism and Judaism came up in the discussion, and I felt that Kaplan was much more radical than his young students, although I do not remember the details.) The issue of women in Judaism is discussed below also in chapter 11.

5. Love obviously exists on all levels: the physical, the psychosocial, and the spiritual.

6. We shall consider the details of Kaplan's ritual guide below in chapter 11, which examines *halakhah.*

7. Kaplan, *Meaning of God,* 63.

8. Ibid., 60.

9. For Kaplan's comments on the Covenant, see Kaplan diaries, April 17, 1946, Jewish Theological Seminary (hereafter JTS), box 4, vol. 13. His comment follows: "Their

writings [the prophets] represent "the passionate outcries of far-seeing divinely inspired men who read their people's fate in the light of a principle it had never occurred to any one to apply to the vicissitudes of nations, viz: the substitution of righteousness for force in all its internal and external affairs."

10. Kaplan, *Meaning of God*, 102.

11. See Kaplan, *Questions Jews Ask* (New York: Reconstructionist Press, 1956), 49, for one version of the proposal. See Kaplan diaries June 20, 1950, JTS, box 4, vol. 15, for the proposal to the Rabbinical Assembly that a special agency be set up. See chapter 5 on this proposal within the total context of Kaplan's Zionism.

12. Kaplan, *Meaning of God*, 105. Kaplan's chapter on Yom Kippur is fascinating and should be read carefully. He traces the development of the day from an emphasis on purity to an emphasis on moral behavior.

13. Ibid., 108.

14. The quotation here and the discussion on kingship are based on the Kaplan diaries, September 21, 1952, JTS, box 5, vol. 16.

15. Kaplan enjoyed using this phrase. It is frequently employed by Spinoza.

16. Kaplan, *Meaning of God*, 244.

17. See chapters 6 and 7 in the current volume.

18. Kaplan, *Meaning of God*, 245.

19. See reference in ibid., 245, to *Berakhot* 6a, 21b.

20. Kaplan, *Meaning of God*, 247.

21. Ibid., 248.

22. Ibid., 249.

23. Ibid., 251.

24. For more on Kaplan's sense of mystery, see chapter 10 in the current volume on Abraham Joshua Heschel and Kaplan.

25. Kaplan, *Meaning of God*, 258.

26. Kaplan quotes this passage from Emerson in ibid., 259.

27. Mordecai Kaplan, *Judaism as a Civilization: Toward a Reconstruction of American Jewish Life,* with a New Introduction by Mel Scult (Philadelphia: Jewish Publication Society, 2010), 426. This work was first published in 1934.

28. The year 2008 witnessed perhaps the best of all Kaplanian worlds, with Michael Strassfeld as rabbi at the Society for the Advancement of Judaism (SAJ) marrying Rabbi Joy Levitt, who is director of the Jewish Community Center (JCC). Both are graduates of the Reconstructionist Rabbinical College. Both the Ninety-Second Street Y and the JCC have synagogues, but prayer is not a major activity at either institution. For an account of Kaplan and the Jewish Center movement, as well as Kaplan at the Ninety-Second Street Y, see Mel Scult, *Judaism Faces the Twentieth Century: A Biography of Mordecai M. Kaplan* (Detroit: Wayne State University Press, 1993).

29. Kaplan quotes Durkheim many times, but see especially *Judaism as a Civilization,* chapter 24 and 333ff.

30. *If Not Now, When? Toward a Reconstitution of the Jewish People: Conversations between Mordecai M. Kaplan and Arthur A. Cohen* (New York: Schocken Books, 1973), 27.

31. Eugene B. Borowitz, *How Can a Jew Speak of Faith Today?* (Philadelphia: Westminster, 1969), 21.

32. Eugene B. Borowitz, *Renewing the Covenant* (Philadelphia: Jewish Publication Society, 1991), 124.

33. For more on these theological questions, see chapters 6 and 7 on Kaplan's conception of God. We should point out what is perhaps quite obvious: the theological questions posed here are never answered. The religious quest is, of course, a life-long process.

34. This excellent metaphor is from my wife, Barbara Gish Scult, who maintains she found it and did not create it but cannot remember where.

35. Kaplan diaries, May 21, 1933, JTS, box 2, vol. 7. Also found in Mordecai M. Kaplan, *Communings of the Spirit: The Journals of Mordecai M. Kaplan, Vol. 1, 1913–1934*, ed. Mel Scult (Detroit: Wayne State University Press, 2001), 505.

36. Kaplan diaries, December 17, 1929, JTS, box 2, vol. 5; Kaplan, *Communings*, 388.

37. Mordecai M. Kaplan, *The Religion of Ethical Nationhood: Judaism's Contribution to World Peace* (New York: The Macmillan Company, 1970), 55.

38. Mordecai M. Kaplan, *The Future of the American Jew* (New York: The Macmillan Co., 1948), 184. We have noted elsewhere that Kaplan sometimes sounds like Abraham Joshua Heschel; this statement is clearly Heschelian in its style and tone.

39. Kaplan, *Questions Jews Ask*, 103–104.

40. Kaplan diaries, January 1, 1940, JTS, box 3, vol 9. The Kaddish, the prayer of mourning, Kaplan is referring to is in the third person and may be translated as follows: "Hallowed and enhanced may He be throughout the world of His own creation," *Baruch Ata*. "Blessed art Thou" is the conventional language of address to God in all prayers.

41. See Alan Miller, *The God of Daniel S: In Search of the American Jew* (London: The Macmillan Company, 1969), 161, for this distinction between affirmation and quotation. See also the very informative article on this matter by Daniel Cedarbaum, "Reconsidering Reconstructionist Liturgy: The Kaplanian Paradox," *Reconstructionism Today* 14, no. 2 (Winter 2006–2007): 17–21; and the response of Elaine Moise in the following issue, "On Our Evolving Liturgy: A Response to Dan Cedarbaum," *Reconstructionism Today* 14, no. 3 (Summer 2007): 9–13.

42. See Cedarbaum, "Reconsidering Reconstructionist Liturgy," 21, and the source of the conversation in Eric Caplan, *From Ideology to Liturgy: Reconstructionist Worship and American Liberal Judaism* (Cincinnati, OH: Hebrew Union College Press, 2002), 120. The comment from Eisenstein is from an interview in 1993. The expression "Those years" probably refers to the years when the prayer books were being published, which would be the 1930s to the '50s.

43. See above chapter 1 for the publication of the Sabbath prayer book in 1945 and Scult, *Judaism Faces the Twentieth Century*, especially chapter 11, for the early revisions of the liturgy. Kaplan worked along with Rabbi Ira Eisenstein and Rabbi Eugene Kohn on the prayer books of the 1940s. The most complete account of the revisions is given in Caplan, *From Ideology to Liturgy*.

44. Kaplan, *Questions Jews Ask*, 103–104.

45. Emmanuel Levinas uses the concept of the "face" in a central way and should be consulted in connection with the matter of address. With Levinas, the "face" of the other is the face of God. For the fullest treatment by Levinas of this concept, see his *Totality and Infinity: An Essay on Exteriority* (Pittsburgh: Duquesne University Press, 1969), 187–254.

46. Marcia Falk, *The Book of Blessings: New Jewish Prayers for Daily Life, the Sabbath, and the New Moon Festival* (New York: Harper San Francisco, 1996), 171.

47. See *Kol Haneshamah, Shabbat Vehagim,* ed. David Teutsch et al., 3d ed. (Wyncote PA: The Reconstructionist Press, 1996).

48. Perhaps it is worth noting that, according to Anne Eisenstein, Ira Eisenstein's daughter, Rabbi Eisenstein much appreciated Marcia Falk's work. Interview with Anne Eisenstein, June 2000.

49. Professor Jack Wertheimer has done us an enormous service by publishing all the documents immediately relevant to the publication of the *The New Haggadah* in 1941. He is one of the few historians who have made full use of the Kaplan diaries. Kaplan's *Haggadah* was revolutionary for its time. He left out the plagues and the hate formula connected to Elijah the prophet and made Moses the center of the *Haggadah* text. Moses quite strangely is never mentioned in the traditional *Haggadah.* Kaplan shifts the focus in his *Haggadah* from God and His power to Moses and freedom. The faculty of the Jewish Theological Seminary wrote Kaplan a nine-page letter criticizing him and "calling him on the carpet" for his departure from tradition. See above chapter 1 for more on *The New Haggadah.* For the relevant documents along with excerpts from the diaries on *The New Haggadah,* see Jack Wertheimer, "Kaplan vs. The Great Do-Nothings: The Inconclusive Battle over *The New Haggadah,*" in *Conservative Judaism* 45 (Summer 1993): 20–37.

50. The signers of the article, *Ha-Do'ar* 24, no. 39, discussed below are Professor Saul Lieberman, Professor Louis Ginzberg, and Professor Alexander Marx.

51. The "Thirteen Wants" can be found on the Internet, specifically, at www.sacred -texts.com; also see my revision of the "Thirteen Wants" in the appendix to this work. It is also found on my website, www.melscult.org/newthings. "Wants," of course, here means goals or ideals. The quotation, which was translated by the author, is from the *Ha-Do'ar* article mentioned below.

52. Though the three signers of the article praise Kaplan for his honesty and his positive intentions, they unfairly characterize him as not being well versed in Talmudic and rabbinic literature. We know that this is an unfounded claim. For more than thirty years, in addition to teaching homiletics, Kaplan taught the traditional rabbinic texts of the midrash. All his students, including Louis Finkelstein, president of the seminary at the time of the excommunication, characterized Kaplan as a master of midrash. These remarks from an interview with Finkelstein and this author, 1985. The same is the case with Robert Gordis and Simon Greenberg. For the relationship of all these individuals to Kaplan, see Scult, *Judaism Faces the Twentieth Century,* chapter 8, "The World as Classroom: The Jewish Theological Seminary." That summer of 1945, *Ha-Do'ar* carried a very lively exchange on the *Herem,* including attempts by Kaplan to justify himself.

53. The original article, signed by Kaplan's colleagues was published in *Ha-Do'ar* 24, no. 39 (*Tishre* 5706). Kaplan's response to the article was also printed in *Ha-Do'ar.*

54. I am indebted to Professor Allan Nadler of Drew University who pointed out Klein's review, "Some Praise the Lord—Some Pass the Ammunition," *Jewish Literature and Culture* 4 (1945): 42–46. Klein also includes the famous poem by Samuel Taylor Coleridge, "He prayeth best who loveth best / All things both great and small, / For the dear God who loveth us / He made and loveth all."

55. See Eric Caplan, *From Ideology to Liturgy,* 50–52, for editing of the prayer book and for the Eisenstein interview quoted here. For details of Milton Steinberg's involvement, see Simon Noveck, *Milton Steinberg: Portrait of a Rabbi* (New York: Ktav Publishing House, Inc., 1978), 179ff. Steinberg was Kaplan's favorite student when he was

in the rabbinical school in the 1920s. See Steinberg in index of Scult, *Judaism Faces the Twentieth Century*. As time passed, Steinberg became one of the outstanding rabbis in the Conservative rabbinate but began to be critical of Kaplan, particularly on matters of theology. It is my belief that Steinberg's criticisms influenced Kaplan significantly. See also Noveck's article, "Kaplan and Milton Steinberg: A Disciple's Agreements and Disagreements," in *The American Judaism of Mordecai Kaplan,* ed. Emanuel Goldsmith, Mel Scult, and Robert Seltzer (New York: New York University Press, 1990), 140–73. Milton Steinberg's papers have been very carefully catalogued and may be found at the Center for Jewish History in New York City. Though Simon Noveck's biography is excellent, there is yet much to be done on Steinberg, particularly as reflected in the Kaplan diary.

56. This statement is made without any explanation and is actually part of another discussion. See Kaplan diaries, July 23, 1944, JTS, box 4, vol. 13.

57. Milton Steinberg, *A Believing Jew: The Selected Writings of Milton Steinberg* (New York: Harcourt, Brace and Company, 1951), 19. This book was edited posthumously from Steinberg's writings and speeches by his wife Edith A. Steinberg.

58. "Introduction to the Reconstructionist Prayer Book" (1945), 6, or in Rabbi Mordecai Waxman, *Tradition and Change: The Development of Conservative Judaism* (New York: The Burning Bush Press, 1958), 341.

59. For a more complete account of the early changes in the liturgy, particularly regarding the chosen people concept, see Scult, *Judaism Faces the Twentieth Century,* chapter 11.

60. For Kaplan's earliest statement on revelation and by implication the issue of chosenness, see his "The Supremacy of Torah," *Students Annual of the Jewish Theological Seminary of New York, 1914* (New York: The Jewish Theological Seminary, 1914), 180–92. The standard work on chosenness is, of course, Arnold Eisen, *The Chosen People in America: A Study in Jewish Religious Ideology* (Bloomington: Indiana University Press, 1983).

61. Jews have always dealt with their suffering with humor, and there are many Yiddish proverbs that ask God, if their present life is a result of their being chosen, perhaps He would like to choose somebody else.

62. See Kaplan, *The Future of the American Jew,* chapter 13, for an extended discussion of chosenness. We find here Kaplan's most complete treatment of the subject, and our discussion comes primarily from this source.

63. Emmanuel Levinas, "A Religion for Adults," in *Difficult Freedom: Essays on Judaism* (Baltimore: The Johns Hopkins University Press, 1990), 22.

64. Talmud *Bavli, Berachot,* 17a, as cited in Kaplan, *The Future of the American Jew,* 229.

65. Ibid.

66. Recent Jewish communal advocacy for Darfur has stressed this theme.

67. This expression, which Kaplan substitutes for the chosenness formula, is taken from the additional prayers (*Musaf Amidah*) for a Sabbath on *Rosh Hodesh*. See, for example, *Siddur Sim Shalom: A Prayerbook for Shabbat Festivals and Weekdays,* ed. Rabbi Jules Harlow (New York: The Rabbinical Assembly and the United Synagogue of Conservative Judaism, 1985), 496. The actual language in the *Musaf* is *ve-keyravtanu malkeynu la-avodatehkah.*

68. This story, which I heard from a third party, was verified by Professor Brisman in a private letter to me on November 15, 2008, which is quoted here.

69. Mordecai M. Kaplan, *Sabbath Prayer Book* (New York: The Jewish Reconstructionist Foundation, 1945), 44–45. As we have indicated, all these changes are detailed in Eric Caplan's work.

70. The fascinating details of Kaplan's correspondence with Judah David Eisenstein and the *Kol Nidre* may be found in Scult, *Judaism Faces the Twentieth Century,* 286ff., and need not be repeated here.

71. Kaplan diaries, October 2, 1942, JTS, box 3, vol.11.

10. MORDECAI THE PIOUS

The epigraph is from Kaplan diaries, October 12, 1943, JTS, box 4, vol. 11.

1. See Mel Scult, "Kaplan's Heschel: A View from the Kaplan Diary," *Conservative Judaism* 54, no. 4 (Summer 2002): 3–15, for another version of the Kaplan-Heschel relationship.

2. Edward K. Kaplan and Samuel H. Dresner, *Abraham Joshua Heschel: Prophetic Witness* (New Haven, CT: Yale University Press, 1998), 292 ff. Heschel wrote a letter to Louis Finkelstein within a few days after landing in New York. See also Edward Kaplan, *Spiritual Radical: Abraham Joshua Heschel in America, 1940–1972* (New Haven, CT: Yale University Press, 2007).

3. Sylvia Heschel mentioned in a conversation with this author (fall 2005) Heschel's close relationship with Louis Ginzberg and the latter's desire to bring him to the seminary.

4. Abraham Joshua Heschel, "An Analysis of Piety," *The Review of Religion* 6, no. 3 (March 1942): 293–307, reprinted in *Moral Grandeur and Spiritual Audacity: Essays— Abraham Joshua Heschel,* ed. Susannah Heschel (New York: Farrar Straus and Giroux, 1996), 305–18.

5. The text inside the square bracket is in Heschel's essay but not quoted by Kaplan in his diary.

6. Kaplan diaries, September 19, 1942, Jewish Theological Seminary (hereafter JTS), box 4, vol. 11.

7. Quotation on reading is from Barbara L. Packer, *Emerson's Fall: A New Interpretation of the Major Essays* (New York: The Continuum Publishing Co., 1982), 119. See the same thought in Ralph Waldo Emerson, *Representative Men: Seven Lectures,* ed. Douglas Emory Wilson and Andrew Delbanco (Cambridge, MA: Harvard University Press, 1996), 4. At this time, in proofreading the text, I am at the New Jersey shore a few miles from where Kaplan summered in 1940. One might say that I am *davvening* from Kaplan.

8. Abraham J. Heschel to Mordecai M. Kaplan, April 1943, Kaplan letter file at Reconstructionist Rabbinical College (hereafter RRC).

9. Kaplan later noted that he thought his favorable recommendation of Heschel played a key role in Heschel's invitation to the seminary. See Kaplan diary, January 16, 1955, JTS, box 5, vol. 17. The Teachers Institute was organized in 1909, with Kaplan as its head. It met during the day and trained teachers for afternoon Hebrew schools. The Seminary College, which met at night, was organized for students who attended a regular college during the day. The curricula of the Teachers Institute and the Seminary College were the same, but there were no education courses in the Seminary College. By the 1920s, the language of instruction at the Teachers Institute was Hebrew. When the Teachers Institute was founded, the language of instruction was English.

10. Conversation with Dr. Baila Shargel, June 2000. Professor Shargel reports in a private conversation that Heschel taught only one course in the rabbinical school.

11. The social visit is found in Kaplan diaries, March 14, 1949, JTS, box 4, vol. 14. Kaplan feeling more relaxed in Kaplan diaries, JTS, December 18, 1951, box 4, vol. 15.

12. Kaplan diaries, January 25, 1950, JTS, box 4, vol. 14. The language of Kaplan's journal has not been changed even when sentences are not complete or are awkward. Phrases in square brackets are by this author.

13. Kaplan diaries, June 6, 1951, JTS, box 4, vol. 15.

14. Kaplan diaries, November 6, 1952, JTS, box 5, vol. 16. Kaplan notes in this entry that he had "heard" about these interviews. We must allow for the possibility that such things were happening, however unlikely they might seem.

15. *Symbols and Society: Fourteenth Symposium of the Conference on Science, Philosophy and Religion in Their Relationship to the Democratic Way of Life,* ed. Lyman Bryson et al. (New York: The Conference, 1955).

16. Kaplan diaries, February 10, 1953, JTS, box 5, vol. 16.

17. Many years ago, I found this statement on the back of an envelope among Kaplan's papers. The writing was clearly his.

18. Kaplan diaries, February 10, 1963, JTS, box 6, vol. 22.

19. "The Spirit of Jewish Prayer," *Proceedings of the Rabbinical Assembly of America* 17 (1953), reprinted in *Moral Grandeur and Spiritual Audacity,* 126.

20. Kaplan diaries, September 15, 1955, JTS, box 5, vol. 17.

21. Kaplan diaries, August 3, 1943, JTS, box 4, vol. 12.

22. Kaplan diaries, April 14, 1946, JTS, box 4, vol. 13.

23. See "To Be a Jew: What Is It?" *Zionist Quarterly* 1, no. 1 (Summer 1951): 78–84, reprinted in *Moral Grandeur and Spiritual Audacity,* 10.

24. Ibid., 9.

25. This phrase has become quite well known and was one of Kaplan's *bon mots.* He repeated it many times in his lectures and sermons. In print, it actually appears as follows: "The ancient authorities are entitled to a vote but not a veto." Mordecai Kaplan, *Not So Random Thoughts* (New York: The Reconstructionist Press, 1966), 263.

26. See "To Be a Jew: What Is It?" *Moral Grandeur and Spiritual Audacity,* 9.

27. See "The Spirit of Jewish Prayer," *Moral Grandeur and Spiritual Audacity,* 109, for the quotations in this paragraph.

28. Kaplan diaries, November, 12, 1930, JTS, box 2, vol. 6; also found in *Communings of the Spirit: The Journals of Mordecai M. Kaplan, Vol 1, 1913–1934,* ed. Mel Scult (Detroit: Wayne State University Press, 2001), 429. It is interesting to note that the rabbis of ancient times also felt this matter of excessive mechanical piety that Kaplan refers to as "yarmulke piety." See *Midrash Rabbah, Bereshit,* 39:12, where the midrash notes that excessive bowing during the *Shimonah Esrei* is not a sign of genuine piety and should be discouraged. The king and the high priest who might be more arrogant than they should be are, on the other hand, encouraged to bow frequently. I am much indebted to my colleague and *haver* Rabbi Shel Schiffman. We have been studying midrash together for many years.

29. "Spirit of Jewish Prayer," in *Moral Grandeur and Spiritual Audacity,* 107.

30. Ibid., 109.

31. *In Praise of Mortality: Selections from Rainer Maria Rilke's Duino Elegies and Sonnets to Orpheus,* trans. and ed. Anita Barrows and Joanna Macy (New York: Riverhead Books, 2005), 10.

32. "Spirit of Jewish Prayer," *in Moral Grandeur and Spiritual Audacity*, 104.

33. See chapter 7 for a discussion of Ames and Kaplan and his students.

34. "Spirit of Jewish Prayer," in *Moral Grandeur and Spiritual Audacity*, 105.

11. THE LAW

The epigraph is from Kaplan diaries, December 6, 1942, JTS, box 4, vol. 12.

1. See *A Guide to Jewish Ritual*, introduction by Ira Eisenstein (New York: Reconstructionist Press, 1962). It is not clear who actually wrote this pamphlet, though of course, Kaplan would have had final approval. In Kaplan's *The Future of the American Jew* (New York: The Macmillan Company, 1948), there is a chapter titled "Toward a Guide for Ritual Usage" that deals with ritual in a general way but does not outline specific recommendations. The contents of the pamphlet also appeared in an earlier version; see "Toward a Guide for Ritual Usage," *The Reconstructionist* 7 (November 14, 1941): 7–13. See also *The Reconstructionist* 7 (December 12, 1941): 10–17; 8 (January 9, 1942): 4–6. For the most recent efforts to offer a guide to religious practice, see David Teutsch, *A Guide to Jewish Practice* (Wyncote, PA: The Reconstructionist Press, 1989). Teutsch's most recent work supersedes and will eventually incorporate all the previous guides. The format of this most recent book is extremely provocative, with a central text on ritual and ethical issues together with reactions by selected rabbis and laymen within the Jewish community. See Teutsch, *A Guide to Jewish Practice: Everyday Living, Volume 1* (Wyncote, PA: Reconstructionist College Press, 2011). Rabbi Teutsch has also edited guides on *kashrut*, bioethics, *tzedaka*, and "The Ethics of Speech." Rabbi Richard Hirsh, executive director of the Reconstructionist Rabbinical Association, has edited a booklet titled "Welcoming Children," which helps provide a meaningful ritual context for arrival of children. See the web site of the Reconstructionist Rabbinical College for more information, http://www.rrc.edu/.

2. Ira Eisenstein was less strict. He did eat kosher types of meat outside the home in restaurants that were not kosher. Kaplan was uncomfortable with Eisenstein's custom. This information is according to Miriam Eisenstein, Ira's eldest daughter, and Rabbi Richard Hirsh, a close associate of Eisenstein. Conversation with Miriam Eisenstein June 2000.

3. Kaplan, *A Guide*, 45.

4. See Kaplan diaries, March 28, 1922, Jewish Theological Seminary (hereafter JTS), box 1, vol. 2. Here I must make a confession. There are some very significant entries in the Kaplan diary that I neglected to enter into the published diary, *Communings of the Spirit: The Journals of Mordecai M. Kaplan, Vol. 1: 1913–1934*, ed. Mel Scult (Detroit: Wayne State University Press, 2001). When I come across such entries, I am deeply pained. The selection here on *kashrut* is one of those diary entries that is not in *Communings*.

5. Kaplan preparing sermons on Friday night, Kaplan diaries, February 20, 1925, JTS, box 1, vol. 2. Selma finds Kaplan writing on the Sabbath, Kaplan diaries, September 21, 1934, JTS, box 2, vol. 7. Regarding other aspects of Kaplan's regimen, he *davenned* daily and often studied a *blatt gemorah* (folio of Talmud), Kaplan diaries, July 3, 1925, JTS, box 1, vol. 3; also *Communings of the Spirit*, 209. We should note that Kaplan wore the four-fringed undergarment throughout his life. In his later life, he was fond of showing people the *tzitzit* (tassles) of this undergarment (*arba kanfot*), which he had had dyed purple, the color of royalty. Although today all *tzitzit* are white, in ancient times they were purple (*tehelet*), which was supposed to symbolize the power of God. For Kaplan it

symbolized that all Jews were royalty. The Orthodox used to tell the story with great rel-ish that all Kaplan's children wore *tzizit*. The story is not true, of course, because Kaplan had four daughters. Heschel, at the celebration of Kaplan's ninetieth birthday, told the audience that he, like Kaplan, wore purple *tzitzit* (recording of this event). My thanks to Edward Kaplan for sharing a copy of the recording with me. The word about this oc-casion is that Heschel was drunk. While he laughed a lot and was very entertaining, his great appreciation for Kaplan seemed genuine and his remarks truthful.

6. In the margin, Kaplan quotes Numbers 11:21, where Moses questions God's ability to provide food for all the Israelites. This questioning was in private, whereas Moses's doubting of God's ability to provide water by striking the rock at Meriba was in public.

7. Kaplan diaries, August 16, 1931, JTS, box 2, vol. 6; also *Communings*, 452.

8. On the Sabbath in general, see *A Guide*, 14–18. The statements in this paragraph are paraphrases from these pages.

9. This story from an interview with Naomi Kaplan Wenner, z"l, July 1985.

10. I am indebted to Dr. Nancy Fuchs-Kramer of the Reconstructionist College for emphasizing this point in our many conversations.

11. See Kaplan, *A Guide*, 12.

12. Mordecai M. Kaplan, *The Future of the American Jew*, 425.

13. See Mel Scult, *Judaism Faces the Twentieth Century: A Biography of Mordecai Kap-lan* (Detroit: Wayne State University Press, 1993), 301, for a more detailed account of the event. The account here is based primarily on Judith's memoir as published, "Judith Kaplan Eisenstein: Becomes the First Bas Mitzvah 1921 (*sic*)," in *Eyewitnesses to Ameri-can Jewish History, Part IV, The American Jew, 1915–1969*, ed. Azriel Eisenberg (New York: Union of American Hebrew Congregations, 1977), 29–32. The Bat Mitzvah, of course, was in 1922, not 1921. Both the Kaplan journal and the *SAJ Bulletin* confirm that the Bat Mitzvah was in March and not May, as Judith's account has it. When asked about this, Judith remembered that, when she published her account, she asked her father about the date, and he apparently did not look in the journal and, thus, gave Judith the wrong day (May 5) and the wrong *Parsha*. He said it was *Kedoshim* but again, according to the *SAJ Bulletin* no. 5, March 1922, it was *Ki Tissah*.

14. Several witnesses attest to this fact of women not being called to the Torah. I first heard about it from Judge Benjamin William Mehlman, z"l, in a private conversation, June 1990.

15. This sense of the congregation from an interview with Kaplan in 1972.

16. This notion was suggested by Riv Ellen-Prell, "The Vision of Woman in Classical Reform Judaism," *Journal of the American Academy of Religion* 50, no. 4 (December 1982), particularly 576, as cited in Ellen Umansky, "Feminism and American Reform Judaism," in *The Americanization of the Jews*, ed. Robert M. Seltzer and Norman J. Cohen (New York: New York University Press, 1995), 280.

17. The Nineteenth Amendment to the Constitution was finally ratified on August 18, 1920, and prohibits the federal government or any state from denying a citizen the right to vote because of that person's sex.

18. "Dedication Ceremonies and Sefer Torah," *Center Journal* 1 (May 10, 1918): 3.

19. Men were seated in the middle section, with women on both sides. The sections were separated by a transparent curtain.

20. The material here that is not in quotation marks is a summation of Kaplan's re-marks in the sermon.

21. "The Sermon on the Emancipation of Women" was delivered at the Jewish Center on November 2, 1918. The sermon is at Reconstructionist Rabbinical College (hereafter RRC). The concept of the chosennness of women is clearly in the text of the sermon, although the word *chosen* is not used there but supplied by this author. The verse is from I Samuel 2:16. The translations from Genesis are from Everett Fox, *In the Beginning: A New English Rendition of the Book of Genesis* (New York: Schocken Books, Inc., 1983). The verse in Zachariah 4:6 expresses the same thought about power and was a favorite of Kaplan's, although he did not use it here: "Not by might nor by power but by My spirit, sayeth the Lord of Hosts."

22. The best book on this period is Henry Feingold, *A Time for Searching: Entering the Mainstream, 1920–1945* (Baltimore: Johns Hopkins University Press, 1992). This work is part of the five-volume history of American Jewry, *The Jewish People in America* (Baltimore: Johns Hopkins University Press, 1992).

23. See the full quotation from Kaplan's diary in Carole S. Kessner, "Kaplan and the Role of Women in Judaism," in *The American Judaism of Mordecai Kaplan,* ed. Emanuel Goldsmith, Mel Scult, and Robert Seltzer (New York: New York University Press, 1990), 344.

24. See Mordecai Kaplan, *Judaism as a Civilization: Toward a Reconstruction of American Jewish Life,* with a New Introduction by Mel Scult (Philadelphia: Jewish Publication Society, 2010), 548, which is also cited in Kessner, "Kaplan and the Role of Women in Judaism," 341.

25. The editorial originally appeared in the *Reconstructionist* 2, no. 3 (March 20, 1936): 3–4. It was reprinted in a little known but very valuable work, *The Reconstructionist Papers,* ed. Mordecai Kaplan (New York: Behrman's Jewish Book House, 1936), 253–54.

26. The article originally appeared in the *Reconstructionist* 2, no. 1 (February 21, 1936): 7–14. It was reprinted in *The Reconstructionist Papers,* 129–141.

27. *The Reconstructionist Papers,* 129.

28. Ibid., 131.

29. Ibid., 133. Kaplan's article on the status of the Jewish woman is also found in *The Future of the American Jew,* 402–12. These two essays are substantially the same except that the material in *The Future of the American Jew* contains the specific references to the status of women in rabbinic and Talmudic texts.

30. David Philipson, *The Reform Movement in Judaism: A New Issue with an Introduction by Solomon Freehof* (New York: Ktav, 1967), as cited in Umansky, "Feminism and American Reform Judaism," 267–83. The standard text on the history of Reform Judaism is Michael Meyer, *Response to Modernity: A History of the Reform Movement in Judaism* (New York: Oxford University Press, 1988).

31. Umansky, "Feminism and American Reform Judaism," 267.

32. For the place of women in the Reconstructionist movement in the postwar world, see Deborah Waxman, "A Lady Sometimes Blows the Shofar: Women's Equality in the Postwar Reconstructionist Movement," in *A Jewish Feminine Mystique? Jewish Women in Postwar America,* ed. Hasia Diner, Shira M. Kohn, and Rachel Kranson (New Brunswick, NJ: Rutgers University Press, 2010), 87–105. My thanks to Rabbi Waxman for making this paper available.

33. Kaplan diaries, January 2, 1945, JTS, box 4, vol. 13. This is one of many examples where Kaplan sounds like Heschel.

34. Kaplan, *The Future of the American Jew,* 423, 426.

35. Kaplan diaries, July 29, 1943, JTS, box 4, vol. 12.

36. Kaplan diaries, December 6, 1942, JTS, box 4, vol. 12.

37. The synopsis here is based on *The Future of the American Jew*, 387. It is interesting to note that Kaplan in his assertion here regarding *halakhah* refers the reader to the work of his arch rival at the seminary, Louis Ginzberg, who was much more traditional than Kaplan on the status of the *halakhah*. For a discussion of Kaplan and Ginzberg on the *halakhah*, see Scult, *Judaism Faces the Twentieth Century*, especially 209–13.

38. Kaplan diaries, July 7, 1927, JTS, box 1, vol. 3. For a report on the convention at which Ginzberg made these remarks, see *Communings of the Spirit*, 245–48. The interested reader will find a group photo of the rabbis at this convention on 246–47 of *Communings*.

39. Kaplan, *The Future of the American Jew*, 391.

40. Ibid., 377, 381.

41. Mordecai M. Kaplan, *The Greater Judaism in the Making: A Study of the Modern Evolution of Judaism* (New York: The Reconstructionist Press, 1960), 488.

42. Mordecai M. Kaplan, *Questions Jews Ask: Reconstructionist Answers* (New York: The Reconstructionist Press, 1956), 33.

43. Kaplan, *The Future of the American Jew*, 381.

44. Kaplan, *Judaism as a Civilization*, 346.

45. In Jewish law, one must wait six hours after a meat meal before eating dairy and one hour after a dairy meal before eating any meat. So, at any given moment, the question becomes whether a person is "dairy" (*milshig*) or "meat" (*fleishig*). The Kaplan family tradition was to pronounce the meat and dairy in this way.

46. It is perhaps noteworthy that, though Kaplan was conversant with the traditional sources, he taught and devoted his energies not to Talmud or *halakhah* but to midrash. Although there are legal *midrashim,* he never taught them. The *midrashim* that Kaplan taught to his classes at the seminary were homiletical, such as the *midrashim* on the Song of Songs or on Genesis. For more on Kaplan and his teaching of midrash, see the index to Scult, *Judaism Faces the Twentieth Century*, and the index to *Communings of the Spirit*. It is also interesting to note that, in the 1920s, the bulletin of the Society for the Advancement of Judaism, called the *SAJ Review,* contained quotations from the midrash, translated and analyzed by Kaplan. For the particular issues where these selections are found, see the Kaplan bibliography in *The American Judaism of Mordecai M. Kaplan*, ed. Emanuel S. Goldsmith, Mel Scult, and Robert Seltzer (New York: New York University Press, 1990) for the years 1924 and 1925.

47. See Eric Caplan, *From Ideology to Liturgy: Reconstructionist Worship and American Liberal Judaism* (Cincinnati, OH: Hebrew Union College Press, 2002). See also his article, "Kaplan and Obligation," *Conservative Judaism* 59, no. 4 (Summer 2007): 42–60. See also the provocative article by Dan Goldman Cedarbaum, "The Role of *Halakha* in Reconstructionist Decision Making," *The Reconstructionist* 65, no. 2 (Spring 2001): 29–38, adapted as "Reconstructing *Halakha*," *Reconstructionism Today* 9, no. 3 (Spring 2002): 1–7.

48. Kaplan, *The Future of the American Jew*, 393.

49. Ibid., 395.

50. Schulweis, "The Character of Halakhah Entering the Twenty-first Century," *Conservative Judaism* 45, no. 4 (Summer 1993): 7.

51. Ira F. Stone, *A Responsible Life: The Spiritual Path of Mussar* (New York: Aviv Press, 2006), introduction. Stone is a Conservative rabbi with a congregation in Philadelphia. It is perhaps no accident that he now teaches *Mussar* to rabbinical students at the Reconstructionist Rabbinical College. His teaching has been very successful, and it may be that, in future years, *Mussar* will be a major component of the Reconstructionist rabbinate.

52. This volume was published by the Jewish Publication Society as part of the Schiff Library of Jewish Classics. *Mesillat Yesharim—The Path of the Upright, by Moses Hayim Luzzatto—A* Critical Edition Provided with a Translation and Notes by Mordecai M. Kaplan (Philadelphia: Jewish Publication Society, 1936). Kaplan received the letter informing him of the project on November 19, 1915, the day that Schechter died. Schechter's letter in the Kaplan diaries, November 21, 1915, JTS, box 1, vol. 1. For more details on the publication of *Mesillat Yesharim* see Jonathan Sarna, *JPS: The Americanization of Jewish Culture, 1888–1988: A Centennial History of the Jewish Publication Society* (Philadelphia: Jewish Publication Society, 1989), 157–58.

53. See Mordecai Kaplan, "A Philosophy of Jewish Ethics," in *The Jews: Their History, Culture and Religion*, Vol. 2, ed. Louis Finkelstein (Philadelphia: The Jewish Publication Society, 1960),1010–1043.

54. Ibid., 1017–18.

55. Ibid., 1018.

56. Jacob Agus, *"Torah M'Sinai,"* in *Guideposts in Modern Judaism* (New York: Bloch & Co., 1954), 289–90.

57. Among Kaplan's papers, there is a letter of commendation from his philosophy professor that mentions his outstanding grasp of Kant's philosophy.

58. Upon his retirement at the age of seventy, Cohen moved to Berlin where he taught Jewish philosophy at the Academy for the Advancement of the Science of Judaism. His lectures resulted in his most comprehensive and representative Jewish work, *Die Religion der Vernunft aus den quellen des Judentums* (The Religion of Reason, Derived from the Sources of Judaism), which was completed before his death in 1918 and published a year later.

59. Mordecai M. Kaplan, *The Purpose and Meaning of Jewish Existence: A People in the Image of God* (Philadelphia: The Jewish Publication Society, 1964), 12.

60. Ibid., 62. The structure of Kaplan's book is rather unusual. On each page, Cohen's work is presented, in Kaplan's translation, above the line. Below the line, we find Kaplan's comments on selected concepts and passages. Some have been quite critical of Kaplan's presentation of Cohen, which is reduced to selected sentences from Cohen's magnum opus. See especially Alexander Kohanski, "Hermann Cohen and Mordecai Kaplan, *Jewish Social Studies* 29 (1967): 155–70.

61. This is the central concept in Kaplan's Hebrew work, *"Ha'emunah vehamusar— hayim ke-amanut ha'elyonah* (Jerusalem: Rubin Mass, 1954). The title may be translated as "Faith and Ethics: Life as Transcendent Art." It is interesting to note that the epigraph for the book comes from A. D. Gordon, the great Zionist ideologue, and emphasizes the notion of life as a work of art. There are many similarities between Gordon and Kaplan, and it is no accident that Kaplan uses Gordon in the epigraph. I have been

aided in my understanding of Gordon by Professor Einat Ramon of the Schechter In-sititute in Jerusalem. My belief is that this Hebrew work is a translation of Kaplan's un-published English manuscript "Soterics." There are scattered parts of this manuscript among Kaplan's papers.

62. Kaplan, *The Future of the American Jew*, 331.

12. KAPLAN AND THE PROBLEM OF EVIL

The epigraph is from the Kaplan diaries, July 24, 1940, JTS, box 3, vol. 9.

1. We shall detail the works of Eliezer Berkovits and Richard Rubenstein below. These are the two major critics of Kaplan's theory of evil.

2. Quotation here from Kaplan's "Soterics," 208, Reconstructionist Rabbinical Col-lege (hereafter RRC).

3. For Kaplan's preaching on economic issues, see Kaplan diaries, July 28, 1919, Jew-ish Theological Seminary (hereafter JTS), box 1, vol. 1. Also found in *Communings of the Spirit: The Journals of Mordecai M. Kaplan, Vol. 1, 1913–1934*, ed. Mel Scult (Detroit: Wayne State University Press, 2001), 137. Kaplan analyzes Communism in a little-known work titled *Judaism in Transition* (New York: Covici, Friede Publishers, 1936), 96–114. This work also contains a very interesting chapter on Maimonides (185–206), titled "How Maimonides Reconstructed Judaism."

4. Kaplan, "Soterics," 209, RRC.

5. Mordecai M. Kaplan, *The Future of the American Jew* (New York: Macmillan Co., 1948), 235 and 237.

6. Kaplan diaries, February 18, 1926, JTS, box 1, vol. 3; also *Communings of the Spirit*, 218.

7. One of the most insightful books I have read on evil as a psychological, social and religious problem is David Blumenthal, *The Banality of Good and Evil: Moral Lessons from the Shoah and Jewish Tradition* (Washington, DC: Georgetown University Press, 1999).

8. In terms of the general problem of evil in the modern period, the reader will find Susan Neiman's *Evil in Modern Thought: An Alternative History of Philosophy* (Princeton, NJ: Princeton University Press, 2002) very useful.

9. Kaplan diaries, May 3, 1943, JTS, box 4, vol. 12.

10. The Lamport family gave strong support to many Jewish institutions, and some of the family members were members of the Society for the Advancement of Judaism. Solo-mon Lamport's son, Montague Lamport, is the subject of this journal entry.

11. Kaplan diaries, July 20, 1927, JTS, box 1, vol. 3; also *Communings of the Spirit*, 248.

12. The full Mishna in the Danby translation reads, "R. Meir said: When man is sore troubled, what says the Shekinah? My head is ill at ease, my arm is ill at ease. If God is sore troubled at the blood of the ungodly that is shed, how much more at the blood of the righteous." Herbert Danby, *The Mishna: Translated from the Hebrew with Introduction and Brief Explanatory Notes* (London: Oxford University Press, 1938), 390–91.

13. Kaplan, "Soterics," 199, RRC.

14. Kaplan diaries, July 20, 1927, JTS, box 1, vol. 3; also *Communings of the Spirit*, 248–29.

15. Kaplan quotes the psalmist who tells us about losing his faith: "I almost slipped; I nearly lost my footing, in anger at the godless and their arrogance, at the sight of their

ease. No pain is theirs but sound strong health, no part have they in human cares, no blows like other men" (Psalms 73:2–5).

16. See Jeremiah 12:1–2. Quoted in Mordecai M. Kaplan, "The Unsolved Problem of Evil: Part 1," *The Reconstructionist* 29, no. 7 (May 16, 1963): 7.

17. See ibid., 8.

18. Ibid., 9.

19. I should think that Kaplan would have liked the interpretation of the book of Job given by the poet Robert Frost. In the verse play *The Masque of Reason*, we find Job conversing with God many years after his torment. At one point, God says to Job,

> I've had you on my mind a thousand years
> to thank you someday for the way you helped me
> establish once for all the principle
>
> there's no connection man can reason out
> between his just deserts and what he gets.
> Virtue may fail and wickedness succeed. . . .
> my thanks are to you for releasing me from moral bondage to the human race.

See Robert Frost, *A Masque of Reason*, in *The Poetry of Robert Frost*, ed. Edward Connery Lathem (New York: Henry Holt and Company, 1969), 475. This reference was first pointed out by my teacher, Dr. Nahum Glatzer, in a course he gave on Job.

20. See Mordecai Kaplan, "The Unsolved Problem of Evil: Part 2," *The Reconstructionist* 29, no. 8 (May 31, 1963): 15. Italics are mine.

21. Kaplan, "Soterics," 208, RRC.

22. This from conversations and also statements in class at Jewish Theological Seminary (fall 2008).

23. Rubenstein studied at the Jewish Theological Seminary with both Kaplan and Heschel. He was ordained in 1952. The account of his spiritual autobiography may be found in *Power Struggle: An Autobiographical Discussion* (New York: Charles Scribner's Sons, Inc., 1974). In his journal, Kaplan comments on Rubenstein as a student: "The student, Richard Rubinstein, came to see me at my office at the Seminary after class to read to me a paper in which he sets forth his attitude toward Judaism. He is one of the two students who had come under Heschel's influence at HUC. The other student is Dresner. I could never warm up to Dresner. He seems to be both arrogant and intolerantly orthodox. Rubenstein is humbly and tolerantly orthodox. He seems to have been under Herberg's influence for a time but was repelled by Herberg's presumption to teach Judaism, despite his ignorance of its sources, as well as by his uncritical acceptance of the basic ideology of Christian neo-Orthodoxy. Rubenstein said to me this afternoon that for a year-and-a-half he was laboring under a sense of guilt for attending the Seminary where he feels out of place. His place should have been at the Yeshivah." (November 27, 1950, JTS, box 4, vol. 15)

24. Richard Rubenstein, "Reconstructionism and the Problem of Evil," in *After Auschwitz: Radical Theology and Contemporary Judaism* (New York: Bobbs-Merrill Co., Inc., 1966), 86. This essay has been expunged from the most recent edition of Rubenstein's book.

25. Ibid., 89.

26. Ibid., 90.

27. Richard Hirsh, "Letter to the Editor," *Conservative Judaism* 35, no. 2 (Winter 1982): 95. The Kaplan quotation on the actual and the possible is mentioned by Hirsh and is from *The Meaning of God in Modern Jewish Religion* (Detroit: Wayne State University Press, 1994), 130.

28. Kaplan diaries, July 24, 1930, JTS, box 6, vol.6; also *Communings of the Spirit*, 417.

29. Eliezer Berkovits, *Major Themes in Modern Jewish Philosophy* (New York: Ktav Publishing House, Inc., 1974), 162. Kaplan's statement " . . . are simply . . ." is found in *The Meaning of God in Modern Jewish Religion*, 76. Berkovits does not quote Kaplan in full and somewhat distorts Kaplan's meaning. Here is the Kaplan quotation in full: "The modern man cannot possibly view earthquakes and volcanic eruptions, devastating storms and floods, famines and plagues, noxious plants and animals *as 'necessary' to any preconceived plan or purpose*. They are simply that phase of the universe which has not yet been completely penetrated by godhood." Italics have been added.

30. Kaplan diaries, August 16, 1944, JTS, box 4, vol. 13. Kaplan does not state clearly what he is commenting on. From what I know of Steinberg, I think Kaplan is distorting Steinberg's position here. See the very significant essay by Steinberg, "God and the World's Evil," *The Reconstructionist* 9, no. 6 (April 30, 1943): 9–16.

31. See cover page for vol. 13 (April 1944, box 4) of the Kaplan diaries, where Kaplan quotes a poem by Robert Nathan (1894–1985), titled "Prayer in the Evil Time." Kaplan makes it clear that he refuses to assent to the hope expressed in the poem that God will intervene to save the Jewish people.

32. Kaplan diaries, May 8, 1943, box 4, vol. 12. Kaplan's good feeling here was due to things going well at the Society for the Advancement of Judaism and at the Jewish Theological Seminary.

33. Kaplan diaries, September 4, 1939, JTS, box 3, vol. 9.

34. Kaplan diaries, April 19, 1943, JTS, box 4, vol. 12. Kaplan does not mention the Warsaw Ghetto Uprising itself.

35. See especially Kaplan diaries, March 8, 1939, JTS, box 3, vol. 8.

36. Kaplan diaries, February 19, 1939, JTS, box 3, vol. 8.

37. See the multitude of references to "Chosen People" in the index to *Judaism as a Civilization: Toward a Reconstruction of American Jewish Life*, with a New Introduction by Mel Scult (Philadelphia: Jewish Publication Society, 2010). The book was first published in 1934.

38. The white paper issued by the British government, which held the mandate over Palestine, asserted that an independent Palestine governed by Palestinian Arabs and Jews would be created in proportion to the population in 1949 (section I). A limit of 75,000 Jewish immigrants was set for the five-year period between 1940 and 1944, consisting of a regular yearly quota of 10,000 and a supplementary quota of 25,000, spread out over the same period, to cover refugee emergencies. (The Arabs and their oil were obviously more strategically important to the British than the Jews and their need for a refuge.)

39. Kaplan diaries, May 17, 1939, JTS, box 3, vol. 8.

40. Kaplan diaries, July 20, 1927, JTS, box 1, vol. 3; also *Communings*, 249. My wife Barbara Gish Scult is primarily responsible for the summary here.

41. Zachariah 4:6. It is interesting to note that this chapter from Zachariah is recited on the Shabbat of Chanukah.

42. See Kaplan diaries, September 14, 1944, JTS, box 4, vol. 13, where he discusses domination.

43. Kaplan diary, March 19, 1943, JTS, box 4, vol. 12. When we deal with the "other" in a Jewish context, we inevitably think of Emmanuel Levinas. Kaplan did not know of Levinas, but he does hold many beliefs in common with his "Lithuanian brother."

44. Milton Steinberg, "God and the World's Evil," *The Reconstructionist* 9, no. 6 (April 30, 1943): 12. All the quotations from Steinberg are taken from this one article. See also the article by Stephen Katz, "Mordecai Kaplan's Theology and the Problem of Evil," *Jewish Social Studies: History, Culture, Society* n.s. 12, no. 2 (Winter 2006): 115–26. This issue of *Jewish Social Studies* contains all the papers presented at the Stanford Conference on Mordecai Kaplan held in 2004.

45. It is also well to remember that it may be that Steinberg himself wrote the very theistic introduction to the 1945 prayer book we are referring to. See chapter 9 for a discussion of the prayer book.

46. Kaplan knew Magnes from the early years of the twentieth century when Magnes was head of the New York Kehillah. Although there was much mutual respect between them, both Magnes and Kaplan were critical of each other. For Kaplan on Magnes, see the index of *Communings of the Spirit*. For Magnes on Kaplan, see the index of *Dissenter in Zion: From the Writings of Judah L. Magnes*, ed. Arthur Goren (Cambridge, MA: Harvard University Press, 1982). The selection here is from the Kaplan diaries, March 25, 1951, JTS, box 4, vol. 15. I mentioned in the chapter on Heschel that sometimes we find a very elegant moving passage where we have "Kaplan as Heschel." This selection is obviously an example. Kaplan is truly the eloquent thinker here.

47. Roy Morris, *The Better Angel: Walt Whitman in the Civil War* (New York: Oxford University Press, 2000), 102. The Whitman selection is from *Leaves of Grass*. Morris does not give a specific line reference to *Leaves of Grass*.

CONCLUSION

1. Arthur Hertzberg, "Introduction to the 1981 Edition—In Celebration of the Hundredth Birthday of Mordecai M. Kaplan," in Mordecai Kaplan, *Judaism as a Civilization: Toward a Reconstruction of American Jewish Life*, with a New Introduction by Mel Scult (Philadelphia: Jewish Publication Society, 2010), xxxiv.

2. Kaplan, *Judaism as a Civilization*, 215.

3. Kaplan, "Soterics," 239, Reconstructionist Rabbinical College (hereafter RRC).

4. Mordecai M. Kaplan, "Our God as Our Collective Conscience," *The Reconstructionist* 41, no. 1 (February 1975): 15–16. We should mention that, although Kaplan does deal with the matter of conscience, here it is clear from the article that he intends to focus on consciousness. Meir Ben Horin in his seminal work on Kaplan, *Transnature's God: Studies in Mordecai Kaplan's Theology* (Wilton, CT: Adar Nisan Books, 2004), points out that Kaplan elaborated the rabbinic references where the rabbis refer to God as the *shekhina* and the collective consciousness is obviously implied. See Talmud Bavli, *Megilah*, 29:b and *Bamidbar Rabbah*, 12:4.

5. The expression "international nation" is found in Meir Ben Horin, *Transnature's God*, 352. The quotation here is from ibid., 232.

6. "Soterics," 230, RRC.

7. John Dewey, *Human Nature and Conduct* (New York: Random House, 1957), 226.

8. Oliver Wendell Holmes, "Letter to Lewis Einstein's Daughter, May 6, 1925," in *The Essential Holmes: Selections from the Letters, Speeches, Judicial Opinions, and Other Writ-*

ings of Oliver Wendell Holmes, Jr., ed. with an introduction by Richard A. Posner (Chicago: University of Chicago Press, 1992), 75.

9. See chapter 7, "God as Felt Presence," in Mordecai Kaplan, *The Meaning of God in Modern Jewish Religion* (Detroit: Wayne State University Press, 1994). The quotation here is on page 244.

10. The thought is found many times in Kaplan's *The Meaning of God in Modern Jewish Religion.* It is also found in the Kaplan diaries, February 18, 1926, quoted in chapter 12 above. The thought is also found many times in Arthur Green's *Seek My Face, Speak My Name* (Northvale, NJ: Jason Aronson, Inc., 1992), especially 109ff. Green's latest work also reflects this notion: see *Radical Judaism: Rethinking God and Tradition* (New Haven, CT: Yale University Press, 2010).

11. Hertzberg, "Introduction to the 1981 Edition," in Kaplan, *Judaism as a Civilization,* xxxv.

SELECTED BIBLIOGRAPHY
AND NOTE ON SOURCES

WORKS BY MORDECAI M. KAPLAN

Communings of the Spirit: The Journals of Mordecai M. Kaplan, edited by Mel Scult. Volume 1, *1913–1934*. Detroit: Wayne State University Press, 2001. Volume 2, *1934–1941*, in preparation.

The Future of the American Jew. New York: Macmillan and Company, 1948.

The Greater Judaism in the Making: A Study in the Evolution of Modern Judaism. New York: The Reconstructionist Press, 1960.

A Guide to Jewish Ritual, introduction by Ira Eisenstein. New York: Reconstructionist Press, 1962.

Judaism as a Civilization: Toward a Reconstruction of American Jewish Life, with a New Introduction by Mel Scult. Philadelphia: Jewish Publication Society, 2010. Original publication: New York: Macmillan and Company, 1934.

Judaism in Transition. New York: Covici, Friede Publishers, 1936.

Judaism without Supernaturalism: The Only Alternative to Orthodoxy and Secularism. New York: The Reconstructionist Press, 1958.

The Meaning of God in Modern Jewish Religion. Detroit: Wayne State University Press, 1994. Original publication: New York: Behrman, 1937.

The New Haggadah. New York: Behrman House, Inc., 1941.

The New Zionism. New York: The Herzl Press and the Jewish Reconstructionist Press, 1959). Original publication: New York: Herzl Press, 1955.

Not So Random Thoughts: Witty and Profound Observations on Society, Religion and Jewish Life by America's Leading Jewish Thinker. New York: The Reconstructionist Press, 1966.

The Purpose and Meaning of Jewish Existence: A People in the Image of God. Philadelphia: The Jewish Publication Society, 1964.

Questions Jews Ask: Reconstructionist Answers. New York: The Reconstructionist Press, 1956.

The Religion of Ethical Nationhood: Judaism's Contribution to World Peace. New York: Macmillan Co., 1970.

OTHER

Eisenstein, Ira, and Eugene Kohn, eds. *Mordecai Kaplan: An Evaluation.* New York: Jewish Reconstructionist Press, 1952.

Scult, Mel. *Judaism Faces the Twentieth Century: A Biography of Mordecai Kaplan.* Detroit: Wayne State University Press, 1993.

———. "Schechter's Seminary." In *Tradition Renewed: A History of the Jewish Theological Seminary, Volume 1,* edited by Jack Wertheimer, 43–102. New York: The Jewish Theological Seminary of America, 1997.

A full bibliography of Kaplan's published works is found in *The American Judaism of Mordecai M. Kaplan,* edited by Emanuel S. Goldsmith, Mel Scult, and Robert Seltzer (New York: New York University Press, 1990). A bibliography of published works about Kaplan is found in *Dynamic Judaism,* edited by Emanuel S. Goldsmith and Mel Scult (New York: Schocken and the Reconstructionist Press, 1985).

This bibliography has been updated in the Hebrew version of *Dynamic Judaism: Yahadut Dynamit* (Tel Aviv: Yediot Ahronot, 2011).

MANUSCRIPT SOURCES

The Kaplan papers are housed at the Reconstructionist Rabbinical College (RRC) in the Ira and Judith Kaplan Eisenstein Reconstructionist Archives. This archive is referred to in this work as simply RRC. The Kaplan papers at RRC are extensive and are in the process of being catalogued. Finding aids for the papers of the RRC itself and for the papers of Ira Eisenstein can be found on the web site of the RRC, http://www.rrc.edu/.

There are also some 12,000 letters in the Kaplan letter file at RRC. The catalogue of the Kaplan correspondence was assembled by Richard Libowitz and may be found in *Jewish Civilization: Essays and Studies,* Volume 2: *Jewish Law: Honoring the One-Hundredth Birthday of Rabbi Mordecai M. Kaplan,* edited by Ronald A. Brauner (Philadelphia: Reconstructionist Rabbinical College, 1981).

KAPLAN'S DIARIES

Early Diary. This early diary, which runs from 1904 to 1907, is short and in one volume. It is found only at RRC.

Major Kaplan Diary. Covering 1913–78, this diary is referred to here as simply the "Kaplan diaries." Kaplan was a compulsive diary keeper throughout his life. His major diary begins in 1913 and ends in the late 1970s. This diary comprises a total of twenty-seven volumes. The books are large, accountant-type volumes and have about three hundred pages each. The originals of the first twenty-five volumes are housed at the Jewish Theological Seminary (JTS). The originals of volumes 26 and 27 (from 1973 onward) are located at the RRC. There are microfilms of the first twenty-five volumes at the RRC, the American Jewish Archives in Cincinnati, and Hebrew Union College in Jerusalem. My personal copy of the microfilm, which I gave to the Jewish Theological Seminary, is available in the reading room. The diary can be accessed online at www.jtsa.edu/library/searchdigital/archives/kaplan/html.

Throughout the present work, when I quote a statement from the diary that is included in *Communings of the Spirit,* I indicate the location and page number. For citations to the major diary, I indicate the box and volume number at JTS in addition to the date. For some diary entries, only the month is given. Sometimes Kaplan included days of the week, sometimes not. A second volume of selections from the Kaplan diary, covering the period from 1934 to 1941, is in the final stages of preparation; the third volume will cover 1941–51. Professor Eric Caplan of McGill University is working on a fourth volume which will cover from 1951 until the final pages of the diary in 1978. The Littauer Foundation, the Kaplan family, and others have contributed toward the publication of the "Kaplan Journal," a project which is in process.

"Soterics" is the name Kaplan gave to his ideology in the 1940s. *Soter* in Greek means save, and he wanted to say that his system was a scientific system of religion and salvation. In a diary entry of May 12, 1943, Kaplan gave a definition of his system: "Soterics might be described as a normative science. It is an organic synthesis of whatever has a bearing in the way of knowledge, attitude and action on the purpose of making the optimum use of life." When Kaplan discusses his ideas in the diaries for the 1940s, he frequently uses the word "Soterics"; Kaplan rarely used this word in his published writings.

Kaplan authored a manuscript that he called "Soterics." Parts of it are found in the archive at the RRC. It has different names: sometimes it is called "Religious Humanism," sometimes "A Humanist Approach to Religion," and sometimes simply "Soterics." My sense is that this unpublished manuscript is the original of the Hebrew work Kaplan published in 1954 titled *Ha-emunah veha-musar*, published by Rubin Mass. The translator is not identified. I refer to it as "Soterics" and include page numbers when available. Portions of this manuscript are found at the RRC.

Publication data for other works cited in this book are given in full in the notes.

TRANSLITERATION

The transliterations in this book follow the guidelines of the *Encyclopedia Judaica*.

INDEX

Abraham, 232

Abramovich, Sholem, 47

Adam, 38

Adler, Cyrus, 54, 55, 101, 296n34

Adler, Felix, 66–87, 114, 169, 268

Agudat Rabbanim (Union of Orthodox Rabbis of the United States and Canada), 9, 10, 14–15, 16, 17–18, 196

Agus, Rabbi Jacob, 246, 294n13

Aher (Elisha Ben Avuya), Rabbi, 303n27

Ahlstrom, Sidney, 29

Akiba, Rabbi, 38, 234, 303n27

Albo, Joseph, 28, 35, 149

Americanization of Judaism, Kaplan as manifestation of: approach to theology, 3, 269; and *halakhah* and ethics, 229, 237–238; and Judaism as a civilization, 89–90, 94, 101–102, 105; and nationalism and righteousness, 46, 49–50, 61; and relationship between Kaplan and Heschel, 207–208, 214; and salvation as the goal of religion, 170, 171, 174; and salvation embodied as *mitzvot*, 188; and universalism and pragmatism, 66–68

Ames, Edward, 138, 224–225

Amichai, Yehuda, 127

apRoberts, Ruth, 58

Aristotle, 36, 56, 61, 83, 161, 163, 245

Arnold, Matthew: influence on Adler, 72–73; influence on Kaplan, 279n6; and Kaplan's ambivalent relationship with God, 110, 127, 298n1; nationalism and

righteousness of, 46–65; and salvation as the goal of religion, 157; and self-reliance, 33; on the transcendent, 76

Baal Shem Tov, 22, 197, 220

Baeck, Leo, 29–30

Battle of France, 34

Believing Jew, A (Steinberg), 198

Ben Azzai, Rabbi, 303n27

Ben Horin, Meir, 323n4

Ben Zakkai, Rabbi Yochanon, 220

Ben Zoma, Rabbi, 303n27

Benderly, Samson, 51, 288n14

Ben-Gurion, David, 8, 102, 296n41

Bentham, Jeremy, 76

Bentwich, Norman, 114, 299n14

Bergson, Henri, 29, 140–142, 286n40

Berkovits, Eliezer, 258–259, 322n29

Beruriah, 234

Bialik, Chaim Nahman, 47, 48, 127

Bible. *See* Torah

bildung, 33, 58–60, 61

Bloom, Harold, 50, 288n12

B'nai B'rith, 52

Bonhoeffer, Dietrich, 190

Borowitz, Eugene, 189

Brisman, Leslie, 202

Browning, Robert, 56

Buber, Martin: on the binational state, 297n53; and excommunications of Kaplan and Spinoza, 24; and Judaism as a civilization, 105; and Kaplan's theology beyond supernaturalism, 138, 142, 147–

MEL SCULT, the biographer of Mordecai Kaplan, is Professor Emeritus in Judaic Studies at Brooklyn College of the City University of New York. His biography of Kaplan, *Judaism Faces the Twentieth Century,* appeared a number of years ago. He is also the editor of a selection from Kaplan's twenty-seven-volume diary, titled *Communings of the Spirit: The Journals of Mordecai M. Kaplan, Volume 1: 1913–1934.* With Professor Emanuel S. Goldsmith, he edited a selection from Kaplan's published works, titled *Dynamic Judaism.* His biography of Kaplan and *Dynamic Judaism* have been translated into Hebrew and are published in Israel by Yediot Ahronot. His account of Solomon Schechter's presidency at the Jewish Theological Seminary appeared in the two-volume work, *Tradition Renewed: A History of the Jewish Theological Seminary of America.* He has also published on Henrietta Szold and on the "London Society for the Promotion of Christianity among the Jews."